Port Cities, Pollution, and Public Health

Port cities of the world are critical nodes for international trade and socio-economic development. Yet they bear several costs, including congestion and pollution, which affect the local environment and population. In certain places, living near the port – together with related industrial and logistical activities – is a synonym of adverse health outcomes, resulting in several diseases and above-average unplanned hospital admissions and mortality. Decades of port-city physical separation have not eliminated such issues, since deep-water facilities, even outside urban cores, impact local populations and reach port and non-port cities through extensive trucking flows. Specific traffic, like cruise, keeps operating within dense urban environments.

This book is one of the first dedicated volumes on such matters, with contributions from scholars on several continents (Europe, Asia, the Americas, Africa, and Oceania). It is highly interdisciplinary, covering geography, history, economics, management sciences, regional science, sociology, public and comparative law, physics, energy and industrial engineering, urban and spatial planning, epidemiology, architecture, biology, and environmental sciences. This volume offers an overview of current environmental and health issues in port cities. It starts by presenting the mitigation and perception of port pollution. Next, it examines the health impacts of ports from a historical perspective and reviews and synthesizes the variety of existing approaches to measure the health impacts of ports and shipping. Finally, it proposes a reflection on multilevel governance and policies.

This book is a comprehensive resource for a wide readership, including academics and upper-level students interested in maritime transport, port management, and sustainability, as well as those in public management, planning, and governance.

Mariantonia Lo Prete is Assistant Professor in Coastal Planning and Port Geography at Dunkirk University (University of the Littoral Opal Coast – ULCO), France, and a member of the research unit Territories, Cities, Environment and Society (TVES ULR 4477).

César Ducruet is Geographer and Senior Researcher at the French National Centre for Scientific Research (CNRS), France. He is currently working at the EconomiX laboratory (Paris-Nanterre) on the local impact of contemporary maritime globalization.

Routledge Studies in Transport Analysis

25 **Port Management Strategy for Enhancing Cybersecurity and Resilience**
Learning from Case Studies
Chalermpong Senarak

26 **Electric Vehicle Supply Chain Management**
Edited by Muhammad Shujaat Mubarik, Jyri Vilko, and Sajid Nazir

27 **Airline Pilots in the Age of AI**
A Global Study of Work, Safety and Technology
Geraint Harvey

28 **Electric Vehicle Supply Chain Management**
Edited by Muhammad Shujaat Mubarik, Jyri Vilko, Sajid Nazir

29 **The Psychology of Traffic**
Edited by Ralf Risser and Matus Sucha

30 **Ports in the Polycrisis**
Navigating Geopolitical, Ecological, and Institutional Challenges
Edited by Marine Chouquet, Nathan Gouin and Laurent Livolsi

31 **European Seaports in the Energy Transition**
Flows, Infrastructure, and Strategy
Noemi Van Meir, Edwin van Hassel and Thierry Vanelslander

32 **Port Cities, Pollution, and Public Health**
Environmental Health Issues from Shipping and Ports
Edited by Mariantonia Lo Prete and César Ducruet

For more information about this series, please visit: www.routledge.com/Routledge-Studies-in-Transport-Analysis/book-series/RSTA

Port Cities, Pollution, and Public Health

Environmental Health Issues from Shipping and Ports

Edited by Mariantonia Lo Prete and César Ducruet

Routledge
Taylor & Francis Group
LONDON AND NEW YORK

First published 2027
by Routledge
4 Park Square, Milton Park, Abingdon, Oxon OX14 4RN

and by Routledge
605 Third Avenue, New York, NY 10158

Routledge is an imprint of the Taylor & Francis Group, an informa business

British Library Cataloguing-in-Publication Data
A catalogue record for this book is available from the British Library

ISBN: 978-1-041-07255-3 (hbk)
ISBN: 978-1-041-07256-0 (pbk)
ISBN: 978-1-003-63958-9 (ebk)

DOI: 10.4324/9781003639589

Typeset in Sabon
by codeMantra

Contents

Figures

Tables

About the editors

Mariantonia Lo Prete

Since 2015, she has been an assistant professor in Coastal Planning and Port Geography at Dunkirk University (University of the Littoral Opal Coast – ULCO) and a member of the research unit Territories, Cities, Environment and Society (ULR 4477 TVES). She is the deputy director of the Federative Research Structure dedicated to the sea and the coastline in the Hauts-de-France (SFR Campus de la Mer) and a co-leader of the POrt and MARitime research group (POMAR) of the French National Centre for Scientific Research (CNRS).

In the continuity of her PhD about the relationship between trading ports and the environment at the French Institute of Science and Technology for Transport, Development and Networks (IFSTTAR) with the National School of Bridges and Roads (ENPC), her work has focused on port, maritime, and coastal issues, particularly from the angle of conflicts of use and development from the perspective of environmental and health issues to understand how the environment and the health of the local residents are taken into account in port development, coastal planning, and public policy. She is the working package leader dedicated to the environmental and health impacts of ports and shipping on local populations in the ANR-funded research project "Maritime Globalization, Network Externalities and Transport Impacts on Cities" (MAGNETICS) (2022–2026). She is also involved in a number of national and international research projects relating to maritime, port, straits, environmental, and coastal issues (DÉCODÉ, Life MARHA, RECREAFISH, PAGENS, etc.), and she has been an expert for various international organizations (WHO, AFD).

César Ducruet

César Ducruet, geographer, is a senior researcher at the French National Centre for Scientific Research (CNRS). He is currently working at the EconomiX laboratory (Paris-Nanterre) on the local impact of contemporary maritime globalization. His research focuses on technological innovation, connectivity, employment, vulnerability, environment, and public health issues in a port and port-city context. He is the principal investigator of the ANR-funded research project "Maritime Globalization, Network Externalities and Transport Impacts on Cities" (MAGNETICS) (2022–2026). César has been an expert for various international organizations (OECD, World Bank, and WHO) and works regularly with numerous partners in Asia (Korea Maritime Institute, JETRO, ASEM, Chinese Academy of Sciences, ECNU, Fudan University, and Shanghai Maritime University). His publications include three edited volumes on *Maritime Networks* (2015), *Shipping Data Analysis* (2017), and *Port Systems* (2023) in the Routledge Studies in Transport Analysis. He is also an associate member of porteconomics.eu, scientific board member of RETE Association, international advisory board member of PortCityFutures, area editor of *Networks and Spatial Economics*, and editorial board member of *Journal of Transport Geography*, *Maritime Business Review*, *International Journal of Transport Economics*, *WMU Journal of Maritime Affairs*, and *Portus*.

Contributors

Charbel Alkhoury is a PhD researcher in Economics at the University of Paris and the University of Paris 1 Panthéon Sorbonne. Specializing in maritime, health, and environmental economics, his research focuses on the impact of port infrastructure and activities on economic growth, the environment, and health at both local and global levels. His research highlights that ports are critical for global trade but create significant environmental and health challenges that are often externalized in traditional economic analyses. His work seeks to develop a comprehensive understanding of the trade-offs between economic benefits and environmental/health costs, providing insights for sustainable and equitable port policies. Additionally, he is a member of the ANR-funded MAGNETICS project (2022–2026) and teaches the course *Analytical Tools in Economic Sciences* at the undergraduate level (L2) at the University of Paris Nanterre, and trade and international finance at Sciences Po.

Julia Appercelle is a recent graduate of the Institut Supérieur d'Etudes Logistiques (ISEL) in Le Havre. She completed two years of preparatory classes and three years of engineering studies at the school, which is part of the University of Le Havre Normandie. She was one of the four members of the project team that carried out the study on the population's perception of the impact of port pollution. This study was proposed to this group of students by Normandie Innovation Marché Entreprise Consommation (NIMEC), as part of one of their fifth-year courses.

Marie-Laure Baron is Full Professor of Management Sciences at the University of Le Havre Normandie, at the Institut Supérieur d'Études Logistiques (ISEL). Her teaching focuses on financial issues related to supply chain management, integrating the challenges of sustainable development and new business models. Her research has focused on inter-company coordination and, more recently, collective strategies. Her location in Le Havre and her involvement in various research projects linked to the port environment make port clusters one of her preferred areas of research.

Olivier Bueno is a generalist logistics engineer graduate of the Institut Supérieur d'Études Logistiques (ISEL) in Le Havre, class of 2024. He is currently specializing in Supply Chain Design & Management at the École Nationale des Ponts et Chaussées (ENPC), Paris. He has shown a strong interest in the decarbonization of transportation and sustainability challenges in industrial supply chains activities within the Safran Group during two years. Today, he contributes to Supply Chain data monitoring and analysis as an Inventory Management Analyst at Sanofi.

Marine Chouquet is Assistant Professor in Public Law at the University of Le Havre Normandy and Member of the Centre de recherche sur les mutations du droit et les mutations sociales (CERMUD). She co-leads the POMAR working group on seaports (GDR OMER, CNRS). Her teaching and research activities cover a wide range of disciplines, including administrative law, public property law, and health law. However, most of her research in recent years has focused on port law. She is the author of several publications that analyse how the legal environment of seaports is evolving in the face of globalization and climate change (governance methods, terminal operating contracts, legal regime of port assets, etc.).

Claude Comtois is Emeritus Professor of Geography at the University of Montreal. He holds a degree in Political Science, an M.Sc. in Geography, and a PhD from the University of Hong Kong for his research in the field of transportation. He is a senior member of the Interuniversity Research Centre on Enterprise Networks, Logistics and Transportation (CIRRELT), Academic Advisor for the Port of Montreal, and member of the Québec Maritime Network on "Intelligent port and maritime transport". His visiting professorships include more than 15 foreign universities. His teaching and research are centred on ports and maritime transport. He is the author or the co-author of over 240 scientific publications and 250 communications. He has supervised or participated in more than 40 research projects and collaborated in the transfer of knowledge and methodologies applied to transport systems for government agencies and private corporations. He currently supervises projects on innovations and the competitiveness of port systems, adaptation measures of ports and maritime transport to climate changes, green shipping corridors, and decarbonation strategies.

Daniele Contini obtained his M.Sc. in Physics in 1994 and his PhD in Energy Engineering in 1999 from the University of Florence. He became a researcher at the Institute of Atmospheric Sciences and Climate of the National Research Council (ISAC-CNR in Lecce) in 2001, and he is now (from 2019) Research Director at ISAC-CNR. He is the coordinator of the macroarea of ISAC-CNR research in atmospheric composition, climate forcing, and air quality. His research activity is mainly experimental and focused on atmospheric sciences. Currently, his research interests could be summarized in four main lines: (i) Identification and characterization of atmospheric particulate matter sources, using both high-resolution temporal measurements and receptor models based on the chemical composition of the particulate, and their spatial and temporal trends; (ii) health and toxicological effects of atmospheric particulate matter due to both natural and anthropogenic sources; (iii) study of atmospheric particulate dynamics in the surface boundary layer with particular attention to nucleation, emission, and deposition processes; (iv) analysis and parameterization of the dispersion of atmospheric pollutants also using physical modelling on a reduced scale in a wind tunnel and/or in a hydraulic vein. Throughout his career, he has established numerous and successful research collaborations with leading international groups in the field of atmospheric and climate sciences. He had coordination responsibility in a number of research projects at regional, national, and international levels. Daniele Contini is President (since 2018) of the Italian Aerosol Society (IAS), and he is the Chair of the working group "Atmospheric Aerosol Studies" of the European Aerosol Assembly (since 2022). He is PI of the Environmental-Climate Observatory (ECO) of Lecce, regional station of the GAW/WMO-Global Atmosphere Watch network, and national facility of the ACTRIS network.

Sophie Cros is Full Professor of Management Sciences. After more than 20 years teaching at the Université Paris 1 Panthéon Sorbonne and at Sciences Po Paris, she now teaches at the Institut Supérieur d'Etudes Logistiques (ISEL), University of Le Havre Normandy, Normandy University. She is the director of the Normandie Innovation Marché Entreprise Consommation (NIMEC), a management science research center, which brings together 12 university sites. She is a specialist in global risk assessment and crisis management. She is currently conducting research on decision-making, risk diagnostics, risk perception, and anticipation of the unlikely in the fields of Environment, Security/Defence/Education of populations.

Frédéric Davansant is an Associate Professor at the School of Law of the University of Littoral Côte d'Opale. He holds an Advanced Master's and a PhD in Legal History from Rennes University. He is currently Member of the Scientific Board of the French Scientific Interest Group of Maritime History and Sea Sciences (Lorient) and a member of the Association des Historiens des Facultés de Droit. Since 2003, he has been the author of scientific publications about Maritime History dealing with Criminal Law, Admiralty Law, and Military justice.

Magali Dumontet is Associate Professor of Economics at Paris Nanterre University and a member of the research unit EconomiX (UMR 7235) since September 2017. Specializing in microeconometrics applied to health economics, her research spans health economics, labour economics, and, more recently, behavioural economics. She focuses on health determinants, the regulation of ambulatory care, and the decision-making processes of healthcare professionals regarding labour supply, including specialty choices, activity choices, and location decisions. Her expertise includes the econometric analysis of both survey and administrative data.

Severine Frère is Professor of Spatial Planning and Urban Development at the Université du Littoral Côte d'Opale (ULCO). She is co-responsible for the "Thinking and building territories" axis of the Territoires Villes Environnement et Société (TVES) laboratory. Her research focuses on air governance, in particular perception, citizen consultation, and behaviour in the field of air quality. She co-chairs the scientific board of the AQACIA research programme (Amélioration de la Qualité de l'Air: Comprendre, Innover, Agir).

Lorena Garcia-Alonso is Associate Professor at the Applied Economics Department of the University of Oviedo (Spain) and holds a PhD from the same University in 2005. Her main line of research includes the analysis of the inter-port competition process in Spain. Her main subjects of teaching are International Trade, Maritime Economics, and World Economy. She has presented numerous papers in international conferences, and she has also published several articles in international journals. She is Member of the International Association of Maritime Economics (IAME), Regional Science Association International (RSAI), European Regional Science Association (ERSA), Spanish Association of Regional Science (AECR), and Economics Free Association (ALDE). She is the founding partner of the journal *Regional Studies* and a founding member of the researching group Regional Economic Analysis Laboratory (REGIOlab).

Christos Hadjichristodoulou is currently the President of the Hellenic National Public Health Organization (NPHO), where he oversees the organization's epidemiological surveillance, risk assessment, scientific consultation, preparedness, and response. He is also Professor of Hygiene and Epidemiology at the University of Thessaly's Laboratory of Hygiene and Epidemiology in Larissa, Greece, where he previously served as Director from 2006 to 2023. He has extensive expertise and over 25 years of experience related to infectious diseases, epidemiology, points of entry, maritime health, mass gatherings, and environmental health. As a medical doctor with a PhD in Brucellosis surveillance and prevention, he further trained as a field epidemiologist through EPIET in Glasgow (1996–1997). For nearly 20 years, he has coordinated European-funded projects and joint actions related to public health and maritime transport, beginning with SHIPSAN TRAINET (2006–2008), SHIPSAN (2008–2011), EU SHIPSAN ACT Joint Action (2013–2016), and EU HEALTHY GATEWAYS Joint Action (2018–2022). He currently coordinates the European Commission-funded Horizon Research and Innovation Action HEALTHY SAILING for prevention, mitigation, and management of infectious diseases on large passenger ships. He is also the President of the European Scientific Association for Health and Hygiene in Maritime Transport (EU SHIPSAN Association) and Head of the WHO Collaborating Center for the International Health Regulations: points of entry (GRE-27). He currently serves as the Deputy Director for the Master of Science (MSc) programme in Public Health and Maritime Transport established at the University of Thessaly.

Alicia Jacquette is an engineer specializing in logistics, and a recent graduate of the Institut d'Études Supérieures Logistiques (ISEL) in Le Havre. During her studies, she became interested in Supply Chain sustainability issues, in particular that of stock management for a major oil group, with the aim of improving and adapting processes to the climatic and environmental challenges of our century. Since graduating, she began her professional career with PETROSERVICES, as a production planning and scheduling manager, whose aim is to ensure responsible and sustainable production, in particular by reducing its ecological footprint.

Carola Hein is Professor of History of Architecture and Urban Planning at Delft University of Technology and Professor at Leiden and Erasmus University. She is the director of the Leiden-Delft-Erasmus PortCityFutures Centre. She holds the UNESCO Chair of Water, Ports, and Historic Cities and leads the LDE PortCityFutures Centre. She has published widely in the field of architectural, urban, and planning history, tying historical analysis to contemporary development. Her recent (co-)edited books include: *Port City Atlas* (2023), *Oil Spaces* (2021), *Urbanisation of the Sea* (2020), *Adaptive Strategies for Water Heritage* (2020), and *The Routledge Planning History Handbook* (2018).

Sarah E. Hinman is an assistant professor at Leiden University College, The Hague, the international honors college of Leiden University, where she teaches across a number of domains in the programme including the majors of Global Public Health and Earth, Energy, and Sustainability. She is a broadly trained geographer who earned her PhD from Louisiana State University and maintains research interests at the intersections of urban-environmental interactions, public health, historical geography, and geographic information systems. Her current teaching and work with students includes an emphasis on the role of green space in cities from the perspectives of ecosystem health, public health, and policies related to such spaces.

Grażyna Liczbińska is a human biologist and an associate professor at the Faculty of Biology, Adam Mickiewicz University in Poznań, Poland. Her main scientific interests are related to biology and demography of populations from the past, with a special emphasis on the impact of social inequalities and environmental stress related to biological and health status and social mobility, as well as positive and negative determinants of health. She is a member of the network of SHiP+ Studying the History of Health in (Port) Cities, a Committee Member in the COST Action CA22116, a Council Member of the European Society of Historical Demography, and a Board Member of the International Commission for Historical Demography.

Sarah Lutfy obtained her Bachelor's degree in Geography at the University of Montreal. She is a researcher for the Interuniversity Research Centre on Enterprise Networks, Logistics and Transportation (CIRRELT). She is currently undertaking an M.Sc. in Geography on green shipping corridors.

Milena Machado undertook her PhD studies at the Federal University of Espirito Santo (UFES), investigating air pollution impacts on health and quality of life in industrialized urban areas. She is an industrial engineer (UFOP) and has a master's degree in Production Engineering (UFMG). She is an associate professor at the Federal Institute of Science and Technology of Espirito Santo. She teaches undergraduate engineering and business courses. Besides the teaching activities, she conducts several kinds of research in the Air Quality Research Lab (NQualiAr) and Stochastically Process Research Lab (Nunes) at the Federal University of Espirito Santo, where she has performed experimental and statistical investigations in many different areas. She has the skills and experience acquired during almost ten years in developing surveys, citizen science studies, applying regression models, and time series analysis and their predictive modelling.

Hervé Sourya Malazoue is at the end of his professional master 2 course at the Maritime University of Togo, option: management of maritime and port activities. He is the head of maritime and logistics operations at GEMINI transport. He also has humanitarian skills and holds several international certificates, such as security risk management (national level) from INSSA (International NGO Safety and Security Association) issued in 2024; certificate in supply and logistics from the Chartered Institute of Logistics and Transport Accredited course of UK, London, issued in 2024. His scientific topics essentially concern logistics and transport, the making of the city, and the practices of appropriation and use of urban and peri-urban spaces. He has also contributed through various projects to improve freight operations between landlocked countries in the Sahel.

Eva Merico got her Master's degree in "Environmental impact assessment and certification" in 2010 and her PhD in Environmental Sciences in 2017 from the University Ca' Foscari in Venice with a Thesis titled: "Assessment of air pollutants contribution of harbour activities in Venice and Brindisi areas", which was awarded as the best PhD Thesis by the Italian Aerosol Society in 2018. In 2012, she started her career research in atmospheric and climate sciences with two post-degree position scholarships at the Institute of Atmospheric Sciences and Climate of the National Research Council (ISAC-CNR in Lecce), until becoming a post-doc researcher from 2018. Her research activity is both field and laboratory experimental and was extensively devoted to estimating the relative contribution of ship emissions to particulate matter and gaseous concentrations in different sites (in the framework of international projects). Currently, her research is focused on different aspects such as: (i) identification, characterization of atmospheric particulate sources, using both high-resolution temporal measurements and statistical analysis/receptor models based on chemical composition and meteorology; (ii) spatial and temporal trends of particulate concentration and source contribution; (iii) health and toxicological effects of atmospheric particulate matter due to both natural and anthropogenic sources; and (iv) evaluation of temporal and spatial pattern of carbonaceous particulate fractions (i.e., elemental carbon, organic carbon, equivalent black carbon), determined by optical and thermo-optical methods, and other elements (i.e., metals) with ED-XRF technique.

She is a member of the Italian Aerosol Society (since 2015) in the WGs "Sampling techniques and analysis of PMx" and "Aerosol generation sources and processes"; of the macroarea of ISAC-CNR research in Atmospheric composition, climate forcing and air quality; of the WG "Atmospheric Aerosol Studies" of the European Aerosol Assembly (since 2022). In 2022, she was Guest Editor of Special Issue "Environmental Footprint of Shipping—Characteristics and Mitigation Strategies" of the *Journal of Marine Science and Engineering (JMSE)* – Open Access Journal by MDPI.

She worked in a number of research projects at the regional, national, and international levels, attending many conferences, and also establishing fruitful collaborations with leading international groups in the field of atmospheric sciences, which led to over 25 publications.

Matteo Nicolini is Full Professor of Comparative Law at the University of Verona (Italy) and Visiting Lecturer at the Newcastle University Law School (UK). His fields of research cover comparative law and methodology, law and humanities, and law and geography. He is the author of monographs, essays, and books in English, Spanish, and Italian. His most recent contributions in the field of legal geography are: *Legal Geography: Comparative Law and the Production of Space* (Cham, 2022); "The Land, the Sea, and the Colonial Production of Space within the Anglo/British Empire", in *Legalities: The Australian and New Zealand Journal of Law and Society*, vol. 4.1, 2024, pp. 43–67; M. Nicolini, "When the Sea Does Have Character: Post-Brexit Maritime Cooperation as Place-Consciousness", in *Belgeo. Revue Belge de Géographie*, vol. 4, 2024, pp. 1–25.

Theo Notteboom is Professor of Port and Maritime Economics. He is Chair Professor of 'North Sea Port' at the Maritime Institute of Ghent University, and a professor at the Faculty of Business and Economics at the University of Antwerp and Antwerp Maritime Academy. He previously held positions as Professor and Foreign Expert at universities in Dalian and Shanghai, China, and as an MPA Visiting Professor at Nanyang Technological University in Singapore. He is a former President (2010–2014) of the International Association of Maritime Economists (IAME). He is the co-founder and co-director of Porteconomics.eu and a member of the Risk and Resilience Committee of the International Association of Ports and Harbors (IAPH). He is an Associate Editor of *Maritime Economics & Logistics* and serves on the editorial boards of eight other leading academic journals in the field. He has published extensively in top-tier academic journals, as well as in reports, book contributions, proceedings, and specialized press. He is the editor/author of about a dozen academic books, including the handbook *Port Economics, Management and Policy* (Notteboom, Pallis & Rodrigue, 2022; Routledge). He is among the most cited maritime economists worldwide. Theo Notteboom has participated as promoter or co-promoter in more than 100 academic research programmes related to the port and maritime industry and logistics topics.

Serge Novikov obtained his bachelor's and his M.Sc. degrees in Geography at the University of Montreal. He is a researcher for the Interuniversity Research Centre on Enterprise Networks, Logistics and Transportation (CIRRELT). He has worked on different research projects related to the maritime industry, including advanced technologies in health safety of the cruise shipping industry, best practices for shipping logistics and decarbonation strategies for shipping companies and ports.

Athanasios Pallis is Professor of Ports and Shipping Economics and Policy at the Department of Maritime Studies, University of Piraeus, Greece. Co-director of the web-knowledge platform PortEconomics, and Vice-Chair of the global Port Performance Research Network (PPRN), in 2022, he was listed in the top 2% of most cited researchers in the realm of transportation and logistics around the globe. A regular advisor of international institutions on projects shaping maritime shipping and ports in North America, South America, Asia, and Europe, he led UN research on the impact of the pandemic on maritime supply chains. He served as President of the International Association of Maritime Economists (IAME), Fulbright Scholar at Columbia University, US, Secretary General of MedCruise, and General Secretary for Ports & Port Policy, Ministry of Shipping, Greece. He co-authored the book *Port Economics, Management and Policy*. He is currently a member of the IAPH Risk & Resilience Committee and co-authors the IAPH World Ports Tracker.

Barbara Polo Martin holds a degree in History from the University of Valladolid (UVA) (2013) and a PhD in Geography, Territorial Planning, and Environmental Management (2020) from the University of Barcelona (UB). Since 2025, she is Assistant Professor at the Autonomous University of Madrid (Spain).

She has nine years of academic experience, with professional ties to various universities. In 2023–2024, she worked as a post-doc at the CNRS (National Center for Scientific Research) in Paris as part of the ANR-funded MAGNETICS project (2022–2026). During this time, she has combined scientific research and teaching activities, as well as educational innovation. Her research specialization began in the fields of the history of cartography, territorial planning, and geomatics, and is currently expanding her knowledge into the fields of geomatics and spatial analysis applied to socio-economic sciences, health, and sustainable development.

Giuseppe Rigobello is a PhD candidate in Comparative Public Law at the University of Verona (Italy) and at the University of Valladolid (Spain). His research concerns the cultural dimension of environmental protection and the constitutional value of the landscape.

Catherine Roche is member of the management team of the Maison Européenne des Sciences de l'Homme et de la Société Lille – Nord de France. She is also the Head of the "Pôle de Recherche Humanités" (House of Humanities) at ULCO and Deputy Director of the Doctoral School in Human and Social Sciences at the Universities of Amiens – Picardie, Artois, and ULCO. Her research has a specific focus on environmental law and marine renewable energies. Among her publications are: *Le droit de la pêche, embryon colbertiste de la préoccupation environnementale (XVIème siècle – XXIème siècle)*, with F. Davansant; *Sharing Is Caring, but Is the Shore Cared for? The Sharing Paradox of the French Coast*, with S. J. Hauser; *La croisière en Méditerranée: un levier de développement pour les ports mineurs ? Le cas des villes-ports espagnoles, françaises et monégasques,* with M. Lo Prete, A. Dubois, Ph. Chagnon & R. Lacoste.

Jane Meri Santos is Full Professor in Air Pollution at the Department of Environmental Engineering at the Federal University of Espírito Santo (UFES), Brazil. She earned her PhD from the University of Manchester (UMIST) in England, where she specialized in dispersion modelling in urban areas. She holds a degree in Mechanical Engineering from UFES and a Master's in Mechanical Engineering from PUC-Rio, Brazil.

At UFES, she has undertaken several international appointments: as a visiting scholar at the École des Mines d'Alès in France, where she investigated odour emissions from wastewater treatment plants; and as a visiting professor at the University of New South Wales in Australia, where she studied momentum and mass transfer at the air–liquid interface to parameterize atmospheric emissions from passive surfaces. She also held a visiting position at the University of Southampton, UK, where she modelled mass transfer in urban canopies. She has also held several administrative roles at UFES, including Director of the International Office for six years, Head of Department for eight years, and Coordinator of the PhD Programme in Environmental Engineering for four years.

She is a recipient of the CNPq Research Scholarship, and her research portfolio includes approximately 100 peer-reviewed journal articles, an h-index of 25 with around 2,000 citations, and the successful supervision of ten PhD students. She leads the Air Quality Research Group (GPQA) at UFES, which comprises eight academic staff (four of whom also hold

CNPq research grants), three postdoctoral researchers, and over 30 PhD candidates.

Ling Sun, PhD in Engineering, is an Associate Professor at College of Transport & Communications, Shanghai Maritime University, and has served as the Deputy Director of the Department of International Shipping. He is also a Postdoctoral Fellow in Business Administration at the School of Management, Fudan University, and a Visiting Scholar at the French National Center for Scientific Research EconomiX (UMR 7235).

His expertise includes port and shipping logistics, sustainable development of ports and shipping, and cruise ship management. In the past five years, he has presided over national projects with a total amount of 2.6 million yuan, including a sub-topic of the National Key R&D Program – Statistical Monitoring and Supervision Technology for Cross-Border Trade (2022YFF0903403); he has also presided over or participated in ten other national and provincial-level projects, published over 30 papers, with 24 indexed in SCI/SSCI (18 as the first author), granted six utility model patents and participated in one related standard.

Currently, he is seconded to the construction of a national high-end think tank, the "Sustainable Transportation Innovation Center", within the "China International Center for Sustainable Transportation Innovation and Knowledge", and serves as a young editor for both the *Journal of Changsha University of Science & Technology* and the *Journal of Metropolitan Development Research.*

Mathias Tranchant is Professor of Medieval History at the University of South Brittany (Lorient), specialist in maritime history, Mathias Tranchant focuses his work on maritime economies, the relationship to risk, port trajectories, and the technological means of coastal societies in Atlantic France. He is currently director of the "GIS Humanités et sciences de la mer" and co-director of the *Revue d'Histoire Maritime.*

Patrick Verhoeven is the managing director of the International Association of Ports and Harbors (IAPH). The organization represents 201 ports and 175 port-related businesses in 94 countries. Prior to joining IAPH in 2017, Patrick spent 24 years in Brussels representing the interests of shipowners, port authorities, terminal operators, and ship agents at the EU level. He started his career in 1991 with the Antwerp-based ship agent Grisar & Velge. From 2019 to 2022, Patrick served on the supervisory board of the Ukrainian Sea Ports Authority as deputy chairman. Patrick holds a PhD in applied economics and a bachelor's in law from the University of Antwerp. He is an associate professor at the university's Centre for Maritime and Air Transport Management (C-MAT).

Jörg Vögele is Professor of Modern History and Member of the Medical Faculty at the Department of History, Philosophy and Ethics of Medicine of the Heinrich-Heine University of Düsseldorf, Germany. From 2003 to

2015, he acted as Managing Director of the Institute for the History of Medicine, and from 2016 to 2022 as Deputy Director of the Department of History, Philosophy and Ethics of Medicine, University of Düsseldorf. He was a Fellow of the University of Liverpool and a Visiting Professor at Charles University in Prague. His recent research focuses on epidemics and pandemics, on health and disease in urban areas, and on the Danse Macabre.

Liehui Wang is a professor at the School of Geographic Sciences, East China Normal University. He is also the Vice President of the Institute for Global Innovation and Development of ECNU, and a researcher of the Center for Modern Chinese City studies, a key research base of Humanities and Social Sciences of the Ministry of Education.

In 2008, he graduated from the Institute of Historical Geography of Fudan University and received a doctoral degree in history. From 2008 to 2010, he was a postdoctoral fellow at ECNU, where he has worked since 2010. The main research directions are transportation geography, big data analysis, such as AIS (Automatic Identification System), which can accurately track global shipping flows, etc.

He has published nearly 60 papers in journals such as *Transport Reviews*, *Growth and Change*, *Acta Geographica Sinica*, and other publications. He has published two books, *Forming the New Hub: Geographical Study on the Relationship between Shanghai and Ningbo ports (1843–1941)* and *The Structure and Evolution of China's Shipping Network*. He is leading a major project of the National Social Science Foundation of China and a general project of the National Natural Science Foundation.

Sheng Zhang is a PhD candidate at the School of Geographic Sciences, East China Normal University, Shanghai, China. His research interests include port geography, the 21st Century Maritime Silk Road, and the impact of maritime logistics on urban development. He has published his work in SSCI Q1 journals such as *Ocean & Coastal Management and Applied Geography* and Chinese Geographical CSSCI journals such as *Acta Geographica Sinica*, *Geographical Research*, and *Urban Planning Forum*. From 2024 to 2025, he is a visiting doctoral researcher at the EconomiX Laboratory, University of Nanterre.

Sabah Zrari Djellid is the director of the Observatorio y Prospectiva research office as well as the International Institute of Ports and Cities. With extensive experience in urban planning and public policy, she has been involved in various international projects related to urban development and port infrastructure management.

Foreword

Christos Hadjichristodoulou

Ports and port cities have long stood at the crossroads of global mobility, trade, and human health. From the earliest maritime routes that connected continents and cultures to today's highly interconnected shipping networks, ports have functioned as both engines of economic development and gateways for environmental and health risks. The COVID-19 pandemic, alongside accelerating climate change and persistent pollution challenges, has once again brought this dual role into sharp focus. In this context, *Port Cities, Pollution, and Public Health* is both timely and necessary.

This volume offers a comprehensive and interdisciplinary examination of the complex relationships between port activities, environmental pressures, and health outcomes in port cities. It moves beyond narrow or sectoral perspectives by bringing together historical analysis, empirical research, qualitative insights, and policy-oriented reflections. In doing so, it demonstrates that the health impacts of ports cannot be understood in isolation from their social, economic, environmental, and governance contexts.

By exploring the long history of ports as sites of disease control, quarantine, and public health innovation, this volume reminds us that contemporary challenges are not entirely new. From medieval and early modern responses to epidemics in European ports to the development and implementation of quarantine and sanitary measures, ports have consistently served as laboratories for public health governance. These historical perspectives enrich our understanding of present-day debates, showing how institutional memory has shaped responses to health threats over centuries.

At the same time, the volume is firmly grounded in contemporary evidence. Robust empirical analyses of air pollution and other environmental stressors linked to shipping and port-related activities demonstrate their associations with chronic disease and quality of life. The geographical scope – spanning Europe, Africa, Asia, and Latin America – underscores the global relevance of these issues while also highlighting important regional differences in exposure, vulnerability, and policy responses. Particularly valuable are the contributions that integrate environmental data with health and social indicators, offering more nuanced insights into how port activity affects populations living and working in port cities.

Beyond measuring impacts, the volume engages critically with governance and policy. Ports operate within complex institutional landscapes, where responsibilities for environmental protection, public health, transport, and economic development are often fragmented. Addressing governance, legal frameworks, and performance indicators illuminates both the progress made and the gaps that remain in integrating health considerations into port decision-making.

The COVID-19 pandemic provides a particularly powerful lens through which to view these challenges. Ports were not only affected by the pandemic; they were also central to maintaining essential supply chains and managing unprecedented public health risks at points of entry. Examining port resilience and the response of global port networks during COVID-19 offers important lessons on preparedness, coordination, and real-time information sharing.

What emerges from this volume is a clear message: port cities must be understood as living environments, not merely as nodes in global logistics chains. The health of port workers, nearby communities, and travelling populations is shaped by cumulative exposures to pollution, occupational risks, and governance choices. Addressing these challenges requires interdisciplinary collaboration and sustained dialogue between researchers, port authorities, public health professionals, policymakers, and affected communities.

Port Cities, Pollution, and Public Health makes a significant contribution to this dialogue. By combining historical insight with contemporary analysis and forward-looking perspectives, it provides readers with the tools to better understand – and ultimately to mitigate – the health impacts of ports and shipping. The volume will be of interest not only to scholars in public health, environmental studies, and transport research, but also to practitioners and decision-makers seeking evidence-based approaches to healthier and more sustainable port cities. In an era defined by global mobility, climate change, and emerging health threats, the questions addressed in this volume are no longer peripheral. They are central to how we conceive the future of ports, cities, and public health.

Acknowledgement

This work is supported by the research project "Maritime Globalization, Network Externalities and Transport Impacts on Cities" (MAGNETICS) (ANR-22-CE22-0002, 2022–2026) funded by the French National Research Agency (ANR).

Introduction

Mariantonia Lo Prete and César Ducruet

As essential nodes in supply chains, seaports are intricate systems. This is because seaports are vital connecting hubs for international trade, port-related industry and passenger travel. They connect land-based and maritime transportation networks and can handle both passengers and freight. They are also a critical link in maintaining territorial cohesion between continents and particularly with insular areas. A wide range of activities in or near ports are common to the majority of industrial areas (e.g., oil terminals, rail and road traffic, chemical and petrochemical plants, manufacturing and industry), but several are specific to a harbour setting, such as loading and unloading of goods, oil jetties, shipyards, fishing fleets, marinas, dredging and the building of port infrastructures (Lecue and Darbra, 2019). As such, they attract thousands of employees both offshore during maritime voyages and onshore to operate various port-related activities. If maritime transport and port-related activities are vectors of industrial, technological, energy and ecological transitions (Serry, 2017; Chouquet and Motte-Baumvol, 2021; Notteboom et al., 2022) as well as promoters of economic growth and innovation at local, regional and global levels, they also may cause several environmental and health impacts on neighbouring territories such as cities and their populations.

Historically, port cities have had a prominent role in the transmission of diseases through flows of goods and people (Vögele and Umehara, 2015; Schubert et al., 2021). In addition, different forms of pollution, such as air, noise, visual, olfactive, soil and water pollution, can result from such activities with negative consequences for human health and the environment (Lo Prete, 2012). Environmental aspects are inherent in port activities and may have direct or indirect negative health impacts (Lo Prete, 2015; Lees et al., 2022). Different activities within port operations affect the environment in varying ways and degrees: health and safety issues, habitat disturbance and biodiversity loss and depletion of non-renewable resources. Although these different forms of pollution and impacts vary from port to port, it is possible to establish a general classification of the environmental impacts associated with port activities and operations, ranging from offshore to onshore port activities.

DOI: 10.4324/9781003639589-1

This introduction to the volume *Port Cities, Pollution, and Public Health: Environmental Health Issues from Shipping and Ports* aims to show that ports are no longer just spaces adapted to the local biophysical environment, as they were in the early stages of their development, but also spaces that modify this environment and evolve in terms of planning. Their development is inexorably linked to considerations of the environment and public health. So, this volume raises a fundamental question: how can we understand the relationship that exists today between port cities, pollution and public health? Indeed, port cities must now comply with an increasing number of obligations from different and complementary angles: moving towards the decarbonization of maritime transport and industrial activities, implementing environmental and health policies, and adapting to global changes with correlated port strategies.

The International Maritime Organization regulates maritime transport activities globally and has adopted several international treaties to protect the marine environment and reduce air and water pollution in coastal communities and seaports. As part of the United Nations, it also supports the implementation of the 14 Sustainable Development Goals (SDGs) while, at the same time, promotes world trade and facilitates the global economy. The World Port Climate Initiative of the International Association of Ports and Harbors (IAPH) fosters awareness, studies and information exchange about environmental issues in ports globally. The International Association of Cities and Ports (IACP/AIVP) has developed the Agenda 2030 for sustainable port cities, including 150 best practices learned from 30 years of collective experience. In accordance with the World Health Organization (WHO) International Health Regulations, the spread of infectious diseases at points of entry, including seaports, is surveyed and controlled, based on the Maritime Declaration of Health and the Ship Sanitation Certificate for both goods and passengers. In Europe, the EU Healthy Gateways project supports coordination between EU Member States to address cross-border health risks, including at seaports, through a network of communication and rapid notification of events with health risks, a catalogue of best practices, guidelines and action plans, and facilitates their implementation in ports. Also in Europe, the EcoPorts initiative of the European Sea Ports Organization encourages ports to use a "self-diagnosis method" to benchmark their environmental footprint and submit it to the Port Environmental Review System, which is independently certified and renewable every two years.

While sectoral approaches are useful, they do not provide a comprehensive understanding of the complex relationship between port cities, pollution and public health. So, the methodological orientation adopted by the volume is founded on an interdisciplinary, multilevel and systemic approach, while drawing on geographical diversity through the analysis of a wide literature and the selection of case studies. To lay the cornerstone for reflection before going into detail about each contribution to this book, this introduction is structured as follows. First, we set the scene and mobilize the approaches and concepts necessary to understand this relationship. We next propose a discussion about the gaps and limitations of current efforts, both academic and practical, towards building greener and healthier port cities in Europe. The structure of the book is then presented, before opening the discussion on the perspectives with a look into the future.

The city-port relationship through the lens of environmental and public health issues

The first approach necessary to understand environmental and health issues is to consider development not only from the perspective of the port itself (Charlier, 1992; Lo Prete, 2012; Lavaud-Letilleul, 2012), but also from the perspective of its relationship with the city and the quality of life of local populations (Lo Prete, 2015). In fact, this issue of the city-port relationship is characteristic of the approach that has emerged since the 2000s: one that considers port development and the environment together.

The significance of the pioneering work of Claude Comtois and Brian Slack (2003, 2005) lies in their demonstration that the link between port development and the environment operates along two axes: technical, i.e. through technological innovation in equipment and infrastructure, and spatial, i.e. through the regulation of spaces already under the control of port operators or in their development plans. However, the work of these same authors on changes in the missions of port authorities (Comtois and Slack, 2003), as well as the work of Cyril Chédot on changes in the practices of port operators (2001), also identifies a third, socio-economic axis. Many port authorities now integrate the environment into their management, even though this integration entails external costs to the market (Frémont, 2019; Lacoste and Lo Prete, 2024).

While global maritime trade was expected to slow down following the COVID-19 crisis (UNCTAD, 2021), ports handle increasing quantities of products, putting pressure on existing transport infrastructures. For cities hosting ports, a tension persists between the economic advantages of direct sea access and the social and environmental costs of cargo transshipment (OECD, 2014; Ducruet et al., 2024a). Port migration outside urban cores had been initially a response to port expansion schemes in the 1960s and 1970s, for modern terminals to reach deep-water sites, in a context of rapid technological change in shipping, such as growing vessel size (Hayuth, 1982). It also provided an opportunity for traditional port cities to redevelop their waterfront for new urban uses (Hoyle, 1989). The motivation of municipal actors and private land developers was both economic, to take advantage of the high land rents near the water (West, 1989), and environmental, to profit from cleaner air making waterside areas even more attractive.

However, port migration and waterfront redevelopment did not fully eradicate environmental impacts. On the one hand, if not by ships, traditional port cities became served by trucks to/from distant port terminals, often causing congestion and pollution along land-based transport corridors and within urban agglomerations, especially when mixed with commuter flows at peak hours. On the other hand, modern ports and related industrial complexes are still surrounded by local communities, which are often socially disadvantaged (Bertoncello and Hagel, 2016). A worldwide analysis of port migration showed that between 1977 and 2008, the proportion of inner city port traffic in total port city traffic remained the lowest and even decreased for liquid bulk (from 48.5% in 1977 to 39.1% in 2008) and solid bulk (from 65.6% to 47.3%), while containers (from 82.0% to 61.4%) and general cargo (79.7% to 64.2%) remained dominantly urban (Ducruet et al., 2023). This is because the latter traffics are more likely to be manufactured goods, imported and consumed by densely populated environments (Ducruet and Itoh, 2016).

As ports are often magnets for industrial activity, pollution may also come from a variety of sites, such as power plants, shipbuilding plants, iron and steel plants, nonferrous metal plants, paper and paper pulp plants, oil refineries and chemical and petrochemical plants. The health implications of residing near such activities have been the focus of numerous studies, including a dedicated WHO report (Mudu et al., 2014). However, these studies do not discuss the specific role of port and related transport/logistics activities (Domingo et al., 2020; Marquès et al., 2020; Martuzzi et al., 2014). Heavy industrial sites are of key concern as accidents and hazards frequently occur in these locations. At the same time, the risks associated with the transport of hazardous materials to and from such sites should not be overlooked. According to a report published by the United Nations, this form of pollution not only has a major impact on the environment and human health, but also contributes to global warming and extreme weather conditions (UNCTAD, 2021).

This consideration has continued to evolve, in line with the affirmation of the concept of sustainable development, particularly through the process of developing and applying environmental and health policies in port development. In light of the recent COVID-19 pandemic and of these different forms of pollution, the enforcement of public health capacity, both in terms of prevention and answer of pollutions and infectious diseases, is today a crucial need for port city development. We can therefore see that not only does the relationship between the port and the city continue to exist despite the process of spatial separation, but also that environmental and health issues have become an intrinsic condition for the balance and therefore the success of this relationship.

The usefulness of a systemic vision

The second approach is to integrate studies on socio-economic systems on the one hand, and studies on natural systems on the other. The priority interactions between socio-economic systems and natural systems can be understood through two key concepts. The first concept explicitly advocates that what is often divided into natural and human systems should be considered a single, complex Social-Ecological System (SES). The SES (Redman et al., 2004) considers the complexity of human systems in strong interaction with the environmental system that serves as life matrix. The second concept is One Health, which aims to promote a pluridisciplinary and global approach of health challenges, at the interface between animal health, human health and the environment, allowing to tackle both health and environmental challenges. The concept of One Health, historically coming from medical and veterinary sciences, sheds light on the interconnections between human health, animal health, and the health of ecosystems. Taking actions on climate change, and contributing to sustainable development, this concept mobilizes multiple sectors, disciplines and communities at varying levels of society.

In the marine and coastal context in which maritime and port activities operate and develop, this approach sheds an essential light on health challenges linked to the environmental pressures produced by the presence of a port with all its activities in a given territory. If the SES offer a systemic vision of the relationships between human societies and their marine and coastal environments, One Health introduces a specific entry through health as sustainability indicator and as major vigilance point. The articulation between SES and OneHealth allows linking immediate sanitary challenges (e.g., exposure to pollutants) to the socio-economic governance of port-city uses, to understand how to reinforce port-city cooperation and thus, the resilience of these marine and coastal socio-ecosystems which are the ports. On these elements depend not only the economic vitality of territories concerned by maritime and port activities, but also, and above all, the public health of populations.

This book enhances our current knowledge by adding a systemic perspective on environmental and health issues linking offshore and onshore, a comprehensive review of the sources and types of port-related pollutions and impacts, an up-to-date review of technical, technological and organizational solutions, and an international perspective blending quantitative and qualitative analyses. As the port industry is global, the related environmental and health issues interest actors at all levels:

- international organizations dealing with maritime transport and port city development;
- European and national associations of port and other supply chain actors;
- coastal WHO Member States and inland countries that possess river port cities;
- urban metropolitan areas and smaller municipalities hosting ports; and
- port authorities, terminal operators, transport and logistics firms and infrastructure providers.

The port–city interface, in particular, deserves attention from a multiplicity of stakeholders:

- environment and/or health practitioners at local level involved with management of the waterfront;
- planners and local decision-makers, politicians and public authorities with responsibility for urban and port development, environmental management, social affairs and public health;
- civil society organizations, local initiatives and citizens concerned with the impact of port activities on urban settings and the local quality of life; and
- researchers, landowners, environmental consultancies, engineers and developers.

Ports are distinguished by a very diverse range of features: morphology, site and situation, land area, water depth, traffic size and specialization (bulks, passengers, containers), multimodal linkages (road, rail, river), hinterland coverage, logistics capabilities, productivity, administrative status (public, private) and type of ownership (local, national). Such differences also apply to the different terminals within a port, which are often operated by distinct entities (Slack and Frémont, 2009). Cities hosting a port – and in some cases, several ports – also differ greatly in their demographic size, population density and economic structure. Distance between port and city, the pattern of transport networks, topography and wind direction also influence the level of exposure to pollutions. Life quality and health concerns extend from port labour to local populations and the rest of the city region, which can be affected by operations along the whole supply chain. Thus, improvement of environmental health conditions does not only concern port areas and adjacent urban neighbourhoods. Greener and healthier planning and management of port cities help to address wider issues of freight and people mobility, socio-spatial cohesion and reduction of inequalities for the whole agglomeration. Addressing these key challenges requires that dialogue between multiple actors and disciplines be strengthened or built.

Gaps and limitations of current research

Research on the local environmental and health impacts of ports is vast and manifold, yet it faces a number of challenges. First, it is often difficult to separate port-related pollution from other pollutions in a port city, given the intermingling of different sources (carried in the air, into water, etc.). The quality of data for research and action delivered by air quality or noise level sensors in and around port areas will depend on careful study of their location, in terms of recurrent wind patterns, the presence of buildings and other obstacles, etc. Second, defining the population at risk is inevitably partial. Residents living near port-industrial complexes are potential targets for surveys, but to reach firm conclusions, medical studies need a wider population sample, including people working or living further from the port. Third, a port is a transshipment node in constant evolution and movement, whose activity consists in adapting to rapidly changing trade patterns and technical, technological and managerial requirements of the supply chain. This implies that flows vary in composition and intensity on different timescales, with daily peak hours and seasonality. Heavy industries around ports have their own fluctuations, from the waxing and waning of global commodity prices to the on-site necessity of temporarily shutting down for maintenance.

Two main bodies of research coexist and need further integration: environmental studies and health studies (Ducruet et al., 2024b). They differ greatly in every aspect, from disciplinary specialization to time and spatial scale and consideration of health impacts. The health consequences of port and port-related activities on local populations are not well explored in the literature, compared with the multiplicity of works assessing and discussing pollutions and the measures used to lower them. Health impacts are often implicit in relation to onshore or offshore pollution sources, which are not addressed simultaneously or through their accumulated impact.

The following gaps will need to be filled to create a more robust evidence base for policymaking. First, the vast literature on "healthy cities" overlooked the port function, despite the maritime character of studied cities. This is the case, for instance, of Helsinki, Liverpool, London and Vancouver in the work of Otgaar and Klijs (2010). Elsewhere, a lot has been written in relation with the Healthy Cities program of the WHO. This project was launched in 1978, with the ambition to promote health and well-being through action at the level of individual local authorities. There are currently more than 2,000 municipalities linked through national Healthy City networks in Europe – with similar networks across all the regions of the globe.

A related book on health and urban planning tackled issues such as climate change and unhealthy lifestyles, leading to obesity, mental illness and growing health inequalities on four continents (Barton et al., 2015). Like for urban studies in general, except for city logistics, this literature tended to ignore material flows and freight movement, including ports (Birtchnell et al., 2015; Hall and Hesse, 2013). When it comes to transport and urban health, more likely are studies dealing with walking and cycling (Pucher and Buehler, 2010), the improvement of public transport to reduce heat islands, car use, noise and air pollution (Nieuwenhuijsen, 2020), and the trend towards compact and mixed-used urban designs (Sallis et al., 2016).

A whole literature investigated similar changes occurring at the port–city interface or "urban waterfront", where former sailortowns were transformed to accommodate new urban uses (Norcliffe et al., 1996; Chaline, 1994; Baudouin et al., 1997), mentioning environmental issues but not health explicitly. Former port activities and transport facilities may have been maintained in the current era (Bruttomesso, 2001), while even new port uses may have been developed instead of postmodern activities like tourism and recreation (Charlier, 1992). Research about port cities and sustainability has grown apace in recent years. In particular, increasingly precise sensor data allow measuring and mapping the intensity of pollutions across urban areas with explicit mention of the port origin (see, Sorte et al., 2019; Paschalidou et al., 2019; Fameli et al., 2020; Ramacher et al., 2020; Soggiu et al., 2020, for recent European case studies). But scientific works correlating port pollution and local population health remain scarce, partly due to lack of data, and because disentangling pollution sources on the one hand and assessing causal effects of disease/mortality on the other hand is difficult over such a large territory (Gianicolo et al., 2013; Vigotti et al., 2014; Bauleo et al., 2019; Lloret et al., 2021). A transition of port cities and maritime transport towards greener, low-carbon and health-oriented development is inevitable.

The literature about the greening of port operations is vast and is being regularly synthesized (see, Azarkamand et al., 2020, for a recent review); it mainly concerns how the different actors of the port community act in favour of sustainability, through both technical and organizational improvements. But efforts to address environmental problems are often carried out without consideration of health. Moreover, evidence on the health benefits of any interventions tackling port- or shipping-related activities is largely missing. Similarly, monitoring and evaluating the (un)intended health and environmental effects of interventions such as relocation of port activities away from cities which led to massive development of road transport in the following decades, would be warranted. Research on mental health impacts arising from environmental hazards from port-related activities is also missing, based on the searches conducted for this book. High-quality evidence on health impacts from shipping and port-related industrial activities on populations living in seaport cities is sparse.

Although some observational studies exist that point towards exposure-response relationships, further research is needed to determine the direction of causality (e.g., self-reported noise exposure and poor mental health). More research on the health effects of exposure to those as well as quantifying the number of people exposed is needed to identify ports as a source of this potential hazard. There are also gaps in local research on the contribution of seaports to infectious disease transmission compared to other points of entry.

Relatedly, no studies could be retrieved that conducted population exposure assessments segregated by onshore and offshore activities or even by different port- and shipping-related activities (such as berthing, manoeuvering) – studies that focused on environmental impacts calculate different levels of emissions from different activities, however, these findings have not consistently been linked to differential population exposures.

Issues relating to environmental (in)justice seem to be under researched, yet it is necessary to examine whether there are population groups that are more vulnerable to environmental health risks related to port activities. It is important to underline that in many places, port and city remain spatially and functionally close today and even geographically adjacent (Hall and Jacobs, 2012). A part of the inner-city port may still be active, and the outport is often located within a radius where certain pollutions can still affect the workers and residents of the traditional port city. Moreover, the populations of smaller municipalities having been the target of new port and terminal development – with related transport infrastructure and industries – are now exposed to acute levels of pollution, given the scale of such logistical complexes. Environmental and health issues caused by the proximity between smaller ports and cities are thus yet to be tackled. So, there is a lack of diversity in health endpoints that are assessed in relation to port-specific hazards. Particularly in smaller port cities, any epidemiological studies are likely to be underpowered due to small numbers of cases.

There is currently not a unified source-apportionment modelling approach to estimate the relative contribution of different port-related activities to air pollution (e.g., road traffic, shipping emissions) and to separate out the contributions of non-port-related activities. Therefore, researchers used different methods, such as dispersion modelling or receptor modelling, which hampers comparability. The relative contribution of port-related emissions is also influenced by the location of monitoring stations, which are not deployed according to uniform standards across countries and ports.

Especially regarding onshore activities, classification of (potentially) hazardous activities as port-related is not straightforward, and it implies governance issues. There is a lack of an integrated assessment approach that includes shipping, port/terminal, city/industry and hinterland. The literature on terminal operations is often disconnected from offshore and onshore dimensions. This also relates to the variety of geographic scales where environmental problems are addressed, from the port terminal itself to the wider city-region, which often hampers comparing assessments. There is a lack of quantification of emissions from port-related road traffic. Most of the modelling studies reviewed did not account for emission contributions from transport vehicles operating between the port and hinterland. The true burden of port-related emissions on health impacts may be under-estimated, as hinterland road traffic does not normally seem be considered in modelling studies quantifying emissions from port-related activities.

The evidence base largely consists of observational and modelling studies. For the former, residual confounding can often not be ruled out entirely. Modelling studies assessing exposure to pollution need to consider not just local pollution at any point in time but also non-static meteorological variables, geographical features such as street canyons and more realistic assumptions about people's movements at any given point in time. This could be achieved by applying population activity profiles, diversified by demographic groups in different microenvironments, such as residential environments, work environments or traffic environments. This would allow for specific considerations relating to outdoor concentrations infiltrating indoor environments in each microenvironment. This requires collection of more comprehensive and granular data sets as well as integration of data from various sources (epidemiology, meteorology, clinical health outcomes, mobility patterns).

In quantifying noise pollution, a-weighting is usually applied to the data, which might bias the conclusions drawn from noise mapping exercises. This may lead to underestimations of health impacts in low-frequency bands. In many cities, the port is a main source of non-audible low frequencies. More research on the health effects of exposure to those as well as quantifying the number of people exposed is needed to identify ports as a source of this potential hazard. More systematic investigations might shed further light on this.

As ports are heterogeneous, varying both in size and function, it is not useful to generalize findings from one port to another. Instead, city-level integrated health and environmental impact assessments in seaport cities are needed to evaluate whether populations in seaports have a greater health burden due to port-related activities than populations in non-seaport cities.

Perspectives and structure of the book

This book synthesizes the lessons learned from a panel of 19 chapters aimed at further understanding the environmental and health impacts of ports on populations in adjacent localities. Case studies cover examples from all over the world and in different time periods. As such, it offers a synthetic view on how port authorities and other decision-makers can ensure that maritime trade – and related landside operations – can prosper without endangering the health of the local community.

It proposes an overview of current environmental and health issues in port cities. It starts by presenting the mitigation and perception of port pollution (Part 1). Next, it examines the health impacts of ports in a historical perspective (Part 2), and it reviews and synthesizes the variety of existing approaches to measure the health impacts of ports and shipping (Part 3). Finally, it offers a reflection on a multilevel governance and policies (Part 4).

The first part focuses on the mitigation and perception of port pollution. It examines developments in solutions enabling the implementation of green port strategies or sustainable facilities. However, despite the various initiatives in place, citizens' perception of pollution caused by ports is also a fundamental factor to be considered in public policy. And while these policies currently focus mainly on the issue of air quality, progress still needs to be made in combating the chronic health effects of maritime and port activities, particularly in some developing countries.

In Chapter 1, César Ducruet and Mariantonia Lo Prete present an overview of existing initiatives in European port cities, whether individual or collective, due to their dispersion in the academic literature. These measures can be classified as "energy transition" or "transport fluidity", two of the three pillars constituting what can be the model of the "healthy, efficient and sustainable port city". If energy transition measures are directly aimed at reducing pollution, especially emissions, transport fluidity measures shall facilitate the flow of goods and people, to limit congestion, thereby reducing pollution.

In Chapter 2, Lorena Garcia-Alonso shows that the transition from polluting port to a sustainable one is a pressing challenge for port cities. Ports are becoming more and more disconnected from the local dynamics of the city. However, most large container ports continue to be located in densely populated areas, causing significant negative externalities, reducing the well-being and damaging the citizens' health. Nevertheless, with the global slowdown in economic activity, competition for spatial resources and pollution in port cities have come into focus, giving rise to a new trend in the literature concerned about greening ports. This chapter provides a literature review on the process of conversion of traditional ports to sustainable facilities, in which some SDGs compliance is now a goal.

In Chapter 3, Julia Appercelle, Marie-Laure Baron, Olivier Bueno, Sophie Cros and Alicia Jacquette examine the perception of the impact of port pollution on the health of its population. A survey conducted with 213 individuals in Le Havre and Rouen port cities found that 60% of respondents prioritize health, with Rouen perceived as more polluted. Moreover, 73% were unaware of environmental projects, indicating a lack of communication.

In Chapter 4, Milena Machado, Severine Frère and Jane Meri Santos study the impacts of air pollution on health and quality of life in a port and industrialised region located on the east coast of Brazil. The main findings highlight a gap between regulatory standards and citizens' perceived well-being. So, evidence suggests the need to integrate public perception into air quality policies and actions aiming at the improvement of air quality.

In Chapter 5, Hervé Sourya Malazoue focuses on the correlation between overall exposure to particulate matter (PM) generated by port traffic and chronic respiratory conditions observed in two groups of port workers at the port of Lomé. Interviews conducted in this qualitative study of harbour pilots and dockworkers highlight the absence of regulatory policy, the lack of personal protective equipment and related medical-social centre. The observed chronic diseases (bronchitis, asthma, back pain, cardiovascular disease) highlight the need to produce air quality monitoring data and related health information. The port of Lomé must anticipate its implication at the long-term by energy transition strategies and by the practice of social dialogue with regard to local residents who are also collateral victims of this port air pollution.

The second part focuses on the health impacts on ports and port cities from a historical perspective. With a variety of case studies analysed from different periods, the contributions reveal both the capacity of ports and cities to implement concrete solutions to health concerns and the inadequacies of port organizational models. In this setting of historical evidence, ports with their different historical testimonies also become a laboratory for resilience in the face of the intensity and diversity of health challenges.

In Chapter 6, Mathias Tranchant analyses the health challenges in the ports and port cities spread along the French coasts of Ponant in the Middle Ages. Territories of movement of people, ships and goods, but also places of production and storage, seaports constituted sensitive spaces exposed to all kinds of pollution but also likely to constitute hotbeds and nodes of transmission of various diseases faced by the users and managers of these ports. The study of these phenomena, their consequences and the attempts made to deal with them has never been carried out for Atlantic France.

In Chapter 7, Frédéric Davansant examines the mechanisms of epidemic control in 18th-century French commercial ports. Drawing on normative sources and administrative practice, it first reconstructs the fragmented legal framework through which the crown sought to regulate the sanitary risks associated with long-distance shipping. The Marseille model serves as a reference point against which the more improvised arrangements of Atlantic ports are measured. The study then turns to the concrete implementation of quarantines, sanitary cordons, inspection boats and religious rituals, highlighting both their empirical foundations and their uneven effectiveness. Particular attention is given to the roles of intendants, municipal officers, naval authorities and merchant elites, whose interests often collided when epidemic defence threatened to paralyse trade. By following several critical episodes, the chapter argues that the Ancien Régime did not construct a coherent "sanitary state", but rather a negotiated and adaptive system that nonetheless helped prevent large-scale epidemic conflagrations along France's maritime frontiers.

In Chapter 8, Sarah E. Hinman highlights spatial aspects of quarantine in port cities until the 20th century. Quarantine is typically associated with what was established among the European shipping powers beginning in the 14th century. Variation in the implementation of this practice and tolerance for its use are evident in the literature and in the outcomes of the International Sanitary Congresses held throughout the 19th and early 20th centuries. How port cities provided space for quarantine and its facilities is rather overlooked in the broader debates around the medical, legal and economic aspects of this practice that generally was viewed as a historical artefact during the 20th century. With emerging infectious respiratory diseases in the first two decades of the 21st century quarantine returned as means of controlling disease spread albeit more in the form of (self)isolation. This chapter seeks to explore variations in where quarantined people, vessels and goods were located in port cities in England, Australia and the United States until the early 20th century. In so doing, this will provide an opportunity to compare and contrast how different priorities and attitudes regarding quarantine were implemented and experienced on the port landscape as well as how some of these spaces are now sites of commemoration.

In Chapter 9, Jörg Vögele and Grażyna Liczbińska provide an outline of the major epidemics, health risks and public health strategies in selected European port cities in the 19th and early 20th centuries, and their causative factors. The growing world economy accelerated disease diffusion in coastal areas and dependent hinterlands. At the same time, substantial levels of in-migration aggravated the latent exposure risks of the indigenous population to endemic and epidemic diseases and led to a high background mortality. This situation made the need to confront health risks initially apparent in port cities and played a key role in the development of modern public health strategies. In this sense, port cities can be conceived as a laboratory of modernity where health conditions and the fight against disease in a globalized world can be studied.

The third part focuses on methodological approaches. The results obtained from different methods used to measure the environmental and health impacts of maritime and port activities highlight the correlation between these activities and environmental health issues. However, it raises questions about the relevance and capacity of models and statistical analyses to accurately measure these impacts and the cause-and-effect relationship between ports, the environment and health. To this end, it is necessary to combine qualitative methodological approaches.

In Chapter 10, Daniele Contini and Eva Merico focus on the impact of shipping on atmospheric concentrations of fine and ultrafine particles in coastal areas with potential effects on air quality, health and climate. Over the past two decades, advances in experimental techniques, air quality modelling and emission inventory analyses have improved understanding of the physical and chemical characteristics of ship-emitted pollutants and their transformations in the atmosphere. The implementation of mitigation strategies, focused on the use of low-sulphur fuels as well as in creation of specific Emission Control Areas (ECAs), has effectively reduced the impact of shipping to air quality and health for specific targeting specific pollutants. However, there are potentially negative effects on climate and limited effects on other pollutants such as metals. Further research should target the use of new alternative fuels, exhaust treatment technologies and port-level mitigation strategies to minimise the environmental and health impacts of maritime transport.

In Chapter 11, César Ducruet, Mariantonia Lo Prete, Magali Dumontet, Barbara Polo Martin, Charbel Alkhoury, Ling Sun and Sheng Zhang analyse the influence of multiple vessel traffics on air pollution and public health in European port cities. Confronting environment and public health data to a wide range of socio-economic and traffic characteristics over the period 2000–2019, this chapter provides a typology of 120 European port cities and zooms in on the most emblematic cases in each category based on the case studies found in qualitative literature.

In Chapter 12, Sheng Zhang, César Ducruet and Liehui Wang examine the relationship between maritime transportation and urban health in China where port-city development has not, overall, accorded sufficient priority to green port strategies, and a scale-first orientation remains dominant. The analysis integrates Lloyd's List maritime data on port traffic, air pollution data and CHARS social survey data to examine the associations between port characteristics and urban health in China. The main findings, which underline the negative correlation between different type of maritime traffic and chronic disease incidences, provide empirical support for healthy city development in China and underscore the pivotal role of port cities to reduce multimorbidity.

In Chapter 13, Charbel Alkhoury presents the Port Performance Capability Index (PPCI) as a robust framework designed to capture the multidimensional performances of ports based on economic, environmental, health and social governance perspectives. It also outlines a systematic literature review of the types of Port Performance Indicators that have been created over the years, illustrating their progression in scope, methodology and application. The analysis highlights the need to identify the most important indicators for socio-economic, environmental and health dimensions. This perspective reinforces that development should not be viewed as a singular indicator, but rather as the growth of multidimensional capabilities shaped by institutional, environmental and social contexts. Future stages of this study will develop an econometric model using the PPCI at the national level, and then at the local scale for particular ports. This will allow policymakers for greater understanding of how each of the dimensions of PPCI affects economic growth, the environment and health.

In Chapter 14, Ling Sun focuses on the impact of Chinese ports on local air pollution and public health. Using panel data from 35 Chinese port cities from 2013 to 2023 and by constructing a panel data model incorporating two-way fixed effects, it systematically compares the significant differences in air pollution and public health levels among dry bulk, liquid bulk and container-dominated port cities. The main findings indicate that dry bulk cargo has a relatively large negative environmental impact, while container throughput is positively correlated with economic development. For coastal port cities, developing dry bulk cargo easily leads to environmental problems, making it advisable to vigorously promote container business. Inland river ports may consider developing liquid bulk cargo. For ports with large throughput, dry bulk cargo is strongly associated with environmental pollution, necessitating enhanced environmental technologies to fully explore business potential. For ports with small throughput, container and liquid bulk businesses can be moderately developed where there is industrial demand, while improving safety and environmental protection facilities.

The fourth part focuses on governance and policies. Multiscalar dimension and multifunctionality of maritime and port activities further increase the governance complexity. In this context, it is not easy for stakeholders to adapt their strategies to the new environmental and health policies that contribute to remodelling port operations and the synergy between the port and the city.

In Chapter 15, Claude Comtois, Serge Novikov and Sarah Lutfy offer a reflection on seafarer health safety and security challenges in global shipping. Various international legal frameworks regulate the welfare of sea workers in the global shipping industry. The most significant is the Maritime Labour Convention (MLC) 2006. Port State control ensures compliance with the requirements of MLC 2006. The chapter examines nine regional port State controls reports, concerning deficiencies as grounds for vessel detention in relation to the health protection, medical care, welfare and social security protection of seafarers in ports of call under their jurisdiction for the period 2019–2025. The research has recorded 1,813 occurrences of such deficiencies related to 30 items during roughly 400,000 inspections. The analysis focuses on a detailed examination of the nature of deficiency, the ship type, the flag of registry and the geographical location. Solutions suggested to minimise seafarers' health risks involve assessing ship's assets, using information technology and enhancing automation.

In Chapter 16, Sabah Zrari Djellid analyses quality of life in Chile's port cities, focusing on Valparaíso and San Antonio within the debate on the environmental and social sustainability of port development. It argues that quality of life, conceived as a multidimensional construct encompassing material, environmental and relational dimensions, should become a core principle of port–city governance. Using data from Chilean quality-of-life observatories, the study compares objective and subjective indicators of well-being, revealing that despite gains in port efficiency and infrastructure, territorial and social inequalities persist. These findings demonstrate the value of combining statistical and perceptual approaches to assess territorial well-being and underscore the need for new governance instruments linking port performance with urban liveability. The chapter aligns with the ongoing reflection within UN-Habitat's Quality of Life Initiative, offering insights that support the transition from an impact-mitigation paradigm towards a systemic, quality-of-life-centred approach for sustainable port cities.

In Chapter 17, Matteo Nicolini and Giuseppe Rigobello offer a reflection on a "Collective place consciousness", coastal grabbing and the "toxic heritage" in the Venetian Lagoon. The appropriation of large parts of these coastal territories by supra-local economic actors to meet their financial interests highlights the complex relationships between coastal communities and legal-spatial production. The case study of the industrial pole of Porto Marghera in Venice is an example of coastal grabbing that also has health consequences, as it has altered the environmental equilibrium, leading to what has been termed the "toxic heritage". The degradation of the environment impacts on the health of the local population and, at same time, goes hand in hand with the exploitation of the touristic attractiveness of Venice.

In Chapter 18, Marine Chouquet, Mariantonia Lo Prete and Catherine Roche examine legal approach to taking public health issues into account in port governance. The links between ports and human health differ depending on the types of ports in question. Large seaports in particular require consideration. These ports host industrial activities that are likely to have an impact on surrounding populations' health, as do maritime activities themselves. The health of populations seems to have been largely overlooked in the texts on the safety of ships docking in ports. Beyond the provisions relating to epidemic prevention, the health issue proves to be a fragmented legal corpus. There is also a lack of an integrated assessment approach that includes shipping, port/terminal, city/industry and hinterland health risks. Although these risks are now taken into account, port authorities are rarely the decision-makers in this area.

In Chapter 19, Theo Notteboom, Athanasios Pallis and Patrick Verhoeven examines the early response of the IAPH and its member organisations to the challenges posed by the COVID-19 pandemic. The creation of the "IAPH-WPSP Port Economic Impact Barometer" (designed to collect real-time data on short-term impacts of COVID-19 on ports in the area of vessel calls, hinterland transport, distribution activities, procedural adaptations and workforce availability), highlighted the critical importance of information exchange, best practice sharing and coordinated action among stakeholders. Analysing 17 Barometer reports produced between April 2020 and April 2021 and based on surveys conducted among global ports, this chapter emphasizes the need for a holistic supply chain perspective in port strategy development, aiming to increase their resilience and extending beyond the ship–port interface to encompass landside logistics and nautical services.

Recommendations for drawing up a strategic and operational research programme

A look into the future

European port cities are set to face a wide range of challenges in the foreseeable future, which represent issues but also opportunities. On the long-term and depending on the emission scenario and the measurement method, sea level rise due to global warming is certain to ultimately redraw the map of the world (EEA, 2021). Coastal populations and activities may have to shift inland, while existing port infrastructures would become obsolete, forcing actors to rethink settlement patterns and intercontinental trade. However, the different coasts will be affected in various ways.

The declining use of fossil fuels will pose severe threats to maritime transport as the principal vector of international trade (Economist, 2021). Renewable energies are insufficient to meet the needs of the existing world fleet. New shipping technologies such as wind-propelled vessels may not be able, for technical reasons, to carry the vast quantities of goods that are currently moved around the world. This challenge is closely linked with growing discussion of the nearshoring, or even reshoring, of industrial activities from the Asia-Pacific region to North America and Europe (Consultancy.eu, 2022).

On the medium-term, the higher growth of coastal versus inland populations (Eurostat, 2011), attracted by the natural and cultural amenities offered by the seaside, presents both a threat to the environment in terms of coastal management and an opportunity for port cities to welcome new workers and residents. This trend is accentuated by the ageing population in developed countries. To best prepare for the resumption of global logistical operations after the COVID-19 pandemic, policymakers may propose alternatives to the excessive concentration of the maritime and ports sector (Merk et al., 2022). Other influential aspects include the deployment of the new Europe–Asia maritime silk roads by China, which will accentuate port competition.

In the short-term, the new and upcoming ECAs (Mediterranean, Black Sea, remainder of Norway), intended to further limit environmental and health impacts of shipping, will favour cooperation within Europe and its neighbourhood. Ongoing efforts to bring greater precision to the measurement of the environmental and health impacts of shipping will increase and refine current knowledge and help support decision-making.

Quality of life as a framework for port–city governance

When choosing to focus on the relationship between port cities, pollution and public health, it was intentional, as suggested by the title of the volume, to target an evolving relationship rather than a fixed picture, whether it be the opening of a new terminal or an ecological disaster. In the real world, it is more about a movement, sometimes conflictual (Lo Prete, 2012, 2015; Foulquier, 2016), which, from problems coming from development to adaptation efforts of port actors, determines the consideration of environmental health in port cities.

Considering environmental health in port development must cope with diverging interests, which motivate a systemic approach. The different approaches developed in this book underline the importance of articulating the concept of Socio-Ecological Systems (SES), which considers the complexity of human systems that interacts with the environmental system, which serves as a SES life matrix (Redman et al., 2004). This is also linked with the One Health concept, which aims to promote a pluridisciplinary and global approach to sanitary challenges by considering health at the crossroads between fauna, human and their environment, allowing to answer both health and environmental challenges.

As such, in any coastal territory, in which the port is a strategic and multifunctional tool, the combination of SES and One Health approaches allow to develop an integrated vision, linking ecological sustainability, socio-economic governance, population and environmental health, which are crucial to face climate change and environmental challenges in port cities of today and tomorrow. For this, it is mandatory it is necessary to have a fruitful collaboration between disciplines. Preventing impacts of environmental degradation on human health is thus made through numerous pipelines and actions that remain to be explored.

Related with the previous, a toolkit for environment and health monitoring and management at European ports could be created for benchmarking and monitoring pollution and facilitating comparisons. Such a tool could be based on the creation of a port-city database including both high-quality data on health and environmental outcomes, as well as analyses of barriers and facilitators of improved port governance. This should be generated according to uniform methodological and reporting standards across all countries to facilitate comparability and accountability.

References

Azarkamand S., Wooldridge C., Darbra R.M. (2020) Review of initiatives and methodologies to reduce CO2 emissions and climate change effects in ports. *International Journal of Environmental Research and Public Health*, 17(11): 3858.

Barton H., Thompson S., Burgess S., Grant M. (2015) *The Routledge Handbook of Planning for Health and Well-Being. Shaping a Sustainable and Healthy Future.* London: Routledge.

Baudouin T., Collin M., Prelorenzo C. (1997) *L'Urbanité des Cités Portuaires.* L'Harmattan, Collection 'Maritimes', Paris et Montréal.

Bauleo L., Bucci S., Antonucci C., Sozzi R., Davoli M., Forastiere F., Ancona C. (2019) Long-term exposure to air pollutants from multiple sources and mortality in an industrial area: A cohort study. *Occupational and Environmental Medicine*, 76(1): 48–57.

Bertoncello B., Hagel Z. (2016) Marseille: une relecture de l'interface ville-port au prisme de l'habiter. *Vertigo*, 16(3), https://doi.org/10.4000/vertigo.18162

Birtchnell T., Savitzky S., Urry J. (2015) *Cargomobilities: Moving Materials in a Global Age*. London: Routledge.

Bruttomesso R. (2001) Complexity on the urban waterfront. In: Marshall R. (Ed.), *Waterfronts in Post-Industrial Cities*. London: Taylor & Francis. pp. 39–50.

Chaline C. (1994) *Ces Ports Qui Créèrent des Villes*. L'Harmattan, Collection 'Maritimes', Paris et Montréal.

Charlier J. (1992) The regeneration of old port areas for new port uses. In: Hoyle B.S., Pinder D.A. (Eds.), *European Port Cities in Transition*. London: Belhaven Press, pp. 137-154.

Chédot C. (2001) Port et environnement, régulations et transitions dans les ports de commerce de l'Europe du Nord-Ouest. PhD dissertation in Territorial Planning, Le Havre University, CIRTAI.

Chouquet M., Motte-Baumvol J. (2021) *Les ports maritimes face aux défis du développement durable*. Volume 126, IFJD (Institut Francophone pour la Justice et la Démocratie).

Comtois C., Slack B. (2003) Innover l'autorité portuaire au 21e siècle : un nouvel agenda de gouvernance ». *Les Cahiers Scientifiques du Transport*, 44/2003: 11–24.

Comtois C., Slack B. (2005) Transformations de l'industrie maritime: portrait international de développement durable appliqué. Etudes et Recherche en Transport, Ministère des Transports du Québec, 247 p.

Consultancy.eu (2022) European companies increasingly moving to reshore Asia production. *Consultancy.eu*, 2 March 2022, https://www.consultancy.eu/news/7430/european-companies-increasingly-moving-to-reshore-asia-production

Domingo J.L., Marquès M., Nadal M., Schuhmacher M. (2020) Health risks for the population living near petrochemical industrial complexes. 1. Cancer risks: A review of the scientific literature. *Environmental Research*, 186: 109495.

Ducruet C., Itoh H. (2016) Regions and material flows: Investigating the regional branching and industry relatedness of port traffic in a global perspective. *Journal of Economic Geography*, 16(4): 805–830.

Ducruet C., Juhász R., Nagy D.K., Steinwender C. (2024a) All aboard: The effects of port development. *Journal of International Economics*, 151: 103963.

Ducruet C., Lo Prete, Polo Martin B., Sene M.A., M., Sun L., Itoh H., Pigné Y. (2024b) Ports and their influence on local air pollution and public health: A global analysis. *Science of the Total Environment*, 915: 170099.

Ducruet C., Notteboom T.E., Slack B. (2023) Port migration patterns in the global seaport system since the 1950s. In: Ducruet C., Notteboom T.E. (Eds.), *Port Systems in Global Competition. Spatial-Economic Perspectives on the Co-Development of Seaports*. London & New York: Routledge Studies in Transport Analysis, pp. 122–146.

Economist (2021) The age of fossil-fuel abundance is dead. *The Economist*, 4 October 2021, https://www.economist.com/finance-and-economics/the-age-of-fossil-fuel-abundance-is-dead/21805253

EEA (2021) *Global and European Sea Level Rise*. Copenhagen: European Environment Agency, https://www.eea.europa.eu/ims/global-and-european-sea-level-rise

Eurostat (2011) *Coastal Regions. Eurostat Regional Yearbook 2011*. Luxembourg City: Eurostat, https://ec.europa.eu/eurostat/documents/3217494/5728589/KS-HA-11-001-13-EN.PDF/c0dd33ed-0db2-4d8b-ae03-26d9bf3e57fc?version=1.0

Fameli K.M., Kotrikla A.M., Psanis C., Biskos G., Polydoropoulou A. (2020) Estimation of the emissions by transport in two port cities of the northeastern Mediterranean, Greece. *Environmental Pollution*, 257: 113598.

Foulquier E. (2016) Prendre la mesure de la conflictualité portuaire. *L'Information géographique*, L'Aménagement en débat, 80(4): 56–75.

Frémont A. (2019) Porte-conteneurs : une croissance sans fin? *Transports infrastructures et mobilité*, 513: 37–43.

Gianicolo E.A., Bruni A., Mangia C., Cervino M., Vigotti M.A. (2013) Acute effects of urban and industrial pollution in a government-designated "Environmental risk area": The case of Brindisi, Italy. *International Journal of Environmental Health Research*, 23(5): 446–460.

Hall P.V., Hesse M. (2013) *Cities, Regions and Flows*. London: Routledge.

Hall P.V., Jacobs W. (2012) Why are maritime ports (still) urban, and why should policy-makers care? *Maritime Policy and Management*, 39(2): 189–206.

Hayuth Y. (1982) The port-urban interface: an area in transition. *Area*, 14(3): 219–224.

Hoyle B.S. (1989) The port–city interface: Trends, problems, and examples. *Geoforum*, 20(4): 429–435.

Lacoste R., Lo Prete M. (2024) Les ports secondaires rouliers et ferries en France : le tournant ferroviaire des pré- et post-acheminements de remorques non accompagnées. *Les Cahiers scientifiques du transport*, 82: 21–42, https://doi.org/10.46298/cst.12575, CC-BY 4.0

Lavaud-Letilleul V. (2012) L'aménagement portuaire en débat. *Norois. Environnement, aménagement, société*, 4 : 11–28.

Lecue M., Darbra R.M. (2019) Accidents in European ports involving chemical substances: characteristics and trends. *Safety Science*, 115: 278–284.

Lees J., Jeanjean M., Ferrier Y., Allen B.L. (2022). Rapport final d'étude Epseal (Etude Participative en Santé Environnement Ancrée Localement) – Tome 1. Environnement et santé des habitants du front industriel (Fos-Berre).

Lloret J., Carreño A., Carić H., San J., Fleming L.E. (2021) Environmental and human health impacts of cruise tourism: A review. *Marine Pollution Bulletin*, 173(A): 112979.

Lo Prete M. (2012) Port de commerce et environnement : une relation en évolution. Ce que nous apprennent les recours contentieux dans les ports français et italiens en mer Méditerranée. PhD dissertation in Territorial Planning, ENPC, Paris-Est University.

Lo Prete M. (2015) La vulnérabilité des villes portuaires méditerranéennes françaises et italiennes au prisme des contentieux. *Annales de la Recherche Urbaine*, 110: 206–215.

Marquès M., Domingo J.L., Nadal M., Schuhmacher M. (2020) Health risks for the population living near petrochemical industrial complexes. 2. Adverse health outcomes other than cancer. *Science of the Total Environment*, 730: 139122.

Martuzzi M., Pasetto R., Martin-Olmedo P. (2014) Industrially contaminated sites and health. *Journal of Environmental and Public Health*, 2014: 198574.

Merk O., Hoffmann J., Haralambides H. (2022) Post-COVID-19 scenarios for the governance of maritime transport and ports. *Maritime Economics & Logistics*, 24: 673–685.

Mudu P., Terracini B., Martuzzi M. (2014) Human health in areas with industrial contamination. Copenhagen: WHO Regional Office for Europe, https://apps.who.int/iris/handle/10665/144490

Nieuwenhuijsen M.J. (2020) Urban and transport planning pathways to carbon neutral, liveable and healthy cities; a review of the current evidence. *Environment International*, 140: 105661.

Norcliffe G., Bassett K., Hoare T. (1996) The emergence of postmodernism on the urban waterfront: Geographical perspectives on changing relationships. *Journal of Transport Geography*, 4(2): 123–134.

Notteboom T., Pallis A.A., & Rodrigue J.-P. (2022) *Port Economics, Management and Policy*. Routledge.

OECD (2014) *The Competitiveness of Global Port-Cities*. Paris: OECD Publishing.

Otgaar A., Klijs J. (2010) *Towards Healthy Cities. Comparing Conditions for Change*. London: Routledge.

Paschalidou A.K., Kassomenos P., Chonianaki F. (2019) Strategic noise maps and action plans for the reduction of population exposure in a Mediterranean port city. *Science of the Total Environment*, 654: 144–153.

Pucher J., Buehler R. (2010) Walking and cycling for healthy cities. *Built Environment*, 36(4): 391–414.

Ramacher M.O.P., Matthias V., Aulinger A., Quante M., Bieser J., Karl M. (2020) Contributions of traffic and shipping emissions to city-scale NOX and PM2.5 exposure in Hamburg. *Atmospheric Environment*, 237: 117674.

Redman C., Grove J., Kuby L. (2004) Integrating social science into the long-term ecological research (LTER) network: Social dimensions of ecological change and ecological dimensions of social change. *Ecosystems*, 7: 161–171.

Sallis J.F., Bull F., Burdett R., Frank L.D., Griffiths P., Giles-Corti B., Stevenson M. (2016) Use of science to guide city planning policy and practice: How to achieve healthy and sustainable future cities. *The Lancet*, 388(10062): 2936–2947.

Schubert D., Wagenaar C., Hein C. (2021) "The hoist of the yellow flag": Vulnerable port cities and public health. *Journal of Planning History*, 21(1): 56–78.

Serry A. (2017) Development of liquefied natural gas facilities in the Baltic Sea ports: A geographical perspective. *Regional Formation and Development Studies*, 23(3).

Slack B., Frémont A. (2009) Fifty years of organisational change in container shipping: regional shift and the role of family firms. *GeoJournal*, 74(1): pp 23–34.

Soggiu M.E., Inglessis M., Gagliardi R.V., Settimo G., Marsili G., Notardonato I., Avino P. (2020). PM10 and PM2.5 qualitative source apportionment using selective wind direction sampling in a port-industrial area in Civitavecchia, Italy. *Atmosphere*, 11(1): 94.

Sorte S., Arunachalam S., Naess B., Seppanen C., Rodrigues V., Valencia A., Borrego C., Monteiro A. (2019) Assessment of source contribution to air quality in an urban area close to a harbor: Case-study in Porto, Portugal. *Science of the Total Environment*, 662: 347–360.

UNCTAD (2021) *Review of Maritime Transport 2021*. Geneva: United Nations Conference on Trade and Development.

Vigotti M.A., Mataloni F., Bruni A., Minniti C., Gianicolo E.A. (2014) Mortality analysis by neighbourhood in a city with high levels of industrial air pollution. *International Journal of Public Health*, 59(4): 645–653.

Vögele J., Umehara H. (2015) *Gateways of Disease: Public Health in European and Asian Port Cities at the Birth of the Modern World in the late 19th and early 20th Century*. Göttingen: Cuvillier Verlag.

West N. (1989) Urban-waterfront developments: A geographic problem in search of a model. *Geoforum*, 20(4): 459–468.

Part 1

Mitigation and perception of port pollution

1 Fostering energy transition and transport fluidity in European port cities

César Ducruet and Mariantonia Lo Prete

Introduction

Globally, Europe is recognized as a fertile ground for actions promoting port city sustainability (Puig et al., 2020). As Gonzalez-Aregall et al. (2018) observe, Europe possesses the largest number of green port hinterland strategies. European ports are also frontrunners in terms of emission reduction and energy efficiency measures (Alamoush et al., 2020). Last but not least, the few ports that are certified for energy management (ISO 50001) are dominantly European, while the proportion of European ports that have energy efficiency programs increased from 57% to 75% between 2014 and 2016 (Iris and Lam, 2019).

This chapter provides a panoramic view of port sustainability initiatives, classified as "energy transition" or "transport fluidity", two pillars of the "healthy, efficient and sustainable port city" model (Figure 1.1). Integrated (territorial) planning better relates to wider port-city relationships at the interface, and will not be treated in our chapter. Energy transition measures are directly aimed at reducing pollution, such as by shifting to cleaner fuels, using renewable energies, or electrifying vehicles. Transport fluidity measures shall facilitate the flow of goods and people, to limit congestion, thereby reducing pollution.

But Europe is still a large polluter on a global scale. Ships operating in the European Economic Area (EEA) generated approximately 18% of global CO_2 emissions in 2018, and 16% of global SO_2 emissions in 2019 (EEA/EMSA, 2021). These greenhouse gas (GHG) emissions not only contribute directly to health harms but also exacerbate climate change (Romanello et al., 2021). In the European Union (EU), shipping accounts for 13.5% of all GHG emissions from transport, the third largest contributor following road transport and aviation (EEA/EMSA, 2021). In 2020, the European Commission published its first annual EU report on CO_2 emissions from large merchant ships, which represented 3.7% of total EU CO_2 emissions (EC, 2020).

Yet, European-wide policies have been put in place to palliate such emissions. Nearly the whole of Europe is covered by Emission Control Areas

DOI: 10.4324/9781003639589-3

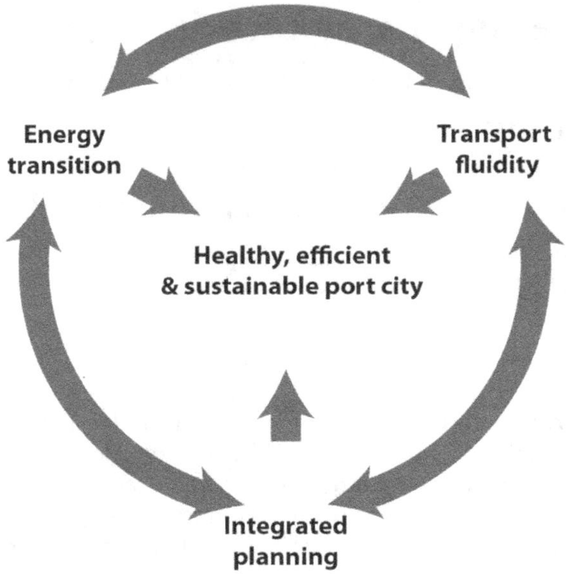

Figure 1.1 Model of the healthy, efficient, and sustainable port city
Source: Own elaboration

(ECAs), created by the International Maritime Organisation (IMO) at successive dates (see Figure 1.2). In the EU, relevant laws include the EU Marine Strategy Framework Directive, the Water Framework Directive, the European Green Deal, and the Ambient Air Quality Directive, which provide stringent enforcement obligations to reduce air and water pollution in EU Member States. The EU-European Trading System (ETS) was extended to the maritime sector in 2024, with the overall objective to reduce GHG emissions by 62% in 2030. In addition, the IMO has proposed a ship greenhouse gas (GHG) emission reduction strategy, aiming to reduce emissions by 20%–30% by 2030 compared to 2008, by 70%–80% by 2040, and achieve net-zero emissions by 2050.

Population exposure to port pollution

Numerous quays and piers remain active today at the very heart of European port cities, despite port migration away from urban cores since the 1950s (Lo Prete, 2012; Ducruet et al., 2023). The average distance between port and city in Europe remains very short, compared with world average and other regions: from 3.46 km in 1880 to 3.88 km in 1960 and 4.31 km in 2020 (Ducruet and Polo Martin, 2026). Antwerp and Hamburg, Europe's second and third largest container ports after Rotterdam, maintained port operations upstream, through massive investment in dredging (Notteboom, 2016). Navarro-Ruiz et al. (2020) showed that the shore excursions of cruise

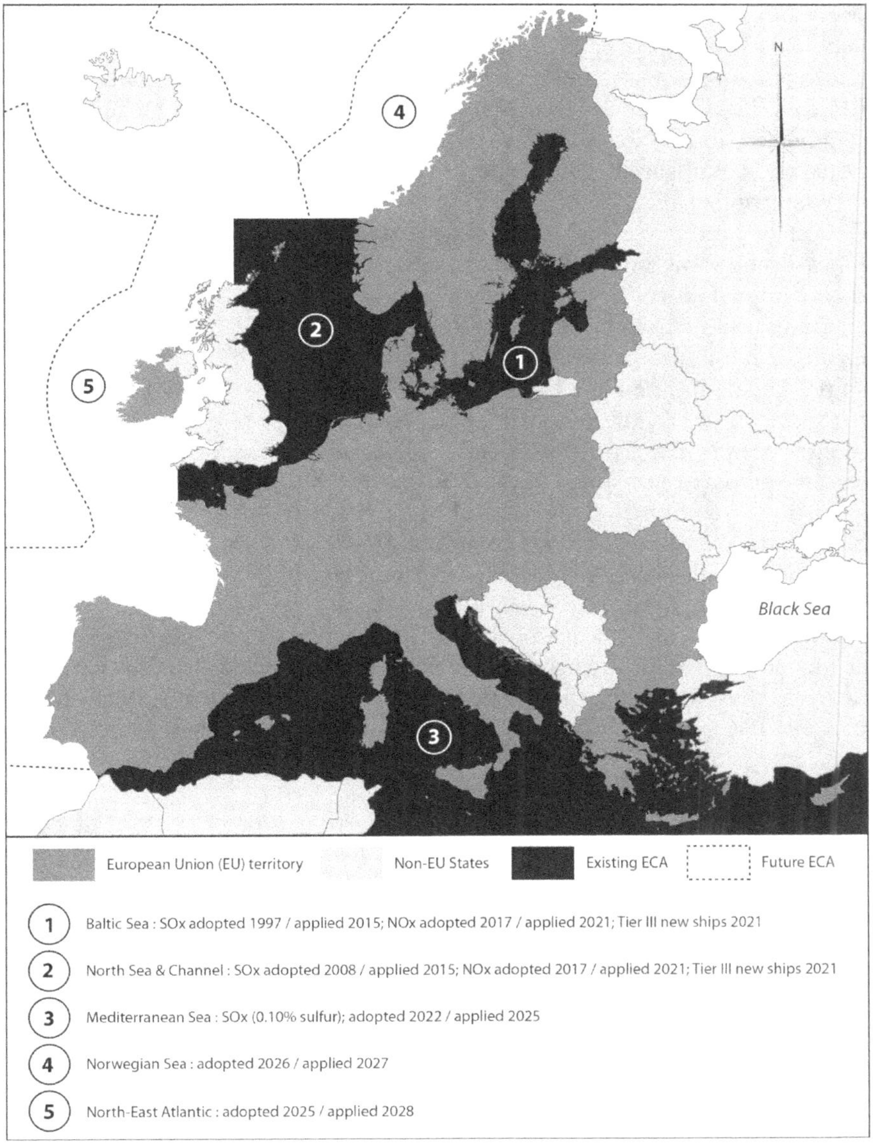

Figure 1.2 Location map of European Emission Control Areas (ECAs)
Source: Own elaboration from various sources

tourists are concentrated in the port cities and cause overcrowding. Bulk and container terminals, like Voltri (Genoa, 19 km) and Fos (Marseilles, 47 km), are much more distant, but serve their coastal cities by trucks, so that environmental impacts have just been displaced and shifted to road. Several epidemiological studies found evidence about the adverse health effects of ports and related industries on local residents (Bauleo et al., 2019; Gianicolo et al., 2013; Viana et al., 2020). Prevailing winds carry pollutions toward populations living near the port, which are often younger and socially deprived (Bertoncello and Hagel, 2016). These evidences confirm that European ports remain very much "urban" (Barberi and Capoani, 2025), implying a superior population exposure to port pollution.

A statistical analysis of 70 European port cities (see Appendix 1.1 for the list of indicators) highlights several trends (Figure 1.3). Group A combines urban congestion, PM, container throughput, population, and total throughput. This confirms that container traffic is likely to generate important trucking flows across cities and to/from the hinterland (Gibbs et al., 2014). Group B combines passengers and roll-on/roll-off with CO_2 emissions from ships. This is in line with CO_2 being the largest emission of cruise shipping for instance (90%, the rest being SO_X, NO_X, and PM). Since CO_2 and passengers are projected positively and significantly on the horizontal axis, they also participate in the mass effect of group A.

Group C combines population, $PM_{2.5}$, dry bulk, and general cargo. Dry bulk ports are the most likely to spread dust clouds during cargo handling or transport between silo/warehouse/plant/factory and terminal (cement, ores, coal, and grain). In Rouen, Europe's largest port for cereals, grain dust clouds used to carry toxic substances like fertilizers and pesticides (Morin et al., 2013). Performing a clustering analysis revealed a particular group of port cities combining high values for containers, total throughput, population, $PM_{2.5}$, congestion, CO_2, and passengers, emblematic of the mass

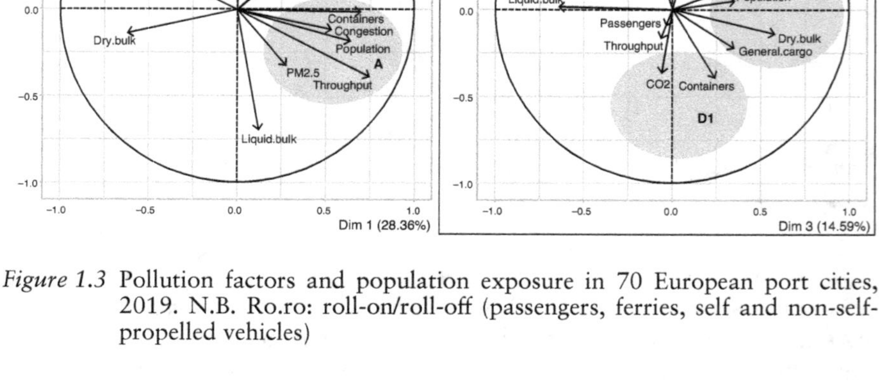

Figure 1.3 Pollution factors and population exposure in 70 European port cities, 2019. N.B. Ro.ro: roll-on/roll-off (passengers, ferries, self and non-self-propelled vehicles)

effect described above, including cities such as Rotterdam, Antwerp, Athens (Piraeus), Barcelona, Genoa, Hamburg, London, and Marseilles.

Sustainability initiatives at a glance: individual and collective actions

This chapter reports initiatives taken by port-city actors in recent years. Individual initiatives may come from one or more actors in one given port city, while collective initiatives involve several port cities carrying one sustainability project (for a full list, see Ducruet and Notteboom, 2023). Our review covers relevant academic and grey literature as well as specific websites such as the World Port Sustainability Program (https://sustainableworldports.org/). The geographic distribution of individual projects is far from being random. There is a strong discrepancy between North and South, and East and West. Among the 129 projects, 92 are located in the North (71.3%) against only 37 in the South. They also concentrate in the major ports, such as Hamburg, Rotterdam, and Antwerp, which combine energy transition and transport fluidity actions.

In terms of collective initiatives, a total of 22 projects were found covering the period 2010–2028. This demonstrates the massive support of the European Commission, since most of these projects were funded by the EC, port cities often being grouped with universities, research institutes, and private firms. Their geographic distribution is radically different; among the 110 occurrences of port cities, 72 are located in the South (65.5%), against 38 in the North. We observe that many more port cities are located in Eastern Europe (Adriatic Sea, Black Sea, East Mediterranean).

Environmental measures related to energy transition

Abatement technologies to reduce ship emissions include exhaust gas cleaning systems (scrubbers) and selective catalytic reduction (SCR) (Gonzalez-Aregall et al., 2018). Scrubbers allow to reduce PM by 85%, SO_X by 50%, and NO_X by 3% (Bjerkan and Seter, 2019). While washing at sea may lead to the acidification and pollution of seawater, scrubbers have the advantage of being adapted to conventional motorization systems, with a recent application between Marseilles and Corsica. Alternative powering options are also explored (wind, solar, and battery propulsion), for hybrid vessels to produce less emissions, like the electrified fleet of La Méridionale in Marseilles.

In terms of cleaner fuels, Sofiev et al. (2018) predicted that cleaner marine fuels would reduce global ship-related premature mortality by 34% and morbidity by 54% in subsequent years, avoiding around 6,400 deaths and 426,000 childhood asthma cases in Europe, although low-sulfur marine fuels would still contribute approximately 250,000 deaths and 6.4 million cases of childhood asthma annually. Several other studies have also suggested that low-sulfur fuel could reduce premature deaths (e.g., Broome et al., 2015; Winebrake et al., 2009). One important measure concerning cleaner fuels is the use of green port dues. The Environmental Ship Index (ESI) is a discount on port dues attributed by the port to shipping companies using cleaner engines and fuels, created by major ports in cooperation with the International Association of Ports and Harbors.

In the last decade, the demand for LNG as an alternative and cleaner marine fuel has increased among shipowners. According to Bergqvist and Monios (2019), this alternative not only reduces SO_x emissions by 100%, but it also reduces NO_x and PM levels by almost 90%. Use of LNG is particularly attractive for ferry and passenger services, which typically occur in close proximity to urban centers, as well as for port service vessels (Styhre et al., 2017). However, LNG produces important quantities of methane, a greenhouse gas (GHG).

On the land side, certification schemes and engine standard incentives aim to reduce emissions from trucks visiting the port, while clean vehicles may gradually replace the older fleet, as in the case of terminal operator HHLA in Hamburg. As part of the European Green Deal, the new Euro 7/VII standard promotes further innovation in the design of emissions control systems. By 2030, new large trucks should emit 30% less CO_2 than today, with an intermediate target of 15% by 2025. Truck emissions may also be reduced by using low-sulfur diesel (cheapest), diesel emulsions, and biodiesel (Bailey and Solomon, 2004). This is also the case for diesel locomotives, for which a tariff system can impose the use of particle filters and noise brakes (Acciaro et al., 2014).

Inland port dues can be levied based on engine data, with five categories of discounts in the Netherlands. Subsidization is also used to reduce GHG emissions of barge operators in Rotterdam: 25% for research projects, 75% for concrete implementations. The *Argonon*, operated by Dutch company Deen Shipping, is the first IWT vessel in Europe to run on dual fuel, using LNG as its main fuel (80%) and diesel as fuel for ignition (20%).

Cold ironing allows ships at berth to connect to shore-side electricity, thereby avoiding running their auxiliary engines during hoteling activities. Electricity can be supplied either by the grid or via renewable sources. EU Directive 2014/94 requires all EU ports to prioritize cold ironing availability. The EU has made it mandatory for Member States to install shore power facilities in ports by 2025. In a major cruise port like Copenhagen (Ballini and Bozzo, 2015), the health benefit of cold ironing technology is considerable, and investments are rapidly profitable, despite their cost and technical requirements (Iris and Lam, 2019). Pioneer European ports include Gothenburg, Ystad, Oslo, and Rotterdam, mostly for passenger vessels.

As noted by Alamoush et al. (2020), 57% of European ports have developed energy efficiency programs, and 20% have adopted measures to utilize renewable energy. Renewable energy installations in the sea for power generation may produce energy from wind turbines on terminal sites or from wind farms (Rotterdam), waves (Mutriku), or tide differentials (Dover). Onshore wind turbines are also used in Antwerp and Amsterdam.

Renewable energies in ports also include the installation of solar panels on available flat surfaces, such as port authority buildings or warehouses, as in Genoa, Hamburg, Rijeka, and Venice. At Ghent, Vlissingen, and Terneuzen, solar panels generate power equivalent to the annual consumption of 28,000 households. In 2020, 1,800 solar panels were installed at the Maasvlakte (Rotterdam), making it self-sufficient for energy needs. At North Sea Port, green hydrogen is produced from wind and solar power, while Rotterdam hosts a sun-powered freezer warehouse (Notteboom et al., 2020). Amsterdam port generates 11 GWh of electricity per year, compared with 55 MWh in Gothenburg, where units lie on top of the port authority's head office. The port of Helsinki (Finland) plans to be carbon-neutral by 2035 by using solar panels.

Geothermal energy is used for heating and cooling, as in the passenger terminal in Portsmouth. More than 60 geothermal energy shafts were placed under the Värtan terminal in Stockholm, while Marseilles hosts the first marine geothermal plant (Thassalia). The latter uses sea geothermal energy to supply heat and cooling to different port buildings connected to its grid, leading to a 70% reduction of associated GHG emissions.

Ports can also use renewable fuels and biomass generation (Alamoush et al., 2020). Biomass production from ports, ships, and industries involves using garbage or other renewable sources (corn, algae, wood pellets, etc.) to generate electricity, heat, biogas, and biofuels. Related facilities are found in Rotterdam, Koper (Greenberth project), and Venice (algae). A dedicated biomass rail wagon carrying wood pellets is in operation in the United Kingdom. The port of Hvide Sande (Denmark) seeks to optimize the production of rest energy from wind, solar, and sea-based power systems by integrating it into the local heating system.

The port can also be a hub for industrial ecology, in association with local industries and adjacent residential areas (Cerceau et al., 2014; Spadaro et al., 2021). Companies utilize each other's waste material or by-products, such as heat (de Langen and Sornn-Friese, 2019; Notteboom et al., 2020), or exchange hydrogen. Industrial ecology is more likely to happen when plants are in close proximity, reinforced by a uniform network of local pipelines, such as through the Hidden Connections project in North Sea Ports. Clustered companies within the port may develop CO_2, water, and biomass synergies. The Warm CO_2 initiative collects the thermal and CO_2 surplus of the chemical company Yara International to feed agricultural and horticultural greenhouses at Zeeland Seaports (Cerceau et al., 2014). In Dunkirk, the DKarbonation project benefits from the support of the central government through the ZIBaC program (low carbon industrial zones), within the framework of France 2030, which is to support energy transition of French industrial areas to make them more competitive while respecting the climate ambitions, both national and European.

The products can then be delivered to residential areas, such as heat from the Shell Pernis refinery to the Katendrecht area of Rotterdam. The port of Rotterdam created a "circularity center", with the aim of reusing CO_2, limiting GHG emissions, and increasing the density of industrial clusters to favor the co-firing of biomass in coal-fired plants. The Smart City project in Rotterdam, in which 60 port companies are participating, plans to reduce emissions by 40% through energy diagnosis, awareness, and the transfer of energy from port to city. Biopark Terneuzen is another example of this kind, while in Amsterdam, residual heat from the coal-fired plant in the port is transferred to the city (Gravagnuolo et al., 2019). The port of Amsterdam has also invested in vapor recovery systems and an emission-laundering system to reduce emissions. It also hosts many recycling companies and has an energy plant where waste is converted into energy.

The LOOP-Ports project is the first of its kind to bring a circular economy approach to EU ports. Coordinated by Fundación Valencia port and funded by the European Institute of Innovation and Technology, its aim is to produce a "circular economy network of ports". Its main outcome is a complete mapping of EU ports characterized according to their circular activities, based on the analysis of more than 450 ports and the identification of 200 circular activities.

Other projects include the Eco-Partnership and smartPORT energy projects in Hamburg, where the port currently hosts 50% of the city's wind production; the attraction of biofuel producers to the port area in Rotterdam; the development of infrastructures to transport and reuse heat, steam and CO_2, also in Rotterdam; the conversion of CO_2 into plastic and CO_2 foam (cardyon) into mattresses and upholstered furniture in Antwerp; and the conversion of CO_2 into bioethanol in North Sea Ports.

In the port of Marseilles, the Jupiter 1000 project is the first industrial pilot of Power to Gas, a process in which electrical current is converted into gas through electrolysis of water. WASh2Emden is a project in which Emden port acts as a laboratory for JadeWeserPort and Niedersachsen Ports to study the feasibility of producing green hydrogen and distributing it to the region.

One recent concrete example of using a smart grid system is the ESTUAIRE project in Nantes Saint-Nazaire, launched in 2019, which promotes energy storage, photovoltaics, and self-consumption based on the concept of smart grid. Used in Amsterdam port, the smart grid relies on information communication technology infrastructure, with high cost, safety, and legal implications, notably in the case of perishable cargo loss or logistics operation crashes due to cyber issues. The microgrid (energy Island) and the virtual power plant are subcomponents of the smart grid.

Some measures are associated with the passive house concept, which requires that port authority and other buildings follow ecobuilding standards. In Genoa, the port acted as a facilitator for the use of seawater as an energy source to supply high-rise residential and office buildings (Acciaro et al., 2014). In Koper, the greening of the heating and hot water preparation system helped to reduce losses in the pipelines. In Aalborg, such standards reduced energy requirements for heating by 94%, while in Ghent, advanced insulation and energy recuperation systems were deployed. Self-energy-preserving warehouses have been built in Immingham. Controlling heating, ventilation, and air-conditioning through a building energy management system is in place at Dover.

The reefer business requires continuous refrigeration of each container to keep products cool. One way to reduce energy consumption is the practice of shading and spacing, which prevents direct sunlight from heating up containers and their immediate surroundings (sun protection roofs). Reefer container plugs are the biggest energy consumer of port terminals (40% of total consumption) (van Duin et al., 2019). In addition, gaps between adjacent reefers can be isolated from the surrounding air by elastic seals (Alamoush et al., 2020).

In port terminals, dynamic lighting systems have been deployed both to improve traffic and to reduce energy consumption. In Moerdijk, Felixstowe, and Finnish ports, light-emitting diode (LED) streetlights equipped with motion sensors are managed by a centralized control system, with different light intensities. Operating costs may be reduced by 80%, and maintenance costs by 50% (Sdoukopoulos et al., 2019). Use of LED lights in buildings, docks, yards, storage areas, warehouses, and tugs has saved 70%–90% of energy in Venice, and reduced CO_2 by 1,000 tons per year in Rotterdam (Alamoush et al., 2020). Another example is the Terminal Dynamic Illumination at the Noatum Terminal in Valencia, which is expected to make an 80% energy saving. The LED-based system in Emden extends along a 10-hectare railway reloading point to reduce light pollution. Outdoor lighting is used in the ports of Amsterdam, Barcelona, Bilbao, and Värtahamnen. The rationale underlying the LED projects in Emden, Vordinborg, and Meppel is to quantify the legally prescribed light quantity for various scenarios (shunting, loading, etc.), thereby reducing visual (light) pollution.

Electrification or hybridization constitutes a further step toward the reduction of pollution (air and noise as well as water and soil). Electric vehicles may even be powered by wind energy, while their consumption can be reduced by automatic start/shut-off technologies and smart charging systems, as in Copenhagen Malmö Port. Smart load management and load shifting can power cargo-handling equipment outside peak hours to reduce electricity consumption, especially in the case of electrified terminals (Alamoush et al., 2020). The electric equipment at APM Terminals in Rotterdam is powered by wind energy, while in Antwerp the terminals run by DP World and PSA International employ hybrid straddle carriers like in Hamburg, Helsingborg, Livorno, and Southampton, while Spanish ports use hybrid-electric rubber-tired gantry cranes. Cold ironing is used in Hamburg to charge battery electric automated guided vehicles (AVGs) and mobility vehicles.

Full terminal electrification was applied in Felixstowe, Hamburg, Koper, Le Havre, Marseille, Oslo, and Piraeus, and through the SEA TERMINALS project in Valencia, resulting in a more efficient transfer of power to wheels than gas or diesel (Green EFFORTS, 2014).

Electrification may extend beyond cargo-handling equipment, such as to port vehicles in general (Barcelona, Koper, and Canary Island ports) or to tourist cars while waiting to board their vessels (e.g., Santa Cruz de Tenerife).

Environmental measures related to transport fluidity

Not all European ports use rail or river as an alternative to road, which represents 75% of all intra-EU freight movements (Eurostat, 2019). Modal shift often consists of traffic transfer from road to rail, waterway, or pipelines, potentially alleviating congestion, air pollution, and the risk of accidents. It often necessitates pricing interventions (taxes and incentives), integrated traffic management systems, infrastructure investments, regulation on emission standards, and liberalization of freight markets (Notteboom et al., 2020).

In green terminal concessions, modal split obligations can be used by port authorities to motivate the terminal operator to favor green modes (van den Berg and de Langen, 2014), while at the same time allowing the port and the terminal to expand their hinterland coverage, since rail and waterway are more profitable over longer distances. The port of Rotterdam was the first to indicate the minimum desired modal split in its proposal request, stating its ambition to shift, between 2015 and 2035, road share from 45% to 35%, rail from 16% to 20%, and inland shipping from 39% to 45%. Pipelines can replace trucking for the transport of hazardous materials such as liquid bulks as well as CO_2, hydrogen, and residual gases, as in the MultiCore pipeline bundle in Rotterdam. At North Sea Ports, the Clean Underground Sustainable Transport study analyzed the feasibility of a pipeline infrastructure in the port area to transport CO_2 and to distribute hydrogen or residual gases.

Another solution is rail shipping. In Amsterdam, the Intermodal Planner digital platform provides customers with information on intermodal line connections via short sea, inland navigation, rail, and road. Hamburg is the largest European port for rail infrastructure; it has 880 switches/sets of points, which are warmed by means of geothermal energy. Rotterdam connects the German border with the 160 km-long Betuwe Rail Line.

Barge or rail shuttle systems, replacing trucks, serve to exchange containers between terminals within the port to avoid congestion onshore (Gonzalez-Aregall et al., 2018), like PortShuttle based on rail and Intercity Barge in Rotterdam, as well as the Amsterdam Barge Shuttle. Barges can be used as floating terminals for bigger cargo ships that cannot enter certain ports, to redistribute containers and replace all transportation by trucks, as seen in Hamburg. The Intelligent Railway Point in Hamburg is a multisensor technology that centrally displays the measured values captured whenever a railway point is switched or crossed. The rail shuttle (RAILPORT) in Gothenburg has reduced transport energy consumption by 70%.

Underground freight transport, which uses electrical (or linear induction) propulsion (Visser, 2018), is also called "port-city underground logistics system (PC-ULS)". It provides more efficient and sustainable freight transport options, and can dramatically reduce negative externalities of port logistics activities, such as environmental pollution, traffic congestion, urban safety, and the scarcity of urban land resources (Hai et al., 2020).

For both road and rail transport, another strategy is to bypass urban areas to avoid mixing passenger car traffic and freight traffic. Creating tunnels or secondary arteries is one solution, as in the Iron Rhine and Liefkenshoek Tunnel in Antwerp, the Vuosaari terminal in Helsinki, and the new motorway at Salerno Porta Ovest. Other approaches include constructing a new entrance for heavy goods vehicles to relieve traffic congestion near the old town center, as in Koper; installing a buffer zone and traffic control office to prevent congestion by trucks, as at Gapsalskiye Gates in Saint Petersburg; or dedicating a specific route for freight, as in the Betuweroute electric rail line in Rotterdam, and the 3-km track for port traffic only in Leixões. A study of the Dublin Port Tunnel in Ireland showed that road emissions fell between 2006 and 2013 thanks to the new infrastructure, as did traffic in the city center (Tang et al., 2017).

Excessive ship turnaround time can be lowered to reduce fuel consumption, but this depends on good coordination of offshore and terminal operations. Several tools can be used in this way. In Finnish, Dutch, and Danish ports, the use of automated mooring systems (AMS) can help to further minimize turnaround time. As reported by Alamoush et al. (2020), the use of AMS in roll-on/roll-off/passenger terminals can reduce mooring CO_2 emissions by 97%.

Virtual arrival (VA) is a process that involves a vessel coordinating with port authorities to reduce its speed at sea and thus change its arrival time if there is a known delay at the destination port. Vessel speed reduction, like for slow steaming, can yield an average 12%–20% saving in fuel consumption, rising as high as 27% (Alamoush et al., 2020). A parent technique is just-in-time arrival, which requires a ship to arrive at the precise time when a berth is available, reducing GHG emissions. Optimal berth allocation, leading to reduced congestion within the port, depends on good coordination between shipping lines, terminal operators, port services (e.g., pilotage), and port authorities.

Optimizing the terminal surface and vehicle mobility, notably through automation, can reduce energy consumption and CO_2 emissions by approximately 70%, as seen at Rotterdam Short Sea Terminal (Geerlings and van Duin, 2011). Such a saving is mainly attributable to the shrinkage of traveled distances across the terminal, under the condition that onshore and offshore operations well synergize. The Secure Truck Parking project in Hamburg turns the parking area of the Cruise Center Steinwerder terminal into a multiuser facility, making an extra 50 spaces available for trucks on days when there are no cruise ship calls.

The concept of ecodriving involves avoiding frequent and/or unnecessary braking and stopping, retaining a steady speed, and shifting gears at low revolutions per minute (Sdoukopoulos et al., 2019). It was found that educating and training machine operators in Copenhagen and Malmö led to a 10%–15% reduction in fuel consumption, lower levels of equipment wear and tear, and a cost saving of €95,000. Automated (or intelligent) transport vehicles not only allow productivity and efficiency gains; they also need less light for navigation, are less noise polluting thanks to improved handling precision (Bjerkan and Seter, 2019), minimize travel distance (Sisson, 2006), and are safer and more secure. Other advantages of automation are reduced box damage, predictable performance, and less dependence on weather conditions, although further automation faces social costs and does not necessarily mean better productivity and performance (ITF, 2021).

Intelligent logistics through digitalization is itself a solution to reduce fuel consumption and optimize traffic (Alamoush et al., 2020). Examples include electronic data interchange (EDI), 3D printing technology used in Hamburg, IoT sensors in Rotterdam to support maintenance and repair, and blockchains used in Antwerp. In Marseilles, the MeRS (Méditerranée Rhône–Saône) project uses blockchain technology to streamline multimodal transport from Marseille-Fos to the hinterland. In Valencia, IoT is used to visualize data from automatic door systems in real time, allowing congestion to be assessed based on truck staying time, or stopping terminal operations when wind speed exceeds a certain threshold.

The Searoutes application was used in the port of Marseilles to calculate optimal and green routes for vessels, based on automatic identification system data and using intermodal solutions to reach their destination. EcoCalculator is a web tool used in Barcelona to calculate CO_2 emissions associated with particular sea and land routes. The PIXEL project, deployed in Monfalcone, Bordeaux, Piraeus, and Thessaloniki, is an IoT-based environmental assessment tool that measures improvement in selected port performance indicators (e.g., energy consumption, average cost per passenger, average waiting time for vessels and trucks). The Green C Ports project developed an IT platform, notably to decrease port traffic congestion and to optimize ship-to-shore crane productivity.

One way to optimize truck time at terminals is automated data capture at entry and exit gates to reduce gate time (Sisson, 2006); examples include the use of optical character recognition gate portals and Vacis X-ray inspection panels for empty containers. In Hamburg, for instance, a connectivity platform (Port Road Management Centre) serves to optimize freight flows. To reduce congestion on port access roads, extended gate operations may benefit from a truck appointment system or vehicle booking system, as in Southampton and Felixstowe. Other systems include, among many others, TERMPoint in Gothenburg, e.Brama in Gdansk, and TAMS in Antwerp. The role of such systems is also to manage road pricing through additional port dues. Fees can be applied to trucks at peak hours to shift activity to evenings and weekends, as in the case of the Deurganckdock terminal in Antwerp, which has extended (night) opening hours.

Reducing congestion and related truck emissions is also enhanced by avoiding empty mileage (for instance, through the Central Booking Platform in Antwerp) or by bundling road cargo within a company or between companies (i.e., horizontal cooperation). An example of the latter is an MDS (mutual distribution system) group of five shipping and haulage companies operating out of Le Havre, which manages their transport flows by pooling their resources to optimize collection and distribution. Idling restrictions reduce fuel use, diesel emissions, and noise; they may be advertised by placement of no-idling signs for trucks and facilitated by automatic idling control devices for locomotives and other vehicles, the cost of which may be recovered by fuel savings.

Conclusion

By combining quantitative and qualitative information and performing a literature review, this chapter offers an original and fully fledged analysis of recent environmental challenges in European port cities. The main findings are as follows. First, the principal differentiating factor of European port cities is a mass effect, whereby congestion, pollution, traffic, and demographic size form a hierarchy dominated by a few large container hubs. Second, although we find a wide variety of sustainability initiatives, they actually concentrate in North Europe at a handful of port gateways, which correspond broadly to such hubs. These two elements raise questions about the possibility for Europe to ensure urban and logistical balance across its territory. The funding of numerous projects by the EC, which include many peripheral port cities, seems to be one important step in such a direction.

Based on our analysis, this chapter provides two key findings. First, leading ports in terms of individual initiatives are often large ports not only in terms of traffic size but also in terms of financial resources. They often operate in North Europe, where containerization is a paramount and stable business, together with strong linkages between bulk trade and industries. Second, collective actions concentrate in South Europe, where ports witness a notable capacity to create synergies and collaborations, allowing them to benefit from financial support from the EC. Such ports are often smaller in terms of traffic size and specialize in passenger traffic (ro-ro, ferry, cruise), while many of them are located on islands and remain peripheral. For these ports, regional balance is a vital stake, as argued by the Conference of Peripheral Maritime Regions that brings together 160 Regions in 24 States from the EU and beyond.

Such findings also appeared during interviews with key stakeholders of the port and maritime industry, whether they should be public or private. Despite the existence of individual or collective initiatives, there is always an issue with financial resources, but also with management and governance. For instance, port governance differs greatly between centralized States, like in Italy, and North Europe, where economies are more liberal. Port governance may allow the emergence of healthy, efficient, and sustainable port cities depending on planning policies at different scales and in close synergy with the city and the communities living in the concerned territories where port and maritime activities prevail.

Appendix 1.1 List of indicators to characterize European port cities

Indicator	*Unit*	*Source*
Total port throughput	Metric tons of cargo handled (LN)	Eurostat
Containers	%	
Dry bulk	%	
General cargo	%	
Liquid bulk	%	
Roll-on/roll-off	%	
Passengers	Number of people (LN)	
Population	Number of inhabitants of the urban area (LN)	Citypopulation.de
Urban congestion	Ratio (%) between excess driving time and uncongested conditions driving time (based on real-time information devices installed in vehicles)	TomTom.com
CO_2	Metric tons (LN)	EMSA
$PM_{2.5}$	Mean population exposure to air pollution in the urban area	OECD

References

Acciaro M., Ghiara H., Cusano M.I. (2014) Energy management in seaports: A new role for port authorities. *Energy Policy*, 71: 4–12.

Alamoush A.S., Ballini F., Ölçer A.I. (2020) Ports' technical and operational measures to reduce greenhouse gas emission and improve energy efficiency: A review. *Marine Pollution Bulletin*, 160: 111508.

Bailey D., Solomon G. (2004) Pollution prevention at ports: Clearing the air. *Environmental Impact Assessment Review*, 24(7–8): 749–774.

Ballini F., Bozzo R. (2015) Air pollution from ships in ports: The socio-economic benefit of cold-ironing technology. *Research in Transportation Business and Management*, 17: 92–98.

Barbieri E., Capoani L. (2025) Renewable energy, resilience, digitalization, and industrial policies in seaborne transport. *Energies*, MDPI, 18(5): 1-28.

Bauleo L., Bucci S., Antonucci C., Sozzi R., Davoli M., Forastiere F., Ancona C. (2019) Long-term exposure to air pollutants from multiple sources and mortality in an industrial area: A cohort study. *Occupational and Environmental Medicine*, 76(1): 48–57.

Bergqvist R., Monios J. (2019) Green ports in theory and practice. In: Bergqvist R., Monios J. (Eds.), *Green Ports: Inland and Seaside Sustainable Transportation Strategies*. Cambridge: Elsevier, pp. 1–17.

Bertoncello B., Hagel Z. (2016) Marseille: une relecture de l'interface ville-port au prisme de l'habiter. *Vertigo*, 16(3), https://doi.org/10.4000/vertigo.18162

Bjerkan K.Y., Seter H. (2019) Reviewing tools and technologies for sustainable ports: Does research enable decision making in ports? *Transportation Research Part D: Transport and Environment*, 72: 243–260.

Broome R.A., Fann N., Cristina T.J., Fulcher C., Duc H., Morgan G.G. (2015) The health benefits of reducing air pollution in Sydney, Australia. *Environmental Research*, 143(A): 19–25.

Cerceau J., Mat N., Junqua G., Lin L., Laforest V., Gonzalez C. (2014) Implementing industrial ecology in port cities: International overview of case studies and cross-case analysis. *Journal of Cleaner Production*, 74: 1–16.

de Langen P., Sornn-Friese H. (2019) Ports and the circular economy. In: Bergqvist R., Monios J. (Eds.), *Green Ports: Inland and Seaside Sustainable Transportation Strategies*. Cambridge: Elsevier, pp. 85–108.

Ducruet C., Notteboom T.E. (2023) A systematic and critical review of port system research. In: Ducruet C., Notteboom T.E. (Eds.), *Port Systems in Global Competition. Spatial-Economic Perspectives on the Co-Development of Seaports*. London and New York: Routledge, pp. 13–54.

Ducruet C., Notteboom T.E., Slack B. (2023) Port migration patterns in the global seaport system since the 1950s. In: Ducruet C., Notteboom T.E. (Eds.), *Port Systems in Global Competition. Spatial-Economic Perspectives on the Co-Development of Seaports*. London and New York: Routledge, pp. 122–146.

Ducruet C., Polo Martin B. (2026) (forthcoming) Port-city evolution in the long-run (1880–2020): Global and regional trends. In: Castillo D.H., Ducruet C. (Eds.), *Port Cities and Globalization*. London: Routledge.

EC (2020) *2019 Annual Report on CO2 Emissions from Maritime Transport*. Brussels: European Commission.

EEA/EMSA (2021) *European Maritime Transport Environmental Report 2021. European Environment Agency/European Maritime Safety Agency*. Luxembourg City: Publications Office of the European Union.

Eurostat (2019) *Maritime Transport*. Brussels: European Commission.

Geerlings H., van Duin R. (2011) A new method for assessing CO_2 emissions from container terminals: A promising approach applied in Rotterdam. *Journal of Cleaner Production*, 19(6–7): 657–666.

Gianicolo E.A., Bruni A., Mangia C., Cervino M., Vigotti M.A. (2013) Acute effects of urban and industrial pollution in a government-designated "Environmental risk area": The case of Brindisi, Italy. *International Journal of Environmental Health Research*, 23(5): 446–460.

Gibbs D., Rigot-Muller P., Mangan J., Lalwani C. (2014) The role of sea ports in end-to-end maritime transport chain emissions. *Energy Policy*, 64: 337–348.

Gonzalez-Aregall M., Bergqvist R., Monios J. (2018) A global review of the hinterland dimension of green port strategies. *Transportation Research Part D: Transport and Environment*, 59: 23–34.

Gravagnuolo A., Angrisano M., Fusco Girard L. (2019) Circular economy strategies in eight historic port cities: Criteria and indicators towards a circular city assessment framework. *Sustainability*, 11(13): 3512.

Green EFFORTS (2014) *Green Efforts: Green and Effective Operations at Terminals and in Ports*. Brussels: European Commission, https://cordis.europa.eu/project/id/285687/reporting

Hai L., Zhang Y., Wang J. (2020) Port-city underground logistics system: A new model for port congestion relief and sustainable development. *Transportation Research Part E*, 140: 101992.

Iris Ç., Lam J.S.L. (2019) A review of energy efficiency in ports: Operational strategies, technologies and energy management systems. *Renewable and Sustainable Energy Reviews*, 112(C): 170–182.

ITF (2021) Container port automation: Impacts and implications. *International Transport Forum Policy Papers, No. 96*. Paris: OECD Publishing, https://www.itf-oecd.org/sites/default/files/docs/container-port-automation.pdf

Lo Prete M. (2012) Port de commerce et environnement : une relation en évolution. Ce que nous apprennent les recours contentieux dans les ports français et italiens en mer Méditerranée. PhD dissertation in Territorial Planning, ENPC, Paris-Est University.

Morin J.P., Preterre D., Gouriou F., Delmas V., François A., Orange N., Grosboillot A., Duclairoir Poc C., Moretti M., Maillot O., Lesouhaitier O. (2013) Particules urbaines et céréalières, micro-organismes, mycotoxines et pesticides. *Pollution Atmosphérique*, 217(1), https://doi.org/10.4267/pollution-atmospherique.759

Navarro-Ruiz S., Casado-Díaz A.B., Ivars-Baidal J. (2020) Cruise tourism: The role of shore excursions in the overcrowding of cities. *International Journal of Tourism Cities*, 6(1): 197–214.

Notteboom T.E. (2016) The adaptive capacity of container ports in an era of mega vessels: The case of upstream seaports Antwerp and Hamburg. *Journal of Transport Geography*, 54: 295–309.

Notteboom T.E., van der Lugt L., van Saase N., Sel S., Neyens K. (2020) The role of seaports in green supply chain management: Initiatives, attitudes, and perspectives in Rotterdam, Antwerp, North Sea Port, and Zeebrugge. *Sustainability*, 12(4): 1688.

Puig M., Raptis S., Wooldridge C., Darbra R.M. (2020) Performance trends of environmental management in European ports. *Marine Pollution Bulletin*, 160: 111686.

Romanello M., van Daalen K., Anto J. M., Dasandi N., Drummond P., Hamilton I. G., Jankin S., Kendrovski V., Lowe R., Rocklöv J., Schmoll O., Semenza J. C., Tonne C., & Nilsson M. (2021) Tracking progress on health and climate change in Europe. *The Lancet*. Public health, 6(11), e858–e865. https://doi.org/10.1016/S2468-2667(21)00207-3

Sdoukopoulos E., Boile M., Tromaras A., Anastasiadis N. (2019) Energy efficiency in European ports: State-of-practice and insights on the way forward. *Sustainability*, 11(18): 4952.

Sisson M. (2006) *The State-of-the-Art for Green Terminals: An Automated Terminal Is a Green Terminal*. Alexandria: American Association of Port Authorities, https://aapa.files.cms-plus.com/seminarpresentations/06_faceng_sisson.pdf

Sofiev M., Winebrake J.J., Johansson L., Carr E.W., Prank M., Soares J., Vira J., Kouznetsov R., Jalkanen J.P., Corbett J.J. (2018) Cleaner fuels for ships provide public health benefits with climate tradeoffs. *Nature Communications*, 9(1): 406.

Spadaro I., Pirlone F., Candia S. (2021) Waste management: New policies for EU port cities. *International Planning Studies*, 26(4): 1–13.

Styhre L., Winnes H., Black J., Lee J., Le-Griffin H. (2017) Greenhouse gas emissions from ships in ports: Case studies in four continents. *Transportation Research Part D: Transport and Environment*, 54: 212–224.

Tang J., McNabola A., Misstear B., Caulfield B. (2017) An evaluation of the impact of the Dublin Port Tunnel and HGV management strategy on air pollution emissions. *Transportation Research Part D: Transport and Environment*, 52: 1–14.

van den Berg R., de Langen P.W. (2014) An exploratory analysis of the effects of modal split obligations in terminal concession contracts. *International Journal of Shipping and Transport Logistics*, 6(6): 571–592.

van Duin J.H.R., Geerlings H., Tavasszy L.A., Bank D.L. (2019) Factors causing peak energy consumption of reefers at container terminals. *Journal of Shipping and Trade*, 4(1), https://doi.org/10.1186/s41072-019-0040-y

Viana M., Rizza V., Tobías A., Carr E., Corbett J., Sofiev M., Karanasiou A., Buonanno G., Fann N. (2020) Estimated health impacts from maritime transport in the Mediterranean region and benefits from the use of cleaner fuels. *Environment International*, 138: 105670.

Visser J.G.S.N. (2018) The development of underground freight transport: An overview. *Tunnel Underground Space Technology*, 80: 123–127.

Winebrake J.J., Corbett J.J., Green E.H., Lauer A., Eyring V. (2009) Mitigating the health impacts of pollution from oceangoing shipping: An assessment of low-sulfur fuel mandates. *Environmental Science and Technology*, 43(13): 4776–4782.

2 From a polluting port to a sustainable one

A pressing challenge for port cities

Lorena Garcia-Alonso

Port-city relationship

Seaports are key infrastructures for a well-functioning economy. At the international level, they are indispensable for world trade; at the national level, they condition the competitiveness of the country's industry; and at the local level, they have a strong impact (direct and indirect) on GDP generation and employment. Their proper functioning is therefore a priority for all levels of administration, as well as for their managers and stakeholders. Ports have also stimulated the growth of cities in which they are located (Fujita & Mori, 1996), acting as drivers of their activity and conditioning their urban development. They serve as a node between maritime and land networks to facilitate the flow of goods and passengers, and in their surrounding areas, industrial, commercial, logistical, fishing and tourist activities are also developed. However, the impetus given by globalization to the growth of maritime traffic has also served to intensify congestion and pollution in their environment, and to highlight the competition for space: increased flows require more facilities, and the world's expanding population tends to be concentrated in coastal areas (Karimpour et al., 2020). Consequently, the port-city relationship is under great stress.

The nature of the relationship between ports and their cities depends on the evolution of their historical links, always unique, although they face similar challenges (Fenton, 2020). On the one hand, the characteristics of the link vary according to their respective size (volume of traffic/population), specialization (type of traffic/secondary or tertiary activity) or relevance (centrality/intermediacy, following the terminology of Fleming & Hayuth [1994]). On the other hand, the development of maritime transport has made port activity increasingly dependent on the logistics chain in which it is integrated,[1] and less so on the dynamics of its city, itself more dependent on local issues and with its own (global) networks, like airlines and multinational firms. Hence, as the pressure of port activity on the urban environment increases, so does the tension between the two spaces. Even so, it is not possible to separate their future: the ports are mostly located in the vicinity of cities, receiving from them the resources they need to develop their activity, and the economic

DOI: 10.4324/9781003639589-4

activity of port cities cannot be disconnected from the presence of these facilities, which connect them with other economic centres and from which they obtain goods and raw materials (Kong & Liu, 2021). That is to say, the ports and their cities feed off each other and maintain a symbiotic relationship (Zhao et al., 2023). Understanding this point is the key to achieving a balanced development of both spaces.

The implications of the different possible relationships between a port and its city are best understood from the matrix developed by Ducruet and Lee (2006), in which the infrastructure is linked to the concept of *intermediation*, and the city to that of *centrality*. In it, the port-city, in a strict sense, results from the intersection of the two diagonals of the matrix, implying an intermediate level both in intermediation and centrality. At the ends of the balance are *coastal towns* (low-low) and *port metropolis* (high-high); and at the ends of imbalance, the hub (high-low) and the *general cities* (low-high). According to these authors, the cases in which *port cities* (medium-medium) are balanced are rarer, while there are plenty of imbalanced profiles: (i) *gateways* (high-medium), highly dependent on the industrial and logistic activity of their hinterland; (ii) *maritime cities* (medium-high), with a very important urban dynamism and minor port activity; and (iii) *outports* (medium-low), dependent on nearby towns and disconnected from their own city. All these combinations mean that there are different possibilities for the development of the port-city relationship, although this is always gradual and requires long-term combined (urban-port) strategies.

In any case, the growth of international trade over the past three decades has led to an intense growth in port activity. This has entailed significant capital investment in the expansion and improvement of infrastructure, boosting the economy of port cities, but also exacerbating existing environmental problems around ports: pollution and high consumption of resources (especially land and energy). In addition, the investment was usually designed independently of the needs of their cities (Doerr, 2011) and the life cycle of ports. This is important as, when faced with rising costs due to land scarcity and congestion of their facilities and transport networks, while also having to compete with better-equipped facilities, these infrastructures can move from a state of maturity to another of obsolescence and decline. In these cases, when it is not possible to develop sustainable port strategies in the long term, a good option could be to free up land for redevelopment (Karimpour et al., 2020).

Negative externalities from port activity

Increased social awareness of the damage caused by negative externalities arising from port activity explains the increasing tension in the port-city relationship. These externalities, shown in Figure 2.1, are manifested through the deterioration of air quality, water pollution, waste generation, congestion of transport routes, noise, light pollution, competition for land and damage

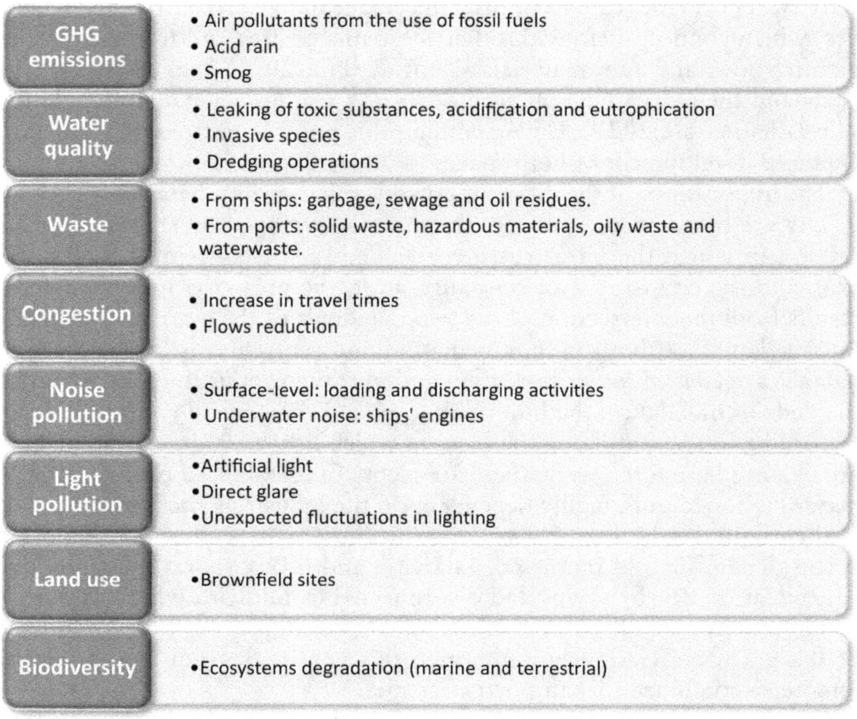

Figure 2.1 Negative externalities from port activity

Source: Own elaboration based on Cullinane and Cullinane (2019), Trozzi and Vaccaro (2000) and World Bank Group (2025)

to biodiversity.[2] The first three are, in the opinion of the port authorities consulted (Hossain et al., 2019), responsible for the main environmental problems caused by the activity of their installations.

The origin of environmental problems caused by port activity is diverse. In addition to those arising from harbour operations are those generated both by the ships that use the installations and by the activities of loading/unloading of the freight, as well as the problems produced by the transport services that connect the installations with their hinterland. Ports are a centre of distribution, which implies a great movement of all kinds of vehicles around them, emitting gases and waste which harm both the population and the environment (Wan et al., 2018). They are estimated to generate around 3% of greenhouse gases (GHGs) (Alamoush et al., 2020), which in turn influence climate change (Azarkamand, Wooldridge, & Darbra, 2020; Lam & Notteboom, 2014). The use of diesel engines also causes local air pollution through emissions of particulate matter, oxides of nitrogen, sulphur dioxide, volatile organic compounds, carbon monoxide, ground-level ozone, polycyclic aromatic hydrocarbons and lead (Monios, 2020; Široka et al., 2021). These emissions are of particular concern due to the poor quality of the bunker fuel used in ships, and due to the fact that these produce higher pollutants per power output (Cullinane & Cullinane, 2019).

Emissions from ships in ports are between three and five times higher than those from ships at sea (Cullinane & Cullinane, 2019), and they represent between 2% and 6% of total maritime transport. This amount, although relatively small in relation to the total, is very important as it is generated close to the population (Mjelde et al., 2019), and it accounts for approximately three-quarters of emissions generated in port facilities. The bulk of the emissions comes from the operation of auxiliary engines, necessary to supply power on board during docking (hence the importance of reducing the time of the vessels in port) (Zhang et al., 2024). The rest of the emissions are generated by land transport vehicles and port activities, which account for less than half of the remaining quarter.

According to their scope, the port activities that generate emissions are classified as shown in Figure 2.2. The sources controlled by the port generate direct emissions (equipment and machinery for cargo handling and storage). Indirect costs are derived from the generation of energy used in the port. Both types of emissions (scope 1 and 2) depend on the nature of the traffic and equipment used, and their control lies with the port authority and terminal operators. Scope 3 emissions are also indirect, generated by port users and external service providers who are responsible for them.

All of these externalities deteriorate the quality of life of the population and damage ecosystems. Their most common effects on human health are related to metabolic, respiratory and cardiovascular diseases, strokes, fertility problems, premature births and deaths, low birth weight, hearing loss,

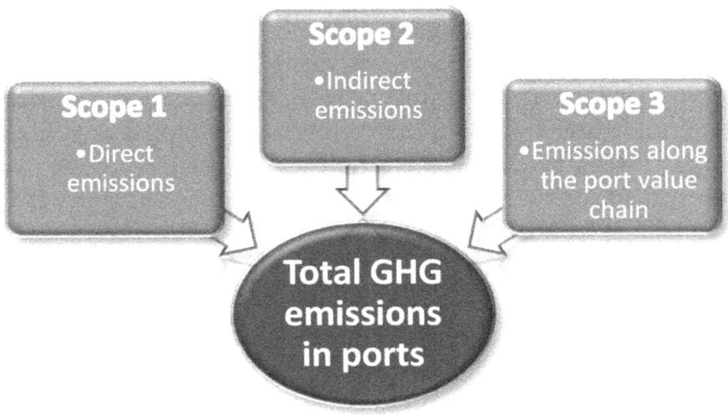

Figure 2.2 Port-related emission sources

Source: Own elaboration based on World Ports Climate Initiative (WPCI) (2010)

high blood pressure, sleep disturbances or decreased performance.[3] However, there are differences between them: while some cause lasting damage (the introduction of invasive species), others are cumulative (GHG emissions), or momentary (noise); some affect the territory in which they occur (degradation of the landscape) and others spread geographically (discharges); some are easily identifiable and measurable (light pollution), and others are more difficult to quantify (impact on biodiversity) (Hou & Geerlings, 2016).

For all these reasons, the business plan of port authorities must also cover the social and environmental aspects of their activity (Rodrigues & Ensslin, 2024). In short, they must pursue a sustainable management of port facilities because many port cities are among the most degraded cities in the world (Ducruet & Lee, 2006), pollution is more intense in coastal areas (Alzahrani et al., 2021), and half of the world's population lives within 60 km of the sea (Mjelde et al., 2019). Furthermore, according to the International Maritime Organization (International Maritime Organization [IMO], 2021), greenhouse gas emissions derived from port activity have increased considerably over the last few years, and are expected to continue to do so over the next quarter century.

Port sustainability versus climate change

Pollution from port activity, in addition to harming the health of the population, degrading the urban environment and damaging the natural environment, also contributes to climate change. In turn, climate change results in damage to health and the environment, and also harms the proper functioning of ports. Although the degree of threat to the ports depends on their geographical location, they will all be affected. For example, two of the most expected effects of climate change, a rise in sea levels and an increase in the number of storm surges, can cause permanent flooding, physical damage to infrastructure, operational delays and a loss of efficiency (Garcia-Alonso et al., 2020).[4] Also, higher temperatures, droughts or changing wave patterns can, respectively, damage the infrastructure (tarmac melting), interior navigation (lowering water levels) and affect berthing conditions (compromising the stability of breakwaters). Preventing these problems involves significant expenditure on protective measures or even the need to relocate facilities (both terminals and storage areas or land roads); but ignoring them may result in higher costs to deal with operational disruptions or reduced useful life of assets (Sierra et al., 2017; World Bank Group, 2025).

Ports can also combat climate change by developing strategies to mitigate it.[5] It is therefore necessary to adopt technical and operational measures, in addition to reducing the GHG emissions linked to their activity. The challenge of decarbonization is particularly difficult to achieve for two main reasons. First, because emissions are expected to soar due to the expected increase in international trade flows (together with the difficulty of introducing alternative fuels to fossil fuels). Second, because there is no unified tool for calculating the carbon footprint of the activity (Azarkamand, Ferré, & Darbra, 2020; Freitas & Gervásio, 2024). Nevertheless, the International Maritime Organization has proposed a target of eliminating GHG emissions from international shipping by 2050. As with previous milestones, it established the need to reduce the emissions by 20%–30% by 2030 and 70%–80% by 2040 (with regard to 2008 levels). In addition, it suggests that fuels and technology with zero (or near-zero) GHG emissions should account for between 5% and 10% of the total in 2030.

The strategies developed to combat the negative effects of port activity externalities, and more specifically to achieve the global target of zero GHG emissions by 2050, also promote the achievement of Sustainable Development Goals (SDGs), established by the United Nations to meet the commitments of the 2030 Agenda. The relationship between the two aspects is shown in Figure 2.3.

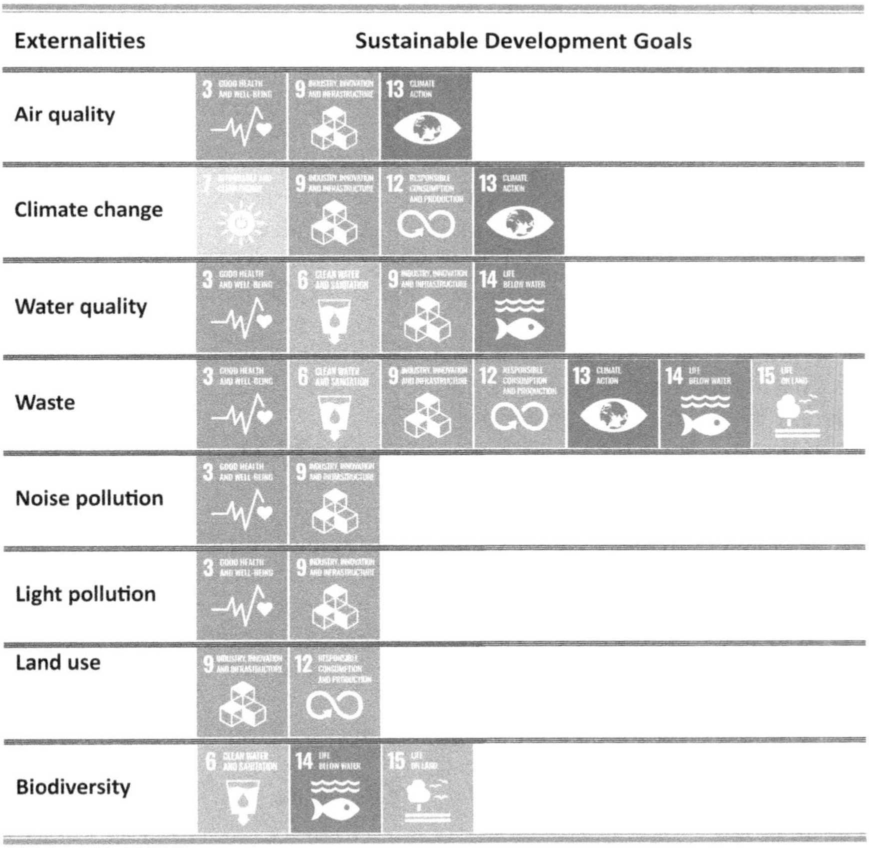

Figure 2.3 The SDGs and their relationship with the negative externalities of port activity

Source: Own elaboration based on World Bank Group (2025)

Greater social awareness in favour of compliance with the SDGs is encouraging the objective of sustainability to be integrated into the development strategies of all types of activity, including that of maritime-port activity (Kong & Liu, 2021). Concern for sustainable development in this area began in the 1990s (González-Laxe et al., 2016). While emissions from this sector were excluded from the commitments of the Kyoto Treaty and the Paris Agreement (Cullinane & Cullinane, 2019; Monios & Wilmsmeier, 2020), international institutions such as the International Maritime Organization, the International Association of Ports and Harbours, or the Organization of European Seaports (ESPO) promote a paradigm shift towards environmental protection, for example, through the World Ports Climate Initiative (WPCI), the World Port Sustainability Program, the World Ports Climate Action Program, the Ship Energy Efficiency Management Plan, the ESPO Environmental Guidelines or the ESPO Green Guidelines (Azarkamand, Ferré, & Darbra, 2020; Azarkamand, Wooldridge, & Darbra, 2020; Kong & Liu, 2021; Ji et al., 2023). The success of these initiatives can be assessed through certified Environmental Management Systems, such as the Eco-Management and Audit Scheme, the Port Environmental Review System or the ISO 14001 (Rodrigues & Ensslin, 2024).[6]

The traditional economic growth model, which did not address the consequences of the indiscriminate use of natural resources, is evolving towards one that takes into account the threat it poses in terms of economic, social and environmental instability (Kong & Liu, 2021). More specifically, this model is being replaced by one based on the concept of *sustainable development* (Hou & Geerlings, 2016). According to the United Nations Brundtland Commission, *sustainable development* implies meeting present needs without compromising the future of future generations (World Commission on Environment and Development, 1987). In other words, its aim is to maximize economic efficiency and social welfare while minimizing the environmental impact of the activity.

In the maritime-port sector, sustainability also implies making environmental management compatible with the economic and social dimensions. It seeks to combat negative externalities through more environmentally friendly practices, while aiming to maximize return on investment, efficiency in the use of facilities and the creation of added value (the economic dimension), and it also contributes to the creation of employment and maximization of welfare of the population around the port facilities (the social dimension) (Asgari et al., 2015; Sislian et al., 2016; Kang & Kim, 2017; Lim et al., 2019). All of this without compromising the capacity of the ecosystem, maintaining financial solvency and facilitating the adaptation of the organization to market changes, as shown in Figure 2.4.

The sustainability of port activity has traditionally been limited due to three reasons: (i) the existence of market failures (lack of competition in some traffic segments and negative externalities) which undermined efficiency in the use of resources; (ii) the pursuit of strictly economic objectives

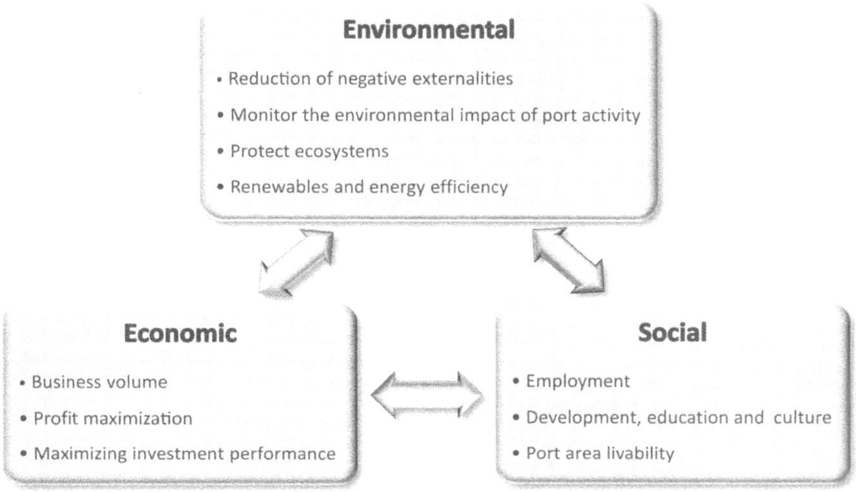

Figure 2.4 General objectives of port sustainability

Source: Own elaboration based on Doerr (2011), Sislian et al. (2016) and Lim et al. (2019)

(prioritizing quantitative growth); and (iii) the use of an obsolete infrastructure/superstructure (Kong & Liu, 2021). It was understood that environmental protection reduced the economic profitability of port activity (Taljaard et al., 2021). However, it is now considered that it promotes the competitiveness of the port in as much that it facilitates efficiency in the use of resources, reduces the risks of accidents, improves the image of the facilities, promotes business with future projection and confers greater economic stability (Kang & Kim, 2017; Lim et al., 2019). And on this path to port sustainability, the concept of *Green ports*[7] is gaining weight.

Strategies for port greening (or "going green")

Sustainable port development focuses on the need to reduce negative externalities arising from the activity of these facilities. It seeks to implement measures that result in environmentally sound behaviour in all areas of action of the ports, and which directly benefit the city in which their facilities are located. This goal led to the concept of *Green port*, coined at the UN Climate Change Conference in 2009 and first implemented at Long Beach Harbor in 2005 (Wan et al., 2018; Ji et al., 2023). This is the name given to ports that, without neglecting the socio-economic dimensions of sustainability, prioritize the use of renewable energies and efficient management of resources to reduce GHG emissions and minimize negative externalities (Styhre & Winnes, 2019; Rodrigues & Ensslin, 2024; Zhang et al., 2024).[8]

Assessment	Identification of the sources
	Measurement of emissions (direct and indirect)
Modernization	Equipment with low/zero emissions
	Electrification
	Generation of renewable energy
Management	Minimize waiting
	Optimization: digitalization, automation, pricing according to objectives
	inter-port collaboration: cooperative development
Regulation	Clear objectives
	Incentives/sanctions
	Incentivization of inland modal shift
	Port-city integration

Figure 2.5 Pillars of decarbonization

Source: Own elaboration based on Mjelde et al. (2019), Alamoush et al. (2020), Wang et al. (2020), Fadiga et al. (2024), Monios et al. (2024) and World Bank Group (2025)

The difficulties in greening traditional ports are linked to the obsolescence of their infrastructure, the difficulty in finding financing for their adaptation, their long service life, the insufficient environmental awareness of many decision-makers, the high level of competition and the lack of unified criteria for evaluating the implementation of this management modality (Wan et al., 2018; Zhang et al., 2024). However, although the strategy of each port depends on its own constraints, the academic literature highlights the four pillars of decarbonization in the field of port activity, listed in Figure 2.5. In short: (i) the measures taken should take into account all activities related to the port, from those taking place within it to those taking place in the hinterland and other facilities connected with it; (ii) there must be precise rules to guide the parties concerned as to the measures to be developed; and (iii) it is necessary to gather all environmental information in order to monitor and analyse the impact of actions taken (Rodrigues & Ensslin, 2024).

The main guidelines to be followed to address negative externalities arising from port activity are shown in Figure 2.6.

The high cost of these measures prevents them from being addressed simultaneously. In addition, the difficulty of passing the costs on to the users of the installations by means of increased charges, together with the fact that terminal operators and shareholders are prioritizing their economic objectives, and that the most adverse effects of climate change remain largely hypothetical, makes it difficult for port managers to carry them out (Esteban et al., 2020; Satta et al., 2025). This gives rise to short-term planning, when what is needed is an ambitious, long-term strategy in which all stakeholders

GHG emissions	• Change from fossil fuels to zero emission energy sources • Energy efficient terminal equipment • Modal shift to low-carbon inland transportation
Water quality	• Wastewater treatment and reuse • Stormwater Pollution Prevention Plan implementation • MARPOL/IMO compliance: oil spillages, ballast water
Waste	• Circular economy • Environmental legislation
Congestion	• Efficient queue and resources management
Noise pollution	• National/regional/local regulation
Light pollution	• LED lighting with shielding • Lighting adjusted to activity level • Motion-sensitive lighting
Land use	• Environmental impact assessment
Biodiversity	• Knowledge of local biodiversity • Proactive restoration

Figure 2.6 Strategies to address negative externalities

Source: Own elaboration based on World Bank Group (2025)

are involved to reorganize their relationships, both with each other and with the city/region where the ports are located (Morris, 2020). The market, therefore, is not capable on its own of meeting the challenge of the green transformation of ports. International norms are needed which, taking into account the different national and local scenarios,[9] facilitate the adaptation of governance structures to efficiently incorporate environmental considerations into management strategies (Monios & Wilmsmeier, 2020; World Bank Group, 2025). In the case of European ports, environmental priorities are set out in Figure 2.7.

Ports are a point of exchange between land and sea transport, so their managers are in the best position to lead, together with local authorities, the green transition of the port-city tandem. In line with Monios et al. (2024), this challenge requires, on the one hand, a more transversal port governance, which redefines and strengthens its relationship with all stakeholders. These key players can be grouped into four blocks: (i) the traditional, which includes all public entities involved in governance; (ii) the commercial, which

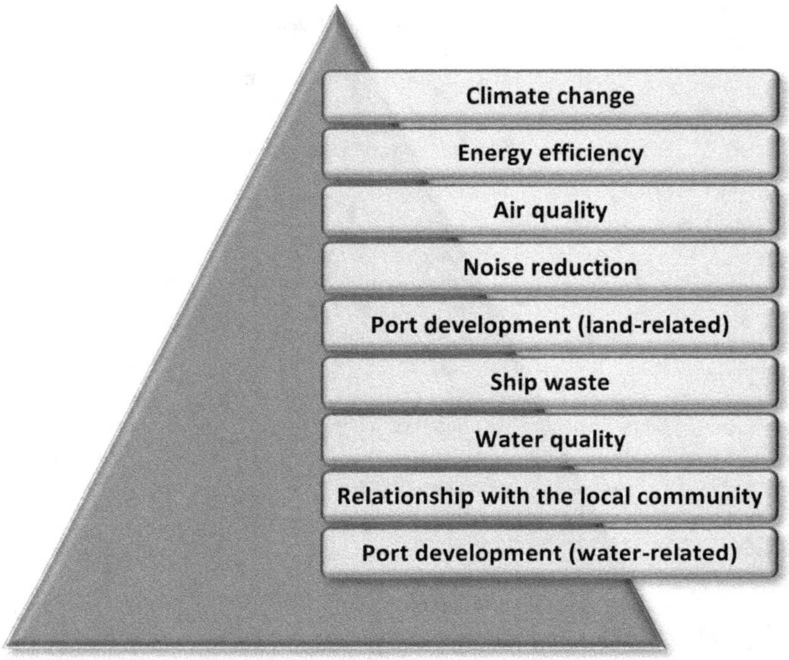

Figure 2.7 European port priorities
Source: Own elaboration based on ESPO (2024)

encompasses all agents responsible for the business related to maritime transport; (iii) the third sector; that brings together all those actors with an indirect interest in the port; and (iv) the international, which includes all the institutions responsible for international regulation in environmental matters. On the other hand, and in order to better meet the challenges arising from environmental problems, it would be positive to stimulate inter-port collaboration. This could be carried out by establishing a common framework in which interests and objectives are shared, such as the consideration of the environment in the design and operation of the facilities (Taljaard et al., 2021). This could be done, for example, by establishing conditions in concession contracts (ESPO, 2021).

Concluding remarks

The traditional port-city symbiosis has weakened. The growth of maritime traffic and urban population within the framework of a non-environmental development model has caused their respective interests to clash. Competition for land use and environmental degradation, stemming from the negative effects of port activity externalities, has been compounded by the threat of climate change. There is therefore an urgent need for a redefinition of the port-city relationship based on sustainability, with environmental management and greenhouse gas emission reduction at the core of local, national and international port strategies. In short, there is an urgent need for a green transformation for ports and their cities.

Notes

1 See Robinson (2002) and the "*new paradigm*".
2 For a detailed description of these effects, see Lam and Notteboom (2014) and World Bank Group (2025).
3 To delve deeper into the effects of port activity on human health, see Mueller et al. (2023) and Ducruet et al. (2024).
4 Global warming is expected to cause a rise in sea level of one metre or more, affecting 80% of ports by 2080. The consequences of this effect, together with those of other predicted phenomena, are not limited to operational problems in ports but rather they will also lead to a significant reduction in GDP and international trade (Esteban et al., 2020; Monios et al., 2024).
5 *Mitigation* implies action aimed at reducing the causes of climate change, while *adaptation* is reactive to it. There is an open debate on whether the two strategies are complementary or mutually exclusive (Lin et al., 2020). In any case, Monios and Wilmsmeier (2020) suggest that there is already a need to go further, and address a process of *deep adaptation*.
6 For a review of both international initiatives to control climate change and the key measurement tools for the environmental performance of ports, see Roos and Kliemann Neto (2017), Azarkamand, Wooldridge, et al. (2020) or Monios (2020).
7 Directly related to this trend is the commitment to the circular economy to facilitate the transition of port-cities towards more environmentally friendly spaces. See Karimpour et al. (2020).
8 See Alzahrani et al. (2021), the Green Guide of ESPO (2021) and Wang et al. (2020) and Zhang et al. (2024) to enhance knowledge, respectively, of the port decarbonization process, green good practices and performance indicators.
9 Ports compete economically with each other, but their exposure to adverse events differs.

References

Alamoush A.S., Ballini F., Ölçer A.I. (2020) Ports' technical and operational measures to reduce greenhouse gas emission and improve energy efficiency: A review. *Marine Pollution Bulletin*, 160: 111508.

Alzahrani A., Petri I., Rezgui Y., Ghoroghi A. (2021) Decarbonisation of seaports: A review and directions for future research. *Energy Strategy Reviews*, 38: 100727.

Asgari N., Hassani A., Jones D., Nguye H.H. (2015) Sustainability ranking of the UK major ports: Methodology and case study. *Transportation Research Part E: Logistics and Transportation Review*, 78: 19–39.

Azarkamand S., Ferré G., Darbra R.M. (2020) Calculating the carbon footprint in ports by using a standardized tool. *Science of the Total Environment*, 734: 139407.

Azarkamand S., Wooldridge C., Darbra R.M. (2020) Review of initiatives and methodologies to reduce CO_2 emissions and climate change effects in ports. *International Journal of Environmental Research and Public Health*, 17(11): 3858.

Cullinane K., Cullinane S. (2019) Policy on reducing shipping emissions: Implications for "Green Ports." In: Bergqvist R., Monios J. (Eds.), *Green Ports: Inland and Seaside Sustainable Transportation Strategies*. Elsevier, pp. 35–62.

Doerr O. (2011) Sustainable port policies. *Bulletin FAL*, 299(7): 1–8.

Ducruet C., Lee S.W. (2006) Frontline soldiers of globalisation: Port–city evolution and regional competition. *Geojournal*, 67(2): 107–122.

Ducruet C., Polo Martin B., Sene M.A., Lo Prete M., Sun L., Itoh H., Pigné Y. (2024) Ports and their influence on local air pollution and public health: A global analysis. *Science of the Total Environment*, 915: 170099.

ESPO (2021) Green Guide 2021. A manual for European Ports towards a green future, https://www.espo.be/publications/espo-green-guide-2021-a-manual-for-european-ports-

ESPO (2024) Environmental Report 2024. EcoPortsinSights 2024, https://www.espo.be/media/ESPO Environmental Report 2024.pdf

Esteban M., Takagi H., Nicholls R.J., Fatma D., Pratama M.B., Kurobe S., Yi X., Ikeda I., Mikami T., Valenzuela P., Avelino E. (2020) Adapting ports to sea-level rise: Empirical lessons based on land subsidence in Indonesia and Japan. *Maritime Policy and Management*, 47(7): 937–952.

Fadiga A., Ferreira L.M.D.F., Bigotte J.F. (2024) Decarbonising maritime ports: A systematic review of the literature and insights for new research opportunities. *Journal of Cleaner Production*, 452: 142209.

Fenton P. (2020) Port-city redevelopment and sustainable development. In: Carpenter A., Lozano R. (Eds.), *European Port Cities in Transition: Moving towards More Sustainable Sea Transport Hubs*. Springer International Publishing, pp. 19–36.

Fleming D.K., Hayuth Y. (1994) Spatial characteristics of transportation hubs: Centrality and intermediacy. *Journal of Transport Geography*, 2(1): 3–18.

Freitas D., Gervásio H. (2024) The challenge of benchmarking carbon emissions in maritime ports. *Environmental Pollution*, 363: 125170.

Fujita M., Mori T. (1996) The role of ports in the making of major cities: Self-agglomeration and hub-effect. *Journal of Development Economics*, 49(1): 93–120.

Garcia-Alonso L., Moura T.G.Z., Roibas D. (2020) The effect of weather conditions on port technical efficiency. *Marine Policy*, 113: 103816.

González-Laxe F., Martín Bermúdez F., Martín Palmero F., Novo-Corti I. (2016) Sustainability and the Spanish port system. Analysis of the relationship between economic and environmental indicators. *Marine Pollution Bulletin*, 113(1): 232–239.

Hossain T., Adams M., Walker T.R. (2019) Sustainability initiatives in Canadian ports. *Marine Policy*, 106: 103519.

Hou L., Geerlings H. (2016) Dynamics in sustainable port and hinterland operations: A conceptual framework and simulation of sustainability measures and their effectiveness, based on an application to the Port of Shanghai. *Journal of Cleaner Production*, 135: 449–456.

International Maritime Organization (IMO) (2021) Fourth Greenhouse Gas Study 2020, https://www.imo.org/en/ourwork/environment/pages/fourth-imo-greenhouse-gas-study-2020.aspx

Ji Z., Wu X., Chen X., Zhou W., Song M. (2023) Finding green performance targets globally closest to management goals for ports experiencing similar circumstances. *Resources Policy*, 85: 103897.

Kang D., Kim S. (2017) Conceptual model development of sustainability practices: The case of port operations for collaboration and governance. *Sustainability*, 9(12): 2333.

Karimpour R., Ballini F., Ölcer A.I. (2020) Port-city redevelopment and the circular economy agenda in Europe. In: Carpenter A., Lozano R. (Eds.), *European Port Cities in Transition: Moving towards More Sustainable Sea Transport Hubs*. Springer International Publishing, pp. 53–71.

Kong Y., Liu J. (2021) Sustainable port cities with coupling coordination and environmental efficiency. *Ocean & Coastal Management*, 205: 105534.

Lam J.S.L., Notteboom T.E. (2014) The greening of ports: A comparison of port management tools used by leading ports in Asia and Europe. *Transport Reviews*, 34(2): 169–189.

Lim S., Pettit S., Abouarghoub W., Beresford A. (2019) Port sustainability and performance: A systematic literature review. *Transportation Research Part D: Transport and Environment*, 72: 47–64.

Lin Y., Ng A.K.Y., Zhang A., Xu Y., He Y. (2020) Climate change adaptation by ports: The attitude of Chinese port organizations. *Maritime Policy and Management*, 47(7): 873–884.

Mjelde A., Endresen Ø., Bjørshol E., Gierløff C.W., Husby E., Solheim J., Mjøs N., Eide M.S. (2019) Differentiating on port fees to accelerate the green maritime transition. *Marine Pollution Bulletin*, 149: 110561.

Monios J. (2020) Environmental governance in shipping and ports: Sustainability and scale challenges. In: Ng A.K.Y., Monios J., Jiang C. (Eds.), *Maritime Transport and Regional Sustainability*. Elsevier, pp. 13–29.

Monios J., Wilmsmeier G. (2020) Deep adaptation to climate change in the maritime transport sector – A new paradigm for maritime economics? *Maritime Policy and Management*, 47(7): 853–872.

Monios J., Wilmsmeier G., Tello G.A.M., Pomaska L. (2024) A new conception of port governance under climate change. *Journal of Transport Geography*, 120: 103988.

Morris L.L. (2020) Stakeholder collaboration as a pathway to climate adaptation at coastal ports. *Maritime Policy and Management*, 47(7): 953–967.

Mueller N., Westerby M., Nieuwenhuijsen M. (2023) Health impact assessments of shipping and port-sourced air pollution on a global scale: A scoping literature review. *Environmental Research*, 216: 114460.

Robinson R. (2002) Ports as elements in value-driven chain systems: The new paradigm. *Maritime Policy and Management*, 29(3): 241–255.

Rodrigues K.T., Ensslin S.R. (2024) Environmental performance evaluation in ports: A literature review and future research guidelines. *Maritime Economics & Logistics*, 26(2): 241–260.

Roos E.C., Kliemann Neto F.J. (2017) Tools for evaluating environmental performance at Brazilian public ports: Analysis and proposal. *Marine Pollution Bulletin*, 115(1): 211–216.

Satta G., Vitellaro F., Njikatoufon A.G., Risitano M. (2025) Green strategies in ports: A stakeholder management perspective. *Maritime Economics & Logistics*, 27(1): 96–122.

Sierra J.P., Genius A., Lionello P., Mestres M., Mösso C., Marzo L. (2017) Modelling the impact of climate change on harbour operability: The Barcelona port case study. *Ocean Engineering*, 141: 64–78.

Široka M., Pilicic S., Miloševic T., Lacalle I., Traven L. (2021) A novel approach for assessing the ports' environmental impacts in real time – The IoT based port environmental index. *Ecological Indicators*, 120: 106949.

Sislian L., Jaegler A., Cariou P. (2016) A literature review on port sustainability and ocean's carrier network problem. *Research in Transportation Business and Management*, 19: 19–26.

Styhre L., Winnes H. (2019) Emissions from ships in ports. In: Bergqvist R., Monios J. (Eds.), *Green Ports: Inland and Seaside Sustainable Transportation Strategies*. Elsevier, pp. 109–124.

Taljaard S., Slinger J.H., Arabi S., Weerts S.P., Vreugdenhil H. (2021) The natural environment in port development: A 'green handbrake' or an equal partner? *Ocean & Coastal Management*, 199: 105390.

Trozzi C., Vaccaro R. (2000) Environmental impact of port activities. In: Brebbia C.A. (Ed.), *Maritime Engineering and Ports II*. Wessex Institute of Technology and J. OLIVELLA, Universitat Politecnica de Catalunya, pp. 151–161.

Wan C., Zhang D., Yan X., Yang Z. (2018) A novel model for the quantitative evaluation of green port development – A case study of major ports in China. *Transportation Research Part D: Transport and Environment*, 61: 431–443.

Wang L., Zhou Z., Yang Y., Wu J. (2020) Green efficiency evaluation and improvement of Chinese ports: A cross-efficiency model. *Transportation Research Part D: Transport and Environment*, 88: 102590.

World Bank Group (2025) Port Reform Toolkit, https://www.worldbank.org/en/topic/transport/publication/port-reform-toolkit

World Commission on Environment and Development (1987) Our common future. UN. Secretary-General.

World Ports Climate Initiative (WPCI) (2010) Carbon footprinting for ports. Guidance document. Carbon Footprinting Working Group, June 2010. https://sustainableworldports.org/wp-content/uploads/Carbon_Footprinting_Guidance_Document.pdf

Zhang Z., Song C., Zhang J., Chen Z., Liu M., Aziz F., Kurniawan T.A., Yap P.S. (2024) Digitalization and innovation in green ports: A review of current issues, contributions and the way forward in promoting sustainable ports and maritime logistics. *Science of the Total Environment*, 912: 169075.

Zhao D., Zhenfu L., Duan W. (2023) Research on the symbiosis of port and city based on symbiosis theory: Empirical evidence from China's coastal port groups. *International Journal of Shipping and Transport Logistics*, 16(1/2): 210–230.

3 Perception of the impact of port pollution on the health of its population

The case of the cities of Le Havre and Rouen – exploratory study

Julia Appercelle, Marie-Laure Baron, Olivier Bueno, Sophie Cros and Alicia Jacquette

Introduction

Some populations perceive air pollution as a danger to their well-being, particularly due to industrial emissions and maritime traffic (Lo Prete, 2023). In Fos-sur-Mer, more than 50 biomarkers analysed from 153 volunteers reported respiratory effects linked to pollutants from the industrial-port zone (Goix et al., 2017). In the Provence Alpes Côte d'Azur (PACA) region, the frequency of ozone pollution episodes accentuates this perception of health risks, influencing residents' sense of vulnerability (Roussel, 2015). This link between pollution and perceived health risks is also observed in Dunkirk, where the proximity of industrial sites has given rise to persistent concerns (Prouvost and Declercq, 2003). Air quality, often perceptible through odours or visible dust, is a powerful vector of awareness for residents, who associate these nuisances with chronic pathologies (Verdin, 2023). The correlation between industrial proximity and an increase in respiratory and cardiovascular disease is fuelling residents' concerns about long-term impacts (Machado et al., 2017; Roussel, 2018). An epidemiological study shows that perceptions of risk are exacerbated by the repetition of incidents and the omnipresence of industrial infrastructures. In Port-Saint-Louis-du-Rhône, a participatory survey revealed a strong concern for the health of children living near port areas, linked to fine particle emissions (Gramaglia and Duchêne, 2020). While studies at European level (Ducruet et al., 2024) have demonstrated significant correlations between industrial port areas and urban pollution, at local level the results remain few. Our research focuses on the population's perception of the impact of port pollution. This exploratory study is based on a graduation report of logistics engineers. We administered a questionnaire to 213 individuals in the cities of Le Havre and Rouen, which are two French port cities in Normandy. The results show that the participants' main concern is health, considered the most important issue by 60% of respondents. Perception of pollution is also a key issue: a majority believe that Rouen is more polluted than Le Havre, partly due to Rouen's geography. When it comes to

DOI: 10.4324/9781003639589-5

raising awareness of environmental projects, 73% of respondents were unaware of regional or European projects, suggesting a lack of communication on the subject. We will present a state-of-the-art on health pollution in port cities, then expose our questionnaire, and discuss its results.

Context

French ports are nowadays considered as a metropolitan asset (Merk and Comtois, 2012). Studies show that residents of port cities are particularly sensitive to air quality issues, as pollutants from shipping and industrial emissions are highly visible. They are also more aware of related nuisances, including noise (Grzelakowski et al., 2024).

The perception of air quality in port cities is a growing concern as maritime activities significantly contribute to air pollution (Wang et al., 2008; Viana et al, 2014). Understanding how local populations perceive air quality is crucial for developing effective environmental management policies.

Air Quality Measurement Systems typically rely on three main types of input data: meteorological conditions, boundary concentrations within the modelled domain, and emission inventories. Since emissions result from the combination of emission-generating processes (economic activity levels) and emission factors (g of CO_2, g of NO_x per kg of fuel, etc), activity levels represent a key determinant in bottom-up emission modelling (Ramacher et al., 2024). The role of human activity in shaping air pollution in coastal cities has been widely documented (Toscano, 2023), but it was particularly highlighted during the COVID-19 lockdowns. In this period, drastic reductions in mobility and industrial operations led to a 30%–50% decrease in NO2 emissions, while paradoxically, ozone concentrations in urban and peri-urban areas sometimes rose by 6%–30% (Gkatzelis et al., 2021).

As part of the APICE project, a year-long monitoring campaign (July 2011–July 2012) was conducted at an urban background site in Marseille to assess air quality and the contribution of different sources to particulate matter (PM) levels. Fine particulate matter ($PM_{2.5}$) is considered more harmful to human health than PM_{10} (dust, pollen, mold,...) contributing to cardiovascular and respiratory diseases. Results showed that shipping accounted for a substantial share of fine particles, contributing about 18% of annual $PM_{2.5}$ mass (3.5 ± 2.3 $\mu g/m^3$) (Toscano, 2023). In this previous research, source apportionment was performed with two chemical transport models – CHIMERE (zero-out method) and CAMx (tracer method, PSAT) – for both winter (February 2011) and summer (August 2011). Maritime contributions to $PM_{2.5}$ were estimated at 7%–10% near the port and 7%–9% at the urban background site. More broadly, studies in France have reported that ship emissions contribute between 7% and 18% of urban $PM_{2.5}$ concentrations (Lo Prete, 2023; Chevet et al., 2024).

Maritime transport is a major contributor to air pollution in port cities, with direct consequences for local air quality and public health. Although this impact is widely recognized, it is less often noted that substituting maritime freight with road transport would likely generate even higher emissions. Beyond these comparisons, maritime activity also sustains local economies and employment. Importantly, the way residents perceive pollution in their daily environment provides crucial information for policymakers, as public perception often shapes awareness, trust and the acceptance of future regulatory measures. It is then interesting to collect the perception of the population living in these urban areas. We then carried out a pilot survey with a questionnaire to collect perceptions of air pollution of people living and/or working in Le Havre and Rouen, the two main ports of Normandy region in France. This study offers indicative results that can guide future research.

Methodology

The questionnaire

Before developing the questionnaire, we held discussions with two port-sector experts to inform its design.

First, we interviewed the president of the AIVP,[1] the worldwide network of coastal cities, M. Bruno Delsalle. He gave us his views, both as a maritime professional and as someone who has lived in Le Havre for over 30 years. According to him, the situation has not changed, but people pay more attention to their surroundings today than they did in the past. They are more sensitive to their everyday environment, including pollution. From a citizen's perspective, he has noticed little change or improvement since moving to the urban area. Although development paths are becoming more sustainable and initiatives in this direction are multiplying, he doubts that the local population perceives them in this way. This discrepancy between sustainable development initiatives and their limited visibility to residents underlines the importance of investigating citizens' perceptions.

The AIVP had not previously explored our specific research topic nor carried out a questionnaire among the relevant population. However, our contact provided valuable insights into the public's likely perceptions and advised us on which questions to include or avoid. His input proved instrumental in shaping the questionnaire, and he also offered constructive feedback before its finalization.

When interviewed on the subject, he underscored that port-related pollution exerts a major impact on public health, whether originating from port activities themselves or from the adjoining industrial area. He further stressed the importance of distinguishing between these two sources of pollution: refinery emissions and industrial accidents are highly visible to the general public, yet, according to him, they cannot be considered specific to port activity.

Second, we interviewed the president of The Nature and Biodiversity Conservation Union (NABU), a major organization with around 900,500 members across Germany's 16 federal states. NABU maintains offices in each of these states. The president of the German branch is primarily based in Hamburg, where he focuses on nature-related issues. As Europe's third-largest port city, Hamburg faces major challenges from shipping, particularly regarding air pollution and public health. NABU's mission extends beyond nature conservation to include human well-being. For the past ten years, its President has overseen environmental policy, notably co-developing the 'Clean Air Ports' project with a colleague from the Berlin office. Within this framework, NABU examined several European port cities and organized workshops that brought together authorities, local communities and policymakers to discuss the impacts of shipping and explore ways to make both ports and shipping cleaner.

From those two experts and our literature review, we built our questionnaire, selecting two types of variables:

- explanatory variables, which represent statistical collected data from the field or academic studies or official websites (e.g. the official meteorological website ATMO);
- consent variables assess the extent of the impact of pollution on the health of the inhabitants of a port city. These variables make it possible to obtain questionnaires about participants' perceptions of the impact of pollution in a port city on their health. We chose two types of consent variable for our questionnaire: the order of importance or priority of several issues, and the participant's perceptions.

The questionnaire was structured into four sections:

- **Part 1 – Perception of health in a port city:** This section aimed to capture residents' general opinions and knowledge about the health situation in Le Havre and Rouen, and whether they believed it affected their own health.
- **Part 2 – Perception of pollution data:** Respondents were presented with figures on pollution levels in Le Havre and Rouen, then asked to share their reactions. This allowed us to assess whether exposure to concrete data led participants to change their initial opinions.
- **Part 3 – Awareness and perception of specific projects:** Here, we explored public awareness of the 'Zero Smoking Stopover' and platform electrification projects, as well as residents' views on whether these measures would benefit their health once implemented.
- **Part 4 – Respondent profiles:** This final section collected demographic and socio-professional information (e.g., age, place of residence, occupation). These variables are essential for analysis, as responses may differ across groups and cannot be directly compared without this context. We placed this section at the end of the questionnaire, as profile questions are relatively straightforward and require less reflection than the preceding sections.

Le Havre and Rouen were divided into four areas each, depending on the compass rose, because the wind disperses air pollution differently in different neighbourhoods (Figure 3.1).

- Le Havre:
    - Area A – North District
    - Area B – East District
    - Area C – South District
    - Area D – West District

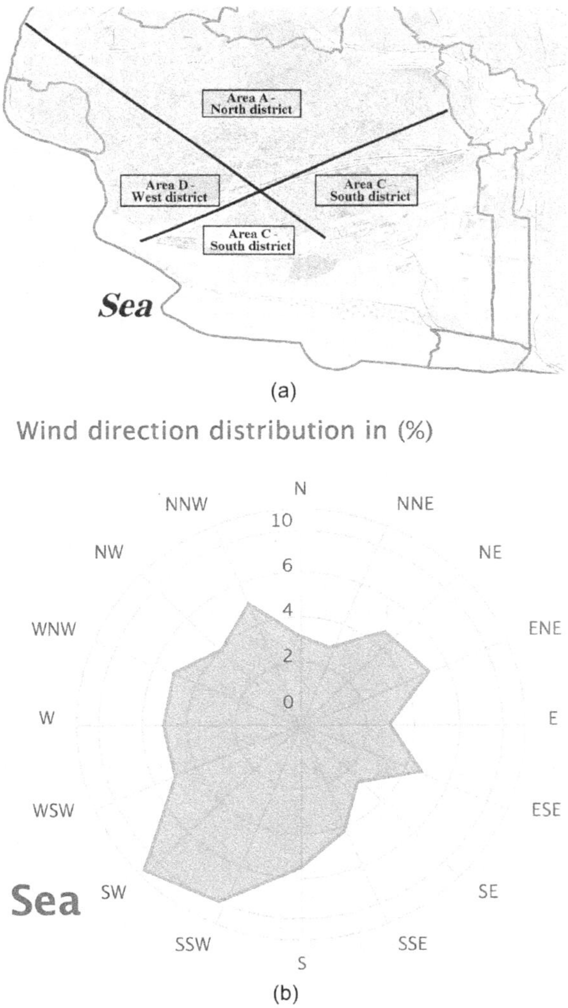

Figure 3.1 Areas identified in Le Havre

Source: Own elaboration

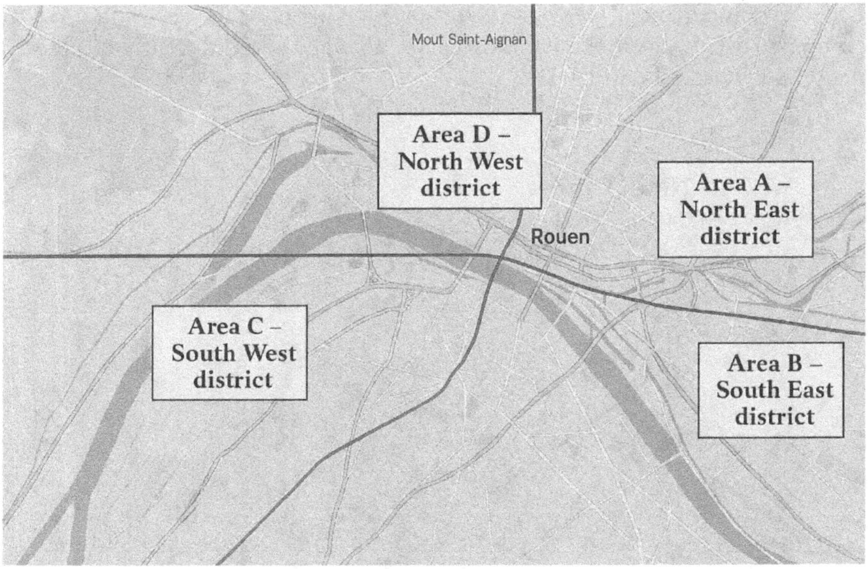

Figure 3.2 Areas in Rouen along the river Seine
Source: Own elaboration

According to the exposure to pollution and the direction of the wind people might perceive pollution differently (Figure 3.2).

- Rouen:
  - Area A – North East District
  - Area B – South East District
  - Zone C – South-West District
  - Zone D – North-West District

The administration

The questionnaire was distributed via social networks, from February to April 2024. Two hundred and thirteen individuals from the port cities of Le Havre and Rouen answered.

Results and discussion

Using R software, we carried out a statistical study.

- **Age of participants (qualitative variable)**

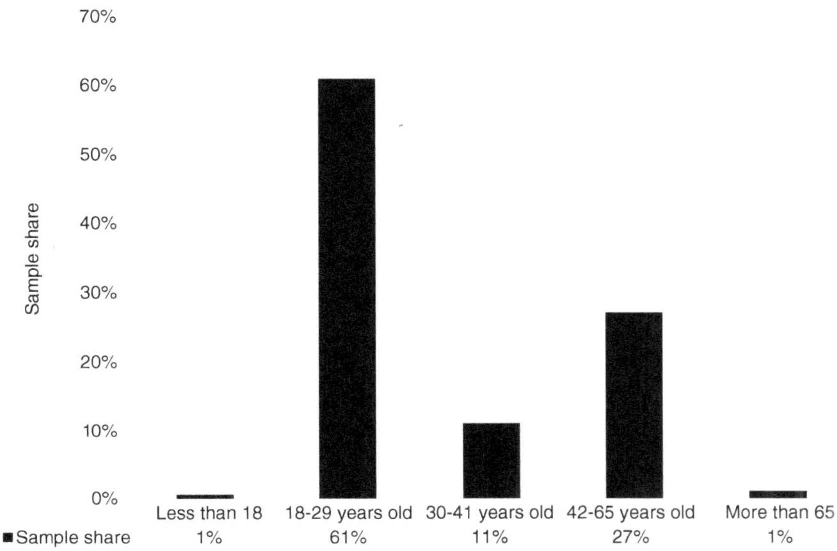

Figure 3.3 Distribution of respondents by age group (percentages)

Source: Own elaboration

We were able to collect responses from a wide range of people: minors, students, juniors, seniors and retired people. We produced a histogram and a frequency table to assess the distribution of participants by age (Figure 3.3).

We quickly observed that the majority of respondents were between 18 and 29 years old, accounting for about 61% of the sample. This strong representation is largely due to the way the questionnaire was disseminated – primarily through schools and universities in Le Havre and Rouen, and subsequently shared via students' social networks. As a result, younger age groups were more likely to participate. The second largest group of respondents was aged 42–65, representing around 27% of the sample.

- **City of respondents (qualitative variable):**

The study focuses on respondents from Rouen and Le Havre. For the purposes of analysing the results and ensuring the relevance of the answers, we have eliminated the 23 people who answered that they live outside these two cities, in neighbouring towns, from this survey. We have nevertheless kept their answers for the other questions, as their opinions may be relevant, despite the fact that they do not live in one of the two towns in the study. The results show that 91% of respondents live in Le Havre. The distribution

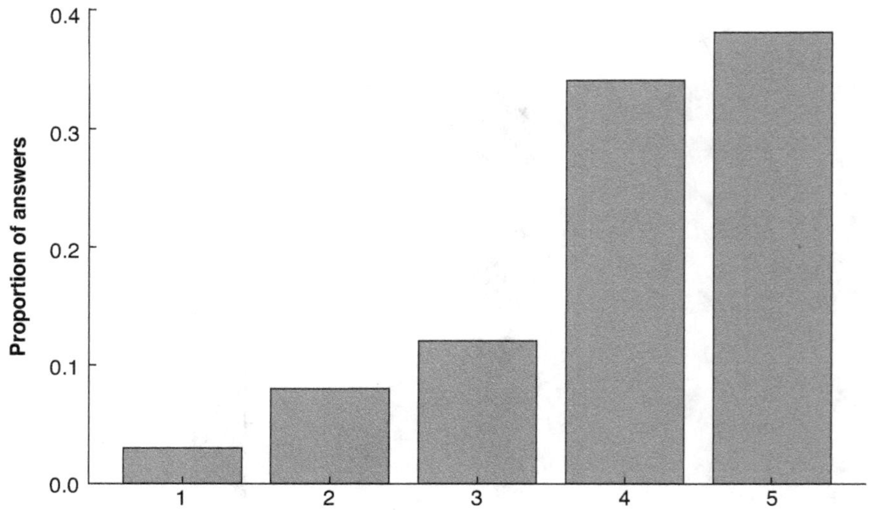

Figure 3.4 Perceived significance of pollution's impact
Source: Own elaboration

of responses between the two cities is of little importance as we are studying the perception of populations in port cities, but the sample is mainly based on the opinions of people from Le Havre (Figure 3.4).

- **Importance of the impact of pollution on participants' lives (quantitative variable).** In this question, we wanted to find out how important participants considered the impact of pollution on their lives to be. For the majority of respondents to the questionnaire, the impact of pollution on their lives is very important (ranked 4 or 5). Conversely, six people considered that the impact of pollution on their lives was not at all important (ranked 1).
- **Importance of health according to respondents** (**quantitative variable**). The purpose of this question was to qualify the importance of health concern better. Respondents were asked to rank 5 themes: health, purchasing power, safety, living environment and the environment.

Most of our 213 respondents, 127 (60%) ranked health as the most important item. Health is therefore the most important factor for the participants. In fact, when we asked why health was placed in this position, the majority of people replied that 'Because without good health, you can't do anything' or 'health is life' (Figure 3.5).

- **Most polluted city: Le Havre or Rouen** (**qualitative variable**). Participants were asked which of the two cities they considered more polluted.

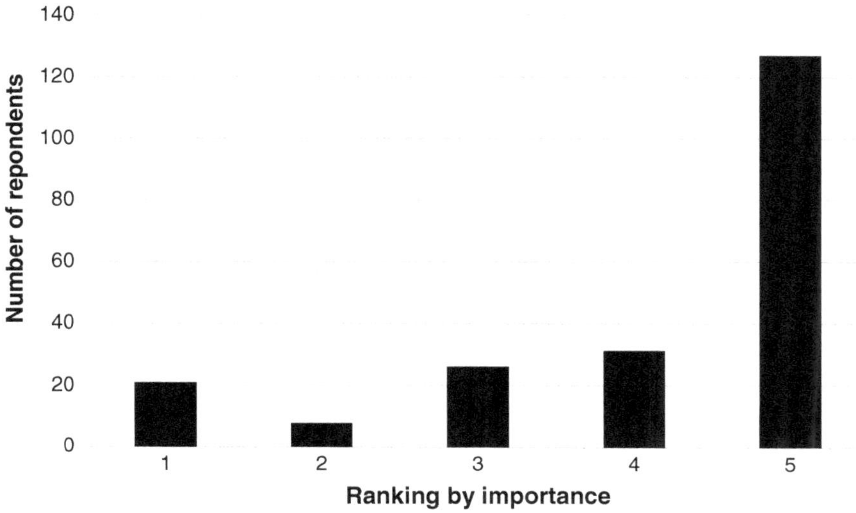

Figure 3.5 Individual's ranking of the importance of health
Source: Own elaboration

Their answers were summarized in a histogram and a frequency table. A majority identified Rouen as more polluted than Le Havre. One reason may be the sample composition, as most respondents were from Le Havre. Another plausible explanation, however, lies in geography: Rouen is situated further inland, in a basin where air circulation is weaker than by the sea, causing pollutants to stagnate. This underlines the potential role of local geography in shaping perceptions of air pollution.

- **Awareness of the Smoke-free stopover project (qualitative variable).** Our questionnaire included a question to find out whether participants were aware of the Smoke-free Stopover. 73% of respondents said they were not aware of this project which shows the local population is not always aware of European and local efforts to deal with environmental issues.
- **Awareness of the local shore-side electricity supply project (qualitative variable).** As with the previous question, we asked participants whether they were aware of the platform electrification project. Again, the majority of respondents (61%) were not aware of the project.
- **Qualitative bivariate analysis of age and health status.**

Firstly, we wanted to find out the link between age and the health condition defined by the individuals. To do this, we used R software to produce two frequency tables from which we obtained an associated 100% diagram (Figure 3.6).

The bars in this diagram are not identical, which shows there is a dependency between the two variables. The older the individual, the more likely they are to report an immune, respiratory or other pathology. In our case, we can

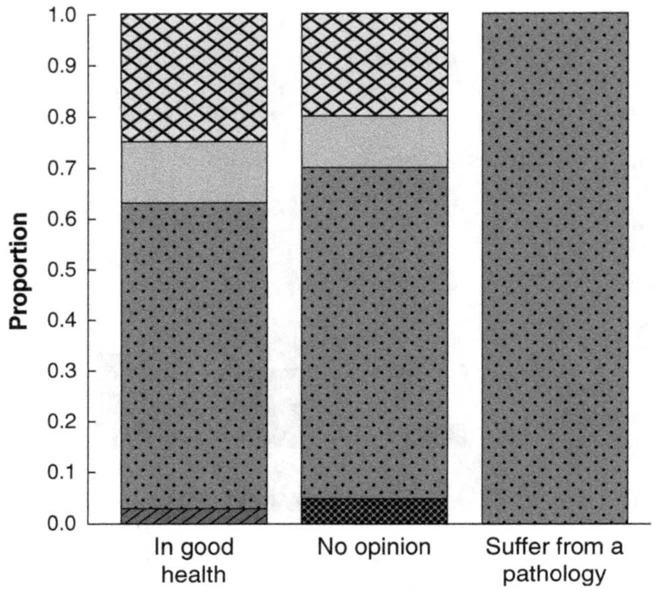

Figure 3.6 Relationship between age and individuals' health condition

Source: Own elaboration

say that the majority of individuals consider themselves to be in good health, but 10.3% of them suffer from a respiratory pathology, and 0.5% declare that they suffer from an immune disease.

- **Quali-quanti bivariate analysis of age and health ranking.** We wanted to know which individuals were more concerned about their health to identify the population most affected by air pollution.

Thanks to the boxplot, we notice, on average, people aged between 18 and over 65 rank health as the most important issue, ahead of purchasing power, environmental concerns, quality of life and safety (Figure 3.7).

- **Quali-quanti bivariate analysis of variables.**

We felt it necessary to understand whether there was a dependency between the perceived impact of pollution on an individual's life and the fact of not going out during periods of heavy air pollution (Figure 3.8).

In other words, individuals who consider the impact of pollution on their lives to be significant do not prevent themselves from going out. This represents 79.3% of the sample. On the other hand, 38.5% of those who consider the impact of pollution on their health to be very important may refrain from

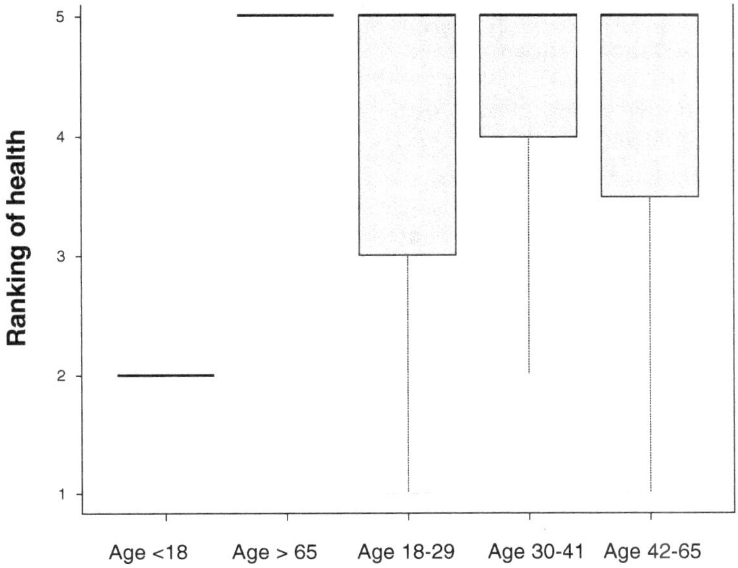

Figure 3.7 Boxplot presenting the ranking of health per age

Source: Own elaboration

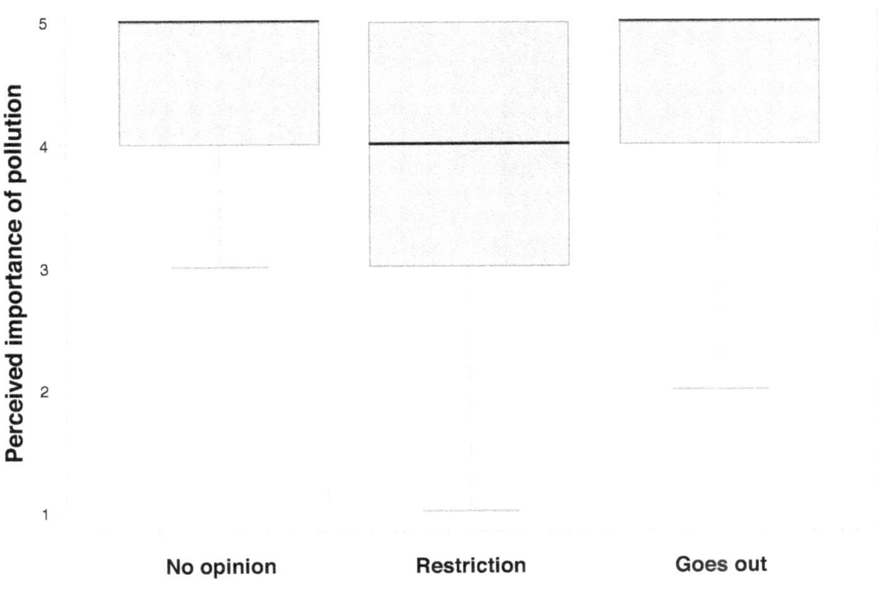

Figure 3.8 Boxplot representing the importance of pollution by restriction of going out

Source: Own elaboration

going out because of the day's air pollution. In the end, the majority of the population did not refuse to go out despite the level of pollution.

- **Quantitative bivariate analysis between 'Do you consider living in a port city that is polluted?'** and the population's opinion of the impact of pollution on their health

For this bivariate analysis, we wanted to know whether individuals who consider that they live in a polluted city think that air pollution has a strong impact on their health. To do this, we used a pivot table to obtain a scatter plot, as shown in Figure 3.9.

The scatterplot does not resemble an elongated, linear pattern, suggesting that there is no relationship between perceiving one's port city as polluted and assigning greater importance to the health impacts of air pollution. In other words, people who consider their city less polluted do not necessarily downplay the health effects of pollution, and the reverse is also true. Thus, the perceived importance of pollution's impact appears unrelated to the actual or perceived pollution level of the city. This implies that other factors weigh more heavily in shaping people's views: media and public discourse of course, trust in local institutions, visibility of pollution sources (ships, smoke, port equipment), sensory nuisances like noise, odours or dust and personal health experience. This highlights the importance of considering social and

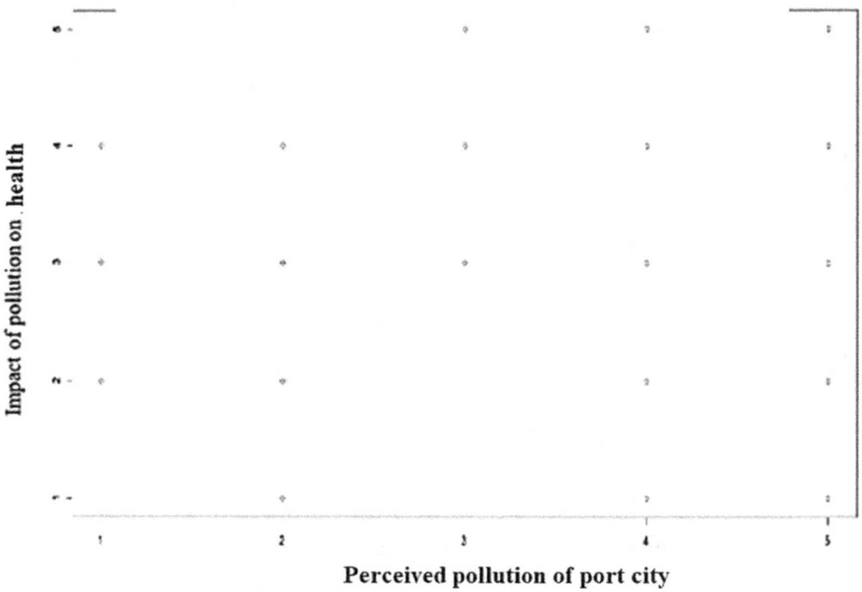

Figure 3.9 Scatterplot of perceived impacts of pollution

Source: Own elaboration

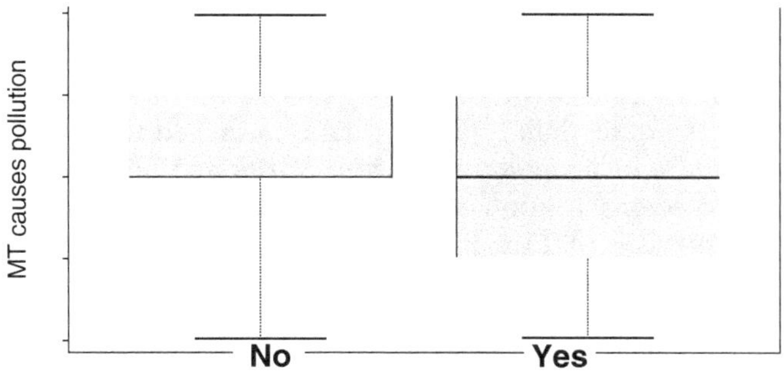

Figure 3.10 Boxplot on perceived air quality improvements

Source: Own elaboration

contextual dimensions, alongside measured pollution levels, when assessing public perception.

- **Quali-quanti bivariate analysis between the extent to which maritime freight transport is responsible for pollution and the opinion regarding improvements to the city's port**

The idea of this analysis is to highlight the link between the population's opinion of the extent to which maritime transport is responsible for pollution and their opinion of the improvements made to the port (Figure 3.10).

Clearly, the majority of the population surveyed seems to agree about the environmental and climatic impact of maritime transport. They believe that it is one of the major causes of pollution in Le Havre and Rouen, after industrial activity in these two cities.

Individuals also seem to be divided on the improvements being made at the port, with 53% believing that improvement projects are not necessary or sufficient for their well-being, compared with 47% who think that, on the contrary, it is important to carry out projects to adapt our port activities to current challenges.

Conclusion

In conclusion, analysis of our questionnaire reveals several clear trends among respondents. The main concern of participants is health, considered to be the most important issue by 60% of respondents. The perception of pollution is also a key point: a majority think that Rouen is more polluted than Le Havre, partly because of Rouen's geography. In terms of awareness of environmental projects, 73% of respondents were not aware of the projects in question, suggesting a possible communication problem.

In addition, the majority of people interviewed seem to recognize the significant environmental and climatic impact of maritime transport, which is considered to be one of the main sources of pollution in Le Havre and Rouen, after industrial activities. Opinions differ as to port improvements.

Statistical analysis shows that there is no correlation between living in a city perceived as polluted and the importance attached to the impact of pollution on health, which suggests port authorities and cities should consider acting on perceptions beyond providing information on pollution levels. The study also reveals that the majority of people do not limit their outdoor activities despite pollution levels. The importance of health varies according to age, with individuals aged 18 to over 65 generally placing health above other concerns such as purchasing power, the environment, the quality of life and safety.

A few limits of our study might be that the majority, 61%, are aged between 18 and 29, which reflects our main distribution within the academic institutions of Le Havre and Rouen. Another notable point is that 91% of respondents live in Le Havre, which explains the predominance of Le Havre-based opinions in our sample.

Nevertheless, these results underline the importance of continuing to monitor and improve environmental and health conditions, while considering the different perceptions and needs of the population living in the considered areas.

Acknowledgments

The authors wishe to express sincere gratitude to Antoine Font de Campos about his contribution to the chapter.

Note

1 Association internationale des villes portuaires (International Association Cities and Ports, IACP).

References

Chevet E., Boiron O., Anselmet F. (2024) Modelling of air pollution due to marine traffic in Mediterranean coastal cities. *Atmospheric Environment*, 329: 120542.

Ducruet C., Martin B.P., Sene M.A., Lo Prete M., Sun L., Itoh H., Pigné Y. (2024) Ports and their influence on local air pollution and public health: A global analysis. *Science of the Total Environment*, 915: 170099.

Gkatzelis G.I., Gilman J.B., Brown S.S., Eskes H., Gomes A.R., Lange A.C., Brian C. McDonald, Peischl J., Petzold A., Thompson C.R., Kiendler-Scharr A. (2021). The global impacts of COVID-19 lockdowns on urban air pollution: A critical review and recommendations. *Elementa: Science of the Anthropocene*, 9(1), https://doi.org/10.1525/elementa.2021.00176

Goix S., Dron J., Raucau A., Chamaret P. (2017) Lancement de l'étude de biosurveillance des populations exposées aux émissions atmosphériques à proximité de la zone industrialo-portuaire de Fos-sur-Mer (INDEX). *Pollution Atmosphérique*, 233, https://www.peren-revues.fr/pollutionatmospherique/5214

Gramaglia C., Duchêne É. (2020) Attachements, pratiques sociales et usages du territoire à l'épreuve des pollutions à Fos-sur-Mer et Port-Saint-Louis-du-Rhône : Comment faire face aux risques industriels chroniques? *Rives Méditerranéennes*, 61: 147–177.

Grzelakowski A.S., Skiba S., Kosiek J. (2024) Noise as environmental nuisance of the seaport activity. *European Research Studies Journal*, 27(4): 1031–1043.

Lo Prete M. (2023) La pollution atmosphérique des navires: une cause majeure de vulnérabilité environnementale. In: Mathlouthi R. B., Pomade A. (Eds.), *Vulnérabilité(s) Environnementale(s): Perspectives Pluridisciplinaires*. L'Harmattan Environnement, pp. 229–250.

Machado M., Méha C. Frère S., Santos J.M. (2017) La perception des nuisances liées à la pollution de l'air: une étude comparative entre Vitoria (Brésil) et Dunkerque (France). In: Frère S., Flanquart H. (Eds.), *La ville et ses risques*. Presses Universitaires du Septentrion, pp. 129–148.

Merk O., Comtois C. (2012) *Competitiveness of port-cities: The case of Marseille-Fos-France*. OECD.

Prouvost H., Declercq C. (2003) *Santé et environnement: Une exploration des enjeux sur le territoire de la Communauté Urbaine de Dunkerque*. ORS Nord – Pas-de-Calais.

Ramacher M.O.P., Badeke R., Fink L., Quante M., Karl M., Oppo, S., Lenartz F., Dury M., Matthias V. (2024) Assessing the effects of significant activity changes on urban-scale air quality across three European cities. *Atmospheric Environment: X*, 22: 100264.

Roussel I. (2015) Les épisodes d'ozone en région PACA, le prix sanitaire du soleil. *Pollution Atmosphérique*, 8: 135–155.

Roussel I. (2018) La ville et ses risques: habiter Dunkerque. In: Frère S., Flanquart H. (Eds.) (2017), *Pollution atmosphérique. Climat, santé, société*. Presses Universitaires du Septentrion, pp. 237–238.

Toscano D. (2023) The impact of shipping on air quality in the port cities of the Mediterranean area: A review. *Atmosphere*, 14(7): 1180.

Verdin M. (2023) Le Dunkerquois se donne les moyens d'aller mieux. *DARD/DARD*, 8: 42–51.

Viana M., Hammingh P., Colette A., Querol X., Degraeuwe B., de Vlieger I., Van Aardenne J. (2014) Impact of maritime transport emissions on coastal air quality in Europe. *Atmospheric Environment*, 90: 96–105.

Wang C., Corbett J.J., Firestone J. (2008) Improving spatial representation of global ship emissions inventories. *Environmental Science and Technology*, 42(1): 193–199.

4 Investigating air pollution-induced annoyance

A case study of a coastal urban region in Brazil

Milena Machado, Severine Frère and Jane Meri Santos

Context of the problem

Air pollution caused by particulate matter (PM) is a major concern in highly urbanized cities, where common sources include construction activities, unpaved roads, wood stoves, fireplaces, and heavy traffic. Indoor environments can also contribute to particle pollution through activities such as cooking, smoking, dusting, and vacuuming. In addition, urban areas are often affected by nearby industrial facilities. Coastal cities face further challenges, as emissions from commercial ports, industrial terminals, container ports, naval bases, and fishing harbours can also contribute to elevated PM levels. Port operations encompass a wide range of activities that can produce particles, for instance, movement, handling, and management of ships and cargo. These operations typically include vessel berthing and unberthing, loading and unloading of containers and bulk materials, cargo storage, customs inspection, and maintenance of port infrastructure.

The size of emitted particles depends on their origin or source. Particles produced by combustion are more likely to be small particles, while particles emitted from material handling, for instance, are more likely to be larger. PM is usually classified as ultrafine particles (smaller than 0.1 µm), fine particles (smaller than 2.5 µm), coarse particles (between 2.5 and 10 µm) and total suspended particles (TSP) (usually smaller than 100 µm depending on the sampling method). All particles suspended in the atmosphere can undergo deposition on different types of surfaces existing in the urban environment. However, large particles are subject to deposition close to the source, while smaller ones tend to settle far from the emitting sources. Therefore, settleable particulate matter (SPM) consists of a wide range of particle sizes, with a predominance, by mass, of larger particles.

SPM represents a chronic challenge in urban areas, where dust can compromise residents' quality of life and damage urban infrastructure. In addition to its health impacts, it can affect the well-being of populations exposed to the daily deposition of dust on homes, vehicles, and leisure areas, causing nuisance associated with long-term exposure and societal

DOI: 10.4324/9781003639589-6

perceptions, as well as individual complaints of annoyance during perceived episodes based on immediate or recurring personal experiences.

The World Health Organization (WHO) has defined health as "a state of complete physical, mental and social well-being and not merely the absence of disease or infirmity". Thus, the nuisance caused by SPM qualifies as a public health problem, as it can be seen as an ambient stressor causing stress and diseases and affecting the quality of life (Jacquemin et al., 2007; Machado et al., 2018; Yang et al., 2018).

The nuisance created by SPM depends on particles characteristics (such as colour, which can vary according to the particles chemical composition and the amount deposited) and on the individual perception. This individual perception, in turn, may be influenced by a person's health, as well as their environment, socioeconomic conditions and cultural background (Forsberg et al., 1997, Rotko et al., 2002; Jacquemin et al., 2007).

Previous studies have demonstrated a complex interplay between air pollutants concentrations and individual perceptions in influencing nuisance. For example, Eek et al. (2010) conducted a study in Sweden and found that individuals who report annoyance due to air pollution also tend to report health complaints related to respiratory illness, higher levels of stress, and lower personal social support compared to those who do not. Similarly, Blanes-Vidal (2015) identified a strong association between exposure to odour sources, reported health symptoms, and annoyance in Spain. Nikolopoulou et al. (2011) found a significant correlation between perceptions of air quality and the visual effects of particulate matter (PM), such as accumulated dust, soot, and smoke, in Greece. Orru et al. (2016) showed that an increase in the annual average PM_{10} concentration was associated with a significant reduction in self-reported life satisfaction in Estonia.

To investigate this relationship further, some authors have utilized questionnaire-based surveys for a detailed analysis of multiple factors related to air pollution perception. For instance, Hayes et al. (2017) conducted a survey to assess community responses to their exposure to an odorant source in their neighbourhood. Li et al. (2020) performed a survey analysis focused on well-being in China, demonstrating that images depicting air pollution caused by particulate matter can negatively affect well-being and induce negative emotions. Similarly, studies by Yang et al. (2018, 2021) in Taiwan and Zhang et al. (2023) in China found that PM_{10} and $PM_{2.5}$ exposure can affect both psychological and physiological reactions, intensifying self-reported unpleasant feelings and reducing overall happiness among citizens.

These studies underscored the importance of complementing perception-based studies with localized epidemiological research. While global and large-scale studies are essential to demonstrate the overall health burden and risks associated with air pollution, city-level research provides more precise insights into local exposure patterns and health impacts. Such localized evidence is crucial for prioritizing policies and designing targeted intervention strategies—actions that municipal authorities can often implement more swiftly and effectively than national governments.

Proposal

This work quantifies the annoyance caused by particulate matter (SPM, PM_{10}, and TSP) in an industrialized coastal urban region of southeastern Brazil. Building upon previous research, it emphasizes the importance of investigating both air quality parameters and subjective factors that influence residents' perceptions of environmental nuisances. The analysis integrates monitored particulate matter data with questionnaire-based surveys to provide a comprehensive assessment of the relationship between objective pollution levels and perceived annoyance.

Data collection and survey analysis

Description of the study area in southeastern Brazil: demography, climate, and air pollution sources

The study area corresponds to the Region of Vitoria located on the southeast coast of Brazil. The region is composed of seven municipalities and spans an area of 2,023 km^2, with a population of approximately 1.9 million inhabitants. The region is characterized by a tropical climate and experiences high temperatures and humidity throughout the year. It has two main seasons: a warm and humid period with heavy rainfall (usually from September to March), and another period milder and drier. The coastal location and sea breezes influence the local weather patterns, but the overall climate remains consistently warm.

The Vitória Region comprises a large port complex system, heavy vehicular traffic, intense building constructions and an industrial park that includes, among others, steel production, pelletizing, quarry, cement, and food industries, chemical industries, and an asphalt plant, that are all potential sources of air pollution (Santos et al., 2017).

The port complex system in the region comprises: (i) The Tubarão Port Complex, which encompasses five terminals. The Tubarão Terminal is the largest and most efficient export terminal for pellets and iron ore worldwide. The Liquid Bulk Terminal specializes in handling petroleum derivatives. The Praia Mole Terminal is dedicated to unloading vessels carrying coal (accounting for 70% of the volume imported by steel manufacturers), coke, and anthracite. The General Cargo Terminal operates an integrated system for receiving, handling, and storing grains (representing 15% of Brazil's exports) and fertilizers (accounting for 8% of imported volume). Lastly, the Steel Products Terminal handles steel products, pig iron, marble/granite blocks, and vehicles. This complex is operated by a consortium comprising

ArcelorMittal Tubarão, Usiminas, and Gerdau Açominas. (ii) The Vitória Port Complex manages general cargo through seven terminals. Among these is the Vila Velha Terminal, which specializes in container handling and is operated by private entities (Log-In International and Logistics). It serves as an excellent hub for container import and export operations and general cargo handling, ranking among the most productive terminals in Brazil within this sector. Additionally, the Vila Velha Port Company supports offshore operations related to oil exploration and production in Espírito Santo.

In addition, there are also other ports located to the north and south of the study area: The Capixaba North Terminal that facilitates the transport of oil from onshore fields. Portocel, that is specialized in pulp production and also handles marble and granite blocks, as well as steel products. The Barra do Riacho Waterway Terminal that manages liquefied petroleum gas and natural gasoline, both derived from natural gas processing and the Ubu Port, which handles pellets and iron ore, solid bulk cargo, and general cargo.

The two main ports located in the region of interest are responsible for intensive operations that require vast storage areas where large piles of raw and processed materials are consistently maintained. These open stockpiles and the necessary material handling logistics are significant sources of suspended particulate matter (dust), with the problem becoming particularly acute during the high-volume ship-loading stages.

These ports were originally constructed to serve existing local heavy industries, establishing a strong interconnection between the ports and surrounding industrial facilities. This relationship has fostered a significant concentration of economic activity in the area. Furthermore, the presence of both direct and indirect employment opportunities in the ports and industries has contributed to a high population density in the region, as workers and their families settle nearby to benefit from these job markets.

Air quality monitoring

To monitor the air quality in the Vitória Region, eight air quality monitoring stations M1–M8 (Figure 4.1) are managed by the state environmental agency providing hourly data of PM_{10} and TSP and monthly data of SPM (the latter measured according to ASTM D-1739 [2004]).

Figure 4.2 presents the time series of SPM. It is evident that the deposition rate of 10 g/m^2.30 days was often exceeded in different monitoring regions. Higher deposition rates were found at M4 and M5 stations, which are located closer to the main industries and port area.

Table 4.1 presents the descriptive statistical values of 24-hour averaged PM_{10} and TSP (maximum, minimum, mean, standard deviation, median). Mean TSP concentration levels are quite high if compared to PM_{10} concentration in all air quality monitoring stations indicating that there is a considerable amount of particles larger than 10 μm. Yet, PM_{10} levels surpass

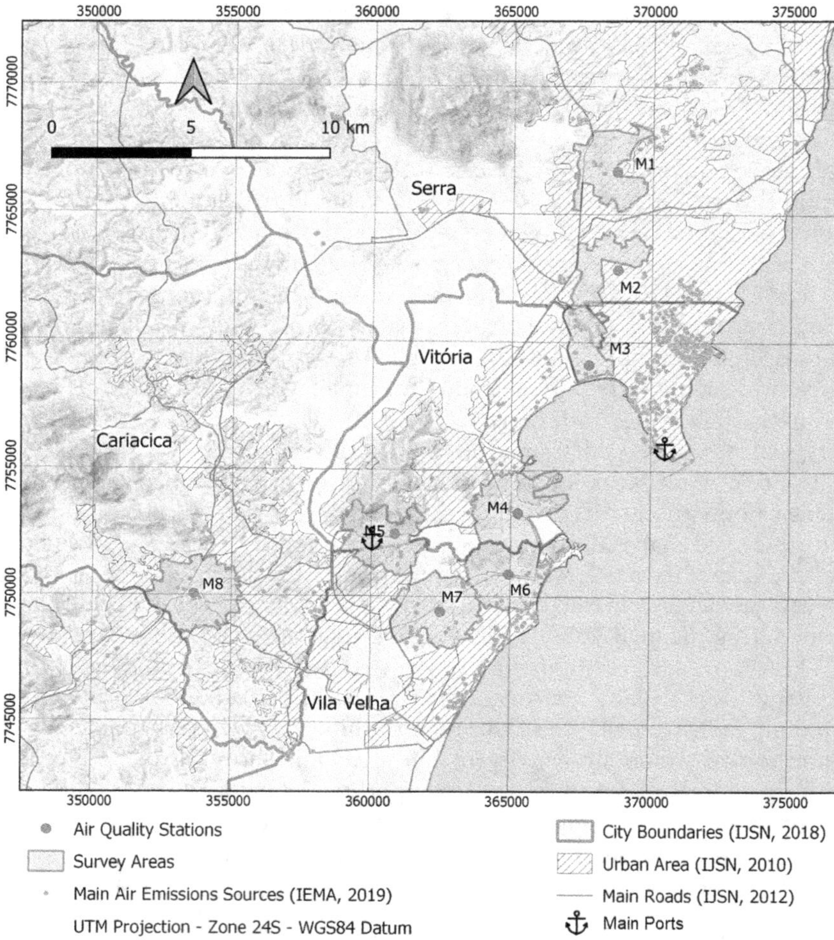

Figure 4.1 Study area, air quality monitoring stations and survey areas

Source: Adapted from Machado et al. (2022)

those recommended by WHO in most stations (45 μg/m³) (World Health Organization [WHO], 2021).

These elevated levels of particulate matter pose a measurable threat to public health, a risk that has been quantified by epidemiological studies conducted in the region that have estimated the relative risk (RR) associated with exposure to air pollutants. From June 2013 to March 2014, Nascimento et al. (2017) have used generalized additive model with Poisson distribution to evaluate the relationship between respiratory outcomes and $PM_{2.5}$ levels in the MRGV. The results showed an increase of 6% of the RR per each $PM_{2.5}$ increment of 4.25 μg m*³. In the same period of study, the authors reported

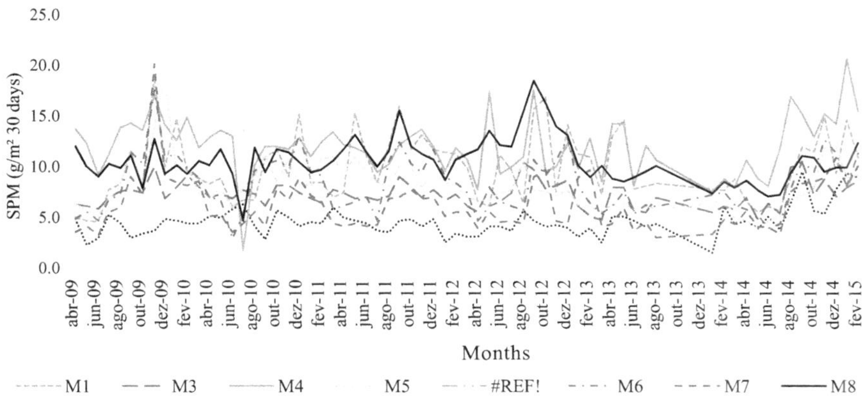

Figure 4.2 Settleable particulate matter. Time series of deposition flux rate

Source: Adapted from Machado et al. (2018)

Table 4.1 Descriptive statistical values (24-h mean) of ambient air pollution levels separated for sub-regions from 2011 to 2014

	M1	*M2*	*M3*	*M4*	*M5*	*M6*	*M7*	*M8*
PM_{10} (μg/m³)								
Minimum	12.0	–	14.0	13.0	10.0	7.0	10.0	11.0
Maximo	69.0	–	34.0	60.0	46.0	51.0	49.0	98.0
Mean	32.8	–	24.8	30.4	28.5	29.3	26.4	56.6
Standard dev.	14.2	–	4.7	8.8	8.0	9.6	7.8	22.2
Median	31.5	–	24.0	31.0	28.0	29.0	26.0	58.0
TSP (μg/m³)								
Minimum	13.0	–	17.0	16.0	17.0	13.0	–	15.0
Maximo	162.0	–	83.0	103.0	121.0	99.0	–	275.0
Mean	62.5	–	38.8	43.6	43.0	45.7	–	88.8
Standard dev.	29.2	–	11.4	15.2	15.6	16.8	–	45.4
Median	59.5	–	37.5	40.5	41.0	43.0	–	82.0

$PM_{2.5}$ level of 11.8 μg m*³, which means that the $PM_{2.5}$ levels MRGV is capable of increasing the RR until 16.6%. Other authors (de Freitas et al. 2016) investigated the impact of PM_{10} on respiratory and cardiovascular morbidity in children and adults, and the results showed an increase of 9.67% in the RR per each increment of 10 μgm^{-3} of PM_{10}. Souza et al. (2018) studied the correlation between hospital admissions for respiratory diseases (in children under six years old) and ambient PM_{10} levels, reporting that an increase of 10.49 μgm^{-3} in PM_{10} levels could increase by 3% the RR. However, effective air quality management requires more than measurement of pollution concentration; it also demands an understanding of how pollution affects citizens' perceived quality of life and daily annoyance.

Survey design and execution

The survey work was executed within a defined geographical area that was divided into several sub-regions (the grey area in Figure 4.1) surrounding the eight air quality monitoring stations. This spatial design was critical, allowing for the direct correlation of residents' subjective perceptions with the objective air quality data from their immediate vicinities.

The field work consisted of 2,638 in-person interviews carried out over a three-year period (from 2011 to 2014). The sample size was determined using simple random sampling with proportional allocation (Barnett, 2002), with households selected randomly (Cochran, 1977) in the areas highlighted in light blue surrounding each air-quality monitoring station (Figure 4.1).

The structured questionnaire was originally developed and validated by Calvo-Mendieta et al. (2008) and adapted by Machado et al. (2018). It contained approximately 50 questions covering the importance and assessment of air quality, risk perception, perceived sources and consequences of air pollution, health symptoms and weather conditions perception, interactions with environmental agencies and personal aspects.

Table 4.2 shows the profile (gender and age groups) of respondents' results from the surveys for each sub-region around the eight air quality monitoring stations. Regarding gender, there are about 62% of women in the sub-regions M5, M7 and M8 and on average 55% in the other areas.

Factors influencing the perception of annoyance

Machado et al. (2021) investigated the relationships between qualitative variables that may influence the behaviour of residents in the Vitória

Table 4.2 Sociodemographic factors in the Vitória Region separated for sub-regions (n = 2638)

	M1	*M2 (n = 297)*	*M3 (n = 284)*	*M4*	*M5*	*M6*	*M7 (n = 420)*	*M8*
	(n = 269)			*(n = 301)*	*(n = 281)*	*(n = 360)*		*(n = 426)*
Gender								
Male (%)	42	46	48	44	36	37	46	35
Female (%)	58	54	52	56	64	63	54	65
Age groups								
16–34 (%)	43	54	56	41	46	43	40	47
35–54 (%)	41	38	34	40	37	38	44	40
54 + (%)	16	8	11	19	17	19	16	13

Region in relation to the annoyance caused by dust. The variables included annoyance reported due to dust and odours, air quality assessment, risk perception, health symptoms, importance attributed to environmental issues, and sociodemographic characteristics. The statistical technique used was Multiple Correspondence Analysis (Greenacre, 2007), which allows the associations between categorical variables to be represented graphically. The results revealed that, in the study region, women and older people showed a greater association with categories of high annoyance, in addition to attributing greater importance to air quality and assessing the environmental situation more negatively. People who answered "yes" to experiencing health symptoms caused by air pollution were associated with reports of being very annoyed by dust. And, the main health symptoms reported were lung/respiratory, allergies, asthma attacks and stress. Another interesting finding reported by respondents was the influence of the northeast wind direction during the summer months, when there are more reports of discomfort. It is worth noting that when the northeast wind prevails, there is a significant influence from emissions from the port of Tubarão towards the residential areas of the city of Vitória. The analysis showed that the perception of dust, combined with a negative assessment of air quality, is central to explaining the annoyance caused by particles and consequently can affect the health status of the population.

Machado et al. (2022) deepened their analyses to identify qualitative factors influencing the perception of annoyance caused by particulate matter. Questionnaire-based surveys were conducted in sub-regions around the air quality monitoring stations in the metropolitan area of Vitoria, Brazil. Logistic regression was used to identify the associations between qualitative questionnaire variables and air pollution expressed by PM concentrations. This tool is suitable for the analysis of this type of data and also allows the estimation of the odds ratio (Baxter et al., 1997 apud Machado et al., 2022).

By applying univariate and multivariate logistic regression, Machado et al. (2022) identified associations between annoyance and the qualitative variables selected in the questionnaire. In Table 4.3, it is possible to compare the results of univariate and multivariate models. According to the odds ratio values given by the univariate model, the significant variables were: gender, age, occupation, have children, importance of air quality, risk perception, assessment of air quality, air pollution perception by dust, seeing doctor, and occurrence of health problems. If all variables are added together (multivariate model), the most significant variables became: age, weather conditions, perceived emission source, assessment of air quality, air pollution perception by dust, seeing a doctor, occurrence of health problems and knowledge about monitoring. Thus, the multivariate model that considers the combined effect of all variables together makes it possible to identify the variables that are significant combined with others (perceived emission sources, assessment of air quality, air pollution perception by dust, occurrence of health problems).

Table 4.3 Coefficients from the logistic regression models to identify determinants of perceived annoyance

Groups	*Variables*	*Univariates models*		*Multivariate model*	
		Odds Ratio	*95% C.I.*	*Odds Ratio*	*95% C.I.*
Socio-demographic factors	Gender (female)	1.156	1.003–1.513	0.921	0.6707–1.265
	Age	1.012	0.982–1.412	1.003	0.982–1.020
	Occupation	1.022	0.9997–1.026	0.999	0.898–1.075
	Have children	1.020	0.931–1.117	0.982	1.005–1.075
Weather conditions	Season (summer)	0.929	0.881–0.980	1.065	0.998– 1.136
Perception	Perceived emission sources	0.83	0.779–0.885	1.161	1.0761–1.253
	Importance of air quality	1.453	1.218–1.734	0.694	0.557–0.863
	Risk perception	1.014	1.003–1.133	0.965	0.886–1.051
	Assessment of air quality	1.508	1.332–1.707	1.203	1.031–1.403
	Air pollution perception by dust	1.723	1.531–1.940	1.585	1.5057–1.677
Life and health effects	Go to the doctor	1.005	1.001–1240	1.005	0.9876–1.203
	Occurrence of health problems	1.05	0.985–1.024	1.238	1.1041–1.388
	Knowledge about monitoring	0.941	0.893–0.991	1.054	0.9967–1.114

Source: Adapted from Machado et al. (2022)

The results presented by Machado et al. (2022) indicated that individuals who consider air quality important are significantly more likely (1.45) to feel annoyed by air pollution. A positive association between risk perception (1.014) and annoyance was found, meaning higher risk awareness correlates with increased annoyance levels, and individuals who assess air quality negatively are more likely (1.5) to report annoyance. Individuals experiencing health issues are more likely (1.05) to report annoyance due to air pollution. Finally, the odds ratios of 1.531–1.940 and 1.5057–1.677 indicate a strong association between the perception of dust pollution and reported annoyance levels.

These findings demonstrate that air pollution annoyance is not solely associated with high particulate concentrations. This makes the results and methodology presented by Machado et al. (2021) highly relevant for planning, serving as a useful resource for stakeholders at the regional or city-planning level who typically don't have access to detailed data for effective micro-management.

Establishing air quality standards based on settleable particulate matter annoyance

Some countries have established their own national standards for SPM, such as the case of Canada, Argentina, Australia, the USA, Spain, and Finland. Standards may vary within the same country, as in the case of the USA and Canada. Brazil, for instance, has no national standard, while the states of Minas Gerais, Rio de Janeiro, Espirito Santo and Amapá have set different SPM standards. Most standards vary between 3.0 and 15.0 g/(m^2·30 days) and take into consideration residential, commercial or industrial areas.

Machado et al. (2018) proposed a guidance to establish air quality standards for annoyance caused by SPM in the Vitoria Region. A new methodology was proposed, featuring monthly measurements of both the particle deposition rate and nuisance perception for a minimum duration of one year. Nuisance data were collected in a two-step process: (i) a first in-person contact followed by (ii) monthly telephone updates. The in-person interviews randomly selected in the areas highlighted surrounding each air-quality monitoring station (Figure 4.1) where SPM was measured. The nonlinear correlation between the perceived annoyance (annoyed and not annoyed) and particles deposition rate (quantitative variable) was modelled by logistic regression. The odds ratio is computed with the estimates of the population parameter β_0 and β_1, that is, with $\hat{\beta}_0$ and $\hat{\beta}_1$ respectively. All estimates, their standard deviation and confidence intervals are displayed in Table 4.3.

Table 4.4 provides the estimates of the odds ratio with confidence intervals and the estimate of the probability of nuisance due to SPM levels of x = 5, 10 and 14 g/(m^2/30 days). One can see that all regression coefficient estimates indicated that the true parameter β_1 is not statistically null for all monitoring stations at a significance level of 5%, that is, all p-values for testing the null hypothesis H0: $\beta_{1j} = 0$ against H1: $\beta_{1j} \neq 0$, j = 1,..., 7, are smaller than 5%.

Analysing the odds ratio (in Table 4.4) one can see that, for example, each unit on the increasing of particles deposition rate at M7 increases the odds of perceived annoyance by a factor of 2.1, implying that the probability of occurrence is almost two times as large as the probability of no occurrence of annoyance. The maximum odds ratio is attained for M3 station in which the probability of annoyance when the SPM rate is equal to 10 g/(m^2/30 days) is 99% and 74% for the overall MRV data set. A critical finding is that a significant portion of the population reports annoyance even at very low SPM levels, for example, 26% of inhabitants report annoyance at particles deposition level of 5 g/(m^2·30 days) MRV.

In short, by modelling the nonlinear relationship using logistic regression, the methodology links a measurable environmental parameter (SPM) directly

Table 4.4 Estimated parameters $\hat{\beta}_0$ and $\hat{\beta}_1$, odds ratio of the logistic regression model and the estimated probabilities at SPM values of 5, 10, and 14 g/m²/30 days

Monitoring stations	$\hat{\beta}_0$ *(sd)*	$\hat{\beta}_1$ *(sd)*	$\hat{\beta}_1$ *P-value for*	*Odds ratio (C.I)*	$\hat{P}(x=5)$ *(%)*	$\hat{P}(x=10)$ *(%)*
M1	*4.57 (1.83)	0.50 (0.194)	0.01	1.656 (1.12–2.41)	11	61
M2	–	–	–	–	–	–
M3	*9.19 (3.58)	1.35 (0.53)	0.01	3.945 (1.35–10.92)	8	99
M4	*4.18 (2.46)	0.46 (0.23)	0.048	1.607 (1.00–2.51)	13	61
M5	*4.39 (2.15)	0.68 (0.31)	0.03	2.045 (1.06–3.69)	28	92
M6	*6.52 (2.35)	0.99 (0.37)	0.009	2.754 (1.28–5.66)	17	97
M7	*4.93 (2.00)	0.74 (0.28)	0.009	2.121 (1.20–3.68)	23	93
M8	*4.48 (2.54)	0.51 (0.26)	0.048	1.721 (0.99–2.76)	13	65
Overall MRV	***3.165** **(0.56)**	**0.419** **(0.071)**	**0.00**	**1.520** **(1.32–1.74)**	**26**	**74**

to a public health/quality of life outcome (annoyance), allowing authorities to set standards based on an acceptable level of public annoyance.

Exposure–response relationship

Machado et al. (2018) presented the prediction curves for the relationship between the levels of exposure to SPM and the likelihood (as a percentage) of annoyance reported by the respondents after exposure to different levels of SPM. Considering the mobility of the population among the sub-regions, it was proposed to perform an analysis with all the data collected in each sub-region into a single logistic regression model to estimate a global model for the Vitória Region (Figure 4.3). The dotted curves indicate the confidence intervals of 95% for each curve. Although the variation of responses was not large, the likelihood of high levels of annoyance could vary depending on the respective confidence intervals (dotted lines).

In the same direction, Machado et al. (2022) conducted a dose-response analysis—using univariate logistic regression models to estimate the probability curve between SPM and citizen-reported annoyance, with further exposure-response curves developed for measured concentrations of PM_{10} and TSP.

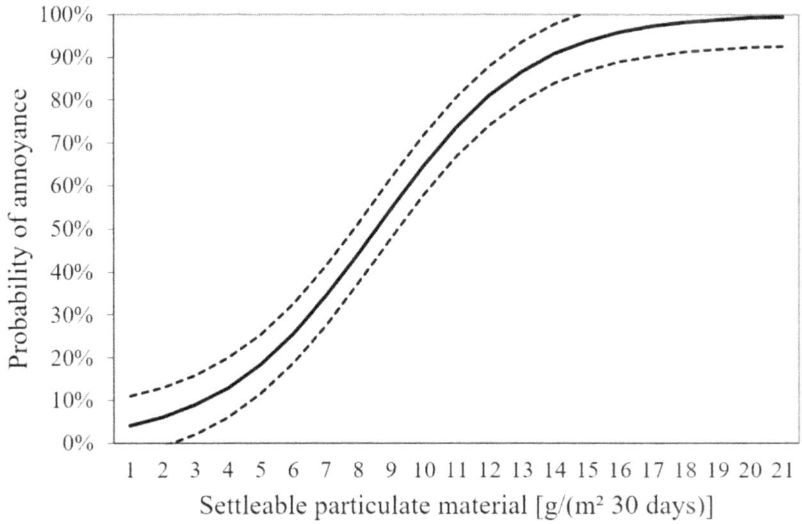

Figure 4.3 Exposure versus response relationship for the overall Vitoria Region

In Figure 4.4(a,b), the curve is cumulative and indicates the probability of annoyance caused by PM. The bands in dotted lines indicate the 95% confidence intervals of the curves. These are the confidence intervals for the relationships, since at each exposure value there is quite large individual variation in the responses. Considering the WHO (2021) guideline for PM_{10} (equal to 45 $\mu g/m^3$, 24-hour mean) about 90% of the population living would report being "annoyed" by air pollution, and for the same concentration of TSP, about 73%. It is worth stating that PM_{10} constitutes about half of the mass in TSP concentration in the region. These results reveal a critical disconnect between international health standards and public perception in the region. Notably, at the WHO (2021) guideline for PM_{10} concentration (45 $\mu g/m^3$), an overwhelming 90% of the population in the region would report being annoyed. Similarly, the annoyance probability is high for TSP (73%).

The results underscore that existing air quality regulations (which are often set to protect against severe health effects) are insufficient to mitigate public nuisance and discomfort. The predictive curves developed in this work serve as an essential tool for local authorities to set perception-based SPM standards that directly address the quality of life and subjective well-being of the exposed community.

Conclusion

Vitória Region stands as one of Brazil's most important industrialized port urban areas. Over the last decades, several studies have been carried out to assess the impact of emission sources to help prevent air quality degradation.

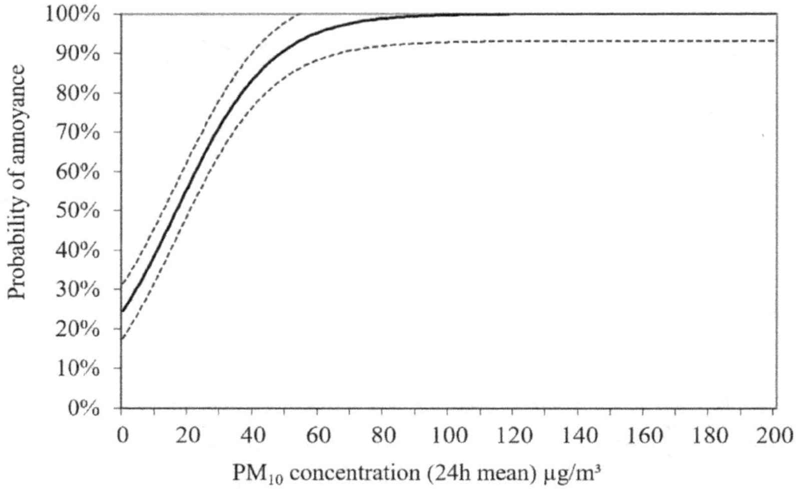

(a)

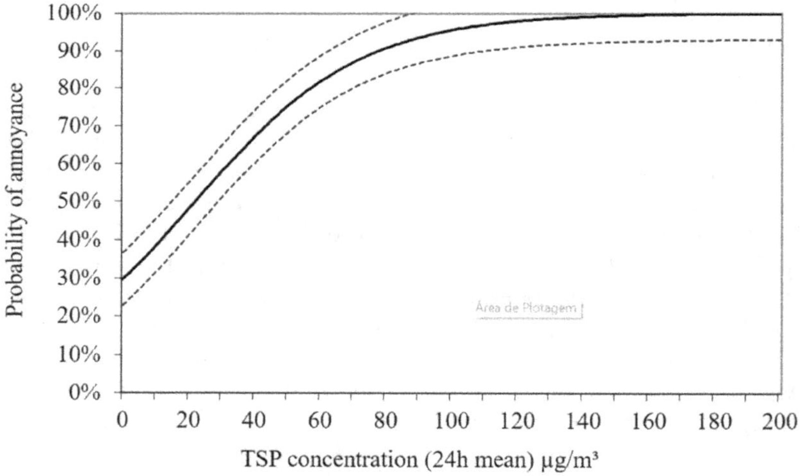

(b)

Figure 4.4 Exposure–response curves for (a) PM_{10} and (b) TSP, showing the relation between pollutant concentrations and the proportion of the population that perceives to be annoyed by air pollution

Continuous air quality monitoring is currently in operation, covering the most critical regulated pollutants. During the study period (2011–2014), exceedances to the limit and target values for SPM, PM_{10}, and TSP concentrations were consistently verified.

However, technical measurement and the verification of exceedances, while essential, do not fully capture the impact of pollution on citizens' daily lives. It is in this context that the surveys become crucial, as they confirm that quantifying air pollution annoyance is a critical social and health indicator, shaped by personal sensitivity, environmental assessment, and direct sensory experience.

The research established a clear exposure–response relationship, demonstrating that as pollutant concentrations increase, so does the probability of public annoyance. This annoyance is a pressing public health concern, as a high percentage of the population reported being affected, with self-reported health symptoms serving as significant predictors.

In conclusion these studies provide a vital framework for policymakers and urban planners. By validating the importance of public perception as a core component of environmental management, the research can be replicated and serve as an essential model for other industrialized coastal regions facing similar environmental challenges. The findings reinforce the need for continuous monitoring and a multifaceted approach that integrates scientific research, public awareness, and effective policy to enhance the quality of life for communities affected by air pollution.

References

ASTM D1739-04 (2004) *Standard Test Method for Collection and Measurement of Dustfall (Settleable Particulate Matter)*. ASTM International.

Barnett V. (2002) *Sample Survey: Principles & Methods* (3rd ed.). John Wiley & Sons.

Baxter L., Finch S., Lipfert F., Yu Q. (1997) Comparing estimates of the effects of air pollution on human mortality obtained using different regression methodologies. *Risk Analysis*, 17(3): 273–278.

Blanes-Vidal V. (2015) Air pollution from biodegradable wastes and non-specific health symptoms among residents: Direct or annoyance-mediated associations? *Chemosphere*, 120: 371–377.

Calvo-Mendieta I., Flaquart H., Frere S., Gonthier F., Hellequin A.P., Le Blanc A. (2008) *Perception du risque industriel par les populations du Dunkerquois: Rapport intermédiaire*. Contrat de recherche pour la Fondation pour une Culture de la Sécurité Industrielle (FonCSI).

Cochran W.G. (1977) *Sampling Techniques* (3rd ed.). Wiley.

de Freitas C. U., de Leon A. P., Juger W., & Gouveia N. (2016) Air pollution and its impacts on health in Vitoria, Espirito Santo, Brazil. *Revista de saude publica*, 50, 4. https://doi.org/10.1590/S1518-8787.2016050005909

Eek F., Karlson B., Österberg K., Ötérgren P. (2010) Factors associated with prospective development of environmental annoyance. *Journal of Psychosomatic Research*, 69(1): 9–15.

Forsberg B., Stjernberg N., Wall S. (1997) People can detect poor air quality well below guideline concentrations: A prevalence study of annoyance reactions and air pollution from traffic. *Occupational and Environmental Medicine*, 54(1): 44–48.

Greenacre M. (2007) *Correspondence Analysis in Practice* (2nd ed.). Chapman & Hall/CRC.

Hayes J.E., Stevenson R.J., Stuetz R.M. (2017) Survey of the effect of odour impact on communities. *Journal of Environmental Management*, 204: 349–354.

Jacquemin B., Sunyer J., Forsberg B., Götschi T., Bayer-Oglesby L., Ackermann-Liebrich U., de Marco R., Heinrich J., Jarvis D., Torén K., Künzli N. (2007) Annoyance due to air pollution in Europe. *International Journal of Epidemiology*, 36(4): 809–820.

Li Y., Zhu K., Wang S. (2020) Polycentric and dispersed population distribution increases PM2.5 concentrations: Evidence from 286 Chinese cities, 2001–2016. *Journal of Cleaner Production*, 248: 119202.

Machado M., Santos J.M., Frere S., Chagnon P., Reisen V.A., Bondon P., Reis Jr. N.C. (2021) Deconstruction of annoyance due to air pollution by multiple correspondence analyses. *Environmental Science and Pollution Research*, 28(35): 47904–47920.

Machado M., Santos J.M., Reisen V.A., Pego e Silva A.F., Reis Junior N.C., Bondon P., Mavroidis I., Prezotti Filho P.R., Frere S., Lima A.T. (2022) Parameters influencing population annoyance pertaining to air pollution. *Journal of Environmental Management*, 323: 115955.

Machado M., Santos J.M., Reisen V.A., Reis N.C., Mavroidis I., Lima A.T. (2018) A new methodology to derive settleable particulate matter guidelines to assist policymakers on reducing public nuisance. *Atmospheric Environment*, 182: 242–251.

Nascimento A.P., Santos J.M., Mill J.G., Souza J.B.D., Reis N.C., Reisen V.A. (2017) Association between the concentration of fine particles in the atmosphere and acute respiratory diseases in children. *Revista de Saúde* Pública, 51(3): 1–9.

Nikolopoulou M., Kleissl J., Linden P.F., Lykoudis S. (2011) Pedestrian's perception of environmental stimuli through field surveys: Focus on particulate pollution. *Science of the Total Environment*, 409(13): 2493–2502.

Orru K., Orru H., Maasikmets M., Hendrikson R., Ainsaar M. (2016) Well-being and environmental quality: Does pollution affect life satisfaction? *Quality of Life Research*, 25(3): 699–705.

Rotko T., Oglesby L., Künzli N., Carrer P., Nieuwenhuijsen M.J., Jantunen M. (2002) Determinants of perceived air pollution annoyance and association between annoyance scores and air pollution (PM2.5, NO2) concentrations in the European EXPOLIS study. *Atmospheric Environment*, 36(29): 4593–4602.

Santos J.M., Reis N.C. Jr., Galvão E.S., Silveira A., Goulart E.V., Lima A.T. (2017) Source apportionment of settleable particles in a mining-impacted urban and industrialized region in Brazil. *Environmental Science and Pollution Research*, 24(27): 22026–22039.

Souza J.B., Reisen V.A., Franco G.C., Ispány M., Bondon P., Santos J.M. (2018) Generalized additive models with principal component analysis: An application to time series of respiratory disease and air pollution data. *Journal of the Royal Statistical Society: Series C (Applied Statistics)*, 67(2): 453–480.

World Health Organization (WHO) (2006) *Air Quality Guidelines for Particulate Matter, Ozone, Nitrogen Dioxide and Sulphur Dioxide*. World Health Organization.

World Health Organization (WHO) (2021) *WHO Global Air Quality Guidelines: Particulate Matter ($PM_{2.5}$ and PM_{10}), Ozone, Nitrogen Dioxide, Sulfur Dioxide and Carbon Monoxide*. World Health Organization.

Yang J., Qu S., Liu M., Liu X., Gao Q., He W., Ji J.S., Bi J. (2021). Gray cityscape caused by particulate matter pollution hampers human stress recovery. *Journal of Cleaner Production*, 279: 123215.

Yang J., Zhou Q., Liu X., Liu M., Qu S., Bi J. (2018) Biased perception misguided by affect: How does emotional experience lead to incorrect judgments about environmental quality? *Global Environmental Change*, 53: 104–113.

Zhang Y., Yang Y., Chen J., Shi M. (2023) Spatiotemporal heterogeneity of the relationships between $PM_{2.5}$ concentrations and their drivers in China's coastal ports. *Journal of Environmental Management*, 345: 118698.

5 Port traffic and chronic diseases

Qualitative study of pilots and dockworkers at the port of Lomé

Hervé Sourya Malazoue

Introduction

Lomé, a city located near the border with Ghana, is the capital of Togo and hosts the port of Lomé, the country's main port (Spire, 2010). Similar to the majority of its West African counterparts, the port of Lomé was first established as a consequence of the spatial restructuring brought about by the arrival of colonists on the African coast. This was a full break from the prevailing pre-colonial paradigm, which was initially focused in the Sahara desert, with a territorial continuity that was nearly accepted by the peoples, and which gave the coastlines a larger role. As a result, this reasoning took root on the Togolese coast between 1899 and 1900 with the establishment of a first wooden quay, 160 m long, that acted as a connection between the German metropolis and the Togolese colony through the Atlantic Ocean. With this, Lomé entered its port age.

In the end, this hub represented Lomé's opening to the rest of the world by centralizing the flow of commodities heading for the metropolis, acting as a distribution channel for completed goods headed for the colony and those intended for the interior. After this wharf, a second and a third were built in 1912, which were in use until 1964, when the deep-water port of Lomé was constructed, paving the way for the present port of Lomé. With significant increases in yearly traffic, the port of Lomé is now the top container port on the West African coast (Figure 5.1). The World Bank's port management reforms, which have led to port concession agreements and the digitization of administrative procedures, are partly responsible for this advancement.

All of these investments have allowed the port of Lomé to reclaim its place as the focal point of attention for major liner shipping companies like Maersk, CMA CGM, MSC, Bolloré, and many others, thereby reestablishing the port of Lomé's connection to the world's main shipping lanes and solidifying its position as the primary gateway to the sea for the hinterland nations. Due to the significance of Lomé's port as a tool for generating national wealth, the city has experienced rapid expansion, drawing in people seeking economic prospects and changing its socio-economic makeup and urban environment (Agbemadon, 2024).

DOI: 10.4324/9781003639589-7

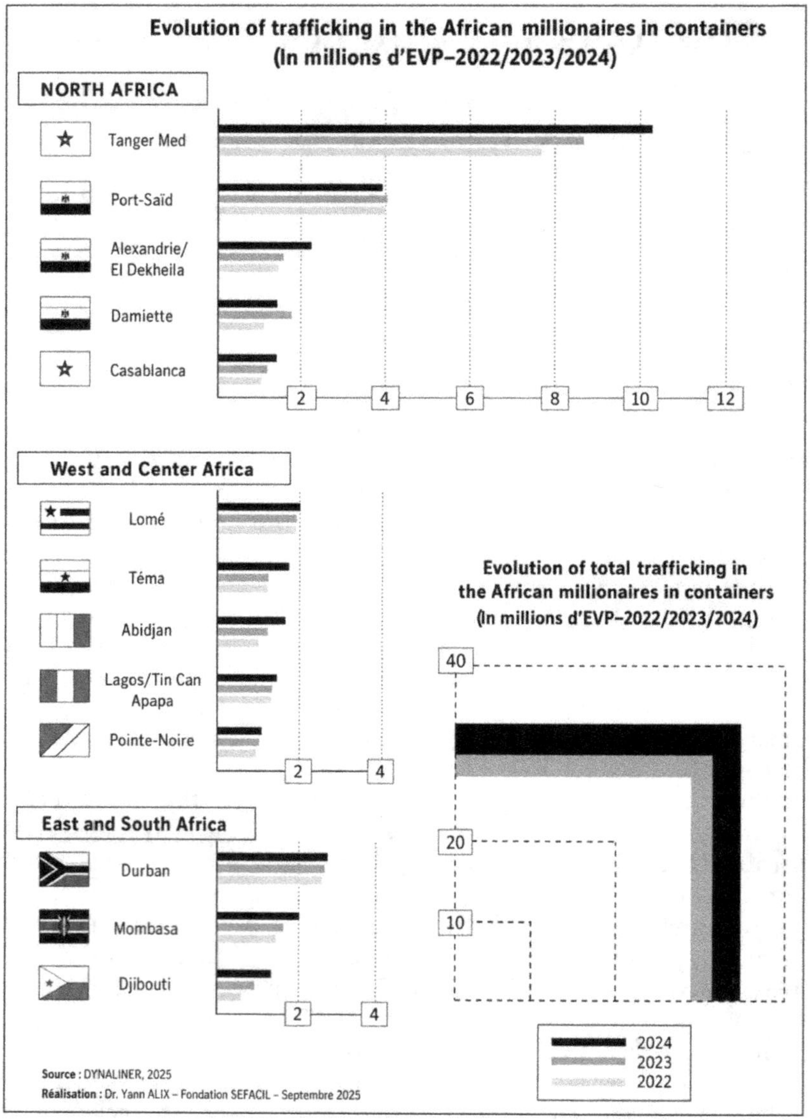

Figure 5.1 Traffic trends at African ports handling millions of containers (millions of TEUs), 2022/2023/2024

Source: SEFACIL (2025)

With its own share of air pollution, however, this direct positive impact has also been accompanied by a decline in the urban environment, which has been experiencing unchecked expansion for over a decade (Agbemadon, 2024). A 2022 study by Garima et al found that 1.4 million people in Lomé are exposed to air pollution. At 10 μg/m^3, the WHO limit, this exposure is four to five times greater (Garima et al., 2022; Raheja et al., 2022).

The relationship between air pollution and urban health, including port health, has been explored in a number of publications from throughout the world (Samet, 2007; Sivertsen et al., 2010; Song et al., 2014; WHO, 2016; IECP, 2018). Articles that address the link between port traffic and health governance in Africa are, however, extremely few. By starting a conversation about the instance of the port of Lomé, this research addresses this gap in the literature. Two socio-professional groups were chosen for the study pilots and dock workers in order to comprehend and pinpoint the relationship between port traffic and illness. Even though there are no air quality standards at the port of Lomé, an observation was made between the exposure of these study targets to fine particulate matter (PM) and volatile organic compounds (VOCs), two health indicators of air pollution, and the chronic respiratory disorders seen during field investigations. Through air pollution, the research at the port of Lomé demonstrated a connection between total exposure to fine and VOCs produced by port activity and chronic respiratory ailments among pilots and dockworkers.

Furthermore, it emphasized two different ways in which the port authority structured these wage groups, both of which came to similar health findings. In contrast, the research itself brings up important concerns about the need for better management of the trio of port traffic, air pollution, and health impacts in light of the shift toward green ports. Furthermore, the study brings up the questions of social discussion inside businesses on the green transition and the social acceptance of industrial hazards by those who reside close to the port of Lomé. The following sections of this book will elaborate on these topics. The Lomé port authority has to weigh the economic interests of the port against health issues.

Study site: the port of Lomé in Togo

Because it is the source of high atmospheric concentrations of gases and aerosols from several sources (CIMTOGO, SIVOP soap factories, DODO cosmetics, smoke from ships at dock, container loading and unloading vehicles, etc.), the study of air pollution caused by port traffic is of major importance, especially considering that it is situated on the coast, where more than 90% of the agglomeration's industrial facilities are concentrated. Not to mention that it is also very close to the city center's major thoroughfares, which experience significant commuter traffic every day. In addition to the ongoing efforts to expand the LCT (Lomé Container Terminal) container transshipment docks at the port of Lomé, the issue of air pollution from port traffic becomes important in terms of the port's profitability, the management of air pollution risks (Diallo et al., 2020), and even the overall health governance of the negative effects of port traffic in Lomé, such as air pollution.

The majority of ports handling millions of containers are strategic transshipment ports, and the leading African representatives are located in the north of the continent, taking advantage of their unbeatable geostrategic positioning. The Gulf of Guinea has been the most dynamic area over the last three years, with 2 million containers handled by the port of Lomé, opposite the port of Tema, the port of Abidjan, and the Nigerian ports (Lagos/Tin Can/Apapa). The eastern and southern coastlines remain the least served in terms of container volumes, despite steady growth in Mombasa and Djibouti.

Methodology

The issue of air quality for port workers is made worse by the absence of measurements from fixed monitoring network sensors that operate continuously over extended periods of time at the port of Lomé and undergo regular calibration, adjustment, and systematic sensitivity checks, since it deprives us of information on the nature of the air that people are actually breathing and the length of time that they are exposed to atmospheric pollutants.

The meteorological station of the Togolese Navy, which is situated on the boundary of the naval base inside the port area, is the sole measuring station in the study region. Nevertheless, air quality is not monitored at this station. It just records wind speed and direction. The Lomé port authority utilizes this information for its operations.

The use of portable sensors in this instance is always beneficial for getting an accurate picture of the spatial distribution of pollutants and making up for the absence of permanent monitoring facilities at the port of Lomé, but most importantly for enabling almost real-time measurements across a rather dense monitoring network like the one at the port of Lomé, even if these measurements are only taken for a short period of time. Based on data on PM_{10}, $PM_{2.5}$, PM_1, and VOCs, this study aims to illustrate the variability and spatiotemporal distribution of air pollution (Diallo et al., 2020) caused by port traffic on pilots and dock workers.

A single stop is equal to two minutes and is comparable to a measurement made during the middle of the day or during morning and nighttime inversion conditions over three days at the port of Lomé and its immediate surroundings in order to determine the variability of the pollutants studied (Tables 5.1–5.3). The Atmotube Pro sensor, a specialized, dependable, and mobile device with well-known technologies like MCERTS-certified Sensirion particle sensors, was used to collect samples. It is ideal for monitoring the aforementioned pollutants, with scientific validation and application in air quality research investigations.

VOCs and small particles were chosen because of their negative impact on human health. $PM_{2.5}$: These particles are the most harmful since they are small enough to pass into the alveoli and then into the bloodstream. Irritation of the eyes, nose, and throat, coughing, and shortness of breath are some of the immediate consequences. Long-term consequences include a decrease in

Table 5.1 First sampling period (day 1)

	PM_1	$PM_{2.5}$	PM_{10}	*VOC*	*Air quality score (AQS)*	*Conclusion*
Morning	12.6	14.5	15.6	1.70	49	Polluted air
Midday	57.3	62.1	63.4	0.24	42	Polluted air
In the evening	12.2	18.4	80.2	0.2	46	Severely polluted air

Source: Own elaboration

Table 5.2 Second sampling period (day 2)

	PM_1	$PM_{2.5}$	PM_{10}	*VOC*	*Air quality score (AQS)*	*Conclusion*
Morning	1.8	1.9	1.9	0.10	94	Air is good
Midday	28.2	32.4	47.2	0.9	46	severely polluted air
In the evening	105	115	118	0.11	0	Severely polluted air

Source: Own elaboration

Table 5.3 Third sampling period (day 3)

	PM_1	$PM_{2.5}$	PM_{10}	*VOC*	*Air quality score (AQS)*	*Conclusion*
Morning	28	32	47	0.99	53	Polluted air
Midday	6.3	8.6	10.3	0.08	92	Moderate air
In the evening	3.5	4.9	6.2	1.04	60	Polluted air

Source: Own elaboration

respiratory function, a higher risk of cardiovascular events and death, lower fertility, higher rates of lung cancer, cognitive impairments, and dementia.

PM_{10} is less severe than $PM_{2.5}$ and can induce transient discomfort in the eyes, throat, and nose, as well as coughing, sneezing, and exacerbation of respiratory conditions. It results in oxidative stress, inflammation, and early mortality over the long run (Weinstein et al., 2010).

PM_1: Their little size makes them extremely dangerous. In the near term, they induce coughing, sneezing, aggravation of asthma episodes, and irritation of the eyes, throat, and nose. They raise the risk of lung cancer and lower life expectancy over time.

VOCs: Irritation of the eyes and throat, nausea, headaches, and respiratory problems can result from brief exposure. Over the long run, they may lead to cancer, liver and kidney damage, as well as problems with the digestive and neurological systems (Turner et al., 2011). They are a reliable indicator of chronic diseases brought on by pollution from port traffic in the port of Lomé, and they may be readily measured using portable sensors.

The measured data is complemented by an individual interview guide for scientific study on cardiorespiratory diseases induced by air pollution linked to port traffic in the port of Lomé (Diallo et al., 2020), which is split into four sections: the first section focuses on warning signs and health issues; the second section focuses on daily life situations and aspects; the third section focuses on perceptions of ambient air quality at the port of Lomé; and the final section addresses the health consequences of bodily exposure to black carbon emitted by ships calling at the port of Lomé, based on a sample of eight harbor pilots out of a total population of 12 pilots working at the port of Lomé harbor master's office. All of this was combined with the pilots' accounts of their health conditions in order to establish the causal relationship between the chronic diseases seen and the measurements made.

Furthermore, the interview guide helped us single out a subgroup of the eight pilots interviewed who experienced even greater clinical impacts as a result of air. The environmental damage brought on by port activity. The study will discuss the testimonies of these pilots. The interviews with the pilots took place at the following times: Phase 1 on August 6, 2025: three pilots interviewed; Phase 2 on August 11, 2025: three pilots interviewed; Phase 3 on August 20, 2025: one pilot interviewed; and lastly, Phase 4: one pilot interviewed.

Furthermore, to cover topics not initially anticipated, a semi-structured interview was held on October 16, 2024, with a union representative for the dockworkers at the port of Lomé. This helped us observe that, regardless of what anyone may say, there is a sort of structure that leaves room for improvement in the Lomé port authority and the dockworkers' profession. The meeting concluded with the gathering of evidence regarding instances of respiratory illnesses among dockworkers that were previously unknown to the port administration, the perplexing realities on the ground, the shortage of personal protective equipment (PPE) for dockworkers, and the dire condition of essential infrastructure like the port's medical and social center, which is completely unable to address this issue.

Results

Using health impact indicators such as VOCs and aerodynamic particles smaller than 10, 2.5, and 1 $\mu g/m^3$, we provide a broad overview of the air pollution produced by port traffic below. Over three consecutive days, samples were collected in three phases.

Results of PM and VOC sampling

Tables 5.1–5.3 for the three consecutive days of sampling show that the air at the port of Lomé is indeed polluted. The air quality index varied from polluted to very polluted during these three days of measurements. From this, we can conclude that there is a positive correlation between the respiratory conditions observed in the following pages of the document among, pilots and dockworkers, and traffic at the port of Lomé.

The medical and social center at the port of Lomé: a fundamental tool against air pollution in a terrible condition

We learned the following about the status of the medical and social center at the port of Lomé throughout the course of our inquiry.

A seaport's medical and social center (CMS) is essential for providing emergency aid, social support, and occupational health services to port workers and maritime workers. Regrettably, the CMS at the port of Lomé is unable to offer health prevention and promotion services due to inadequate working circumstances and a lack of technical resources (e.g., rusty dressing materials, low lighting, no spirometer to monitor respiratory conditions, no dining hall, medical staff eating and drinking in consultation and treatment rooms, increasing the risk of infectious disease contamination, etc.). The CMS at the port of Lomé is now unable to care for the sick or promote a process of port medical health governance, as evidenced by all of these facts.

Results obtained among dockers

Among dockers, the situation is somewhat more complicated than among pilots. There is a lack of PPE when unloading toxic cargo, as shown in Box 5.1, which is an account obtained during an interview with the union representative for dockworkers at the port of Lomé.

Box 5.1

"Yesterday, before your visit this afternoon, a team had left to unload a ship, but the captain refused to let the team board because we don't have PPE. We had to negotiate with him before we could finally unload the ship. Sometimes we cover our faces with our old shirts to unload the ship if the captain is lax, and you end up inhaling all these fumes. At the end, we get boxes of milk if there are any. After a certain period of time, either two or three months, it is not a gift, it is practical training with the dockworkers. Milk is believed to have certain imaginary therapeutic properties in combating the risks associated with frequent unprotected exposure to toxic gases during dockworkers' shifts. This remains to be scientifically proven, and I don't know anything about it, but that's the reality on the ground. We are now negotiating with the new head of service for PPE (personal protective equipment). We'll see what happens."

In addition, we have learned that the regulatory framework governing the dockers' profession at the port of Lomé dates back to 1992 and has never been updated to improve the working conditions of dockers at the port of Lomé. Furthermore, it is not adapted to the new requirements of the port energy transition. Boxes 5.2 and 5.3 provide further details.

Box 5.2

"Regarding the legal framework, every May 1 we submit a report on the regulatory framework for the profession to the minister responsible and the port's CEO, but we never get any feedback. I have been working for 22 years, and in 22 years we have never received a response on this issue, despite our strikes. The same thing happens when we go to the ministry. The Secretary General of the Ministry of Maritime Economy responds by saying, 'Your case is under review,' and that's it. A case that has been under review since 1992. Well, with the appointment of the new minister, who is a former port department director, we hope that this time it will go through."

Box 5.3

"You become a dockworker at the port of Lomé because you need to feed yourself. You read the port's call for tenders, you report to the port's labor office, you register, and you start as soon as there is a ship to unload. The current CEO of the port of Lomé has introduced a policy for us dockworkers: if you are 49 years old, you become a permanent dockworker; if you are 41, you become a professional dockworker. You have to see the arbitrariness and disorder that this creates on the ground." Then, regarding concerns about respiratory conditions and exposure to black carbon emitted by ships during unloading, here is the response provided by the union representative in Box 3.3.1.4 "There are many cases of dockworkers suffering from respiratory diseases, but these are not recorded, and not all cases are included in the database on occupational risks for workers at the port of Lomé. As for black carbon, last time we attended a training course organized by the port, and we raised the issue with the trainer, who replied that he would pass on the information to see what could be done about it." In short, there is a lax attitude on the part of the port of Lomé toward dockworkers, both in terms of organization and working conditions.

Results obtained from port drivers

The results of port drivers' opinions on the relationship between air pollution from port traffic and respiratory diseases are shown in the paragraphs below and in Table 5.4. In the course of our study, we discovered three distinct groups of pilots who experienced symptoms that were much more severe than those of the other pilots. Their testimonies are presented in the following lines.

The data gathered from field studies indicates that none of the pilots questioned, that is, 100% of the sample had a history of respiratory issues prior to joining the merchant navy in the port of Lomé. As seen in Table 5.4, they developed respiratory ailments throughout their time working as pilots.

The various instances of respiratory ailments among pilots at the port of Lomé are shown in Table 5.4. The majority of pilots, or 62.5%, are shown to have sleep apnea. The second category includes 25% of pilots with influenza, while 1.25% of pilots, that is, one pilot has bronchitis. It should be emphasized that the air quality index findings acquired earlier are consistent with the positive correlation between the different respiratory disorders shown in Box 5.4, which is related to port air pollution caused by port traffic.

In contrast, the majority of pilots in the sample, six, or 75% experience eye, throat, and skin irritation as a result of the excessive amount of PM and VOCs in the air in the port. On the other hand, two pilots or 25% of the total experience other symptoms or irritations that are not covered in the paper, rather than irritation. The link is evident once more.

Additionally, the majority of arriving vessels do not have scrubbers, and 50% of pilots claim to be covered in soot numerous times each week when executing port docking operations, while 25% say they are covered several times each day. Additionally, Lomé port has no legislation barring ships that do not have scrubbers from using the port quay, and 25% of respondents say they are rarely exposed to soot from ships.

Additionally, compared to the 37.5% (three pilots) who are unsure of the connection between these two occurrences and the 1.25% (one pilot) who

Table 5.4 List of respiratory diseases reported among port pilots and the number of cases obtained

	Number of cases obtained
Sleep apnea	5
Bronchitis	1
Influenza	2
Chronic obstructive pulmonary disease	0
Cardiovascular Diseases	0
Total	8

Source: Own elaboration

has never had any symptoms after being physically exposed to black carbon released by ships, half of the pilots, 50% or four pilots, have already reported headaches, nausea, and exhaustion just a few minutes after being covered in it. As three of the eight pilots interviewed are even more clinically impacted by air pollution, as they state in Box 5.4.

Box 5.4

"I have trouble climbing stairs, I'm getting more and more short of breath, I have trouble eating, I find it increasingly difficult to have visitors at home because I get tired more quickly, I'm afraid my illness will get worse, I'm afraid of being hospitalized again because of pollution, I'm thinking of moving away from the port city because of pollution."

Discussion

Overall, this research emphasizes the necessity of improving air pollution risk management in light of the port of Lomé's energy transition.

As this is, in the end, a matter of port environmental health governance, raising the broader topic of air pollution from fine particles at the port of Lomé and its short-, medium-, and long-term health effects, the Lomé port authority will have to come up with consistent and sustainable solutions. Not only at the port itself, but also in the urban areas that fall under the radius or sphere of influence of this immediate result of the port of Lomé's operations.

This exposure affects everyone, including the people who live close to the port of Lomé, the majority of whom are also infected but are unaware of it because they lack access to information and are unable to relocate. The current risk management procedures at the port of Lomé begs the question: do local people have an obligation to act as good neighbors to the port, regardless of the negative health consequences it may have on their daily lives?

The several effects of these incidents will eventually result in legal, ethical, and financial concerns related to the corporate social responsibility of the port of Lomé. As a result, the issue is how to arrive at a reasonable agreement that strikes a balance between a reality that can no longer be covered up or ignored and suggestions that are impractical and expensive, given the current industrial environment of the port of Lomé.

Lastly, she brings up the subject of social discourse regarding the port of Lomé's energy transition. To improve their standing with the Lomé port administration, representatives of the workers at the port of Lomé must address the issues and difficulties surrounding the green transition.

Conclusion

The Lomé port authority must seize the initiative and give due consideration to the conflicts of interest between the port economy and port health. The port is not only a conduit for national economic prosperity, but a means of territorial control cover a certain geographical area of the world, or a politically regulated area governed by the laws and norms of international commerce that are recognized and accepted by international players, giving it considerable authority in global trade. The port also has a dual health component. The first is an internal health dimension brought about by endogenous variables brought about by port operations, and the second is an external health dimension brought about by variables outside the port. If policymakers disregard these two factors, the effects might be felt over time in terms of people, money, reputation, or geography.

As seen by the COVID-19 pandemic, which had a direct impact on the national economy, the exogenous health dimension is related to infectious diseases that can cause supply chain disruptions. Second, the port's internal health aspect is derived from its very existence or from its expansion, and it is related to the existence of industrial port sites that produce substantial pollution as a result of maritime transport and industrial operations, to the logistics that affect the air (greenhouse gas emissions), to the atmospheric pollutants from ship engines, port service trucks, handling equipment, and ultimately logistical trains.

Pollutants released by factories at the port contaminate the soil and then the water, which also contributes to community health issues. In the port's territory of origin and geographical area of influence, this indigenous health dimension is typically the center or incubator of diseases. Our research of chronic diseases and respiratory ailments related to port traffic among maritime pilots and dockworkers in the port of Lomé provides evidence of this. Furthermore, the port of Lomé's area of influence is where pilots and dockworkers live around the clock, all year round, and it's also where the pollution indicators that cause the illnesses seen among these port workers are concentrated. Additionally, due to a lack of precise field data (consultation with port workers at competing ports) and in-depth scientific analysis of the health realities linked to port traffic in ports competing with Lomé, the study on health practices at the port of Lomé cannot be directly compared with those in use in other major seaports along the West African coast.

The objective of this study on port traffic and chronic illnesses, using pilots and dockworkers at the port of Lomé as a case study, was to ascertain the health effects of port traffic at the port of Lomé. The study focused on two socio-professional groups: dockworkers and pilots. Despite the lack of air quality regulations at the port of Lomé, the study targets were observed to be exposed to fine PM, VOCs, and chronic respiratory illnesses.

The study highlighted the absence of regulatory policy, the lack of PPE and associated infrastructure, and inadequate field practices, as well as a positive correlation between overall exposure to fine particles and VOCs produced by port traffic and chronic respiratory ailments among pilots and dockworkers. The absence of equipment at the medical-social center in the port of Lomé makes it harder for the attending physician to participate more fully in screening or preventative actions and procedures. The evaluation also highlights the necessity of collecting and analyzing air quality monitoring data and associated health data. Furthermore, the port administration emphasized two separate forms of organization for its wage groups, yet with similar health outcomes. However, the study itself brings up important issues regarding the necessity for improved management of the trio of port traffic, air pollution, and health consequences in light of the green transition in ports. In addition, the research highlights the significance of social discussion on the green transition inside firms, as well as the concept of social acceptability of industrial hazards among people who live close to the port of Lomé. The port authority of Lomé must strike a balance between the port's economy and public health. It would be unfortunate to give up health in order to make a gain.

References

Agbemadon A.K. (2024) *Port Development and Dynamics of Port Cities on the West African Coast: The Case of the Port and City of Lomé in Togo. Geography.* Panthéon-Sorbonne University – Paris I, 2024. French. ffNNT: 2024PA01H057ff. fftel-05045681f.

Diallo A., Hayaka A., Dossou-Yovo K., Assih M., Badjabaissi E., Ketoh K. (2020) Étude de l'impact de la qualité de l'air sur la santé respiratoire des populations à Lomé (Togo). *Toxicologie Analytique et Clinique*, 32(2): 120–126.

Garima R., Kokou S., Hèzouwè S., Kokou E., McFarlane C., Hodoli C. G., Westervelt M. D. (2022) Network of Field-Calibrated Low-Cost Sensor Measurements of PM2.5 in Lomé, Togo, Over One to Two Years. ACS Earth and Space Chemistry, 6(4): 1011-1021. DOI: 10.1021/acsearthspacechem.1c00391

IECP (2018) INDEX – Etude d'imprégnation de la population aux polluants atmosphériques de la zone industrialo-portuaire de Fos-sur-Mer, https://www.institut-ecocitoyen.fr/publication/1/SANTE%20-%202018%20-%20INDEX%20[Rapport%20etude%20Goix].pdf

Raheja G., Sabi K., Sonla H., Gbedjangni E.K., McFarlane C.M., Hodoli C.G., Westervelt D.M. (2022) A network of field-calibrated low-cost sensor measurements of PM2.5 in Lomé, Togo, over one to two years. *ACS Earth and Space Chemistry*, 6(4): 10111021.

Samet J.M. (2007) Traffic, air pollution, and health. *Inhalation Toxicology*, 19(12): 1021–1027.

Sivertsen B., Guerreiro C., Ly I. (2010) Air quality standards for Senegal. Project report on the establishment of a central laboratory and air quality monitoring network, Dakar. https://nilu.com/wp-content/uploads/dnn/49-2010-cbg.pdf

Song Q., Christiani D.C., Wang X., Ren J. (2014) The global contribution of outdoor air pollution to the incidence, prevalence, mortality and hospital admission for chronic obstructive pulmonary disease: A systematic review and meta-analysis. *International Journal of Environmental Research and Public Health*, 11(11): 11822–11832.

Spire A. (2010) Lomé, a post-border city. *EchoGéo*, 14, https://journals.openedition.org/echogeo/11974

Turner M.C., Krewski D., Pope C.A., Chen Y., Gapstur S.M., Thun M.J. (2011) Long term ambient fine particulate matter air pollution and lung cancer in a large cohort of never smokers. *American Journal of Respiratory and Critical Care Medicine*, 184(12): 1374–1381.

Weinstein J.P., Hedges S.R., Kimbrough S. (2010) Characterization and aerosol mass balance of PM2.5 and PM10 collected in Conakry, Guinea during the 2004 Harmattan period. *Chemosphere*, 78(8): 980–988.

WHO (2016) Ambient (outdoor) air quality and health. Retrieved October 2016, https://www.who.int/mediacentre/factsheets/fs313/en/

Part 2

The health impacts of ports in a historical perspective

6 Health challenges in the ports and port cities of Atlantic France (13th–15th centuries)

Mathias Tranchant

Introduction

Ports have long served as hubs of communication where people, ships, and goods converge, but they are also centers of production and storage. Throughout history – and continuing today – these port territories have been highly vulnerable to various health crises. Ships, along with their crews, passengers, and sometimes cargoes, often acted as unwitting carriers of infectious agents from distant regions, which would likely not have spread so far without maritime transport. The so-called "index ship," "zero vessel," or "source ship" was, before the advent of modern land and air transportation, frequently the initial vector through which a pathogen – such as the plague – entered a society, causing sudden and catastrophic mortality. Consequently, maritime ports receiving these infected ships became focal points of contagion.

Beyond the epidemiological dimension, ports also posed environmental and public health challenges. Since antiquity, ports have confronted various forms of pollution, with harbors and basins functioning as de facto dumping grounds for waste generated by port, urban, or peri-urban activities.

Historical scholarship on health has often examined transport as a vector of disease transmission, yet the critical role of ports has been largely overlooked. Ports have typically been regarded merely as transit points through which pathogens passed briefly, triggering major epidemic episodes, rather than as complex environments in their own right. They are systematically overshadowed by broader urban, demographic, epidemiological, and political studies. This blind spot stems, in large part, from the tendency of researchers not to consider ports as distinct territories, separate from the cities they serve. This is particularly true for the medieval period, and, as a result, the study of health-related phenomena, their consequences, and the measures taken to mitigate them remains virtually unexplored for Atlantic France[1] (see Figure 6.1).

The scarcity of sources further complicates research. Epidemic awareness was still emerging during this period, and public authorities were primarily concerned with issues of sanitation, which occasionally left regulatory traces acknowledging a problem and corresponding remedial actions. Jean-Pierre

DOI: 10.4324/9781003639589-9

Figure 6.1 Location map of French Atlantic ports

Leguay's work on urban water systems illustrates this well, even though port-specific issues receive little attention (Leguay, 2002). Similarly, studies by maritime historians on Bayonne, Bordeaux, La Rochelle, Rouen, or Dieppe offer only sporadic evidence (Goyheneche, 1990; Bernard, 1968; Bochaca, 2015; Tranchant, 2003; Lardin, 2008, 2023). Even the ESTRAN database, which compiles some 3,200 documents related to maritime life, provides little additional insight.[2]

This study does not aim to present new archival discoveries. Rather, drawing on the compilation of scattered research, it seeks to reflect on the health challenges faced by ports and their urban hinterlands in Atlantic France during the 13th–15th centuries. In doing so, it highlights the risks encountered by port users and administrators and examines the strategies and measures employed to address these challenges.

A retrospective approach to diseases and epidemics in ports

In the absence of explicit textual and archaeological data, a retrospective approach is necessary to assess the presence of diseases and epidemics in French ports. It is understood, on the one hand, that endemic pathologies persisted for centuries before contemporary remedies were invented, and, on the other hand, that ailments caused by deficiencies resulting from long overseas voyages – xerophthalmia and night blindness, beriberi and pellagra, scurvy – are generally outside the scope of this period.

Although established for the early modern period, the list of major diseases affecting maritime environments likely did not differ significantly at the end of the Middle Ages, particularly since recent studies suggest that no exogenous diseases were introduced in the interim. Recorded pathologies include viral and microbial infections such as influenza, smallpox, typhoid fever, and typhus, as well as diseases caused by parasitic agents (hookworm, tapeworm, and roundworm). That said, neither the extent nor the recurrence of these diseases is known. From the early 14th century onward, the climatic downturn – compounded by food shortages, military conflicts, and political crises – led to a widespread and chronic deterioration of sanitary conditions, resulting in a general demographic decline in the Kingdom of France. Beyond this, little can be said to distinguish seafaring populations from other coastal inhabitants.

Despite the scarcity of knowledge, two issues appear particularly relevant to populations frequenting ports and their associated towns. It is generally acknowledged that, up until the widespread use of antibiotics, venereal diseases (gonorrhea, chlamydia, trichomoniasis) were particularly common in these areas, largely due to the widespread practice of prostitution (Dutour, 2022). Syphilis, whose endemic nature is now considered established, was likely widespread, even though its most severe form appeared only after 1495 among French troops at the siege of Naples. One of the earliest mentions of its spread among sailors in the Atlantic coast region relates to Saint-Macaire, upstream from Bordeaux. In a document dated November 16, 1514, a teenager testified that "a year ago, he experienced a great inconvenience and illness, called from Naples"[3] (Bernard, 1968, p. 627). Brothels frequented by sailors and merchants – key centers for the transmission of venereal diseases – appear sporadically in sources. In Bordeaux, according to notarial records from 1484 to 1514, the municipal jurats managed, "for the good and utility of the public," certain "rooms and houses" located in the parish of Saint-Éloi, collectively forming the "bourdeau" (brothel) called Château-Gaillard, where prostitutes offered their services[4] (Bernard, 1968, pp. 766–767). In La Rochelle, near inns, several brothels operated. A remission from February 1399 mentions a woman named Jehanne Gronzilly "who was a common woman of the brothel," on rue Sainte Catherine.[5] Another royal pardon of June 1417 refers to the "bourdeau" of La Rochelle, naming some of the women: Jehanne Voironne alias Poictevine, Jehanne des Jardins, Jehanne la Gabriele, Perrine la Mareschalle, and Katherine la Normande, called la Piote. They practiced their trade on "the main street of the said brothel."[6] Finally, in Dieppe during the 15th century, there were at least two houses of prostitution within the town and one in Le Pollet, across the harbor (Lardin, 2023, p. 491).

Beyond venereal diseases, plague was the primary disease whose spread significantly involved maritime ports. The pandemic first developed through Mediterranean port networks in 1347, reaching Constantinople from the Black Sea and then spreading westward to Messina, Naples, Pisa, and Genoa. Having arrived in Marseille in November 1347, it traveled via the Garonne valley (which may also have facilitated the spread of syphilis at the turn of the 16th century), as well as the Rhône, Loire, and Seine valleys, with maritime ports soon taking over from river ports. By June–July 1348, the first cases were reported in Bordeaux and Rouen. The contagion quickly spread to other French coasts, from the Bidasoa to the Zwin estuary, striking Calais, Dieppe, La Rochelle, and Bayonne, along a path that cannot be precisely determined. However, it is certain that every port connected to Atlantic trade networks could have contributed to the pandemic's dynamics.

After the catastrophic episode of the Black Death, new outbreaks occurred sporadically along the kingdom's coasts, or at least collective illnesses perceived as such by contemporaries (Biraben, 1976, pp. 71–92, 377–382, 415–417). This is evidenced by the measures and precautions taken by populations and municipal authorities, which will be discussed further. For example, in Dieppe, after 1348, plague reappeared in 1362, 1379, and 1417–1418, killing up to half the local population in some areas, leaving communities debilitated for decades (Lardin, 2023, pp. 155–159). A particularly intense wave, affecting much of the Atlantic coast, continued into the years 1515–1518.

Port unsanitary conditions

As Philippe Lardin aptly writes, "when the city enclosed itself within walls, it also trapped its filth inside" (Lardin, 2023, pp. 369–370). Seeking to dispose of waste beyond the walls, the port became a convenient basin for townspeople wishing to rid themselves of their unwanted materials. As medieval towns grew increasingly cluttered and polluted by the various wastes and refuse produced by human life and activity, ports were no exception, particularly since, located outside the city walls, they lay beyond the sight and smell of most inhabitants.

Many of these disposals compromised the quality of the port waters, their beds, and the surrounding areas. Despite the limited information available, it seems fair to say that pollution was a recurring problem in these territories, regardless of the scale of their traffic. In Bordeaux, the mayor and jurats were concerned from the mid-13th century, and repeatedly over the following two centuries, about certain practices by port users who showed little scruple[7] (Bochaca, 1997, pp. 139–140). They had turned the riverbanks (the "padouens"), the "esteys," and the ditches into genuine public dumps, into which they discarded, indiscriminately, all sorts of items ("aucuna causa"), including earth, straw, or refuse ("terra, palha ni ordura"). Further downstream, at Talmont on the Gironde estuary, the constable of Bordeaux was alerted in 1329 to damage affecting the channel and nearby ditches, which were obstructed by several barrels left there by passing ships (Périsse, 2007; 2011, pp. 333–336).

The harbor of La Rochelle suffered from similar problems. In addition to natural debris brought in by the sea, waste generated by economic activity along the banks and urban areas accumulated in the port. In May 1483, for example, a pardon was granted to Jehan Jeudy, a local butcher, who had pierced the wall along the Maubec channel "with a conduit or opening through which the refuse of the butchery is thrown."[8] One can imagine the stench that must have prevailed in the port during summer, mingling with the odor of other rubbish discarded by residents and sailors. The same inconveniences were observed in Dieppe at the end of the Middle Ages. "It is a fairly beautiful town, located on the coast, but the air is very unhealthy due to the rotting fish, for many sea fish are sold there, and large piles are thrown and decompose," reported in substance a Bohemian ambassador visiting Louis XI in 1464 (Lardin, 2003, p. 7).

Ports confronted with contagion

Faced with diseases whose scale of contagion and mortality struck people with astonishment and terror – and which no medical knowledge could halt – individual and collective reactions were remarkably consistent, whether along the coast or inland. The role and effect of rumor in this context should not be underestimated; the same rumors that sailors usually relied upon to learn the latest commercial news, acts of piracy, or shipwrecks could now announce plague and death (Bernard, 1968, p. 463).

Flight, driven by the belief that the miasmas of contaminated places explained the devastation, seized many and, in fact, often accelerated the spread of epidemics. This reflex is observable in Dieppe during the second half of the 14th century, with some inhabitants leaving the town for Rouen. The recurrence of epidemics led those who could afford it to maintain two residences, one in town and another in the countryside. For instance, according to a 1434 lease, Jean de Rochechouart, resident of La Rochelle, reserved the right to retreat with his family to his châtellenie of Chiche (Deux-Sèvres) if compelled "by mortality or otherwise"[9] (Favreau, 1967, p. 354). In 1515, when the plague was widespread in the West, the contagion in La Rochelle was such that all the notables left the city to take refuge "in the fields," and the mayor, ringing the bell to convene the town council and inform them of royal directives, could gather only six of its 24 members, despite their obligation to comply.[10] Similarly, in 1519, after four years of plague in Labourd, which soon reached Bayonne, the town council decided to relocate to the Brindos district in Anglet.[11] A few years later, from November 12, 1523 to September 21, 1524, the Parliament of Bordeaux temporarily relocated to Libourne due to the plague there (Bernard, 1968, pp. 30, 60).

Notarial contracts in Bordeaux sometimes included clauses requiring shipmasters to first inquire about the sanitary conditions of a port before entering it and, second, to divert if an epidemic threatened. For example, in a document dated October 16, 1493, it was stipulated that on the route of the *Nicholas* of Loctudy to Crotoy, if there was "mortality" at the port, the master was to stop at Dieppe; except "if death occurs at Dieppe and Crotoy," in which case he was required to proceed to the original destination of Crotoy.[12] A similar precaution applied to the *Cristofle* of Crozon, bound for Lisbon in 1506, which was required to divert to Restelo or Setubal in case of "plague danger."[13] However, if disease broke out onboard, panic could overtake the crew. In early 1519, an 80-ton ship from Labourd bound for Portugal experienced plague onboard, resulting in two deaths. "As the master, the boatswain, and the crew dared not remain on board, the ship was looted by pirates" after being abandoned in Lisbon.[14]

Despite the absence of effective remedies, care for the sick was not neglected, motivated by sanitary, social, moral, religious, economic, and political considerations. Since the 12th century, towns had established numerous facilities through religious orders and hospital statutes to receive and aid the sick – a movement soon reinforced by mutual assistance provisions in guild statutes, providing material support in case of illness or death. This was the case, for example, for the bargemen and boatmen in Bordeaux (Bernard, 1968, pp. 668–669). By contrast, Eugène Goyeneche (Goyheneche, 1990, p. 100) notes that in Bayonne "the assistance clauses proper (aid to the sick, widows, and orphans) are virtually absent." These centers, serving both the poor and the wealthy, were tasked with caring for individuals suffering from various ailments. By the late Middle Ages, all port towns had such dedicated facilities. In La Rochelle, for instance, public health was partly managed by the city through the Saint-Barthélemy almonry, a secular hospital under municipal authority, which provided essential care and assistance. In Dieppe, there was a leper hospital and a town-managed hospital, staffed with three attendants to care for patients (Lardin, 2023, p. 54).

Michel Mollat notes that "hospitals at the time received more than they treated," functioning as a form of hospitality for travelers (Mollat, 1978, p. 184). Physicians played only a secondary role alongside religious staff. Nonetheless, port towns were attentive to the presence of barbers, surgeons, and physicians capable of attending to the population. The existence of hospitals and leper houses suggests that healthcare professions, including physicians, surgeons, and barbers, were present, although records are sparse and indicate that no women practiced these trades. Several Dieppe residents practiced medical care, including physicians and barbers who also acted as dentists or performed minor surgeries. In 1425, two such practitioners from Criel-sur-Mer and Neufchâtel-en-Bray became citizens of Dieppe (Lardin, 2023, p. 487). In Bayonne, from the 14th century onward, apothecaries, physicians, barbers, and surgeons were required to take an oath, with plague surgeons taking a special oath (Goyheneche, 1990, p. 287). During the 1518 plague, the town contracted Jean de Saint-Martin and Bernard de Labadie, master barbers and surgeons, agreeing that they "shall remain resident in the present town, both in times of peace and during plague and contagion, and diligently and loyally care for all plague victims and other patients, and shall not leave the town under any circumstances."[15]

In La Rochelle, the Saint-Barthélemy almonry employed physicians and surgeons to visit the sick. In 1471–1472, Symon Texier and Jehan Cadoye, surgeons, and Jehan de Ydeghen, a "doctor of medicine," served in succession, even calling upon an apothecary, Jehan Guerin, to supply ointments, plasters, and other remedies (Pouponnot, 2001, p. 18; Loriaud, 1973). La Rochelle also counted several renowned physicians whose reputation extended across western France, such as masters Joubert Astore and Jehan du Poys, active in the 1340s and 1360s.[16] The aldermen of Saint-Jean-d'Angély readily recommended the services of Rochelais surgeons to their fellow citizens. "Perette, femme Nicaise," was sent there in July 1397 to determine whether she was "tainted with the disease of Saint Ladre [leprosy] or not."[17] By decision of January 11, 1407, the prosecutor of the court of Saint-Jean-d'Angély ordered that the wife of Guillaume Lescot, who was suspected of being "afflicted with the disease of leprosy," which posed a great danger to the town, should go to La Rochelle

> before the master surgeons, namely Master Jehan Noblet, a Carmelite friar, and Master Jehan Lappe, to be examined. And in the event that she does not have the said disease, and that she has been duly examined by them, she shall bring before us proper certification from them under the royal seal or the seal of the town; and in the event that she does have the said disease, she shall no longer sell here and shall depart.[18]

The Rochelais physicians treated for several days a German master who, in 1414, had been struck on the head by one of his sailors.[19] In the mid-15th century, Olivier Gansales, a native of Vivero in Galicia, practiced as a surgeon in La Rochelle for more than 30 years.[20] In Nantes, it was

> pointed out that in this town diseases often spread, both plague and others, and that in the past, due to the dangers and inconveniences arising from these diseases, it was common knowledge that in La Rochelle there was a very good and upright physician, a doctor highly learned and skilled in the medical art and science, experienced and well known to many of the inhabitants of this town, named Master Gouraud.

Consequently, by deliberation of December 15, 1520, the bourgeois of Nantes decided, for a handsome salary, to hire him into their service.[21] History does not tell us whether the people of La Rochelle accepted his departure without protest. When official medicine was not enough, traditional medicine and esoteric remedies took over. An old woman, known as Jehanne la Sauvelle, was known there for her activities in witchcraft. She appears in two cases judged in November 1381 and April 1382.[22] And an act dated September 20, 1459, records the existence of a fortune-teller in La Rochelle.[23]

The first measures of isolation

Jacques Bernard aptly summarizes the attitude of populations and their rulers toward the dangers brought by the sea and rivers: "Everything that came from it, in troubled times, was suspect; everything that was suspect was cast back into its external darkness, where foreigners, potential enemies, quarrelsome sailors, scoundrels, and the plague swarmed together in a single condemnation" (Bernard, 1968, p. 61). Following the Black Death, measures were taken to protect against epidemics – believed to be carried by humors and the wind – just as people protected themselves from all that was strange, by building fortified enclosures in which coastal towns could isolate themselves and control comings and goings through a few well-guarded gates. Considerable financial and human resources were devoted to this effort.

This desire to keep danger at a distance, outside the social, religious, and political body, initially targeted visible threats posed by outsiders. Soon, however, it extended to invisible threats – those that even members of the urban community could inadvertently carry. In July 1515, struck by a plague outbreak, the town of Bayonne postponed its fairs and instructed "all neighbors, residents, and inhabitants of the town that no one should dare to go, speak, converse, or conduct business outside the town with anyone coming from Bordeaux or any other contagious place." Communication with the parishes of Dax, Bidart, Toulouse, Salies, and other plague-stricken locations was also forbidden. Regarding Salies, boatmen and ferrymen were prohibited

> from receiving or transporting to the said town any salt or other hides and goods from Salies, even if the carriers came from elsewhere, and from daring to enter the said town at night or to land without first seeking permission from the lieutenant, so that the said boats could be inspected to determine which persons and goods were aboard, in order to avoid contagion, without any grace.

Subsequently, fearing that goods might have been contaminated during maritime transport or affected by the plague in Bayonne and its surroundings, several merchants explicitly requested permission from the town to unload their goods in various locations, notably at Capbreton. In December 1517 and February 1518, pilgrims to Saint-Jacques were prohibited from crossing the Nive River under penalty of having their transporting ship burned. Some months later, on April 11, 1518, with the disease persisting in Saint-Jean-de-Luz, Bayonne authorities issued an "inhibition and prohibition to all inhabitants and foreigners not to go to, converse in, or frequent the town and parish of Saint-Jean-de-Luz, where some persons had died of plague."[24]

In this context, healthy populations were first isolated within enclosures, and soon thereafter, the practice extended to the sick themselves – confirmed or potential cases – regardless of origin. Gradually, starting in the Western Mediterranean (Venice, Genoa, Barcelona) in the 15th century, and later in the Atlantic but not before the second half of the 16th century, the concept of imposing prolonged isolation outside the city on infected individuals emerged (Biraben, 1976, pp. 205–206). The town of Bayonne, through measures taken in 1515 to combat plague, serves as a precursor. The city council decreed:

> We command, prohibit, and forbid all kinds and classes of people who, being denied entry into the town because they come from dangerous places where there is plague, to remain or dwell anywhere within the jurisdiction of the town, but to retire immediately and without delay, so that they do not converse or interact with the inhabitants of the town or surrounding boroughs. And this under penalty of twenty-five livres tournois, to which they will be condemned, and they are henceforth condemned each time they are found doing the contrary, without any grace.
>
> We also forbid anyone who goes to speak or converse with the aforesaid persons from such contagious places outside the town, wherever they are, from subsequently residing in the town, the boroughs, or the jurisdiction for forty days, under the same penalties as above, and without any grace.

These lines indicate that without gathering actual or suspected plague victims in a single place, they were prohibited from entering the city for 40 days – a practice equivalent to quarantine. A similar measure was imposed on anyone coming from Bordeaux in July 1528.[25] The period of enforced distance could even reach two months, as was the case for pilgrims at the turn of 1517–1518.[26] In Nantes, it was not until 1569 that the town council established a lazaret near the Quai de la Fosse to house the poor afflicted by plague (Guenel, 1982). It should also be noted that, in some respects, leper hospitals and other maladreries – founded in the countryside away from towns between the 11th and 13th centuries – provided an early experience of isolation. These facilities were sometimes used to organize quarantines from the 16th century onward. Ultimately, two key points emerge regarding epidemic control: first, coastal towns served as pioneering laboratories for developing collective protective and remedial measures; second, it took nearly a century – until the early modern period – for Atlantic populations to adopt sanitary solutions devised by Mediterranean authorities.

The first attempts at port hygiene

Regarding the various wastes that could be deposited on the banks or dumped into port waters, specific measures were occasionally implemented. In urgent situations, the priority was to remove identified pollutants from the site. In 1329, for example, the constable of Bordeaux had the channel and ditches near the port of Talmont-sur-Gironde dredged (Périsse, 2007, pp. 90–95; 2011, pp. 333–336). Beyond emergency action, regulatory measures were sometimes introduced, such as for the Bordeaux "padouens," i.e., the strips of land separating the port banks from the city walls. As early as 1253–1254, it was decreed:

> That no one in this place shall create any obstruction, and that if anyone places anything there, it must be removed within three days; and that no ship shall henceforth be or remain in the entire mudflat in front of said padouen in any manner.

In other words, it was forbidden to leave anything abandoned in the Place de l'Ombrière, with offenders given three days to remove what they had deposited. The same regulation applied to the Port Saint-Pierre.[27] In 1336, the commune clarified the penalties in two articles:

> [Art. 3] Likewise, in these matters, we forbid any man or woman to throw soil, straw, or refuse into the large ditches, inside or near the city gates, nor into the Devèze, nor into the estey of Pont-Saint-Jean, nor on the Place Saint-Pierre, nor into the sea, nor [on the Place Saint-Projet, nor] any other public place, under penalty of the said fine.
>
> [Art. 4] Likewise, we order that anyone who has placed a bulky item on the padouen must remove it within eight days, and may place nothing further there without the permission of the mayor and jurats, except as established by customary usage, under the aforementioned penalty, and shall lose the item if they obstruct the padouen.

Thus, dumping refuse or bulky items in the ditches, the Devèze, the Peugue, the Garonne, or on the padouens was punishable by a fine of 65 sous.[28] Nevertheless, some individuals continued to dispose of waste and unwanted goods in port areas. In 1406, the Jurade imposed fines again: "And this, under the penalty of the above-mentioned gage, for each cartload and each pack animal load: XX sous, applicable and enforceable as above"; a provision that was reiterated and strengthened in 1420: "And this, under penalty of sixty-five sous of gage, for any cases in which the padouens were found obstructed" (Bochaca, 1997, pp. 139–140). It is unclear to what extent these injunctions were effective.

Similar regulations existed in Bayonne concerning illegal deposits along the Nive in 1515–1516.[29] In Rouen, the city deliberated on sanitation and pollution roughly once or twice a year, focusing mainly on street paving and cleaning, with the city quays included in these works. In December 1407, it was decided to pave the Quai de la Madeleine up to the Porte Jehan-le-Cœur. According to Pierre Cochon's Chronique Normande, the quays near the old bridge were also cleared of refuse and paved (Lardin, 2008). In both cases, the aim was as much to facilitate movement on these vital commercial spaces as to improve sanitary conditions. In 1435, simultaneously with works in Rouen, "aisements," i.e., toilets enclosed with a wooden door, were installed at the port of Dieppe near the pillory for the use of residents and passing sailors, to prevent them from relieving themselves in the streets (Lardin, 2023, p. 369). For similar hygiene and public health reasons, Marc Ryckaert notes that it was forbidden to throw refuse into certain Flemish ports (Ryckaert, 1988, pp. 366–367).

The issue of potable water, potentially carrying multiple diseases (diarrhea, dysentery, hepatitis A, typhoid fever, poliomyelitis, etc.), remains. Supplying crews with water during port calls was crucial. While wine rations, considered potable, were provided aboard, freshwater was still needed for longer voyages. But it was still necessary to "make water" during a journey of a certain distance. Wells, fountains, and cisterns existed in every port town, but specific access for seafarers, if it existed, is unknown. Many installations belonged to private individuals or ecclesiastical establishments. In Bordeaux, some cellars overlooking the port had private access (Bernard, 1968, p. 64). Additionally, proximity to the sea often made groundwater brackish and unsuitable for drinking. This was the case in Dieppe, where the Puits Salé served more for cleaning than drinking, though a public well at the base of the cliff supplied fresh water (Lardin, 2023, p. 131). In La Rochelle, small surrounding ports, such as the Port du Plomb with its aqueduct, provided important logistical support. Before 1300, the city already had a public basin. The fountain was then a simple reservoir in a large, deep cavity collecting rain and runoff, accessed by a staircase. In 1447, repeated shortages during dry periods led the Rochelais to build a second basin "at the highest and firmest rock of this city, near the fresh waters coming from Lafond, on the site now called the Vieille Fontaine." To finance it, they obtained royal permission on August 22 to levy ten deniers per barrel of wine and five deniers per pipe leaving their suburbs. This substantial hydraulic installation distributed water through 14 conduits in the city and was regularly maintained and cleaned, as in 1499 (Tranchant, 2003, p. 181). These references suggest that a dedicated inventory of potable water resources in these ports would be worthwhile.

Conclusion

If, as was the case everywhere and at all times in the medieval period, prayer to obtain forgiveness, mercy, and the intervention of Almighty God was considered essential during severe health crises, new practices – based on pragmatic observations and economic, political, and social necessities – gradually emerged in port environments during the late Middle Ages. For its users, the port certainly offered a point of connectivity with the sea, through which they sustained their livelihoods, development, and partnerships. As a territory of transit and transition, conducive to exchange, it was an opportunity for its actors. Yet at the same time, as a gateway to the foreign and to all manner of exogenous elements, it posed a potential threat to the society it served. Consequently, its inhabitants were inclined to protect themselves.

It should be noted that ports and their associated towns, by the end of the Middle Ages, constituted unique – and likely pioneering – laboratories for dealing with public health issues. More than elsewhere, as places of population and goods mixing, they exposed people to the transmission of diseases and accelerated contagion. More than elsewhere, as hubs of transit and handling, they required that quays and public spaces be maintained and cleared of encroaching filth. This probably explains the innovative and early nature of the responses implemented by municipal authorities.

However, these few pages alone cannot fill the gaps on a topic too long neglected. To obtain a more comprehensive picture, it would be necessary to systematically review the municipal deliberations of port towns – Bayonne, Bordeaux, La Rochelle, Nantes, and Rouen – from the 14th century, where records exist, through the mid-16th century. In doing so, the variety of issues and necessities, the intensity of crises, and the weight of habits, customs, and preconceived notions about health would become clearer. The quality and pace of the responses by public authorities, as well as the initiatives and reactions of individuals according to their trades and interests, could be specified in greater detail. A comparative analysis of the solutions adopted by other coastal populations should also be considered. For instance, it is known that in St John, Scotland, according to a 1429 letter from the Council of Danzig, a cargo could be burned if it was suspected of carrying pestilence.[30] Moreover, it would be worth tracing the spread of lazaret establishment from the Mediterranean ports northward through Europe. Yet this is, in reality, the pioneering work of a thesis, for which we have outlined in broad strokes – using a few significant examples – the mechanisms and significance.

Notes

1 It should nevertheless be noted that a recent collective study on the subject has been published, even though the Middle Ages are not covered: Pouget (2025).
2 In order to compensate for the deterioration of documentary series that might have specifically reported maritime events, since 2010 we have undertaken the creation of a database, named ESTRAN, intended for the recording, processing, and publication of documents relating to the populations of the Atlantic seaboard of the kingdom of France. It is published with restricted access within the TGIR Huma'num. This database currently brings together more than 3,200 documents.
3 AD33 (Departmental Archives of Gironde), 3E 4990 (16/11/1514).
4 AD33, 3E 86, fol. 4v° (13/10/1484) ; 3E 11015, fol. 155v (20/07/1514).

5 AN (French National Archives), JJ 154, n° 60.
6 AN, JJ 170, n° 94.
7 *Livre des coutumes, publié avec des variantes et des notes*, éd. Henri Barckhausen, *Archives Municipales de Bordeaux*, t. 5, Bordeaux, Imprimerie G. Gounouilhou, 1890, n° XIX, art. 77, p. 304, art. 79, p. 305, n° XX, art. 3, p. 312. *Registre de la Jurade. Délibérations de 1406 à 1409*, éd. Henri Barckhausen, *Archives Municipales de Bordeaux*, t. III, Bordeaux, Imprimerie G. Gounouilhou, 1873, p. 8. *Registre de la Jurade. Délibérations de 1414 à 1416 et de 1420 à 1422*, éd. Henri Barckhausen, *Archives Municipales de Bordeaux*, t. IV, Bordeaux, Imprimerie G. Gounouilhou, 1883, p. 454.
8 *Recueil de documents concernant le Poitou contenus dans les registres de la Chancellerie de France, 1475–1483*, éd. Paul Guérin et Léonce Celier, Poitiers, Société française d'imprimerie et de librairie, 1919 (*Archives Historiques du Poitou*, t. XLI), p. 607–610.
9 AD79 (Departmental Archives of Deux-Sèvres), chartrier de Saint-Loup, B 1822.
10 Barbot Amos, *Histoire de La Rochelle*, éd. Denys d'Aussy, Paris/Saintes, A. Picard/Z. Mortreuil, 1886 (*Archives Historiques de la Saintonge et de l'Aunis*, t. XIV), p. 479–480.
11 *Délibérations du corps de ville. Registres Gascons, t. II (1514–1530)*, éd. Édouard Ducéré, Pierre Yturbide et Charles Bernadou, *Archives Municipales de Bayonne*, Bayonne, A. Lamaignère, 1898, p. 230.
12 AD33, 3 E 4811, fol. 63 v.
13 AD33, 3 E 12214.
14 *Délibérations du corps de ville. Registres Gascons, t. II (1514–1530)*, éd. Édouard Ducéré, Pierre Yturbide et Charles Bernadou, *Archives Municipales de Bayonne*, Bayonne, A. Lamaignère, n° 16, pp. 211–212.
15 *Délibérations du corps de ville. Registres Gascons, t. II (1514–1530)*, éd. Édouard Ducéré, Pierre Yturbide et Charles Bernadou, *Archives Municipales de Bayonne*, Bayonne, A. Lamaignère, n° 351, p. 158. Surgeons specializing in the plague appear in later deliberations of 1522 and 1527.
16 AN, JJ 72, n° 213.
17 *Registres de l'échevinage de Saint-Jean-d'Angély, 1332–1496*, éd. D. d'Aussy, Paris/Saintes, A. Picard/ Z. Mortreuil, 1895, pp. 26–27.
18 *Registres de l'échevinage de Saint-Jean-d'Angély, 1332–1496*, éd. D. d'Aussy, Paris/Saintes, A. Picard/ Z. Mortreuil, 1895, p. 204.
19 AN, JJ 168, n° 3.
20 AN, JJ 191, n° 210. Médiathèque La Rochelle (La Rochelle Media Library), ms 200, f° 33 v°.
21 Archives Municipales de Nantes (Nantes Municipal Archives), GG 765, n° 6. "remonstré que en cestedite ville y avoit souventes fois cours de malladies, tant de peste que autres, et que anciennement pour les dangiers et inconveniens qui se y trouvoint à l'occasion desdites malladies. Or, il estoit bruit notoire que à La Rochelle y avoit ung très homme de bien de médecin, docteur fort bien scavant et cougnoessant en l'art et science de médecine, expérimenté et cougnu de pluseurs des habitans de cestedite ville, nommé missire Gouraud".
22 AN, JJ 119, n° 404 ; JJ 120, n° 170.
23 *Registres des Grands Jours tenus à Bordeaux en 1456 et 1459*, éd. par H. Barckhausen, *Archives historiques du département de la Gironde*, t. 9, Bordeaux, Imprimerie G. Gounouilhou, 1867, pp. 275–278.
24 *Délibérations du corps de ville. Registres Gascons, t. II (1514–1530)*, éd. Édouard Ducéré, Pierre Yturbide et Charles Bernadou, *Archives Municipales de Bayonne*, Bayonne, A. Lamaignère, n° 236, p. 42, n° 245, p. 53, n° 252, p. 59, n° 281, pp. 81–82, n° 330, p. 129, n° 338, pp. 141–142, n° 348, p. 155, n° 27, pp. 229–231, n° 31, pp. 233–234, n° 33, pp. 234–235.

25 *Délibérations du corps de ville. Registres Gascons, t. II (1514–1530)*, éd. Édouard Ducéré, Pierre Yturbide et Charles Bernadou, *Archives Municipales de Bayonne*, Bayonne, A. Lamaignère, n° 238, p. 44, n° 231, pp. 504–505.
26 *Délibérations du corps de ville. Registres Gascons, t. II (1514–1530)*, éd. Édouard Ducéré, Pierre Yturbide et Charles Bernadou, *Archives Municipales de Bayonne*, Bayonne, A. Lamaignère, n° 330, p. 129, n° 338, pp. 141–142.
27 *Livre des coutumes, publié avec des variantes et des notes*, éd. Henri Barckhausen, *Archives Municipales de Bordeaux*, t. 5, Bordeaux, Imprimerie G. Gounouilhou, 1890, n° XIX, art. 77, p. 304, art. 79, p. 305.
28 *Livre des coutumespublié avec des variantes et des notes*, éd. Henri Barckhausen, *Archives Municipales de Bordeaux*, t. 5, Bordeaux, Imprimerie G. Gounouilhou, 1890, n° XX, art. 3, p. 312.
29 *Délibérations du corps de ville. Registres Gascons, t. II (1514–1530)*, éd. Édouard Ducéré, Pierre Yturbide et Charles Bernadou, *Archives Municipales de Bayonne*, Bayonne, A. Lamaignère, n° 236, pp. 42–43, n° 281, pp. 81–82.
30 *Hansisches Urkundenbuch*, vol. 6, 2022, n° 844, p. 470. I thank Tobias Boestad for having communicated this reference to me.

References

Bernard J. (1968) *Navires et gens de mer à Bordeaux (vers 1400-vers 1550)*. Paris: S.E.V.P.E.N.

Biraben J.N. (1976) *Les hommes et la peste en France et dans les pays européens et méditerranéens, Tome I: La peste dans l'histoire*. Paris-La Haye:, Mouton.

Bochaca M. (1997) *La Banlieue de Bordeaux. Formation d'une juridiction municipale suburbaine (vers 1250- vers 1550)*. Paris: L'Harmattan.

Bochaca M. (2015) *Villes et organisation de l'espace en Bordelais (vers 1300-vers 1550)*. Paris: Les Indes Savantes.

Dutour O. (2022) L'origine de la syphilis: Colomb enfin innocenté? *Les Nouvelles de l'Archéologie*, 169: 29–34.

Favreau R. (1967) Épidémies à Poitiers et dans le Centre-Ouest à la fin du Moyen Âge. *Bibliothèque de l'Ecole des Chartes*, 125(2): 349–398.

Goyheneche E. (1990) *Bayonne et la région bayonnaise du xii*[e] *au xv*[e] *siècle. Études d'histoire économique et sociale*. Leioa: Universidad del País Vasco.

Guenel J. (1982) Un hôpital nantais disparu: le Sanitat. In: *Les Annales de Nantes et du Pays Nantais*. Nantes: Société académique de Nantes et de la Loire-Atlantique, 204, pp. 19–23.

Lardin P. (2003) Le poisson de Dieppe au Moyen Âge. In: Thomasset C. (Ed.), *Le poisson, une histoire extraordinaire*. Paris: Connaissance et Mémoire, pp. 6–31.

Lardin P. (2008) Les Rouennais et la pollution à la fin du Moyen Âge. In: Lalou E., Lepeuple B., Roch J. L. (Eds.), *Des châteaux et des sources. Archéologie et histoire dans la Normandie médiévale. Mélanges en l'honneur d'Anne-Marie Flambard-Héricher*. Mont-Saint-Aignan: Presses universitaires de Rouen et du Havre, pp. 399–428.

Lardin P. (2023) *Dieppe au Moyen Âge: des origines à Jehan Ango*. Dieppe, Philippe Lardin.

Leguay J.P. (2002) *L'eau dans la ville au Moyen Âge*. Rennes: Presses universitaires de Rennes.

Loriaud B. (1973) Les pauvres malades et le personnel de l'aumônerie Auffredi à La Rochelle vers 1470. In: *Recueil de la Société Archéologique et Historique de Charente-Maritime*, Saintes: Musée Archéologique, pp. 137–142.

Mollat M. (1978) *Les pauvres au Moyen Âge, étude sociale*. Paris: Hachette.
Périsse S. (2007) Les transformations de la côte saintongeaise et leurs répercussions sur les activités maritimes et portuaires aux xve et xvie siècles. In: Bochaca M., Sarrazin J.L. (Ed.), *Ports et littoraux de l'Europe atlantique. Transformations naturelles et aménagements humains (xive-xvie siècles)*. Rennes: PUR, pp. 81–95.
Périsse S. (2011) *Les campagnes littorales saintongeaises à la fin du Moyen Âge (xie-milieu xvie siècle)*. thèse de doctorat sous la direction de Michel Bochaca, Université de La Rochelle, dactyl.
Pouget B. (Ed.) (2025) *Marine, marins et maladies collectives (xviiie-xxe siècles). Une histoire sur la longue durée. Revue d'Histoire Maritime*, 35.
Pouponnot G. (2001) *L'aumônerie Saint-Barthélemy de La Rochelle au XVe siècle*. mémoire de Maîtrise sous la direction de Mathias Tranchant, Université de La Rochelle.
Ryckaert M. (1988) La gestion des ports flamands au Moyen Âge. In: Cavaciocchi S. (Ed.), *I porti come impresa economica (Secc. xiii-xviii)*, Atti della Diciannovesima Settimana di Studi (Prato, 2–6 maggio 1987). Firenze:, Firenze University Press, pp. 347–368.
Tranchant M. (2003) *Le commerce maritime de La Rochelle à la fin du Moyen Âge*. Rennes: Presses universitaires de Rennes.

7 Controlling epidemics in 18th-century French commercial ports

Frédéric Davansant

Introduction

The 18th-century merchant ship was at once a vehicle of wealth and a carrier of pathogens. Crowded conditions aboard, the length of voyages, and poor nutritional and sanitary provisions fostered the spread of viruses and bacteria that then circulated between sea and shore. The intensification of maritime exchange in the early modern period thus accelerated what one might call an "epidemic import–export," capable of triggering deadly outbreaks both in fleets and among port populations. The "Northern Plague" (1709–1714), the Great Plague of Marseille (1720), smallpox on Île Bourbon (1729), and the typhus epidemic aboard the squadron of Comte Du Bois de la Motte and then at Brest (1757–1758) are among the many examples attesting to the porous boundaries between maritime spaces and coastal urban milieus (Hildesheimer, 1980).

In the Age of Enlightenment, the arrival of ships from places subject to epidemics invariably provoked a "wave of fear," which authorities attempted to contain through preventive devices. This fear of disease arriving from the sea forms part of a long history: from the Black Death (1347) to the Great Plague of Marseille, western European societies were regularly confronted with contagions whose spread owed much to maritime and commercial traffic.

Frequent until the mid-16th century, plague flare-ups became more sporadic, reappearing episodically until the 1670s, before resurfacing spectacularly in 1720 in the Phocaean city. The human toll for southern France was considerable: estimates run to nearly 50,000 dead in Marseille alone and roughly 120,000 deaths in Provence between 1720 and 1722 (Signoli and Tzortzis, 2018; Biraben, 1975–1976)—about a third of the provincial population. Although plague receded over the course of the 18th century, the epidemic threat by no means vanished. It recomposed itself around other diseases—typhus, the "Siamese illness," "pestilential scurvy," peripneumonias, and ill-identified fevers—which continued to circulate along sea routes.

Faced with this persistent danger, commercial states, from the late Middle Ages and even more in the modern era, put in place an array of preventive measures: health boards, port-specific regulations, quarantines, the

DOI: 10.4324/9781003639589-10

multiplication of lazarettos, and tighter control over crews and goods. The Marseille model—with its health board established in the mid-17th century and its rigorous practice of quarantine—exerted a lasting influence on sanitary imaginaries and practices (Demichel, 2023). Yet not all coastal regions possessed this same "familiarity" with contagious diseases and their institutional remedies. On the Atlantic seaboard, notably in the ports of the Ponant or along the Charente coast, comparable measures were mobilized only during exceptional alerts (plagues of the North; epidemics arriving from the Levant, Africa, the Baltic, or the Balkans). At Rochefort, as in the Atlantic islands (Aix, Ré, Groix), accounts of "sick squadrons," disembarking hundreds or even thousands of scurvy- or typhus-ridden sailors, bear witness to an epidemic exposure directly tied to the activity of naval and commercial ports (Even, 2004).

In this context, the 18th century appears as a pivotal moment in the organization of sanitary control in French ports. Under the reign of Louis XIV and then in the early 18th century, the assertion of a more centralized royal administration—concerned with "public sanitary order"—resulted in the gradual consolidation of a legal and regulatory framework: royal ordinances, local regulations, the creation or strengthening of health boards, and the regulation of quarantines and communications with places reputed to be infected. This normative dynamic nevertheless remained dependent on local authorities and initiatives: port cities, intendants, naval officers, merchants, and ecclesiastical authorities devised and adapted their own responses, oscillating between imitation of Mediterranean models and empirical tinkering conditioned by economic and military constraints. Prevention rested as much on vigilance and information (lists of infected places, surveillance of ships and urban boundaries) as on an exceptional arsenal—isolations, closures, quarantines—the implementation of which remained uncertain.

This chapter analyzes the concrete modalities of epidemic control in 18th-century French commercial ports, combining the study of normative texts with that of administrative and sanitary practices. It interrogates the structural weakness of legal responses, the roles of the various institutional actors, and the weight of local resistance in risk management. In doing so, it seeks to gauge the real scope of the devices put in place and to shed light, at the scale of commercial ports, on how the French early modern state learned to cope with the epidemic threat from the sea.

Modest administrative and legal responses in the century of enlightenment

Frequent until the 1530s, plague outbreaks then became more spaced out; the disease returned on average every 15 years until the 1670s. In the first two-thirds of the 17th century—the period of the last major flare-ups—French port cities applied local regulations drafted in the first half of the 16th century and then simply reiterated at each alert. The reign of the Sun King marked a growing awareness of the role the state should assume in combating epidemics. This increasing intervention took the form of national-scope norms that were implemented and supplemented on the ground by royal administrators, municipal authorities, and merchants.

A sketchy national legal framework, supplemented by local regulation

Under the Ancien Régime, the fight against the epidemic risk coming from the sea rested on a normative edifice that was late, fragmentary, and unevenly distributed across the territory. The state's involvement in public health—and particularly in the fight against epidemics—was slow and progressive (Stahl, 2020). For a long time, it was local authorities—municipalities, parlements, provincial estates, dioceses—that took on the front-line management of sanitary crises, before being gradually supervised by a royal power keen to coordinate scattered initiatives.

From the 17th century onward, and more clearly under Louis XIV, an administrative network was put in place to monitor and frame foci of contagion. The central government kept itself informed by its diplomatic agents of the sanitary situation in foreign countries, notably through consulates in the eastern Mediterranean (Panzac, 1987). Information was then transmitted down to the local level by the Controller-General of Finances via the intendant, who informed municipal authorities through his sub-delegates. Required to inform their minister of eruptive fevers, plagues, and epizootics within their jurisdiction, intendants also sent local information back up to the center and helped local authorities finance operations in times of crisis (health boats, burials, food supplies, and care for inhabitants and confined patients). Largely wait-and-see, this system did not amount to a systematic preventive policy, since it was activated only by the irruption of a scourge.

Because the geography of norms followed that of risk, the contrast between the Mediterranean and the Atlantic façade was marked. In Provence, where regular trade with the Orient and North Africa kept plague as a permanent threat, a set of early preventive measures was adopted: as early as 1622, the Parlement of Provence, and later royal authorities, issued rulings and ordinances imposing quarantines, health inspections, and the control of ships coming from regions reputed to be infected. Over the course of the 17th and 18th centuries, these texts organized a genuine sanitary monopoly in favor of Marseille and Toulon, the only places authorized to receive vessels from the Levant and Barbary in quarantine. The Marseille Board of Health and its lazaretto became the linchpin of this system, with a sophisticated regime of "nette" (clean) "suspecte" (suspect) or "brute" (foul) "patentes" (bills of health) determining the duration of quarantine for passengers, ships, and cargoes (Hildesheimer, 1985).

By contrast, on the Ponant coasts, from Dunkirk to Biarritz, a much more lax regime prevailed in the 17th century. With no trade with the eastern Mediterranean, the danger of plague seemed remote to authorities in Channel or

Atlantic ports, and no systematic regulation was put in place. Although the Secretary of State for the Navy was responsible for the sanitary protection of the coasts, he usually contented himself with disseminating notices or letters of recommendation when plague struck in the Baltic, Portugal, or elsewhere in Europe. He invited local authorities to take preventive measures but without imposing a uniform framework. Hence a great diversity of practices, depending on local contexts, economic interests at stake, and the degree of mobilization of urban elites (Even, 2004).

The Enlightenment century only partially broke with this logic. True, royal texts of broader scope multiplied—ordinances of 1712 and 1714 on trade with northern Europe or the "Levantine trading posts" (échelles du Levant); Royal Council rulings, notably that of 14 September 1720 "regarding the contagious disease in Marseille," intended to fix a minimal set of precautions at the kingdom-wide scale without unduly hampering the circulation of people and goods. But these norms, conceived to respond to identified crises, left wide zones of shadow. For the Channel and the Atlantic, several 18th-century texts provided for quarantines and lazarettos without managing to impose themselves durably: many quickly fell into desuetude, to the point that one can consider that, by the early 19th century, there was scarcely any continuous sanitary legislation for the Ocean (Hillemand, 2012).

In practice, therefore, the legal framework of epidemic prevention in ports appeared as an assemblage of norms of uneven scope: Royal Council rulings allowing rapid action while circumventing the parlements; intendants' ordinances limited to their jurisdiction; and municipal regulations—sometimes very draconian—adopted during major alerts. Health boards modeled on Marseille's appeared late in Nantes, Saint-Malo, Morlaix, and Bayonne. They oversaw the day-to-day implementation of these texts, but their existence seems conjunctural. Far from having produced a genuine "sanitary code," the 18th century thus featured a hybrid system in which monarchical centralization oversaw a mosaic of local regulations, more or less inspired by the Mediterranean model.

Municipal officers, magistrates, intendants, and merchants: authorities mobilized against contagion

This weakness of the general normative framework helps explain why prevention largely rested on the initiative of multiple local actors, whose mobilization varied by place and circumstance. The great plagues—and foremost the one in Provence in 1720–1722—offer a privileged laboratory for these configurations of power. The Marseille epidemic generated an unprecedented proliferation of police regulations gathered in a "plague register" in which municipal ordinances, parliamentary rulings, royal letters, and military decisions accumulated. Behind this normative inflation, the municipality—supported by the military commander and the governor-viguiers—was primarily responsible: urban authority, in its different components, managed the epidemic within the city walls (Hildesheimer, 1981; Chaumet, 2011).

The case of Marseille—with its "bureau de santé" (health board) closely tied to the Chamber of Commerce—illustrates the central place of merchant elites in maritime sanitary control: health intendants recruited from among leading merchants and former captains; specialized staff assigned to the lazaretto and to "infirmaries"; and consuls who, in Toulon, became health intendants after leaving office, in charge of sanitary cordons and the control of bills of health. This strong involvement of merchant circles was not without ambiguity: their expertise in maritime traffic and their well-understood interest in preserving trade justified their role, but could also fuel tensions between economic imperatives and sanitary rigor, as the disaster of 1720 would show.

In other ports—particularly on the Atlantic—the institutional configuration proved more fluid. Studies devoted to ports on the Ponant coasts testify to the variability of equilibria: in Dunkirk, the municipality stood at the center of the system; in Carteret, the admiralty and the king's prosecutor played the leading part; in Calais, a genuine "sanitary coalition" brought together municipal bodies, judicial officers, police and admiralty, the navy commissioner, the intendant's sub-delegate, consular judges, and notables; in La Rochelle, measures were taken by the intendant in coordination with the navy commissioner and admiralty officers; in Bayonne, the intendant worked closely with the city, while in Bordeaux he clashed openly with the provincial commander (Hildesheimer, 1980). In Le Havre, finally, the naval intendant gathered the sub-delegate, admiralty, magistrates, and leading merchants (Rioult, 2019). Behind these shifting configurations lies a constant: the state could not intervene effectively without relying on urban powers and local economic actors.

Alerts linked to "plagues from elsewhere" allow one to grasp these mobilizations up close. When plague spread along the Baltic in 1711 or struck Lisbon in 1757, the Secretary of State for the Navy alerted the Breton authorities. In Vannes, the admiralty, municipal officers, representatives of royal justice, navy commissioners, and some notables met to designate places of quarantine, set rules for ship inspection, appoint health commissioners, and forbid any contact with suspect vessels under penalty of sanctions up to the death penalty. At the scale of a small port, one sees the establishment of a device associating royal power (intendant, admiralty), municipality, health officers, and coastal populations (Oger, 1987).

The situation in La Rochelle and Aunis during the 1720–1721 alert offers another telling example. The intendant attempted to frame the local reaction, but urban bodies found themselves on the front line: the city corps armed the health boat, set the pay of health officers, organized the guarding of gates and ramparts, and oversaw the expulsion of foreign beggars presumed to be vectors of contagion; at the same time nobles, magistrates, officers of the finances, members of the présidial, lawyers, and merchants were requisitioned to stand guard at the different gates of the city and at the chain across the harbor entrance. The intendant often merely confirmed by ordinance the measures taken locally, conferring on them royal authority (Even, 2004).

Far from pure and simple centralization, the fight against epidemics instituted a "concentration" of sanitary concerns, in which the state reinforced its prerogatives—particularly through intendants and council rulings—without entirely substituting itself for local authorities. Municipalities remained the essential actors of ordinary sanitary policing; health boards kept watch over ships and travelers; merchants, indispensable to the functioning of ports, participated in decision-making bodies; and parlements exercised limited oversight, focused on the homologation of regulations rather than their concrete execution. In this multilevel game, epidemic prevention in 18th-century ports resulted less from an all-powerful "sanitary state" than from successive compromises among municipal officers, magistrates, intendants, and merchants—under the pressure of crises and the imperatives of maritime commerce.

The relative effectiveness of sanitary devices implemented in the ports

Beyond the difficulties tied to the legal and institutional framework, combating epidemics raised the question of the nature of the measures adopted—necessarily dependent on the state of medical science and on available material and human resources. A second question concerns the concrete effectiveness of restrictive measures, which generated administrative conflicts and resistance on the part of inhabitants and the trading community.

Quarantines, lazarettos, fumigations, and sacraments: an empirical sanitary arsenal

Observation of port sanitary practices in the 18th century reveals an arsenal that was at once sophisticated in its procedures and profoundly empirical in its foundations. Physicians and health authorities operated within an intellectual landscape riven by deep controversies: on one side, contagionists, who emphasized contact with the sick and with "infected" objects; on the other, partisans of "aerialist" theories, who explained epidemics by miasmas and "bad exhalations" and privileged the aeration of places and goods (Fournier, 2008; Demichel, 2023). These doctrinal divergences were not without consequence for practice: the former justified strict isolation of persons and effects, while the latter placed more value on ventilation, perfume, and the purification of air.

The Marseille episode of 1720 is a good illustration of these hesitations. Physicians sent by the Faculty of Montpellier, reluctant to recognize plague, preferably refereed to "pestilential fevers" and did not hesitate, at first, to approach the sick, to touch them, even to handle corpses without particular protection—contrary to some Marseille practitioners more convinced of the disease's contagiousness (Beauvieux, 2021). Today, thanks to the work of historians of medicine, we know that plague is transmitted to humans primarily by fleas from infected rodents, and that the handling of corpses, the inhalation of droplets, or contact with contaminated excreta also play a role.

In this context of etiological ignorance, the measures adopted could only be tentative: they combined intuitions that were sometimes effective (isolation, destruction of clothing, limiting movement) and gestures that were more symbolic or reassuring than truly protective.

The heart of the sanitary arsenal rested on quarantine and the lazaretto. The often-cited model is Venetian in origin. The Serenissima was the first, in the 15th century, to install isolated facilities where people and goods stayed for a period that tended to settle around 40 days. Provence very early inserted itself into this lineage. The Marseille lazaretto, created in the 16th century, was later moved and developed on the islands of Pomègues and Jarre. The Toulon lazaretto appeared in the 17th century, and maritime quarantines were practiced on the Saint-Mandrier peninsula or Île de Sépet (Vergé Franceschi, 2007). The Encyclopédie of Diderot and d'Alembert ratified this definition of the lazaretto as a large but isolated building intended to receive crews and to unload, ventilate, and "purify" cargoes coming from places suspected of plague (Diderot and d'Alembert, 2016).

Around these infrastructures there developed a highly organized system of surveillance supported by bills of health. Issued by municipal authorities or, especially, by French consuls established in Ottoman ports, the bill attested to the sanitary situation of the port of departure and of stopovers: a "clean" bill if no case was reported; a "suspect" bill if rumors or doubtful cases circulated; a "foul" bill in the event of confirmed plague. Each category corresponded to a precise "operation" in the language of health boards: longer or shorter quarantines; stricter or looser isolation of crews; different procedures for treating cargoes. With a clean bill, for example, passengers were confined to the lazaretto under the supervision of guards who quarantined with them, while the merchandise underwent a longer quarantine. For suspect or foul bills, the authorities redoubled vigilance: prior aeration of goods on board; mooring apart from all other vessels; unloading into special halls where ventilation, fumigation, and "perfuming" operations accumulated (Beauvieux, 2021).

This normative apparatus did not preclude a large measure of improvisation, especially in regions less well endowed with infrastructure. In the Mediterranean, Roussillon authorities in 1747 invented an ad hoc solution when a vessel from Barbary put in at Collioure: 15 sailors were isolated for 18 days on a nearby island, perfumed with vinegar and aromatic herbs before being authorized to circulate, bearing a certificate. On the Ponant coasts, where lazarettos remained rare and little used, vigilance focused more on health boats and surveillance at harbor entrances. In La Rochelle, a manned boat met vessels that fired a gun and raised a flag, verified nationality, port of origin, stopovers, papers, and certificates, then directed ships toward quarantine offshore (Île d'Aix, the Bay of Aiguillon) or authorized unloading if no risk was present (Even, 2004). At Le Havre, Dunkirk, or in the Channel Islands, similar boats carried out these inspections before possibly sending suspect ships to a royal lazaretto such as La Hougue on Tatihou Island—whose activity, however, was highly intermittent (Hildesheimer, 1980).

Alongside these "material" measures, a whole register of religious practices persisted: processions, votive masses, public prayers, invocation of plague intercessor saints (the Virgin; Saint Sebastian; above all Saint Roch, whose statue displaying a bubo on the thigh drew Mediterranean crowds, notably in Toulon or Corsica) (Vergé Franceschi, 2007). Urban authorities sometimes hesitated to forbid them, aware of the risk of contagion but also anxious not to offend a religious culture that saw in collective repentance an indispensable bulwark against divine wrath. These practices partook of a logic in which the temporal safeguarding of the community passed by the sacrifice of the individual stricken by the scourge, called to submit to the will of God to save his soul. They reveal a conception of epidemic risk in which medicine, sanitary policing, and religious salvation coexisted more than they contradicted one another (Hildesheimer, 1990).

Reluctance, evasion, and institutional dysfunctions

Given the highly coercive character of the various sanitary measures, their concrete implementation met with serious opposition. Decreeing a general quarantine—closing a port or isolating a city—amounted to provoking a major economic and social crisis. A sanitary state of siege unfailingly produced provisioning difficulties, a halt to commerce, massive unemployment, riot risks, and an explosion of municipal spending devoted to the maintenance of the sick and of confined populations. At sea, the first obstacle to rapid detection of epidemics came from crews, who either failed to identify symptoms or attempted to conceal them from health authorities for fear of being sent to lazarettos or seeing their goods immobilized or destroyed. Another, institutional reluctance appeared at the stage of "publishing" (officially declaring) plague. As long as mortality remained limited, municipalities responsible for collective prophylaxis tended to delay official announcement of disease, hoping the evil would burn out on its own (Belmas, 2017). Although, in theory, since the 17th century parlements required that plague be declared as soon as it was recognized, these regulatory obligations ran up against the weight of local interests and were unevenly applied.

The Marseille epidemic (1720–1722) is paradigmatic in this respect. The role of the ship Grand Saint-Antoine—returning from the Levant, probably contaminated by bales of cotton and by a Turkish passenger who died at sea—is well known. Despite deaths on board and a ban on docking in Livorno, Captain Chataud multiplied maneuvers to shorten quarantine, even stopping clandestinely by night near Toulon to alert his Marseille owners, anxious not to lose a cargo valued at 100,000 écus and destined for the Beaucaire fair. Within the Board of Health itself, some municipal magistrates—most notably the premier échevin Jean-Baptiste Estelle, financially interested in the shipment—are said to have pressured for a regime of "clean bill" and for expediting the unloading of merchandise. The quarantine of the ship, freight, and passengers was accordingly shortened despite suspicious deaths, and the aldermen persisted in minimizing the situation, asserting that the disease was contained at the lazaretto even as it began to strike the city (Poussou, 2017; Belmas, 2017).

This policy of denial and disinformation had dramatic effects. The late decision to concentrate the sick in infirmaries triggered panic at the worst possible moment, when contagion was already well advanced. Religious institutions, arsenals, and fortifications shut themselves up, and notables fled to the countryside. Thousands left Marseille before the Parlement of Aix decided to isolate the city, contributing to the spread of plague throughout Provence. The same Parlement, eager to regain control in the face of municipal failure, multiplied rulings (banning fairs; ordering consuls to declare cases of plague; restricting penitents' processions), producing a normative inflation deemed counterproductive by the Royal Council, which saw in it a source of excessive alarm and a brake on "the ordinary course of commerce" (Stahl, 2020).

The reaction of the central power illustrates the shift toward emergency measures. The Council ruling of 14 September 1720 suspended the powers of sovereign courts and of part of municipal authorities, conferring on intendants and provincial commanders the direction of the fight against the epidemic. The Regent ordered the blockade of Marseille and the establishment of a sanitary cordon to prevent spread beyond Provence, while taking care to maintain the indispensable exchanges with the Levant and to prevent complete economic asphyxia. Commercially, however, the consequences were considerable: closure of French and European ports to Marseille and Provençal vessels; paralysis of the shipyard; misery among fishermen, sailors, and porters; massive city indebtedness to ensure provisioning and assistance to the poorest. The effectiveness of the blockade came at the price of the lasting ruin of the plague-stricken city (Belmas, 2017).

Atlantic ports, less directly touched by plague, did not escape the tensions between sanitary imperatives and economic interests. In La Rochelle or Bordeaux, manning health boats, maintaining a mobilized medical corps, and setting up quarantines offshore or on neighboring islands represented a heavy burden for often fragile urban finances. In times of dearth, as in 1709, the La Rochelle intendant found himself torn between the need to quarantine ships arriving from the Baltic—potential vectors of contagion—and the urgency of unloading the grain they carried as quickly as possible to avoid food riots and social unrest in a province already disturbed by bands of "brigands" and threats of insurrection by workers from the Rochefort arsenal (Even, 2004).

In this context, the temptation to relax vigilance was great, especially when disease remained distant. Captains, shipowners, and crews multiplied frauds: flying false flags; clandestine landings on islands or in small coastal ports; concealing deaths at sea in order to obtain clean bills of health. Coastal populations—living in large part from commerce and smuggling—sometimes abetted these maneuvers. On Île de Ré, throughout the 18th century, captains were observed coming ashore without inspection; goods were sold clandestinely; health officers struggled to enforce regulations and ran up against municipalities' reluctance to pay decent wages or to fund regular patrol boats. Jurisdictional conflicts among admiralty courts, city councils, and intendants compounded these dysfunctions.

Even in the Levantine ports, where controls were tighter, the effectiveness of the system depended largely on the probity of health intendants and on the firmness of municipal magistrates—who were often themselves merchants. The proximity between economic and sanitary power fueled suspicions of indulgence, even corruption, as shown by the Grand Saint-Antoine affair. At the kingdom-wide scale, emergency devices—sanitary cordons, blockades, bans on fairs—also drew criticism in the name of the freedom of commerce and out of fear of nurturing a "fièvre obsidionale" (siege fever) (Poussou, 2017) in cities living barricaded behind their walls, as in Bordeaux and La Rochelle at the height of the Provençal epidemic.

Conclusion

As this survey suggests, the balance sheet of French port sanitary policing in the 18th century is marked by ambivalence. On the one hand, the legal framework remained patchy, unevenly applied, highly dependent on local configurations, and constantly reshaped by economic constraints. Quarantine, lazarettos, bills of health, inspection boats, and sanitary cordons never existed in a pure state: they were continually negotiated, circumvented, or softened under pressure from merchants, municipalities, and coastal populations. On the Ponant coasts, measures promulgated in the 18th century fell quickly into desuetude, to the point that by the early 19th century one can speak, for the Channel and the Atlantic, of a near absence of structured sanitary legislation (Hillemand, 2012). Only with the 1822 law did a homogeneous national device begin to take shape, aiming to make maritime frontiers as impermeable as possible to the invasion of epidemics. On the other hand, a long-term perspective tempers the impression of weakness. After 1722, plague no longer struck Ancien Régime France—lending credence to the idea that the Great Plague of Marseille may have been an "accident" that the failures of the Board of Health and municipal authorities turned into a catastrophe (Poussou, 2017). The singular character of that episode points, in negative, to the relative effectiveness of a system that statistically prevented epidemic conflagration for several decades.

References

Beauvieux F. (2021) Quarantaine, lazarets et hôpitaux: les enfermements sanitaires à Marseille pendant la peste de 1720. *Revue d'Histoire Culturelle*, 3, https://doi.org/10.4000/rhc.648

Belmas E. (2017) Pouvoir politique et catastrophe sanitaire: la 'publication' des épidémies de peste dans la France moderne. *Parlement[s]. Revue d'Histoire Politique*, 25: 31–54.

Biraben J.N. (1975–1976) *Les hommes et la peste en France et dans les pays européens et méditerranéens*. Paris and The Hague: Mouton.

Chaumet P.O. (2011) L'engagement du pouvoir royal contre les risques épidémiques sous l'Ancien Régime (XVIIe–XVIIIe siècles). *Droit et Médecine Bucco-Dentaire*, 1(4): 189–194.

Demichel S. (2023) Risque et vigilance sanitaire. La côte méditerranéenne française face à la peste, 1700–1750, PhD dissertation, Ludwig-Maximilians-Universität München & Université de Fribourg, Vigilanzkulturen/Cultures of Vigilance, Vol. 9, 55.

Diderot D., d'Alembert J.L.R. (2016) *Encyclopédie, ou dictionnaire raisonné des sciences, des arts et des métiers.* ARTFL Encyclopédie Project, University of Chicago, 9: 329, https://encyclopedie.uchicago.edu

Even P. (2004) Le mal venu de la mer. In: Augeron M., Tranchant M. (Eds.), *La violence et la mer dans l'espace atlantique.* Rennes: Presses Universitaires de Rennes, https://doi.org/10.4000/books.pur.19567

Fournier P. (2008) Zones humides et 'aérisme' à l'époque moderne. In: *Zones humides et santé.* GHZH, Arles, pp. 9–23.

Hildesheimer F. (1980) La protection sanitaire des côtes françaises au XVIIIe siècle. *Revue d'Histoire Moderne et Contemporaine*, 27(3): 443–467.

Hildesheimer F. (1981) Prévention de la peste et attitudes mentales en France au XVIIIe siècle. *Revue Historique*, 265(537): 65–67.

Hildesheimer F. (1985) La monarchie administrative face à la peste. *Revue d'Histoire Moderne et Contemporaine*, 32(2): 302–310.

Hildesheimer F. (1990) *La terreur et la pitié. L'Ancien Régime à l'épreuve de la peste.* Paris: Publisud.

Hillemand B. (2012) La police sanitaire maritime française au XIXe siècle. *Histoire des Sciences Médicales*, 46(2): 95–110.

Oger Y. (1987) Les mesures prises au XVIIIe siècle dans l'évêché de Vannes à l'égard des navires en provenance des régions où règne la peste. In: *Société d'Histoire et d'Archéologie de Bretagne*, pp. 185–193. https://m.shabretagne.com/scripts/files/669984c1742349.23818615/1987_09.pdf

Panzac D. (1987) Alexandrie: Peste et croissance urbaine (XVIIe–XIXe siècles). *Revue de l'Occident Musulman et de la Méditerranée*, 46: 81–90.

Poussou J.P. (2017) La peste de Marseille de 1720. *Cahiers Saint Simon*, 45: 47–66.

Rioult C. (2019) Le Havre, le contrôle sanitaire maritime et le problème méditerranéen, années 1750–1780. *Revue d'Histoire Moderne et Contemporaine*, 66(4): 7–31.

Signoli M., Tzortzis S. (2018) La peste à Marseille et dans le sud-est de la France en 1720–1722: les épidémies d'Orient de retour en Europe. *Cahiers de la Méditerranée*, 96: 217–230.

Stahl H. (2020) Le Droit face aux circonstances sanitaires exceptionnelles: La Peste de 1720 en Provence. *Revue des Droits et Libertés Fondamentaux*, Chron. No. 26(3), https://revuedlf.com/droit-administratif/le-droit-face-aux-circonstances-sanitaires-exceptionnelles-la-peste-de-1720-en-provence/

Vergé Franceschi M. (2007) 1720–1721: la peste ravage Toulon. *Annales de Bretagne et des Pays de l'Ouest*, 114(4), https://doi.org/10.4000/abpo.461

8 Spatial aspects of quarantine in port cities until the 20th century

Sarah E. Hinman

Introduction

Quarantine is typically associated with what was established among the European shipping powers beginning in the 14th century initially as a means of stopping, or at least delaying, the spread of plague. Variation in the implementation of this practice and tolerance for its use are evident in the literature and in the outcomes of the International Sanitary Congresses held throughout the 19th and early 20th centuries (Maglen 2003; Bynum 2013). Given the importance of coastal ports to the movement of goods and people since the 14th century and particularly since the 18th century, it is intriguing that how port cities provided space for quarantine and their facilities appear to be overlooked in the broader discussions around the medical, ethical, and economic aspects of this practice. Until the SARS outbreak in 2003, quarantine was effectively relegated by the general population to a historical practice. When asking a classroom of undergraduate students what they knew about quarantine before reading Weber (2019) and prior to the COVID-19 pandemic their responses ranged from something mentioned in a history class briefly to what happens to their emails. Public health offices, such as the Centers for Disease Control (CDC) in the United States, likely maintain a slightly different perspective of the historical nature of quarantine. The CDC currently staffs 20 quarantine hospitals across the country for times when there is concern over individuals arriving at the land or sea border with one of the listed quarantinable diseases such as cholera, yellow fever, or plague. Then in 2020 with the COVID-19 pandemic quarantine practices returned in many places, although much like in past centuries with quite drastic differences in implementation depending upon location.

When considering the history of quarantine at coastal ports there are a few common threads in the discussion of quarantine in historical context. Many scholars begin with the definition of quarantine, the separation of goods and/or people arriving at a port from the local "healthy" population for a given period of time either to determine if disease is present within the traveling population often coming from a port known to have an active epidemic of a notifiable disease or because people arrive symptomatic with a disease of

DOI: 10.4324/9781003639589-11

concern (Bashford 2016; Weber 2019). The definition is almost inevitably followed by reference to the Croatian and Italian roots of quarantine as a practice and the translation of the term from Italian to English as meaning 40 days. The origin story focuses on the spread of plague and particularly the period of the Black Death in Europe from the 1340s until the late 1350s.

The second common thread picks up around the turn of the 19th century when ideas around disease causation begin to provide grounds to call for the end of quarantine as it was deemed ineffective tool and simultaneously economically harmful through the delayed movement of imported goods thus impeding the process of free trade (Maglen 2014; Barnes 2014; Sabhlok et al. 2024). In terms of the theories of disease causation and their connection to arguments for the abolition of quarantine bring us to the pre-germ theory debate between the contagionists and anti-contagionists. The former believed that diseases spread through contact between an infected individual or material and a healthy individual while the latter believed diseases spread through the environment. Specifically, through the breathing in of bad smells or vapors coming from decaying vegetive matter, swamps, or other less pleasant localities. In an average port city of the 18th and 19th centuries such smells were difficult to avoid, particularly near the ports themselves (Boone 2003). Given the belief that diseases were spread via the composition of the local environment rather than contact in the view of anti-contagionists, quarantine was useless against the spread of diseases. From this perspective people arriving by ships at ports were not spreading disease by coming in contact with the healthy population, therefore there was no need to isolate them in quarantine, which at a minimum delayed their journey and at worst exposed them to the disease-causing miasmas by forcing them to remain in a locality near a disease source.

It is in this realm that there is discussion in detail of the quarantine ship's cargo and how these goods were processed (Barnes 2014). Barnes makes the case that while quarantine historiography tends to focus on people, in fact cargo was the primary focus of quarantine activities using the Philadelphia Lazaretto as a case study. He writes that "[t]he stakes were high. Quarantine decisions affected lives and fortunes; their ramifications ranged from inconvenience and boredom to severe financial loss to the spread of illness and death" (Barnes 2014, 81). With so much at stake it is understandable that both public health officials and shipping companies needed to find a balance between delayed movements and economic gain with the preservation of health in the port city. Prevailing ideas of how diseases spread in this pre-bacteriology era provided support for those desiring movement of goods and people to be as smooth as possible.

The third key thread running through much of the literature is that by the 19th century quarantine was a means of maintaining national boundaries and norms between the European nations along with the connection between quarantine and immigration policies/practices in New World ports (Bashford 2016; Maglen 2014). The New World ports that tend to receive the most attention are Australia, albeit usually before the consolidation of the six colonies into a single country, and the United States, both localities being the destination for substantial numbers of immigrants during the 19th and early 20th centuries.

What these three streams of emphasis do not discuss, at least not in detail as it is outside the scope of the work, are the more mundane aspects of quarantine in terms of the location and composition of the facilities themselves. In fact, it seems that that type of information is contained in texts for a more popular audience, albeit one with rather particular interests, than as a part of the academic discourse. For example, in an effort to determine what became of the two artificial quarantine islands for the Port of New York that were in use from the 1870s until 1923, the only sources with some information about their current status are websites about abandoned or lesser known islands around New York City (for example, https://www.untappedcities.com/8-abandoned-islands-near-nyc/) and a little bit on the National Park Service website as they now manage the islands (National Park Service 2020). Nonetheless, the spaces for the quarantine of goods and people were a part of port spaces and the geography of ports until the mid-20th century in some locations. Therefore, as a part of understanding the history of port cities and their environments writ large, it is important to explore these more practical matters of location and composition of quarantine stations in addition to the contexts within which they functioned politically and medically.

Quarantine locations and facilities

Coastal port quarantine spaces generally have at least one feature in common, a lack of contiguity with the port itself. Bashford (2016) refers to the non-contiguous nature of quarantine facilities to the port cities they serve an archipelago of small islands within ports that served this purpose. The lack of adjacency to the port itself and the local community makes logical sense as just like a prison or landfill particularly given ideas of how diseases spread in the 19th century it is a simple matter of "not in my backyard." Generally the facilities regardless of location would include space for passengers to stay the duration of the quarantine and the means of decontaminating the cargo and the vessel either on land or on the ship itself. Depending on when and where, the separation of the healthy and infected passengers varied as well as the variation for passengers of different classes of passage. When exploring these landscapes within the literature it can again be viewed through the three threads already mentioned, those of early quarantine, the English landscape that resisted quarantine, and then in combination with immigration in New World ports. Finding descriptions of these landscapes though is a bit like trying to solve a mystery.

Early facilities

A bit more is discussed with regard to the earlier lazarettos and quarantine stations of the Mediterranean in terms of the buildings and their purposes.

Figure 8.1 Manoel Island, Malta: The Quarantine Station. Etching by A. Benoist after J. Goupy, ca. 1725

Source: Wellcome Collection

For example, Currie (2022) provides short descriptions of the lazarettos in Malta, Corfu and Zakynthos, Venice and Ancona, and Marseilles. The lazaretto in Malta is described as being built on Manoel Island with the permanent structure first being constructed in 1643 with regular improvements over time (Figure 8.1). He writes that "[in] the Malta lazaretto, it is clear that ships could approach and there are two distinct forms – one for the quarantined goods and one with a more open façade to house passengers and crew" (Currie 2022, 19). Here it is clear that this fairly early quarantine station was constructed on an island and thus near, but not adjacent to the port itself. Similarly, Dacome (2024) provides a detailed depiction of the new lazaretto in Ancona, Italy, its construction, and its connections to borderlands, maritime mobility, and port management for the sake of health. In this instance the island for the quarantine station had to be created along with the buildings used to quarantine passengers and goods. While there are more descriptions of the quarantine facilities of Mediterranean ports, typically the composition of the lazaretto is not the focus of the study and therefore is typically included only to support the primary argument.

Anti-quarantine Britain

When trying to determine the location and status of similar quarantine facilities with the United Kingdom, particularly London's port, there seems to be a lack of information and consistent information, more specifically. As the world's largest shipping power, Britain pushed back again the use of quarantine by the 19th century wishing to do away with it on the grounds of anti-contagion theories as it was slowing the movement of goods and thus impacting economic activity through shipping. Krista Maglen (2014) is the most prominent scholar to highlight and discuss the reasoning behind and development of the "English System" which was Britain's alternative to more typical quarantine methods of lazarettos with the creation of the Port Sanitary Authority in 1872. Prior to the new legislation, quarantine for ships arriving in the port of London would keep passengers and crew onboard for between 40 and 60 days along with goods being aired on deck and then placed on land for further airing. Glancing reference is made to other British port cities such as Liverpool and Portsmouth but detailed depictions focus on the capital (Maglen 2002). Following the 1872 Public Health Act, while quarantine remained technically active in law, only passengers with active cases of infectious diseases were hospitalized. The remainder of arrivals were able to disembark and carry on their way while being monitored by the local public health authority in the situation that additional active cases of disease arise. This not only helped to move journeys and trade along at a more acceptable pace, but also better allowed for the separation of the infected from the healthy populations.

A great deal of attention is given to the rules and laws of British quarantine while the discussion of the facilities used and their location is limited if even present. Maglen (2014) makes reference to a lazaretto that was to be built at Chetney Hill but was never completed. Currie (2023) once again provides some additional information about quarantine in London, which involved the use of decommissioned Royal Navy gunships moored in an inlet from the Rivers Medway and Thames and referred to as hospital ships. Figure 8.2 is of the *HMS Dreadnaught*, which, while not a quarantine hospital ship, was a hospital ship for the care of Royal Navy men, and provides an idea of what the quarantine ships would have been like. While discussing Britain, Maglen (2014) acknowledges her focus on London while also alluding to quarantine in Liverpool, but offers no details. Information about the facilities in Liverpool is referenced briefly by Brabin (2020) who focuses on the introduction of smallpox between 1901 and 1903 to Liverpool via its shipping connection with Boston. Here the author includes a photo of a memorial pillar with a plaque describing the isolation hospital that existed between 1875 and 1963 across the River Mersey from the city's port, therefore again not physically adjacent to the port. The plaque describes how the hospital was built to replace the hospital ships in the River Mersey. Considering the importance of Britain to the movement of resources, goods, and passengers during the 18th and 19th centuries along with need to participate in some type of quarantine in order to continue to trade with and stops at other European ports it is interesting that the information on actual facilities is so limited. Perhaps the vagueness stems from having limited facilities as a result of Britain's desire to eliminate quarantine from the port in the first place. What is apparent in the

Figure 8.2 H.M.S. Dreadnought, a hospital ship, being towed to the breakers by tugs. Wood engraving by T. Williams, November 1872

Source: Wellcome Collection

available information is that quarantine in Britain also happened in spaces non-contiguous to their ports be it on a hospital ship in a different part of a river or across the river from the port.

New World ports

When attention shifts to New World ports and quarantine facilities there appears to be both more detail related to some of the major ports such as Sydney and New York and a noticeable lack of information about less prominent yet still active ports such as Baltimore or New Orleans. At times, sickness onboard ships arriving at ports such as Sydney or New York City were grounds to quarantine all passengers onboard regardless of health status. In Sydney this could mean anchoring the ship in a particular part of the harbor and quarantining the infected on the ship while isolating the healthy on land in tents or in the Quarantine Station at North Head completed in 1832 (Foxhall 2011). In New York prior to 1858 this would mean disembarking the ship at the quarantine station, built in 1799, on Staten Island, which at the time was an independent municipality. Both of these ports along with San Francisco feature prominently in literature discussing New World ports, quarantine, and often the connections with immigration. Therefore, each country will be addressed separately below as each has its own specific circumstances. What stands out collectively is again the use of non-contiguous land and in these three cases the preservation of the landscapes today as sights of commemoration.

Sydney

The Quarantine Station at North Head in Sydney was completed in 1832. It provided space to isolate the sick and separate quarters for passengers without symptoms of infectious diseases. It was located on the northern peninsula making up the entrance to Sydney Harbour about 10–15 km from the city center. Therefore, as consistent with most quarantine facilities in a geographically non-contiguous location to the harbor and its daily activities. The most recent sources focused on North Head discuss it as a commemorative landscape (Clarke, Frederick, and Hobbins 2016; Bashford et al. 2016). Comparatively, Foxhall (2011) emphasizes the quarantine station and its role in the immigration journey to New South Wales between 1837 and 1840. Figure 8.3 provides some further insights into the composition of the

Figure 8.3 Sydney, New South Wales: The quarantine station, view from the mainland showing the isolation hospital and the jetty. Reproduction of a photograph, 1880/1910

Source: Wellcome Collection

station with this annotated photo depicting the isolation hospital, quarantine facilities for the healthy and the landing jetty for the arriving ships. Interestingly, the station remains on the landscape, although now on protected land and is currently in use as a hotel, which indicates that the buildings have survived. This is not always the case as will be discussed with regard to New York and other port cities in the United States. The buildings did need to undergo repair after a period of neglect. Perhaps their persistence on the landscape is connected to the fairly recent date for the final closure of the quarantine station, 1984.

New York City and San Francisco

The Port of New York City established its series of quarantine facilities like all of the previous examples on land that was not adjacent to the port and city itself. Two of the three locations for quarantine or at least medical inspection today also serve as commemorative landscapes small or large (Weber 2019; Maddern 2008). The other site is now a bird sanctuary managed by the National Park Service (National Park Service 2020). New York's quarantine history is a great story as the original site was burned to the ground by a mob and, of course, from the late 19th century quarantine, or at least isolation for reportable diseases, was being processed through Ellis Island, which returns us to the theme that connects quarantine with immigration.

In response to a series of yellow fever epidemics that impacted much of the east coast of the United States in the late 18th century, the state government in Albany, New York used eminent domain to convert 30 acres of land on Staten Island into the Port of New York's quarantine station with the first building being completed in 1799. At the time of construction, Staten Island was not yet incorporated into New York City, therefore, in this example not only was the quarantine station at a distance from the port in question, about 24 km from Manhattan, but also located on land adjacent to a separate municipality. While Staten Island is indeed an island, it is large enough to have been home to a number of low-density towns and farming communities, so unlike many other isolation island situations where the island was uninhabited except for the lazaretto, here quarantine was taking place next door to a community. Needless to say the locals were not welcoming to the new neighbors (Weber 2019).

The Staten Island Quarantine Hospital included spaces for the isolation and/or treatment of first and second class passengers and separate smaller spaces for third class passengers to recover from any number of notifiable diseases such as yellow fever, cholera, and smallpox. Weber (2019) and Stephenson (2004) discuss this quarantine hospital with a focus on what is referred to as the Quarantine Wars that led to burning the facility to the ground in 1858. Weber (2019) also discusses how the landscape of this location evolved from the hospital to now a memorial sign by the municipality's courthouse, which commemorates quarantine hospital's cemetery. While the sign commemorates migrants who did not survive the last stage of their journey to the United States, it only mentions the thousands of Irish immigrants who would have passed away at the hospital while not acknowledging immigrants of other nationality who would also did not reach their destination (Weber 2019).

Following the destruction of the Staten Island Quarantine Marine Hospital, new facilities were established on the purpose-built artificial islands just off the coast of Staten Island, Hoffman and Swinburne Islands. These remained in use for quarantine until 1923 and served other purposes after that time (National Park Service 2020). Again following the traditional model of locating lazarettos on harbor islands in use solely for quarantine purposes.

From 1892 Hoffman and Swinburne Islands were used for quarantine in combination with the immigration station opened on Ellis Island. Until 1878 and the passage of the National Quarantine Act, the United States managed port quarantine facilities and legislation at the state level. In the wake of a number of yellow fever epidemics, the most recent of which was in the same year, this act provided means for the then Marine Hospital Service (renamed the Public Health Service in 1912) to oversee and manage all quarantine stations around the nation, although not without controversy (Frierson 2022). In so doing being able to standardize processes across the country. The standardization process took time with some stations being directly managed by the Marine Hospital Service sooner than others (Markel 1974). For example, the quarantine station in Baltimore did not come under the umbrella of the Public Health Service until 1918 (Markel 1974). The 1891 Immigration Act brought immigration processing also under the jurisdiction of the federal government and introduced medical inspection of arriving immigrants for possible medical exclusion. This resulted in port quarantine stations being combined with immigration processing and both the Marine Hospital Service and Immigration Service working together in same space. The facilities constructed from 1892 would have being built with this dual purpose in mind. The most famous of these being Ellis Island in New York Harbor opened in 1892 and secondly Angel Island in San Francisco Harbor opened in 1910.

While perhaps built and intended for effectively the same purpose, the processing of new migrants alongside medical inspection and possible quarantine of new arrivals displaying symptoms of one of the infectious diseases identified for isolation, the operationalization of these goals differed substantially between Ellis Island and Angel Island. This resulted in differences in the composition of the landscapes. A portion of this difference is scale: 12 million immigrants arrived through Ellis Island in the 62 years between 1892 and 1954 while a few hundred thousand to perhaps as many as 1 million individuals entered through Angel Island. The Chinese Exclusion Act of 1882 is one of the reasons for the smaller numbers of immigrants arriving at Angel Island and also a fire burned many of the records in the Administration Building in 1940 resulting in numerical estimates. One result of the scale differential between the two stations is the use of "line medical inspection" at

Ellis Island, which relied on Public Health Service doctors to visually assess the passengers making their way in lines to the Registry Room (Shah 2016; Parascandola 1998). This is in contrast to the more invasive and detailed medical inspections conducted at Angel Island (Shah 2016). Most immigrants spent between two and four hours at Ellis Island. This process only applied to steerage class passengers who were processed through Ellis Island, while doctors would briefly visit first and second class passengers in their cabins when the ship docked at its berth in the port (Parascandola 1998). Shah (2016) describes how on Angel Island medical inspection took longer and the doctors employed more detailed and invasive investigations into arrivals' bodies. This included assessing everything from individuals' naked bodies to using microscopes to check fluids and waste for parasites (Shah 2016). One result of these differing practices was the duration of time that immigrants spent on the respective islands. Most people passing through Ellis Island left within hours unless there was a problem with their paperwork or a need for hospitalization. On Angel Island immigrants stay could be similarly short or could last days, weeks, months, or even years (Shah 2016).

These different medical inspection and immigration processing practices produced two different landscapes. While both sets of facilities were once again at a distance from their respective ports, the variety of buildings included in each location differed. On Ellis Island, a partially artificial island, the primary building was the main hall containing the Registry Room. The island also included a dock, facilities for the overall running of activities, so a power station and restaurant. On the other side of the island was the Hospital Building with all of its wards (Figure 8.4). Angel Island, on the other hand, included not only an administrative building, but also a hospital, detention barracks, cottages for employees, and a power house along with the pier for the arriving ships (Cresswell and Hoskins 2008). Likely the smaller facilities on Ellis Island are also related to the ease with which employees could return to New York City or New Jersey whereas with the detention of hundreds of even healthy individuals at Angel Island there would be more need for residential staff. Additionally, some of the inpatient or detention elements of Ellis Island could have been outsourced to Hoffman and Swinburne Islands, as well.

The commemoration element of Ellis Island is well known after the opening of the Immigration Museum in 1990. The buildings did need substantial restoration after falling into disrepair after the closure of the immigration station in 1954. Today the Immigration Museum tells a version of the American immigration story, but the emphasis is on immigration rather than quarantine or public health or even port history (Maddern 2008). Cresswell and Hoskins (2008) provide a detailed timeline of who maintained the facilities on Angel Island and when in their exploration of the landscape's historical significance. The buildings were left abandoned between 1946 and 1964 when the state of California took over the land. After a lengthy process of being designated a National Historic Landmark in 1997 the buildings were finally renovated, and the Angel Island Immigration Museum was opened in

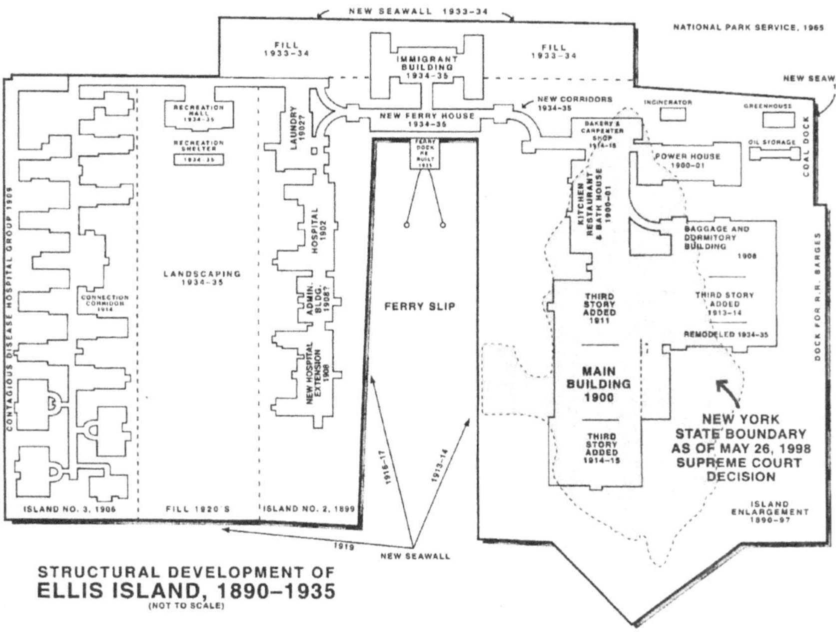

Figure 8.4 Map of the development of Ellis Island between 1890 and 1935, depicting the expansion of buildings and the islands

Source: National Park Service (1965), https://www.nps.gov/elis/learn/historyculture/maps.htm

2022. Again, the emphasis is on immigration and not quarantine on Angel Island. Nonetheless, the museum itself is housed in the old hospital building. Unlike Sydney's North Head Quarantine Station which closed in 1984, the longer period of time between use and renovation for commemorative purposes in both American examples does indicate that a great deal more effort needed to go into the preservation of these landscapes. In all three instances it seems that the restoration of the quarantine facilities themselves was less of a priority with emphasis being placed on migration history.

While the Staten Island Quarantine Hospital and Ellis Island both have some type of commemorative element today, Hoffman and Swinburne Islands were mostly left to decay once they were no longer needed. Both islands served active use by people for some years, but today they are a bird sanctuary, and the buildings are no longer standing (National Park Service 2020). So much like Liverpool's Isolation Hospital, once these spaces were no longer fit for purpose they were either removed from the landscape or allowed to disappear from it. Another example of this erasure from the landscape includes Baltimore. The former's quarantine station was on Leading Point, more than 12 km from Baltimore's Inner Harbor, and was closed in 1961, is now the site of a U.S. Gypsum Plant (Markel 1974).

All of the threads described above are interesting and provide a multitude of insights into the development of public health strategies that utilized the quarantine in order to try and prevent the spread of diseases like plague, cholera, yellow fever, and smallpox across national borders. What does become clear through the sources that do discuss the spatial and compositional aspects of quarantine in more detail are a few commonalities that include being at a distance from the city itself, often on an island, and that most of these landscapes were not maintained after quarantine was discontinued. The exceptions to this latter point are the quarantine and immigration stations that in the late 20th century were renovated and re-opened as museums and landscapes of memory, including Sydney's Quarantine Station, Ellis Island in New York, and Angel Island in San Francisco.

Conclusion

When thinking about quarantine and quarantine stations historically as elements of port cities it quickly becomes clear that we as a general population know more about the underlying concept of the practice than the details of where these facilities were located, what the facilities entailed in terms of buildings and staff, or the diseases listed for quarantine. In terms of location, Bashford quickly makes reference to the usage of harbor islands for quarantine in her introduction to the 2016 edited volume *Quarantine: Local and Global Histories*. Following on from Bashford there is reference in the literature to places such as Angel Island, Staten Island, various islands in Venice, and Tinicum Island near Philadelphia, to name a few (Shah 2016; Frierson 2022; Foxhall 2011; Barnes 2014). These non-contiguous port sites, which were integral to the regional and global movement of goods and people, worked to create a larger port region within the city. The use of hinterland spaces for quarantine activities calls to mind Matthew Gandy's primary argument in his chapter on the building of the Croton Aqueduct in the 2002 book, *Concrete and Clay*. While the book and chapter focus on urban spaces and the natural environment, this particular chapter makes the case for the "capture" of natural resources from non-adjacent parts of New York state, thus making hinterland spaces effectively urbanized or at the extreme end of the line of thinking a part of New York City itself. While islands and other spaces used for quarantine were usually closer than the 65 km distance of the southern reaches of the Croton watershed, they are nonetheless spaces that were converted to a public health use related to movement of people and goods through a maritime port. Conceptually, this increases the physical and regional size of the port to encompass non-contiguous spaces.

Altogether, the history of quarantine and physical manifestation of the practice provide an interesting perspective on the function of port cities and the manifestations of public health practices. Quarantine may no longer operate as it did between the 14th and early 20th centuries, but it certainly returned to our vocabulary through the COVID-19 pandemic. The location of facilities maintained a fairly consistent geography of being in the waters near the associated port, usually on islands. Not surprisingly resistance to slowing down the movement of people and goods via quarantine led Britain to find their alternative to quarantine in light of anti-contagionist theories of disease causation. This is not so different from when some countries offered travelers fewer or shorter self-isolation times if they had been vaccinated against COVID-19. New World ports found ways of connecting quarantine and medical inspection to immigration processes and used this as a means of policing borders and deciding who was or was not deemed welcome with these new countries. While this chapter concretely discussed a number of port cities and their quarantine facilities, so many more ports also maintained quarantine facilities, but they are not as prominent in the literature. This raises questions about the geography of those quarantine stations and why they are not discussed as concretely in the literature. There is a rich opportunity to explore both these prominent examples but more importantly the somewhat overlooked ones, such as Boston, and to map, measure, and catalog the locations, buildings, and what happened once they were no longer fit for use. These are interesting ports and public health landscapes that can tell us a lot about the priorities and concerns of ports and the nations to which they belong.

References

Barnes D. (2014) Cargo, 'infection,' and the logic of quarantine in the nineteenth century. *Bulletin of the History of Medicine*, 88(1): 75–101.

Bashford A. (2016) Maritime quarantine: Linking old world and new world histories. In: Bashford A. (Ed.), *Quarantine: Local and Global Histories*. London: Palgrave, pp. 1–12.

Bashford A., Hobbins P., Clarke A., Frederick U.K. (2016) Geographies of commemoration: Angel Island, San Francisco and North Head, Sydney. *Journal of Historical Geography*, 52: 16–25.

Boone C.G. (2003) Obstacles to infrastructure provision: The struggle to build comprehensive sewer works in Baltimore. *Historical Geography*, 31: 151–168.

Brabin B. (2020) An analysis of the United States and United Kingdom smallpox epidemics (1901–5) – The special relationship that tested public health strategies for disease control. *Medical History*, 64(1): 1–31.

Bynum W.F. (2013) The rise of science in medicine, 1850–1913. In: Bynum W.F., Hardy A., Jacyna S., Lawrence C., Tansey E.M. (Tilli) (Eds.), *The Western Medical Tradition 1800 to 2000*. Cambridge: Cambridge University Press, pp. 111–239.

Clarke A., Frederick U.K., Hobbins P. (2016) Sydney's landscape of quarantine. In: Bashford A. (Ed.), *Quarantine: Local and Global Histories*. London: Palgrave, pp. 175–194.

Cresswell T., Hoskins G. (2008) Place, persistence, and practice: Evaluating historical significance at Angel Island, San Francisco, and Maxwell Street, Chicago. *Annals of the Association of American Geographers*, 98(2): 392–413.

Currie J.M. (2022) Isolation, quarantine, infection control. In: Bliss A., Kopec D. (Eds.), *Architectural Factors for Infection and Disease Control*. New York: Routledge, pp. 13–29.

Dacome L. (2024) An island in the city: Ancona's new lazaretto as a medical, political, and religious borderland. *Eighteenth-Century Studies*, 57(3): 325–352.

Foxhall K. (2011) Fever, immigration and quarantine in New South Wales, 1837–1840. *Social History of Medicine*, 24(3): 624–642.

Frierson J.G. (2022) *Guarding the Golden Gate: A History of the U.S. Quarantine Station in San Francisco Bay*. Las Vegas: University of Nevada Press.

Gandy M. (2002) *Concrete and Clay: Reworking Nature in New York City*. Cambridge: Massachusetts Institute of Technology Press.

Maddern F.J. (2008) Spectres of migration and the ghosts of Ellis Island. *Cultural Geographies*, 15(3): 359–381.

Maglen K. (2002) 'The first line of defence': British quarantine and the port sanitary authorities in the nineteenth century. *Social History of Medicine*, 15(3): 413–428.

Maglen K. (2003) Politics of quarantine in the 19th century. *JAMA: The Journal of the American Medical Association*, 290(21): 2873.

Maglen K. (2014) *The English System: Quarantine, Immigration and the Making of the Port Sanitary Zone*. Manchester University Press.

Markel H. (1974) A gate to the city: The Baltimore quarantine station, 1918–28. *Public Health Reports*, 110(2): 218–219.

National Park Service (2020) Hoffman and Swinburne Islands, https://www.nps.gov/gate/learn/historyculture/hoffman-and-swinburne-islands.htm

Parascandola J. (1998) Doctors at the gate: PHS at Ellis Island. *Public Health Reports*, 113: 83–86.

Sabhlok S., Frijters P., Foster G., Bhattacharya J., Joffe A.R. (2024) The failed history of quarantines, and its implications for public health. IZA Discussion Papers, No. 17100. Bonn.

Shah N. (2016) The empire of medical investigation on Angel Island, California. In: Bashford A. (Ed.), *Quarantine: Local and Global Histories*. London: Palgrave, pp. 103–120.

Stephenson K. (2004) The quarantine war: The burning of the New York marine hospital in 1858. *Public Health Reports*, 119(1): 79–92.

Weber A. (2019) A forgotten quarantine landscape. *Material Culture*, 51(2): 18–41.

9 Health and disease in European port cities, ca. 1850–1930

Jörg Vögele and Grażyna Liczbińska

Portals of death

In the 19th and early 20th century European port cities served as the nexus and hubs of the growing world economy. As a consequence of this function, port cities were invariably prone to an increased risk of exposure, particularly to infectious diseases. Many of the predominant epidemic diseases, such as plague, cholera, typhoid and yellow fever, followed trade routes and were imported via port cities, which, in turn, accelerated disease diffusion in coastal areas and dependent hinterlands. At the same time, substantial levels of in-migration, the predominance of casual labor, which resulted in a high population density in the areas close to the harbor, aggravated the latent exposure risks of the indigenous population to endemic and epidemic diseases and led to a high background mortality. In this sense port cities can be perceived as "portals of death", as "gateways of disease", and an analysis of health in port cities must take into account as the global as well as the local perspective, in a modern phrase it has to focus on the "glocal approach" – which is superbly reflected by the cover illustration of Tony Lanes's History of Liverpool.

With the acceleration of trade and mass migration during the first wave of globalization the diffusion of pathogens increased and accelerated – and included those of infectious diseases with a short incubation period (such as cholera) and a high infection rate. Originating in the Ganges delta, cholera spread from there and swept through Europe from the 1830s onwards in various pandemic waves until the early 20th century (Figure 9.1) (Haeser, 1882; Sticker, 1912; Spink, 1978). In the first wave, cholera was imported via ships to St. Petersburg in 1831 and claimed more than 6,000 casualties within the region until the end of the year (Olzscha, 1940). In April, cholera had reached Warsaw, and in May, Gdansk/Danzig and other German port cities of the Baltic and the North Sea (Creighton, 1965). From there the disease moved further westward along the trade routes via rivers and coastal areas toward English and Scottish port cities and from there – with the Irish emigration – to North and Middle America as well as to Canada. In the south-west Spain, Portugal and Northern Africa were affected. Another

DOI: 10.4324/9781003639589-12

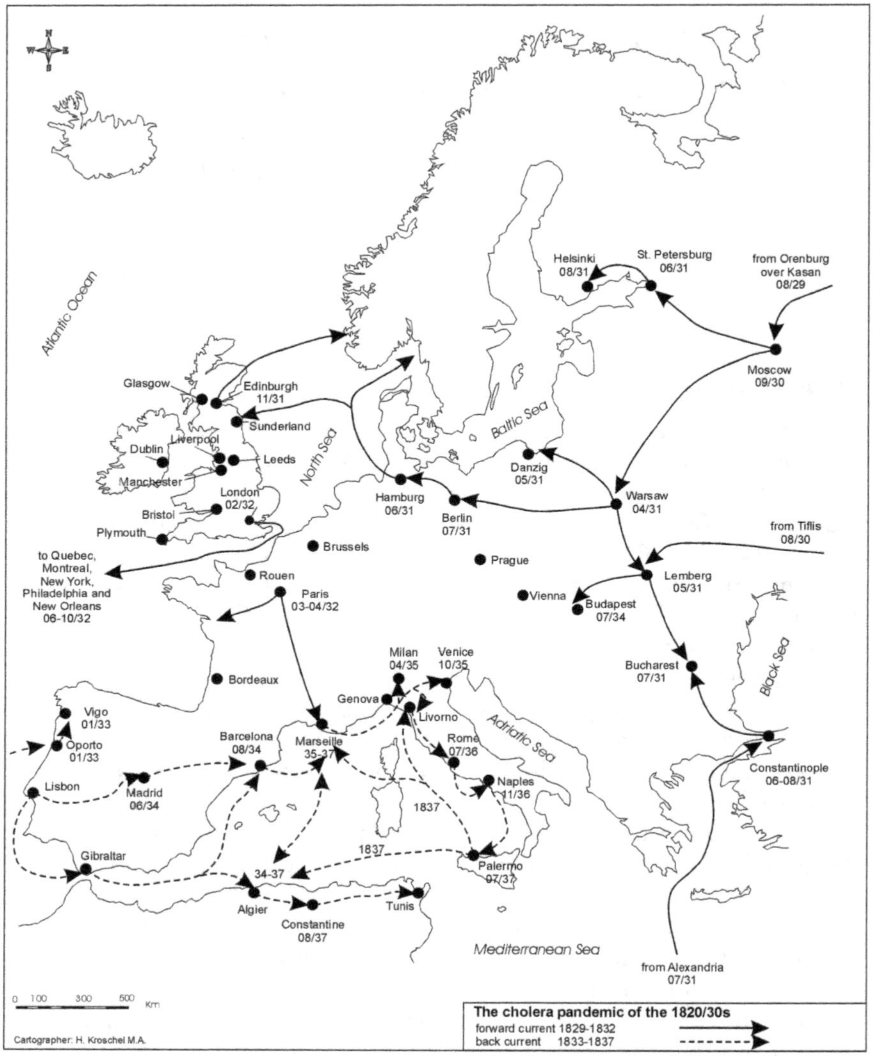

Figure 9.1 Cholera pandemic in Europe, 1829–1837

Source: Data collected from the Institute for the History of Medicine, University of Düsseldorf

highly affected area was southern France, particularly Marseille and Toulon; from there ships carried the pathogen to Italian port cities such as Genoa, Torino, Florence and Livorno (Haeser, 1882, Stolberg, 1995). Similarly, the subsequent pandemics followed the trade and shipping routes with devastating effects to the population of port cities: Hamburg, for example, was heavily affected by cholera in the 1890s, with more than 8,000 victims within six weeks (Evans, 1987). The large emigration ports were particularly at risk.

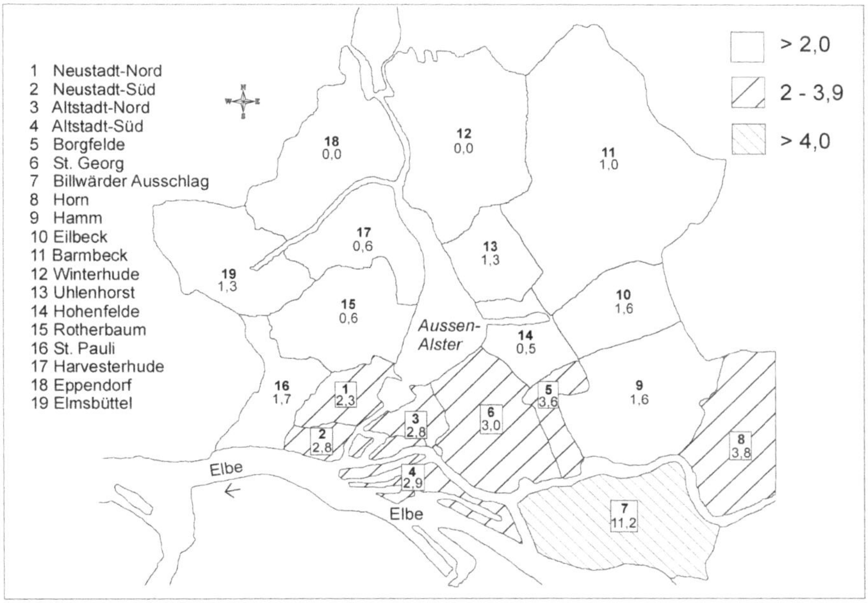

Figure 9.2 Cholera death rates in Hamburg City Districts (per 1,000 living), 1873

Source: Statistik des Hamburgischen Staates 7 (1875), pp. 49–50

In Naples, the most important transit port in the Mediterranean for emigrants to Argentina and the US, cholera demanded about 20,000 casualties in 1884 (Snowden, 1995); Liverpool, the classic English emigration port, was repeatedly hit by severe epidemics. Differentiated within the city, the close connection to trade and shipping is also evident in the fact that the districts located directly on the water were often the most affected by cholera or typhus epidemics: in Odessa, for example, the Peresip district, in Hamburg the Neustadt, the Altstadt and St. Georg (Figure 9.2). In Liverpool in 1832, 5,000 of the 230,000 residents became ill, of which 1,523 ultimately died, most of them in the basement apartments or "back-to-back houses" near the harbor. Over 2,000 deaths were registered in Marseille in 1834/1835, mostly children and dock workers (Bourdelais and Raulot, 1987).

So, port cities were notorious as places of intrusion and profusion of worldwide threatening acute epidemics like plague and cholera. Yet, not only the scandalized killers represented a threat, but also "ordinary", rather endemic infections or local epidemics, like typhoid fever, typhus or malaria received more attention. At the heights of imperialism many ports on the way to and also in the colonies had newly been built – mainly to subject the old or even newly gained territories to a global economic exchange, where the colonies produced the basic materials, which were processed in the industrialized countries into products and then sold to the colonies. The growth of steam shipping accelerated these developments even further. Thus, as the commercial web became more densely woven, not only did worldwide commerce increase but also the spread of pathogens and deadly infectious diseases became more intense (Echenberg, 2007; Harrison, 2012; Vögele and Umehara, 2015).

Disease and social class

The economic prosperity resulting from the expanding maritime trade led to a remarkable population growth in the port cities and made them core elements in the European urbanization process. Marketing and trade were important factors that affected the pattern of urban expansion or decline, and ports, after capital cities, frequently registered the greatest growth (Lee, 1998; Lawton and Lee, 2002). The dominance of trade had far-reaching consequences for the development of the port cities, as domestic and foreign trade provided only a small basis for the broad scale of industrialization. As a consequence trade and finance remained the economic basis for many port cities. Rather, the local economic structure was determined by the typical shipping industry, and in addition to this, by the processing of goods as well as banking and insurance companies. No substantial diversification of the industry took place. The economic sectors remained extremely one-sided and essentially depended on imported raw materials. As a result, port cities were extremely dependent on the routes and the structures of the emerging world market. Trade and finance remained the economic basis of Naples, the largest and most populous maritime city in the Mediterranean. In Constantinople, the concentration of commercial and financial activities even increased after the economic collapse of the Ottoman Empire, which brought complete dependence on foreign capital. The dominance of grain exports prevented Odessa from transforming from a trading to an industrial city. At the beginning of the 20th century it was said about Liverpool: "There is probably no city of anything like equal size in which so small a proportion of the population is maintained by permanent and stable industrial work" (Muir, 1907).

This meant that the port cities became extremely dependent on the routes of world trade: with the entry of American grain onto the European market, Ukraine was replaced as the granary hub, and thus Odessa as the central export port. Northern Europe turned away from the Mediterranean and looked across the Atlantic, important grain markets shifted from Marseilles to Le Havre and Nantes, from London to Liverpool. General economic development – especially in the urban hinterland – also played a central role: the fate of the port of Liverpool, for example, was closely linked to Lancashire's cotton industry, and when the textile manufacturing crisis began there, it had a lasting impact on the city.

The wealth that arose with the rise of the port cities remained extremely unevenly distributed: it was limited to the few merchants, while "… the great majority of the inhabitants had little share of this golden shower" (Muir,

1907). On the contrary, many social problems that manifested themselves in the 18th and 19th centuries seemed to culminate in the port cities. The dominant role that the port played for the city shaped the local labor market structure: work on the docks required no qualifications, which created a labor market with low wages and unskilled employment. Casual work was another feature: sailors were only hired for the duration of a passage, ship repairs were limited to the short time a ship was in port, and finally dock workers were only hired to load or unload a specific cargo. In 1913, in the port of Hamburg, there were said to be an average of 32 job placements per employee per year. According to the 1921 census, 20% of Liverpool's male workers remained without permanent employment, compared to just 5% in neighboring Manchester (Lane, 1987).

Adding irregular work, moving goods between ships, warehouses and the railway network, carried out by unskilled workers, including around 25,000 dock workers, was the main source of income in Liverpool in the early 20th century. At the same time, the dominance of unskilled and irregular work meant that women and children had to contribute disproportionately to the family income. While the importance of child labor decreased as compulsory schooling became more practical, the contribution of married women to the family income played a crucial role. Especially in seafaring families, the wives had a significant responsibility for the family due to the frequent absence of the men. Since there was a fundamental lack of appropriate employment opportunities for women in the regular labor market – until after the Second World War, "domestic service" was the main employment for women in Liverpool– they were pushed into the informal labor market (Harrison, 1904; Ayers, 1990). So women often had no choice but to contribute to the family income in other ways: they worked as laundresses, sewed, did handicrafts, helped out in the household, chopped and sold firewood. Prostitution also needs to be mentioned in sailortowns.

The specific labor market structure in turn influenced the settlement structure and housing conditions, as it forced those affected to live near the port, always looking for casual and at least short-term employment. Dense, low-standard residential areas are therefore typical of many port cities in the 19th century. In Liverpool, this led to the highest population density in England around the middle of the 19th century (Taylor, 1974). The city was notorious for its high proportion of "court houses" (tenements) and basement apartments near the docks. In his famous report on the situation of the working class in England (1844), Friedrich Engels stated that a fifth of the population, more than 45,000 people, lived in cramped, dark, damp and poorly ventilated basement apartments, of which there were almost 8,000 in the city (Engels, 1892). In 1880, 70,000 people are said to have lived in "court houses" that were actually considered uninhabitable (Waller, 1981). In Hamburg, dock workers and day laborers in particular remained in the notorious "Gängeviertel", while many craftsmen and industrial workers moved to the new residential areas on the outskirts of the city. When Robert Koch visited Hamburg in the course of the Cholera epidemic in 1892, he remarked that in no other city he had come across such unhealthy dwelling, such plague-spots, such breeding place of infection. Gentleman, he concluded, "I forget that I am in Europe" (Meine Herren, ich vergesse, dass ich in Europa bin) (Evans, 1987). It was only after the cholera epidemic of 1892 and the dock workers' strike of 1896/1897 that it was finally decided to demolish these quarters.

Epidemics and pandemics, therefore, hit a densely packed, emaciated city population. Strong population growth and geographical expansion options limited by the economic structure led to cramped living conditions, which, together with the low standard of living, resulted in exorbitantly high death rates. High unemployment, poor living conditions in slums, a lack of water supply and sewerage were just some of the problems that created an ideal breeding ground for epidemics and at the same time ensured high "background mortality". Even without taking crisis mortality into account, life expectancy in port cities was often low. Naples was one of the unhealthiest European cities; Liverpool had one of the highest death rates in England until the 20th century (Figure 9.3) (Vögele, 1998).

Not only were the big "killers" of the time, such as tuberculosis, responsible for this, but almost all fatal diseases resulted in drastic excess mortality among the inhabitants. This particularly affected adult men who were exposed to an increased risk of death due to poor and dangerous working conditions on land and at sea. High migration rates and a high proportion of unmarried young men went hand in hand with a high level of prostitution, encouraged by the mentioned monostructural orientation of the labor

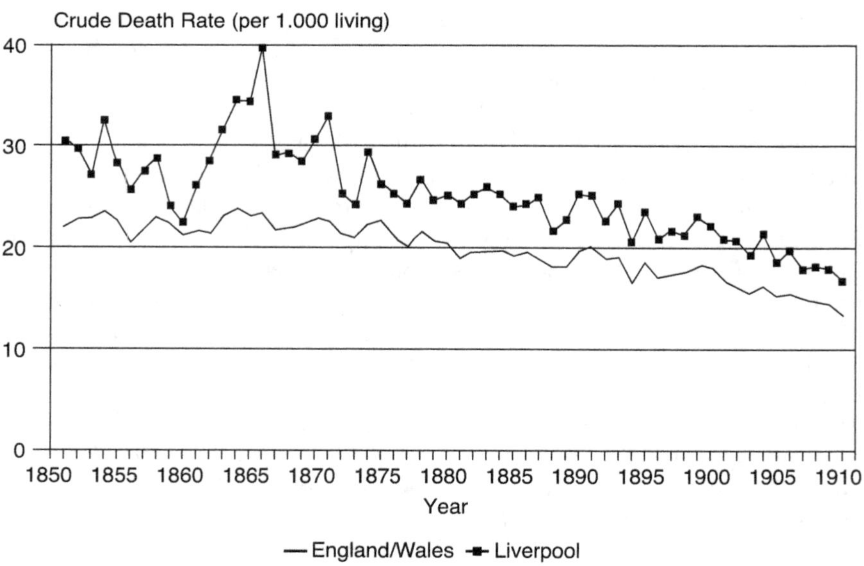

Figure 9.3 Crude death rates in Liverpool and England and Wales, 1851–1910

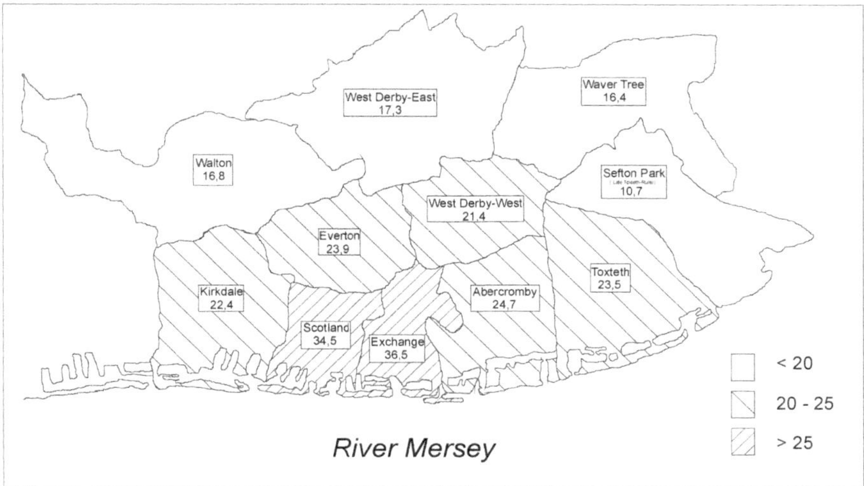

Figure 9.4 Crude death rates in Liverpool Districts (per 1,000 Living), 1900

Source: Report on the Health of the City of Liverpool during 1900. Liverpool Health Department

market toward the port, which made it more difficult for women to access the regular labor market. The result was an increased incidence of sexually transmitted diseases. Another characteristic was generally high infant and child mortality. In the mid-19th century, less than half of all children born in Liverpool reached the age of ten.

At the same time, many ports were characterized by flexible labor markets, a strong reliance on casual work, extensive in-migration and a broad ethnic mix. Female participation in the official labor market was low; however, women were burdened with a multitude of tasks to contribute to the family income. Prostitution was a typical element of port cities. This narrow structure of the labor market had a profound impact on the settlement structure and the living conditions. The constant search for immediate and short-time work in the docks forced the people concerned to live close to the ports in often densely populated, over-crowed city districts near the waterfront, which again increased the risk of acute and also chronic infectious diseases, such as tuberculosis, and proffered additionally a high background mortality risk among the population of port cities, with particularly high death rates in the inner city districts near the port – as is shown for the crude death rates in Figure 9.4 for Liverpool in 1900.

Public health

In European port cities, the dominance of merchant capital directly affected the contemporary response to public health issues and had a profound impact on the selection and implementation of specific strategies. On the one hand the need to confront health risks was initially apparent in port cities; on the other hand there was an unusually high dependency on charity and philanthropy, and a general absence of collective commitment to social welfare provision (Muir, 1907). Beyond the functioning of the business, merchants, as world citizens had only limited interest in local affairs.

At the same time, any interruption of trade and commerce should be avoided. Traditional methods of state intervention, such as quarantine or isolation (Cordon Sanitaire), which were still predominant at the combat of the 1830/1831 cholera pandemic, became increasingly contra-productive within the framework of a modern economy, based on the free exchange of goods and services. Max von Pettenkofer, an influential Munich-based hygienist and the main protagonist of experimental hygiene, claimed that infectious diseases were the result of miasmatic evaporations from the soil. He recommended the control of groundwater via sanitation to avoid miasmatic diseases, such as cholera and typhoid fever, whereas quarantine measures were not helpful and therefore not necessary. He emphasized that an interruption of trade, in order to stop the diffusion of cholera, was a greater vice than the cholera itself, and that most people would prefer to be exposed to an epidemic than to suffer a substantial restriction of their living standard (von Pettenkofer, 1873). In this sense, his public health approach was ideal for trade oriented cites in the rising world economy.

Following similar considerations, many port cities of the 19th century suffered a critical shortage of medical supply and public health devices (Hietala, 1987). It was only hesitantly that these cities developed a modern professional administration, and specific measures were mostly introduced when they were related to trade and commerce. In many places, tropical medical schools were installed rather to protect European port cities from the intrusion of exotic colonial diseases then to fight the diseases at loco (Power, 1999). The lucrative emigration business in Bremen, for example, encouraged the municipal officials to establish health examinations and controls particularly where Eastern European trans-migration was concerned (Leidinger, 2000). In contrast, measures which run contrary to commercial interests were savagely blocked, as, for example plans to establish public baths in the port area of Liverpool (Sheard, 1993). Similar problems arose in Hamburg. The city had an early central water supply; however, no appropriate filter plant was installed. Hamburg's merchant elite was orientated toward Max von Pettenkofer's experimental hygiene, and considered the erection of a costly filter plant unnecessary and superfluous. Consequently, Hamburg became the only large European city to fall victim of the great cholera epidemic of 1892 with more than 8,000 deaths (Evans, 1987; Vögele, 1998). In the wake of the epidemic a filter plant was constructed in day and night shifts in record time. Against this background cost-benefit calculations, on the basis of Pettenkofer's human capital economy became increasingly applied in the years to follow: A total loss of 430 million marks was offset by the seemingly modest costs of 22.6 million marks for the waterworks equipped with a filter system in the following year (Gottstein, 1929). In addition, city districts were renovated, and further hygienic measures were taken. Since the city was spared further cholera epidemics, it can be concluded that the great cholera epidemic accelerated Hamburg's transformation into a modern trading metropolis.

In Naples, all plans to improve the city's environment, which were elaborated due to earlier cholera epidemics, became diluted or even completely negated by mismanagement or corruption. As a consequence, there was no protection when cholera returned to Italy in 1910 and 1911. As city officials were afraid of financial losses – Naples being the most important Mediterranean transition point for emigrants to Argentina and the US – and tried to camouflage the outbreak of the epidemic (Snowden, 1995).

All in all, however, the days of miasmatic theories had been counted, and municipal governments returned to classic measures to control disease, such as disinfection, cordon sanitaire, quarantine and isolation. The cartoon of Friedrich Graetz, publishes in Puck Magazine in 18th of July 1883 depicts "The Kind of assisted emigrant we can not afford to admit", where a skeletal figure in Turkish clothing, carrying a scythe, with a belt labeled "cholera", sails toward land, while a battery armed with the disinfectant carbolic acid and a line of men place themselves between the immigrant's ship and land (Figure 9.5).

Figure 9.5 "The Kind of assisted emigrant we cannot afford to admit"

Source: PUCK Magazine, 18th of July 1883. Public Domain

In the course of the 20th century, the situation changed fundamentally. First of all, with the end of the traditional passenger ships during the 1930s, an important economic base of many port cities disappeared. Then, the structure of labor-intensive and time-consuming port work changed with the replacement of traditional cargo ships in the 1960s. The new container ships enabled faster loading and unloading with significantly lower personnel costs, but required well-trained workers. Economic activities in the port changed and at the same time the port increasingly withdrew from the city. The port and port city decoupled economically, socially and epidemiologically. Today, in the age of Covid and other modern infectious diseases, the epidemiologic focus is directed toward airports as the new hubs of world traffic.

Summary and conclusion

Interactions between socioeconomic change and the average health status of a population were clearly manifested in the European port cities, which developed into hubs of the emerging European world trade in the 19th century. On the one hand, they were gateways for plagues and epidemics that moved along trade routes and migration flows. On the other hand, the socioeconomic situation of the population in the port cities resulted in increased background mortality: high mobility, dangerous working conditions, casual work, low living standards and poor and cramped living conditions caused death rates to rise. Those residents who could have politically shaped the health situation through appropriate measures had long since become independent of the specific urban living conditions. The merchants who had the power to shape politics had little interest in a functioning urban environment because their capital was based primarily on international maritime trade. Immigration and emigration in the port cities remained largely unregulated; the only regulation was economic necessity. Public health measures fluctuated and often had to find a balance between control (quarantine) and the free movement of goods and people. All in all, many port cities can be conceived as archetype places where the origins of modern health conditions and modern public health strategies can be analyzed.

References

Ayers P. (1990) The hidden economy of dockland families: Liverpool in the 1930s. In: Hudson P., Lee W. R. (Eds.), *Women's Work and the Family Economy in Historical Perspective*. Manchester, pp. 271–290.

Bourdelais P., Raulot J. Y. (1987) *Une peur bleue: histoire du choléra en France, 1832–1854*. Paris: Payot.

Creighton C. (1965) *A History of Epidemics in Britain*, 2 Bde. Cambridge 1894 and London 1965 (2), Bd. 2.

Echenberg M. (2007) *Plague Ports. The Global Urban Impact of Bubonic Plague, 1894–1901*. New York: NYU Press.

Engels F. (1892) *The Condition of the Working-Class in England in 1844*. London, UK: Swan Sonnenschein & Co.

Evans R. (1987) *Death in Hamburg. Society and Politics in the Cholera Years 1830–1910*. 1st Ed. Oxford University Press.

Gottstein A. (1929) *Die Lehre von den Epidemien*. Berlin: Springer.

Haeser H. (1882) *Lehrbuch der Geschichte der Medizin und der Epidemischen Krankheiten*, Vol. 3. Jena: Fischer.

Harrison A. (1904) *Women's Trades in Liverpool*. Liverpool: University Press of Liverpool.

Harrison M. (2012) *Contagion. How Commerce Has Spread Disease*. New Heaven.

Hietala M. (1987) *Services and Urbanization at the Turn of the Century. The Diffusion of Innovations*. Helsinki: Suomen Historiallinen Seura.

Lane T. (1987) *Liverpool. City of the Sea*. London: Lawrence & Wishart Ltd.

Lawton R., Lee R. (Eds.) (2002) *Population and Society in Western European Port Cities, c. 1650–1939*. Liverpool: University Press of Liverpool.

Lee R. (1998) The socio-economic and demographic characteristics of port cities: A typology for comparative analysis. *Urban History*, 25: 147–172.

Leidinger B. (2000) Auswanderergeschäft und Gesundheitspolitik – Auswanderungskontrollen in der Allgemeinen Krankenanstalt Bremen um 1900. In: Vögele J., Woelk W. (Eds.), *Stadt, Krankheit und Tod. Zur Geschichte städtischer Gesundheitsverhältnisse während der Epidemiologischen Transition* (vom 18. bis ins frühe 20. Jahrhundert). Berlin, pp. 383–397.

Muir R. (1907) *A History of Liverpool*. London.

Olzscha R. (1940) *Die Epidemiologie und Epidemiographie der Cholera in Rußland*. Berlin.

Power H.J. (1999) *Tropical Medicine in the Twentieth Century. A History of the Liverpool School of Tropical Medicine 1898–1990*. London.

Sheard S. (1993) Nineteenth century public health. A study of Liverpool, Belfast and Glasgow. Unpublished Ph.D.-thesis, University of Liverpool.

Snowden F.M. (1995) *Naples in the Time of Cholera. 1884–1911*. Cambridge.

Spink W.W. (1978) *Infectious Diseases. Prevention and Treatment in the Nineteenth and Twentieth Centuries*. Minnesota.

Sticker G. (1912) *Abhandlungen aus der Seuchengeschichte und Seuchenlehre*, Bd. 2. Gießen: Die Cholera.

Stolberg M. (1995) *Die Cholera im Großherzogtum Toskana. Zur historischen Wissenssoziologie einer tödlichen Seuche*. Landsberg/Lech.

Taylor I.C. (1974) The insanitary housing question and tenement dwellings in nineteenth-century Liverpool. In: Sutcliffe A. (Ed.), *Multi-Storey Living. The British Working-Class Experience*. London, pp. 41–87.

Vögele J. (1998) *Urban Mortality Change in England and Germany, 1870–1910*. Liverpool.

Vögele J., Umehara H. (Eds.) (2015) *Gateways of Disease. Public Health in European and Asian Port Cities at the Birth of the Modern World in the Late 19th and Early 20th Century*. Göttingen.

von Pettenkofer M. (1873) *Was Man gegen die Cholera thun kann*. Munich.

Waller P.J. (1981) *Democracy and Sectarianism*. Liverpool.

Part 3

Measuring the health impacts of ports and shipping

10 Impact of shipping on atmospheric concentrations of fine and ultrafine particles in coastal areas

Daniele Contini and Eva Merico

Introduction

More than 80% of global trade volumes are carried by sea, with a rapid growth from 3.7 billion tonnes in 1980 to 12 billion tonnes in 2021 as total volume of shipping transportation (UNCTAD, 2022). Unlike airports and other industrial areas of emissions, most of the ports are urban, being usually placed near the city centre (Ducruet et al., 2024).

Currently, several aspects have been discussed on environmental and health issues in port cities in the past two decades (Carpenter and Lozano, 2020; Wagner, 2019; Zheng et al., 2020) such as: the green transformation of industrial maritime transport, industrial ecology, environmental conflicts (Bartlomiejski, 2016), urban vulnerability in port cities, the sustainability of port and port-city plans and stakeholder perspectives on the sustainable development of port cities (Lam and Yap, 2019).

Although ports and related activities can favour the development of the territory in economic, commercial and tourist terms, they are also pollution sources since they operate continuously throughout the year. Because of this, daily emission sources are from ships, trains and diesel-burning trucks that transport goods to and from ports.

The 2020 global Fourth IMO Greenhouse Gas (GHG) study projects a strong growth of shipping activity up to 2050, with GHG emission levels ranging from 90% to 150% of 2008 levels regardless of the measures currently in force.

The impact of maritime traffic and port activities on atmospheric pollutant concentrations is certainly not negligible, especially in areas closest to ship docking piers. The coastal population is at high density and more exposed to port activities emissions than from other sea transportation processes (Mueller et al., 2023). In fact, vessel operations such as hotelling, manoeuvring and cruising operations in harbour areas generate a large share of local and global pollution, external costs and public health issues (Viana et al., 2020), leading to deterioration of air quality and increasing the risk of illness and death for port city residents (i.e., affecting average life expectancy). However, the different jurisdictions, the continuing increase in marine

DOI: 10.4324/9781003639589-14

port operations, and the scarcity or lack of regulations to control emissions suggest the need to increasing efforts at all levels, from institutions such as the International Maritime Organization (IMO), the International Association of Ports and Harbors (IAPH) and the European Seaports Organization (ESPO), to promote sustainability in ports through a broader environmental vision that encompasses both climate change and health issues.

State-of-the-art shipping emissions studies

An in-depth understanding of the complex characteristics of ship-combustion products can help to identify viable ship-related pollutants measurement techniques and instrumentation for marine engines, thereby enhancing emission regulation.

The most used ship fuel, HFO (Heavy Fuel Oil), generates a high amount of fine particles (diameter <0.3 μm), ultrafine particles (UFPs, diameter <0.1 μm) and nanoparticles (diameter <0.05 μm), mainly composed of Organic Carbon (OC), Elemental Carbon (EC), transition metals, Polycyclic Aromatic Hydrocarbons (PAHs) and nitro-PAHs. Increased VOCs and SO_2 emissions result in the formation of secondary particles via nucleation and condensation processes (Figure 10.1). Moreover, particle size distribution within the plume of ships may cover a size range from nanoparticles (5 nm) to coarse particles (3 μm) (Merico et al., 2016).

Over the past 20 years, different methods are complementary and ideally all of them are needed to achieve a solid knowledge of aerosol emissions from ships and to provide useful input on how to develop legislation and

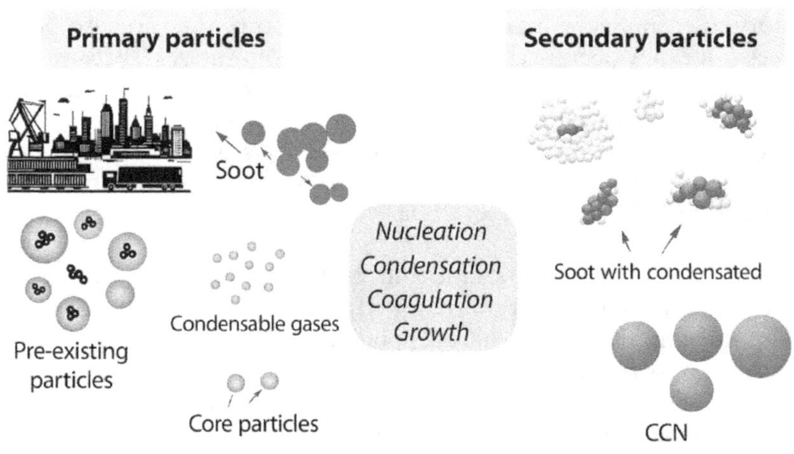

Figure 10.1 Exhaust emission-related particle types – primary particles (left) as particles are in the hot exhaust, these include delayed primary particles, and secondary particles (right) formed from gaseous emissions (organics and sulphates) after atmospheric oxidation and nucleation/condensation processes

technology. In particular, the following approaches are typical: (i) experimental observations with various methodologies: laboratory engine studies, on board measurements on an individual ship running at different operating conditions, measurements using aircrafts/drones or ships to follow individual plumes, and stationary measurements in environments affected by ship activities with application of source apportionment approaches such as receptor models (Contini et al., 2011; Gobbi et al., 2020; Merico et al., 2016, 2017; Murena et al., 2018; Prati et al., 2015); (ii) the use of air quality models (Aulinger et al., 2016; Deniz and Kilic, 2010; Nunes et al., 2020; Tang et al., 2020; Ramacher et al., 2020) and (iii) emission inventory analysis (Russo et al., 2018). In recent years, the availability of detailed shipping information through the Automatic Identification System (AIS) has allowed to infer emissions at high temporal and spatial resolution (Li et al., 2016; Merico et al., 2019).

Current mitigation policies and strategies

From a regulatory point of view, the reference is Annex VI of the MARPOL 73/78 Convention by the IMO, entered into force in 2005 and signed by 97 countries representing about 97% of the global fleet's tonnage. It set global limits on maximum Fuel Sulphur Content (FSC) and NO_x emissions from ships of above 400 GT (gross tonnage). Briefly, the MARPOL treaty establishes: zones where the FSC was limited to 0.1% by mass after January 1, 2015, called Sulphur Emission Control Areas (SECAs), that includes North America, the United States, the Caribbean Sea, the Baltic Sea and the North Sea; global waters outside the regions mentioned above, where the regulation of FSC to below 0.5% became effective on January 1, 2020. The 2020 Fourth IMO GHG Study aimed to reduce the carbon intensity of international shipping, stressing the importance of renewable energy, alternative fuels and technological development. The goal is to reach the net-zero GHG emissions by 2050, although the IMO Initial Strategy was the reduction of GHG emissions from ships, by at least 50% by 2050 compared to 2008 (Di Natale and Carotenuto, 2015).

Alternative mitigation measures are allowed, also in combination, to reduce shipping emissions using exhaust gas cleaners (Marine Exhaust Carbon Capture Systems for reducing CO_2 and SOx emissions) (Stec et al., 2021), alternative fuels, i.e., Methanol (Helgason et al., 2020), Ammonia (NH_3) (Hansson et al., 2020), hydrogen (H_2) (Sürer and Arat, 2022; Long et al., 2022) and other technological and operational solutions to apply on board. The use of new fuels, such as ammonia (NH_3), although offering some advantages, implies other negative effects (i.e., potentially higher secondary particulate formation compared to HFO) due to production, bunkering activity and fugitive emissions (Rathod et al., 2023). Contrarily, cold-ironing (i.e. furnishing electricity on shore) may correspondingly lead to significant cuts, at local scale, of 3%, 12% and 25%–30% in $PM_{2.5}$, SO_2 and NO_2 emissions by 2040 (Jonson et al., 2019).

In this perspective, European ports are recognized ahead of North American and Asian ones in terms of active policies and programmes for emission reduction and energy efficiency improvement (Alamoush et al., 2020; Iris and Lam, 2019). Europe, which has the highest density of metropolitan harbours (areas with a concentration of population, socio-economic activities, traffic volume – notably containers, and GHG emissions), is recognized as a fertile ground for actions promoting port city sustainability (Ducruet et al., 2024).

Research results suggest that implementation of IMO's policies to curb ship emissions has improved environmental, health and societal impacts (Roy and Chakraborty 2025). For example, since 2020, in Japan it was observed a downward trend of nss-SO_4^{2-} and NH_4^+ and of the particle exposure risk levels for As, W, Sb, V, Ni and Cd and for non-carcinogenic risk and carcinogenic risk for both adults and children (Zhang and Aikawa, 2023). Moreover, the introduction of ECA has resulted in a significant decrease of both primary particulate matter emissions and secondary formation of $PM_{2.5}$ (–35%–37%) from shipping, even not proportional to sulphur reduction regulation (Karl et al., 2019). The use of low-sulphur content fuels leads to reduction of the impact of shipping on SO_2, and particulate matter however, no significant changes were observed for total metals and PAHs in gaseous and particulate phase in PM_{10} (Gregoris et al., 2016).

The combined designation of a SECA and a NECA in European seas could have a $PM_{2.5}$ reduction potential of 50% and 65% in 2030 and 2050, respectively (Cofala et al., 2018). However, efforts towards lower emissions from the shipping sector in the South Europe are opposed (and, often, exceeded) by changes due to climate change (Russo et al., 2023). In light of these changes, the introduction of an ECA is proposed for the Mediterranean, which would help us to make great strides to reduce the impact of the shipping sector in the region and aid in counteracting the effects of climate change, although a number of peculiarities need to be accounted for (Testa, 2020). Although mitigating $PM_{2.5}$ and O_3 pollution from shipping should be a priority, the shipping-related VOC emissions should also be controlled because several new fuels with low-sulphur content often lead to high VOC emissions, therefore not reducing O_3 formation (Sun et al., 2024).

Another recently investigated phenomenon has been the impact of COVID-19 lockdown (period 2019–2020), in terms of air pollutants reduction and health benefits. Sun et al. (2024) suggested that shipping-related global $PM_{2.5}$, NO_2 and O_3 levels reduced by 14%, 85% and 1%, respectively, even if with large spatial inhomogeneity. In particular, $PM_{2.5}$ and NO_2 levels decreased in China, India, Europe and the United States by 6.5% (NO_2: 9%), 7.4% (8%), 11% (8.6%) and 15% (10%), with slight changes for O_3 (+0.7%, *12.9%, +16.6% and *4.8%). Globally, the all-cause premature mortalities caused by shipping-related $PM_{2.5}$ exposures reached 40,464 and 39,035 cases in early 2019 and 2020, respectively. The combined health benefits of $PM_{2.5}$, NO_2 and O_3 linked with shipping emission reduction strategies in China, India, Europe and the United States reached 476, 3,341, 2,194 and 311, respectively.

Impacts of shipping on air quality and health

Shipping affects concentrations of several air pollutants in gaseous and particulate phases (Merico et al., 2021). Relative contributions to SO_2 and NO_x are generally larger compared to those of particulate matter (PM) and CO, which are comparable to each other (Merico et al., 2017). Overall, air quality and health impacts of harbour activities and shipping are larger in coastal areas, where shipping emissions could contribute to 1%–14% of the $PM_{2.5}$ levels and 7%–24% of the NO_2 levels in port cities in Europe (Viana et al., 2014). However, a significant contribution was also reported in inland zones (Nunes et al., 2020). Aksoyoglu et al. (2016) found the contribution to the total $PM_{2.5}$ to be the largest in Western Mediterranean (up to 14%), compared to Northern European coasts (1%–5%), U.S. harbours (3%–9%) and the worldwide busiest Chinese harbours (2.4%–25%) (Contini and Merico, 2021). Shipping and shipping-related harbour emissions have high spatial gradient of their contributions to local pollution with larger impact on harbour areas and nearby zones. Near the emission sources, their effect could be a reduction of ozone due to titration; however, at larger distance from the emissions this source can increase summer ozone concentrations (Merico et al., 2016).

There are considerably less studies on the contribution of shipping to the concentrations of UFP or, more in general, to the atmospheric particle number concentration (PNC) that is dominated by UFP. UFP emissions from ships are strongly influenced by fuels and by the variability in ship activities and conditions (i.e., the effect of technology, fuel and operating load of diesel engine). It would be useful to increase the ability to model and measure the time evolution of the number size distributions and chemical composition of UFPs in ship exhaust to assess the resulting exposure in the vicinity of shipping routes. However, there are also other sources of NPs in harbour areas, such as vessel refit and repair activities including abrasive removal of filler and paint, or spray painting with antifouling coatings, primers and topcoats. These different types of NPs summed with ship emissions may result in PNC in the range of industrial activities (up to $5 \times 10^5/cm^3$, mean diameters <30 nm). Vallabani et al. (2023) emphasizes the current limited knowledge of the health impacts of source-specific UFPs related to different transport modes, especially about toxic effects linked to some sources (shipping, road and tyre wear, subway). A summary of comparison of shipping contributions to particles of different sizes and to PNC and $PM_{2.5}$ (or PM_1) is reported in Figure 10.2 for several coastal cities in Europe. Results were obtained with different instruments and different approaches and suggest that the impact of shipping and harbour emissions on PNC is significantly larger (three times or

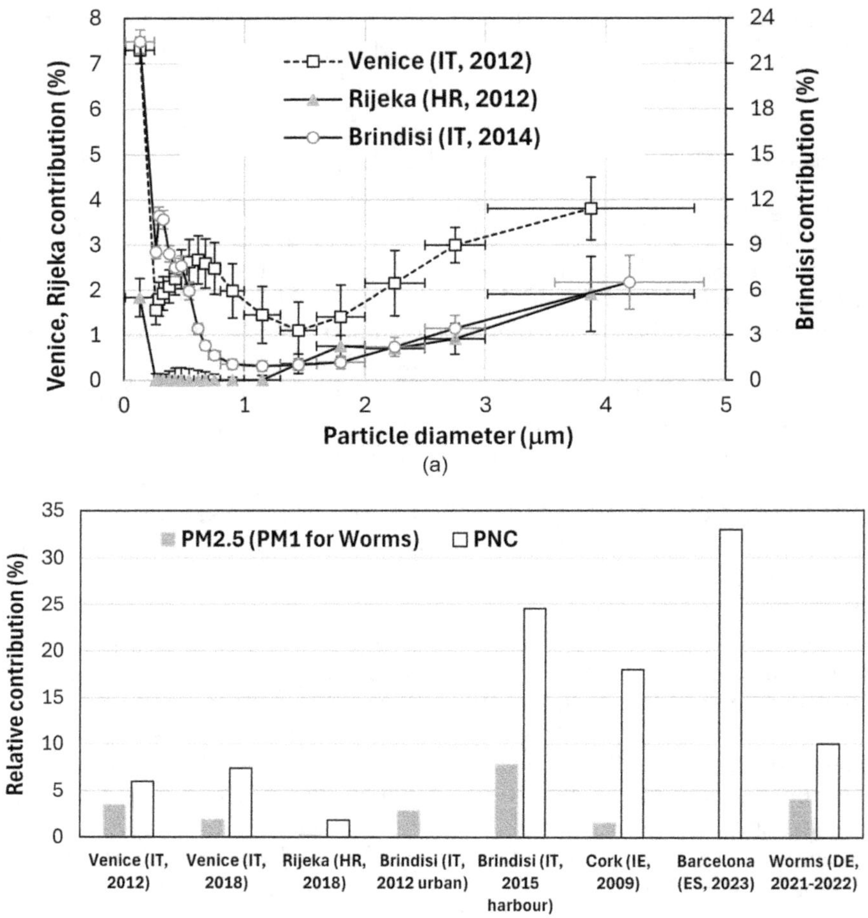

Figure 10.2 Contributions of shipping and harbour emissions to particle number concentration of different sizes (left). Average contributions to PNC and mass concentrations in different EU harbours (right)

Source: Own realization based on data collected from different studies: Cesari et al. (2014), Eger et al. (2023), Healy et al. (2009), Merico et al. (2016, 2020) and Ridolfo et al. (2025)

more) than the impact on mass concentrations (either PM_1 or $PM_{2.5}$). Moreover, even if in some areas a decrease in the impact on $PM_{2.5}$ concentrations was observed, this was not the case for PNC.

PNC is a metric that has only recently been included in the European Air Quality Directive (Directive-EU-2024/2881). Different epidemiological studies have shown significant associations between health effects of both long- and short-term exposure. In 2021, the World Health Organization (WHO) recommended integrating UFP monitoring, measured as the total number of particles, into the existing air quality monitoring stations. World Health Organization [WHO] (2021) Air Quality Guidelines states that high UFP concentrations can be considered as a health issue if daily averages exceed 10,000 # cm*[3], or 20,000 # cm*[3] on one-hour mean. A large variety of health effects have been linked to inhalation of nanoparticles, including respiratory and cardiovascular diseases as well as cancer. Many of these effects have been linked to the ability of nanoparticles to cause oxidative stress, inflammation and genotoxicity (Leikauf et al., 2020; Miller and Newby, 2020) and a more reactive surface area than larger particles, which makes them more prone to stimulate toxic effects. The increased concentrations of UFP attributed to ship plumes significantly increase the short-term exposures of the population in the vicinity of the harbour areas.

Epidemiological studies indicate that emissions related to shipping can trigger biological effects, such as oxidative stress and cytotoxicity. One study showed that $PM_{2.5}$ emissions from the combustion of HFO showed cytotoxicity and ROS generation in lung cancer cells (A549) (Wu et al., 2018). Overall harbour emissions of $PM_{0.25}$ (including emissions from ships, locomotives and heavy-duty vehicles) accounted for 16% ± 3% of the overall oxidative potential of the ambient $PM_{0.25}$ samples in three U.S. harbours (Mousavi et al., 2019). Recent systematic reviews to synthesize the existing knowledge on the effects of shipping emissions on public health are available (Ducruet et al., 2024; Mueller et al., 2023; Roy and Chakraborty, 2025; Sun et al., 2025; Kiihamäki et al., 2024). All studies, while agreeing on the shipping impact on health and environment (up to 0.5% of global mortality), point to significant critical points in the variety of methodologies used (in the evaluation of emissions, dispersion and exposure) and the comparability of results.

Ducruet et al. (2024) conducted a global empirical analysis including port traffic typology (i.e., containers, bulk and passenger ships), data on natural conditions, air pollution, socio-economic indicators and public health. Health impacts in port cities are shown to vary according to the size and specialization of the harbour region (industrial, intermediate and metropolitan). In this study some aspects are highlighted to improve health assessment of the impact of air pollution: the need of deconstruction by age groups of population, data about access to and availability of medical care (i.e., number of doctors and hospital beds), data on vessel movements combined with engine and fuel type, disaggregation of port activities by ship types (i.e., crude oil, chemicals, tanker, general cargo, port services, cruise, ferries, etc.), metropolitan database including socio-economic and environmental indicators such as port city topography and morphology, land use, distance between port and city, wind direction and data on urban congestion.

Health impact assessment applies exposure distributions of the studied populations and exposure-response functions, while epidemiological studies, including time-series analyses, apply empirical data on both exposures and health outcomes and estimate empirical exposure-response functions. They can be applied in elucidating the temporal dynamics of exposure and health outcomes, allowing for a more detailed understanding of the relationships between shipping emissions, air pollution and mortality.

Health outcome predominantly studied was mortality (all-cause, cause-specific, loss in life expectancy, years of life lost [YLLs]), but also morbidity (disease cases, hospital admissions, years lived with disability [YLDs]), disability-adjusted life-years (DALYs), restricted activity days and work loss days.

For Europe, Brandt et al. (2013) estimated that up to 50,000 premature deaths per year can be associated with emissions from shipping, while a study focused on the Baltic Sea region estimated that $PM_{2.5}$ emissions from shipping caused up to 2,300 premature deaths in the Baltic countries in 2016, resulting in a reduction of 37% compared to before a SECA was enforced in the area (Barregard et al., 2019).

The implementation of stricter sulphur cap, that is the reduction of the cap from 1% to 0.1% of sulphur fuel content in the SECA of North Sea and English Channel on January 1, 2015, demonstrated to reduce the risk of low birthweight of 7%, associated to a SO_2 and $PM_{2.5}$ decrease of 22% and 6%, respectively (Lindgren, 2021).

In Iberian Peninsula, it was estimated that the number of premature deaths and years of life lost (YLL) due to NO_2 ship-related emissions was similar to those of $PM_{2.5}$ ship-related emissions (Nunes et al., 2021). Estimated all-cause premature deaths attributable to $PM_{2.5}$ ship-related emissions represented an average increase of 7.7% for the Iberian Peninsula when compared to the scenario without shipping contribution. Estimates showed that the IMO2020 could reduce shipping $PM_{2.5}$ attributable mortality by 6% and shipping PM_{10} attributable post-neonatal deaths by 10% among the Spanish and Portuguese population and around 50% and 30%, respectively, of $PM_{2.5}$ and NO_2 ship-related mortality would been avoided.

A health assessment analysis conducted Viana et al. (2020) in height European Mediterranean port cities indicated that adopting the IMO2020 regulation, can potentially decrease premature deaths, caused by $PM_{2.5}$ pollution by 15% compared to 430 premature deaths per year (about 5.5 premature deaths per year for every 100,000 inhabitants) due to long-term exposure to ship-sourced $PM_{2.5}$. Finally, on a global scale, implementing the IMO2020 policy could decrease approximately 34% in annual premature deaths and reduce an asthma morbidity by around 54% (Sofiev et al., 2018). However, shipping was found to be responsible of decreasing human health effects by 137,000 deaths, especially in Asia and India but to a significantly lower extent in areas already regulated by existing SECAs (i.e., Northern Hemisphere).

In Australia, an estimated 220 YLLs in 2010/2011 were reported as a result of ship exhaust-related exposure. However, requiring ships to use 0.1% low-sulphur fuel within 300 km of Sydney more than doubles the health benefits (as population weighted-mean concentration of $PM_{2.5}$) compared to applying the same fuel standard only at berth (*25%), over a 20 year-period (Broome et al., 2016).

Implementing SECA (in 2015) in the Baltic and North Sea regions reduced premature deaths by about 35% and, in addition, 1,500 non-fatal cases of ischaemic heart disease and 1,500 non-fatal cases of stroke in 2014 caused by Baltic shipping emissions were reduced by the same extent in 2016 (Barregard et al., 2019). Projections suggest that implementing a North Sea ECA will reduce approximately 1% premature mortality throughout the North Sea countries by 2030, doubling by 2040 (Ramacher et al., 2020). In the Mediterranean region, the potential implementation of an ECA could avoid nearly 1,730 premature deaths per year (Rouïl et al., 2019).

It should be emphasized that mitigation strategies targeting the reduction of sulphur content in marine fuels have yielded improvements in local air quality within regions influenced by shipping emissions, thereby contributing to a potential decrease in ship-related adverse health outcomes. From a climatic standpoint, the net radiative forcing (RF) attributable to the shipping sector has been estimated at approximately –0.4 W m^{-2}, indicating a short-term cooling effect resulting from the combined influence of negative (SO_2) and positive (CO_2, black carbon) RF components associated with ship emissions. Nevertheless, over longer timescales, the slow atmospheric removal of CO_2 may reverse this balance, leading to a net warming effect. This potential warming could be further exacerbated by the transition to low-sulphur fuels, which inherently reduce the formation of secondary sulphate aerosols generated from ship emissions (Sofiev et al., 2018).

Conclusions

Although most ship emissions take place at open sea, a non-negligible fraction of these involve harbour cities and coastal communities, exposing them to PM and gaseous pollutants with potential negative effects on health. Ship traffic contribution to PM pollutants is found generally to be lower than that to gaseous pollutants such as NO_X, CO and SO_2. In particular, $PM_{2.5}$ impact ranges typically between 0.2% and 14% (Europe); between 3% and 9% in North America; and from 2.4% to 25% in Asian regions. Relative contributions to PNC are generally several times larger than those to PM mass concentrations suggesting that this is a metric that should be carefully monitored and possibly targeted in future mitigation strategies.

At the international level, regulatory measures/strategies have been adopted to lower the sulphur content of marine fuels and to designate specific Emission Control Areas (ECAs and NECAs) at the regional scale. The most recent IMO regulation, enforced on 1 January 2020, is anticipated to substantially decrease ship-related emissions of sulphur dioxide (SO_2) and primary PM with a beneficial effect also on the formation of secondary sulphate aerosols within PM. In contrast, only limited reductions are expected in emissions of nitrogen oxides (NO_x), trace metals and PAHs associated with both gaseous and particulate phases.

Global assessments suggest that the implementation of the IMO 2020 regulation could reduce ship-related premature mortality and morbidity by approximately 34% and 54%, respectively. Despite these improvements, the residual health burden attributable to maritime emissions is estimated to remain significant. Moreover, the decrease in SO_2 emissions resulting from the transition to low-sulphur fuels is expected to increase the RF linked to ship-derived aerosols, potentially offsetting some of the climatic benefits.

Therefore, while the current regulatory framework represents a major step towards cleaner shipping, additional mitigation efforts are required. The concurrent expansion of maritime trade, population growth and urbanization in coastal zones calls for integrated policy approaches capable of addressing the combined impacts on air quality, human health and climate. Advancing a comprehensive "green port" vision, based on the integration of local, regional and global perspectives, will be useful to achieve sustainable maritime development in the near future.

References

Aksoyoglu S., Baltensperger U., Prévôt A.S.H. (2016) Contribution of ship emissions to the concentration and deposition of air pollutants in Europe. *Atmospheric Chemistry and Physics*, 16: 1895–1906.

Alamoush A.S., Ballini F., Ölçer A.I. (2020) Ports' technical and operational measures to reduce greenhouse gas emission and improve energy efficiency: A review. *Marine Pollution Bulletin*, 160: 111508.

Aulinger A., Matthias V., Zeretzke M., Bieser J., Quante M., Backes A. (2016) The impact of shipping emissions on air pollution in the greater North Sea region—Part 1: Current emissions and concentrations. *Atmospheric Chemistry and Physics*, 16(2): 739–758.

Barregard L., Molnàr P., Jonson J.E., Stockfelt L. (2019) Impact on population health of Baltic shipping emissions. *International Journal of Environmental Research and Public Health*, 16(11): 1954.

Bartlomiejski R. (2016) Environmental conflicts in port cities. *Opuscula Sociologica*, 18(4): 33–44.

Brandt J., Silver J.D., Christensen J.H., Andersen M.S., Bønløkke J.H., Sigsgaard T., Geels C., Gross A., Hansen A.B., Hansen K.M., Hedegaard G.B., Kaas E., Frohn L.M. (2013) Assessment of past, present and future health-cost externalities of air pollution in Europe and the contribution from international ship traffic using the EVA model system (Aug.). *Atmospheric Chemistry and Physics*, 13(15): 7747–7764.

Broome R.A., Cope M.E., Goldsworthy B., Goldsworthy L., Emmerson K., Jegasothy E., Morgan G.G. (2016) The mortality effect of ship-related fine particulate matter in the Sydney greater metropolitan region of NSW, Australia. *Environment International*, 87: 85–93.

Carpenter A., Lozano R. (2020) Proposing a framework for anchoring sustainability relationships between ports and cities. In: Carpenter A., Lozano R. (Eds.), *European Port Cities in Transition*, New York: Springer, pp. 37–51.

Cesari D., Genga A., Ielpo P., Siciliano M., Mascolo G., Grasso F.M., Contini D. (2014) Source apportionment of $PM_{2.5}$ in the harbour-industrial area of Brindisi (Italy): Identification and estimation of the contribution of in-port ship emissions. *Science of the Total Environment*, 497–498: 392–400.

Cofala J., Amann M., Borken-Kleefeld J., Gomez-Sanabria A., Heyes C., Kiesewetter G., Sander R., Schoepp W., Holland M., Fagerli H., Nyiri A. (2018) The potential for cost-effective air emission reductions from international shipping through designation of further Emission Control Areas in EU waters with focus on the Mediterranean Sea: IIASA Research Report. International Institute for Applied Systems Analysis (IIASA), Laxenburg, Austria.

Contini D., Gambaro A., Belosi F., Pieri S. De, Cairns W.R.L., Donateo A., Zanotto E., Citron M. (2011) The direct influence of ship traffic on atmospheric $PM_{2.5}$, PM_{10} and PAH in Venice. *Journal of Environmental Management*, 92: 2119–2129.

Contini D., Merico E. (2021) Recent advances in studying air quality and health effects of shipping emissions. *Atmosphere*, 12(1): 92.

Deniz C., Kilic A. (2010) Estimation and assessment of shipping emissions in the region of Ambarlı Port, Turkey. *Environmental Progress and Sustainable Energy*, 29(1): 107–115.

Di Natale F., Carotenuto C. (2015) Particulate matter in marine diesel engines exhausts: Emissions and control strategies. *Transportation Research Part D: Transport and Environment*, 40: 166–191.

Ducruet C., Lo Prete M., Polo Martin B., Sene M.A., Sun L., Itoh H., Pigné Y. (2024) Ports and their influence on local air pollution and public health. A global analysis. *Science of the Total Environment*, 915: 170099.

Eger P., Mathes T., Zavarsky A., Duester L. (2023) Measurement report: Inland ship emissions and their contribution to NO_x and ultrafine particle concentrations at the Rhine. *Atmospheric Chemistry and Physics*, 23: 8769–8788.

Gobbi G.P., Di Liberto L., Barnaba F. (2020) Impact of port emissions on EU-regulated and non-regulated air quality indicators: The case of Civitavecchia (Italy). *Science of the Total Environment*, 719: 134984.

Gregoris E., Barbaro E., Morabito E., Toscano G., Donateo A., Cesari D., Contini D., Gambaro A. (2016) Impact of maritime traffic on polycyclic aromatic hydrocarbons, metals and particulate matter in Venice air. *Environmental Science and Pollution Research*, 23: 6951–6959.

Hansson J., Brynolf S., Fridell E., Lehtveer M. (2020) The potential role of ammonia as marine fuel—Based on energy systems modeling and multi-criteria decision analysis. *Sustainability*, 12(8): 3265.

Healy R.M., O'Connor I.P., Hellebust S., Allanic A., Sodeau J.R., Wenger J.C. (2009) Characterisation of single particles from in-port ship emissions. *Atmospheric Environment*, 43: 6408–6414.

Helgason R., Cook D., Davíðsdóttir B. (2020) An evaluation of the cost-competitiveness of maritime fuels – A comparison of heavy fuel oil and methanol (renewable and natural gas) in Iceland. *Sustainable Production and Consumption*, 23: 236–248.

IMO (2020) *Fourth IMO GHG Study, International Maritime Organization*. London, UK, https://greenvoyage2050.imo.org/wp-content/uploads/2021/07/Fourth-IMO-GHG-Study-2020-Full-report-and-annexes_compressed.pdf

Iris Ç., Lam J.S.L. (2019) A review of energy efficiency in ports: Operational strategies, technologies and energy management systems. *Renewable and Sustainable Energy Reviews*, 112(C): 170–182.

Jonson J.E., Gauss M., Jalkanen J.P., Johansson L. (2019) Effects of strengthening the Baltic Sea ECA regulations. *Atmospheric Chemistry and Physics*, 19(21): 13469–13487.

Karl M., Jonson J.E., Uppstu A., Aulinger A., Prank M., Sofiev M., Jalkanen J.P., Johansson L., Quante M., Matthias V. (2019) Effects of ship emissions on air quality in the Baltic Sea region simulated with three different chemistry transport models. *Atmospheric Chemistry and Physics*, 19: 7019–7053.

Kiihamäki S.P., Korhonen M., Kukkonen J., Shiue I., Jaakkola J.J.K. (2024) Effects of ambient air pollution from shipping on mortality: A systematic review. *Science of the Total Environment*, 945: 173714.

Lam J.S.L., Yap W.Y. (2019) A stakeholder perspective of port city sustainable development. *Sustainability*, 11(2): 447.

Leikauf G.D., Kim S.H., Jang A.S. (2020) Mechanisms of ultrafine particle-induced respiratory health effects. *Experimental & Molecular Medicine*, 52: 329–337.

Li C., Yuan Z., Ou J., Fan X., Ye S., Xiao T., Shi Y., Huang Z., Ng S.K.W., Zhong Z., Zheng J. (2016) An AIS-based high-resolution ship emission inventory and its uncertainty in Pearl River Delta region, China. *Science of the Total Environment*, 573: 1–10.

Lindgren S. (2021) The coast is clear: Shipping emission standards, air quality and infant health. *Transportation Research Part D: Transport and Environment*, 100: 103067.

Long Y., Li G., Zhang Z., Wei W., Liang J. (2022) Hydrogen-rich gas generation via the exhaust gas-fuel reformer for the marine LNG engine. *International Journal of Hydrogen Energy*, 47(32): 14674–14686.

Merico E., Cesari D., Gregoris E., Gambaro A., Cordella M., Contini D. (2021) Shipping and air quality in Italian port cities: State-of-the-art analysis of available results of estimated impacts. *Atmosphere*, 12(5): 536.

Merico E., Conte M., Grasso F.M., Cesari D., Gambaro A., Morabito E., Gregoris E., Orlando S., Alebic-Juretic A., Zubak V., Mifka B., Contini D. (2020) Comparison of the impact of ships to size-segregated particle concentrations in two harbour cities of northern Adriatic Sea. *Environmental Pollution*, 266(3): 115175.

Merico E., Dinoi A., Contini D. (2019) Development of an integrated modelling measurement system for near-real-time estimates of harbour activity impact to atmospheric pollution in coastal cities. *Transportation Research Part D: Transport and Environment*, 73: 108–119.

Merico E., Donateo A., Gambaro A., Cesari D., Gregoris E., Barbaro E., Dinoi A., Giovanelli G., Masieri S., Contini D. (2016) Influence of in-port ships emissions to gaseous atmospheric pollutants and to particulate matter of different sizes in a Mediterranean harbour in Italy. *Atmospheric Environment*, 139: 1–10.

Merico E., Gambaro A., Argiriou A., Alebic-Juretic A., Barbaro E., Cesari D., Chasapidis L., Dimopoulos S., Dinoi A., Donateo A., Giannaros C., Gregoris E., Karagiannidis A., Konstandopoulos A.G., Ivošević T., Liora N., Melas D., Mifka B., Orlić I., Poupkou A., Sarovic K., Tsakis A., Giua R., Pastore T., Nocioni A., Contini D. (2017) Atmospheric impact of ship traffic in four Adriatic-Ionian portcities: Comparison and harmonization of different approaches. *Transportation Research Part D: Transport and Environment*, 50: 431–445.

Miller M.R., Newby D.E. (2020) Air pollution and cardiovascular disease: Car sick. *Cardiovascular Research*, 116: 279–294.

Mousavi A., Sowlat M.H., Lovett C., Rauber M., Szidat S., Boffi R., Borgini A., De Marco C., Ruprecht A.A., Sioutas C. (2019) Source apportionment of black carbon (BC) from fossil fuel and biomass burning in metropolitan Milan, Italy. *Atmospheric Environment*, 203: 252–261.

Mueller N., Westerby M., Nieuwenhuijsen M. (2023) Health impact assessments of shipping and port-sourced air pollution on a global scale: A scoping literature review. *Environmental Research*, 216(1): 114460.

Murena F., Mocerino L., Quaranta F., Toscano D. (2018) Impact on air quality of cruise ship emissions in Naples, Italy. *Atmospheric Environment*, 187: 70–83.

Nunes R.A.O., Alvim-Ferraz M.C.M., Martins F.G., Calderay-Cayetano F., Durán-Grados V., Moreno-Gutiérrez J., Jalkanen J.P., Hannuniemi H., Sousa S.I.V. (2020) Shipping emissions in the Iberian Peninsula and its impacts on air quality. *Atmospheric Chemistry and Physics*, 20(15): 9473–9489.

Nunes R.A.O., Alvim-Ferraz M.C.M., Martins F.G., Peñuelas A.L., Durán-Grados V., Moreno-Gutiérrez J., Jalkanen J.P., Hannuniemi H., Sousa S.I.V. (2021) Estimating the health and economic burden of shipping related air pollution in the Iberian Peninsula. *Environment International*, 156: 106763.

Prati M.V., Costagliola M.A., Quaranta F., Murena F. (2015) Assessment of ambient air quality in the port of Naples. *Journal of the Air & Waste Management Association*, 65: 970–979.

Ramacher M.O.P., Tang L., Moldanová J., Matthias V., Karl M., Fridell E., Johansson L. (2020) The impact of ship emissions on air quality and human health in the Gothenburg area – Part II: Scenarios for 2040. *Atmospheric Chemistry and Physics*, 20(17): 10667–10686.

Rathod S., Edwards M., Roy C., Wieser L., Rafaj P., Kiesewetter G., Klimont Z. (2023) Air quality and health effects of a transition to ammonia-fueled shipping in Singapore. *Environmental Research: Health*, 1: 041002.

Ridolfo S., Querol X., Karanasiou A., Rodríguez-Luque A., Perez N., Alastuey A., Jaén C., van Drooge B.L., Pandolfi M., Cortes J., Amato F. (2025) Concentrations and origins of ultrafine particles at a major European harbor. *Science of the Total Environment*, 963: 178467.

Rouïl L., Ratsivalaka C., André J.M., Allemand N. (2019) ECAMED: A technical feasibility study for the implementation of an emission control area (ECA) in the Mediterranean Sea. IMO Report MEPC 74/INF.5.

Roy A., Chakraborty M. (2025) A review of ship emissions impacts on environmental, health, societal impacts and IMO's mitigation policies. *Regional Studies in Marine Science*, 81: 103964.

Russo M., Carvalho D., Jalkanen J.P., Monteiro A. (2023) The future impact of shipping emissions on air quality in Europe under climate change. *Atmosphere*, 14(7): 1126.

Russo M.A., Leitão J., Gama C., Ferreira J., Monteiro A. (2018) Shipping emissions over Europe: A state-of-the-art and comparative analysis. *Atmospheric Environment*, 177: 187–194.

Sofiev M., Winebrake J.J., Johansson L., Carr E.W., Prank M., Soares J., Vira J., Kouznetsov R., Jalkanen J.P., Corbett J.J. (2018) Cleaner fuels for ships provide public health benefits with climate tradeoffs. *Nature Communications*, 9(1): 406.

Stec M., Tatarczuk A., Iluk T., Szul M. (2021) Reducing the energy efficiency design index for ships through a post-combustion carbon capture process. *International Journal of Greenhouse Gas Control*, 108: 103333.

Sun W., Jiang W., Li R. (2024) Global health benefits of shipping emission reduction in early 2020. *Atmospheric Environment*, 333: 120648.

Sun L., Zhang J., Ducruet C., Itoh H., Liu X. (2025) The impact of shipping activities on air quality and residents' health in China's port cities. *Journal of Transport Geography*, 123: 104099.

Sürer M.G., Arat H.T. (2022) Advancements and current technologies on hydrogen fuel cell applications for marine vehicles. *International Journal of Hydrogen Energy*, 47(45): 19865–19875.

Tang L., Ramacher M.O.P., Moldanová J., Matthias V., Karl M., Johansson L., Jalkanen J.P., Yaramenka K., Aulinger A., Gustafsson M. (2020) The impact of ship emissions on air quality and human health in the Gothenburg area – Part I: 2012 emissions. *Atmospheric Chemistry and Physics*, 20(12): 7509–7530.

Testa D. (2020) A note on the potential designation of the Mediterranean Sea as a sulphur emission control area. *Marine Policy*, 121: 104145.

UNCTAD (2022) *Maritime Transport Indicators – Handbook of Statistics 2022, UNCTAD Handbook of Statistics 2022*. Accessed: July 15, 2025. [Online], https://hbs.unctad.org/maritime-transport-indicators/#Note1

Vallabani N.V.S., Gruzieva O., Elihn K., Juárez-Facio A.T., Steimer S.S., Kuhn J., Silvergren S., Portugal J., Piña B., Olofsson U., Johansson C., Karlsson H.L. (2023) Toxicity and health effects of ultrafine particles: Towards an understanding of the relative impacts of different transport modes. *Environmental Research*, 231(2): 116186.

Viana M., Hammingh P., Colette A., Querol X., Degraeuwe B., de Vlieger I., van Aardenne J. (2014) Impact of maritime transport emissions on coastal air quality in Europe. *Atmospheric Environment*, 90: 96–105.

Viana M., Rizza V., Tobías A., Carr E., Corbett J., Sofiev M., Karanasiou A., Buonanno G., Fann N. (2020) Estimated health impacts from maritime transport in the Mediterranean region and benefits from the use of cleaner fuels. *Environment International*, 138: 105670.

Wagner N. (2019) Sustainability in port cities: S bibliometric approach. *Transportation Research Procedia*, 39: 587–596.

World Health Organization (WHO) (2021) *WHO Global Air Quality Guidelines, 2021*. Particulate matter ($PM_{2.5}$ and PM_{10}), ozone, nitrogen dioxide, sulfur dioxide and carbon monoxide. Geneva: World Health Organization. Licence: CC BY-NC-SA 3.0 IGO.

Wu D., Li Q., Ding X., Sun J., Li D., Fu H., Teich M., Ye X., Chen J. (2018) Primary particulate matter emitted from heavy fuel and diesel oil combustion in a typical container ship: Characteristics and toxicity. *Environmental Science and Technology*, 52(21): 12943–12951.

Zhang X., Aikawa M. (2023) The variation of $PM_{2.5}$ from ship emission under low-sulfur regulation: A case study in the coastal suburbs of Kitakyushu, Japan. *Science of the Total Environment*, 858(2): 159968.

Zheng Y., Zhao J., Shao G. (2020) Port city sustainability: A review of its research trends. *Sustainability*, 12(20): 8355.

11 Maritime traffic specialization and environmental health impacts in European port cities

César Ducruet, Mariantonia Lo Prete, Magali Dumontet, Barbara Polo Martin, Charbel Alkhoury, Ling Sun and Sheng Zhang

Introduction

Port cities are critical hubs of maritime commerce and logistics, featuring a wide spectrum of activities such as cargo handling, oil terminals, shipyards, fishing fleets, and marinas, which collectively generate complex environmental pressures (Lo Prete, 2015; Hernández et al., 2024). Unlike other industrial urban zones, ports uniquely influence air, water, and soil quality through diverse emissions and resource consumption (Lo Prete, 2023).

Maritime shipping is a major source of coastal air pollution worldwide, emitting significant amounts of sulfur oxides (SO_x), nitrogen oxides (NO_x), particulate matter (PM), carbon monoxide (CO), and volatile organic compounds (VOCs) (Ledoux et al., 2018; Athul et al., 2025; Calgaro et al., 2025). Prior to the implementation of International Maritime Organization sulfur emission controls, ship emissions accounted for 4%–9% of global SO_x emissions, rising to 30%–40% of NO_x in some coastal regions (Hernández et al., 2024). In European ports, shipping contributes notably to particulate emissions, with $PM_{2.5}$ and PM_{10} shares reaching 45% and 28% respectively (Merico et al., 2021; D'Amico et al., 2024).

The high emission intensity of cruise liners and ferries further exacerbates pollution hotspots near European ports such as Barcelona, Venice, and Southampton, affecting both port workers and adjacent residents (Merico et al., 2021).

This chapter innovates in two ways. First, it proposes a simultaneous analysis of different traffic types as most existing studies consider traffics separately (see also Chapter 1). Second, it considers such traffics as revelatory of the presence of onshore activities, which also contribute to pollution, of which hinterland trucking for containers, tourism flows for cruise and passengers, factories and storage for solid bulks, and heavy industrial transformation for liquid bulks. Each traffic thus reflects the presence of a particular supply chain, and larger ports are often more diversified.

Traffic specialization is partly a reflection of port hinterlands. Solid bulks like grain, coal, and ores often imply the presence of raw material

DOI: 10.4324/9781003639589-15

production, while port cities with a large population attract manufactured goods in containers to meet local demand. The heritage of capital and historic port cities is a magnet for cruise tourism and passenger traffic in general. Such traffic creates important influx of visitors also toward the hinterland for tourism, resulting in crowding and congestion along city arteries and highways. Hinterland traffic and the logistics sector in general also contribute to local pollution, depending on the modal split (Mueller et al., 2023; Rowangould et al., 2018; Sun et al., 2025). In Europe, 75% of all freight movements occur by road, so that a large majority of ports are served by trucks to carry containers for import-export (and also transshipment). Thus, ports specialized in container traffic are potentially congested and polluted by such heavy-duty vehicles, especially at peak hours, when mixed with automobile traffic. In Le Havre, 90% of hinterland traffic occurs by road, while Antwerp uses barges for about 40% but still faces significant air quality challenges (Yu et al., 2025).

The cargo type influences pollutant profiles. Heavy industries, such as petro-chemical complexes or steelworks, have in common with (liquid) bulk terminals to emit VOCs during storage, transfer, and transformation. Solid bulk terminals as well as related silos, warehouses, plants, and factories may generate dust clouds containing hazardous substances like fertilizers and pesticides in the case of grain (Yuan et al., 2022; Sathish and Patterson, 2025). The growing cruise industry adds further strain to air quality and local health, increasing exposure to harmful emissions among passengers, crew, and residents (Lloret et al., 2021; Lo Prete et al., 2024).

The goal of this chapter is to confront environment and public health data to a wide range of socio-economic and traffic characteristics, in order to detect the relative impacts of the latter simultaneously. A sample of 120 European cities, or Functional Urban Areas (FUAs), is analyzed over the period 2000–2019 with the main objective to provide a typology of port cities and discuss particular cases.

The impacts of main traffic types and their related supply chains

Container ships represent 4% of the world's shipping fleet; however, they contribute to 22% of CO_2 emissions (Corbett et al., 2009). Utilizing container technologies at ports reduces staying times and improves vessels' efficiency, thereby lowering ship-related pollutants (Agarwala et al., 2021).

At the local scale, the handling of containers on terminals for ships, locomotives, trucks, and shuttles for storage used to rely on heavy fuel with negative effects on health and the environment, before recent efforts toward terminal electrification and the use of cleaner fuels (Lo Prete, 2023).

Moreover, the combination of trucking and automobile flows increases congestion and emissions, also because of the fast economic development of cities themselves (Kotowska and Kubowicz, 2019). Taken as a whole, hinterland transport represents twice the emissions of a port on average, as seen with the large container port of Felixstowe in the United Kingdom (Gibbs et al., 2014). At the regional scale, empty container repositioning is a major cause of congestion and pollution in certain regions, such as Southern California, which had been the focus of many researches on truck routing optimization (Englert et al., 2011).

According to Paoli et al. (2017), the Euro Zone cruise ship market played an important role in the global cruise market in 2013, accounting for about 30% of European passengers, and generating 31.2 million passenger visits on both the Baltic Sea and the Mediterranean. Yet, cruise is among the most energy-intensive types of tourism and generates a high pollution load (Lloret et al., 2021). Investigation showed that carbon emissions from cruise passengers are more than five times those of luxury hotels and four times those of economy-class flights (Howitt et al., 2010). Cruise ships are significant emitters of nitrogen oxides (NO_x), sulfur oxides (SO_x), particulate matter (PM_{10} and ultrafine particulates), and carbon dioxide (CO_2) (Lansø et al., 2023). Emissions are particularly high during the "hotelling" phase, where ships remain berthed for hours, continuously running auxiliary engines. For instance, in 2018, 345 cruise ships in Copenhagen Port emitted 291 tons of NO_x, accounting for 52% of the port's total vessel emissions (Lansø et al., 2023).

In Copenhagen, cruise emissions of NO_2 exceeded EU limits by five times (Lansø et al., 2023). These emissions contribute to respiratory diseases and increased cardiopulmonary mortality (Lloret et al.,2021; Mendoza-Lara et al., 2023). A typical seven-day cruise in the Baltic Sea emits approximately 590 kg CO_2 per passenger (Olaniyi et al., 2022). This is compounded by emissions from port-related land transport, such as diesel-powered shuttle buses, which can add 6,852 tons of CO_2 annually for short excursions (Olaniyi et al., 2022).

The phenomenon of "overtourism" manifests as severe congestion in historic city centers (e.g., Venice, Dubrovnik, Lisbon, Barcelona), diminishing the quality of life for residents and eroding the authentic visitor experience (Abeal-Vázquez et al., 2024). In Barcelona and Valencia, Navarro-Ruiz et al. (2020) showed that the shore excursions of cruise tourists are concentrated in the port cities and cause overcrowding.

The high demand for bulk commodities such as iron ore, grain, and coal has become an important driver of global trade (Van Vianen et al., 2014). According to Hoffmann et al. (2018), in 2018, solid bulk represented about 53.3% of nearly 11 billion tons of global handled cargo. The increase in air PM in ports and surrounding communities is linked to smoke and dust emissions from loading, unloading, and the transportation of bulk materials (Merico et al., 2019; Santos et al., 2019). PM can decrease visibility, contribute to acid rain, and impact ecosystem diversity; all of this depends on the chemical and physical composition of particles. In addition, PM emissions can directly affect health. For example, fine particles with an aerodynamic diameter below 10 microns can enter the lungs and even the bloodstream, and can induce severe acute or chronic disease (Cao et al., 2013).

The case of grain is peculiar as it may be mixed with contaminated earth (fertilizers, pesticides used in agriculture, mycotoxins, and microflora), which spread through the air in the absence of filters between silos and ships. Conveyor belts carrying coal (between port and power plant) or iron ore, if not closed, cause spillage and fugitive dust emissions at feeding, transfer and discharge points.

As ports are often magnets for industrial activity, pollution may also come from a variety of sites, such as oil refineries and chemical and petrochemical plants. The health implications of residing near such activities have been the focus of numerous studies, although they do not discuss the specific role of port and related transport/logistics activities.

Especially during the loading and unloading of tanker ships, VOCs (methane and nonmethane) contribute to GHG emissions. Among them, the heavier components (nonmethane VOCs) contribute to low-level photochemical oxidants, such as ozone, which affect human health and the environment. Ship demolition or modification can emit asbestos, heavy metals, hydrocarbons and ozone-depleting substances. Additional pollutants include oil itself (accidental discharge, loss from deposit tankers and pipeline), oil and rubber (spill from bulk-handling device), oily and toxic sludges (fuel deposits), as well as polychlorinated biphenyls, hydrofluorocarbons, and hydrocarbons (ship demolition in developing countries) (Trozzi and Vaccaro, 2000).

A series of case studies was conducted in industrial port cities in Italy in the past decade or so, demonstrating the health effects of ports but also of the associated industrial areas. In Brindisi, increased health risk was observed when the prevailing wind came from the port and the industrial area (Gianicolo et al., 2013). In Civitavecchia, people living near the port, with higher concentrations of PM10 or NOX, were younger (18–44 years old) and had a lower socio-economic profile, with higher mortality from all cancers and neurological diseases (Bauleo et al., 2019).

Heavy industrial sites are also of key concern as accidents and hazards frequently occur in these locations. For France, Georgeault (2015) demonstrated that a large share of all industrial accidents since the 1960s had occurred at seaport-industrial complexes (e.g., Bordeaux, Brest, Calais, Dunkirk, Le Havre, Marseille, Rouen). Darbra and Casal (2004) highlighted a drastic increase in events in European ports between the 1960s and 2002s, of which loss of containment (51%), fire (29%), explosion (17%) and gas cloud (3%), while the main activities were transport (57%), loading and unloading (15%), storage (12%), processing (11%) and warehousing (4%).

Lecue and Darbra (2019) analyzed about 650 accidents in European ports between 1961 and 2017, involving release of oil or derivatives (57%) and chemicals (24%). A minority of these accidents caused death (20%) or injuries (30%). The main activity involved was transport (42%) and transfer (32%), and the main types of accident were chemical release (61%), fire (23%), explosion (16%), and gas cloud (3%).

Data and methodology

This study investigates the environmental and health impacts of maritime traffic on FUAs. FUAs are defined using the harmonized OECD-EU framework, which delineates urban cores and commuting zones based on daily mobility patterns. FUAs are composed of:

- City core: Defined by urban centers according to the degree of urbanization, adapted to the closest local administrative units.
- Commuting zone: Includes all local areas where at least 15% of employed residents commute to work in the city.

To integrate ports into the FUA framework, we applied a 20 km buffer around each FUA. This adjustment accounts for cases where port coordinates fall outside the strict FUA boundaries due to physical expansion, while remaining functionally part of the urban area. All variables were spatially matched to FUAs and ports using R and GIS techniques. Demographic and economic indicators were aggregated at the FUA level, while maritime and environmental data were linked to port locations. Derived indicators, such as proportions and rates, were calculated using standard statistical methods. To ensure comparability across FUAs and to avoid the country bias, Location Quotients (LQ) were calculated. LQ transformations allow the study to capture the functional intensity of different types of maritime traffic relative to broader regional or national patterns.

To quantify shipping-related CO_2 emissions within each urban area, a 12-nautical-mile buffer was generated outward from the boundary of each FUA to delineate the near-shore zone in which maritime activities are most likely to exert environmental influence on the city. For emission data, this study draws on the shipping-related CO_2 emissions reported in the EDGAR database under the IPCC 1996 categories 1A3d (international navigation) and 1C2 (domestic navigation). These two categories are merged in EDGAR and jointly provide a comprehensive representation of CO_2 emissions from maritime fuel combustion. For each year, the gridded emission layer for the shipping sector was spatially intersected with the 12-nautical-mile buffer of each FUA, and all grid cells falling within the buffer were extracted. Annual statistics were then computed for each FUA, including total emissions, mean emission intensity, maximum value, median value, the number of intersected grids, and the area covered. Together, these indicators characterize not only the overall magnitude of shipping emissions around each city but also their spatial concentration patterns.

In order to better understand the relationships among the numerous demographic, environmental, economic, and maritime variables, the study applies Principal Component Analysis (PCA). PCA is used to reduce the dimensionality of the dataset while preserving the maximum possible variance. This technique identifies underlying patterns by transforming the original correlated variables into a smaller set of uncorrelated components. These components

Table 11.1 Selected indicators on European port cities

Category	*Variable*	*Unit of measure*	*Source*
Demographic	Proportion of 65 years old	Percentage (%)	Own calculations
	Population density	Persons/km²	OECD
	Mortality rate	Deaths per capita	NUTS3
	Life expectancy	Years at birth	NUTS3
Economic	GDP per capita	Currency per person	OECD
	Unemployment rate	Percentage (%)	NUTS2/OECD
	Education level (ISCED ≥ 5)	Percentage (%)	NUTS2
Environmental	$PM_{2.5}$ concentration	μg/m³ (micrograms per cubic meter)	Atmospheric Composition Analysis Group
	NO_2 concentration	ppm (parts per million)	Atmospheric Composition Analysis Group
	Ship CO_2 emissions	kt (kiloton)	EDGAR
Maritime	Total traffic	Gross Registered Tons	Lloyd's List
	Container	Gross Registered Tons	Lloyd's List
	Cruise	Gross Registered Tons	Lloyd's List
	Liquid bulk	Gross Registered Tons	Lloyd's List
	Passenger	Gross Registered Tons	Lloyd's List
	Solid bulk	Gross Registered Tons	Lloyd's List
	Other	Gross Registered Tons	Lloyd's List

summarize the dominant gradients of variation across FUAs, facilitating interpretation and subsequent analysis. Following PCA, a clustering procedure was performed to group FUAs according to their shared characteristics. Clustering allows FUAs with similar profiles to be classified into coherent groups. This step helps reveal distinct types of port–city systems, such as high-traffic cruise hubs, industrial cargo-oriented ports, or low-exposure urban areas. These clusters are then used to interpret how different port–city typologies relate to environmental pressures and potential health impacts.

Given the panel structure of the data (multiple FUAs observed over time), two econometric models are proposed. A Fixed Effects (FE) model is preferred, as it controls for unobserved, time-invariant characteristics of each FUA (e.g., geographic location, historical infrastructure). This approach allows for robust estimation of the traffic effect while accounting for latent heterogeneity. A Random Effects (RE) model may be used for comparison, and a Hausman test will be conducted to validate model choice (Table 11.1).

Main results

Panel data regression results (2000–2019)

As seen in Figure 11.1, population density is the major cause of all three emissions, in general ($PM_{2.5}$, NO_2) and from ships (CO_2), followed by GDP.

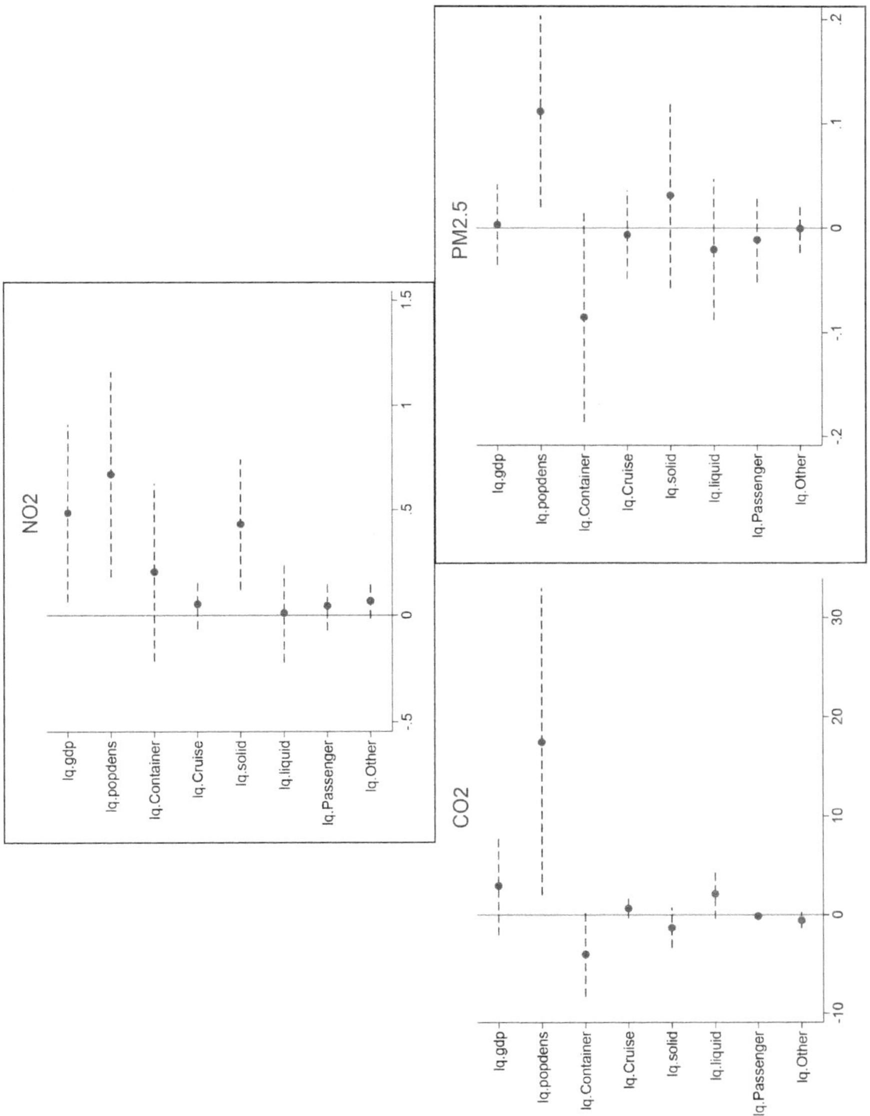

Figure 11.1 The influence of maritime traffic on local air pollution

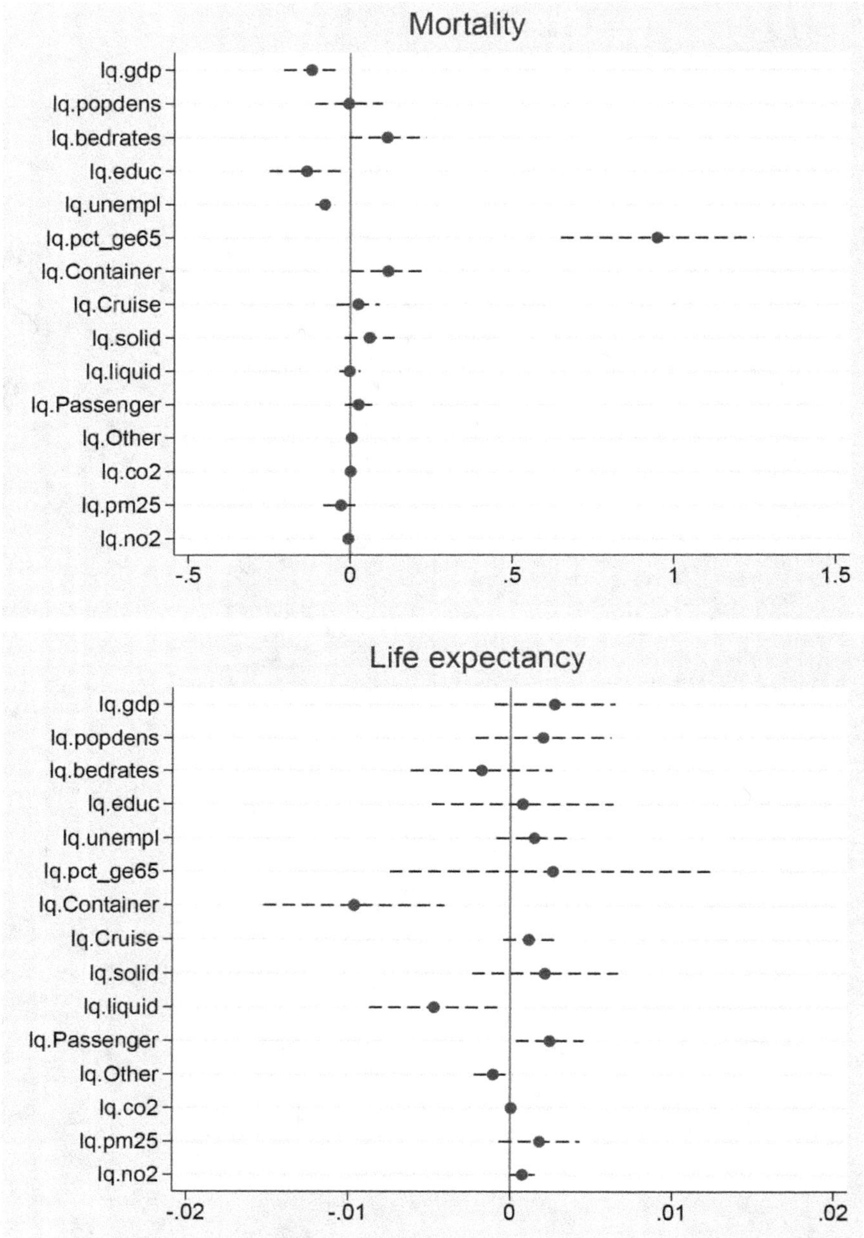

Figure 11.2 The influence of maritime traffic and pollutions on mortality and life expectancy

Such a result means that the nature of the socio-economic environment is far more important than maritime activities to explain local air pollution. Highly concentrated and productive urban environments tend to emit more than others, due to the agglomeration of people and economic activities. In turn, this agglomeration fosters intensive commuter flows, which may lead to congestion and pollution at peak hours. Solid bulks have a minor but positive influence on $PM_{2.5}$ and NO_2. This importance for emissions in general can be explained by the production of dust clouds from coal, ores, and grain during cargo handling, transport, and storage, as specified earlier.

The age category over 65 years old has a positive influence on both mortality and life expectancy (Figure 11.2). This means that aging cities are more likely to have deaths than other cities, but at the same time, aging cities witness a longer-than-average lifespan. In terms of traffic, containers slightly increase mortality and strongly reduce life expectancy, while solid bulks increase both, and liquid bulks reduce life expectancy. The high and negative influence of containers and liquid bulks on life expectancy suggests the presence of heavy industries and logistics facilities that exacerbate congestion and pollution within port cities. When it comes to the socio-economic environment, GDP, educational level, and unemployment reduce mortality, while GDP, population density, and unemployment increase life expectancy. The scores of pollutions are not significant, except for $PM_{2.5}$, which positively influences life expectancy.

PCA and port city typology

Results from the PCA underline several interesting trends about the intermingling of health, environment, and socio-economic dimensions in European port cities (Figure 11.3). The most negative scores on the second component (vertical axis) include unemployment, cruise, and passengers (including roll-on/roll-off and vehicles).

In the related literature, the relationship between cruise/passenger shipping and employment is ambivalent. On the one hand, several studies confirmed that cruise has direct, indirect, and induced benefits on local employment. Globally, Arlı et al. (2023) found that a 1% change in the number of world cruise tourists reduces the world unemployment rate by 7.6%, suggesting a correlation between cruise activity and employment (see also McWay, 2022). Positive effects of cruise and passenger shipping on employment were found at the local level in diverse port cities, such as Valletta (McCarthy, 2003), Zadar (Jugović, 2021), and Barcelona (Vayá et al., 2018). On the other hand, Bottasso et al. (2013) found that regional employment in Europe is positively correlated to overall port throughput, but not to the number of passengers. The authors argue that transit passengers do not generate significant local expenditure, and the ferry industry is capital-intensive. Chang et al. (2016) demonstrated that cruise ship visits to the Port of Incheon (South Korea) primarily benefit the Seoul economy in terms of job creation and value added, rather than the local port city itself, which implies a limited direct correlation with local employment in Incheon. This "hinterland effect", which can be found in other places (e.g., Civitavecchia and Rome in Italy), is aggravated by the "seasonal effect", due to the rise of unemployment during the off-season, and its effects on sales, profitability, and investment (Espinet-Rius et al., 2024).

A second trend is the correlation between solid bulks, liquid bulks, other traffics, and mortality in the upper-left quadrant of Figure 11.3. As mentioned in our literature review, existing works have already discussed the health risks related with the transport of dangerous goods and hazardous materials. Other works have been conducted, focusing on specific places. For instance, the port of Barcelona is a leading regional distribution hub for hydrocarbons and a vital part of the metropolitan energy production and distribution systems, suggesting a link between bulk cargo (like hydrocarbons/LNG) and urban environments (Nogué-Algueró, 2020). Focusing

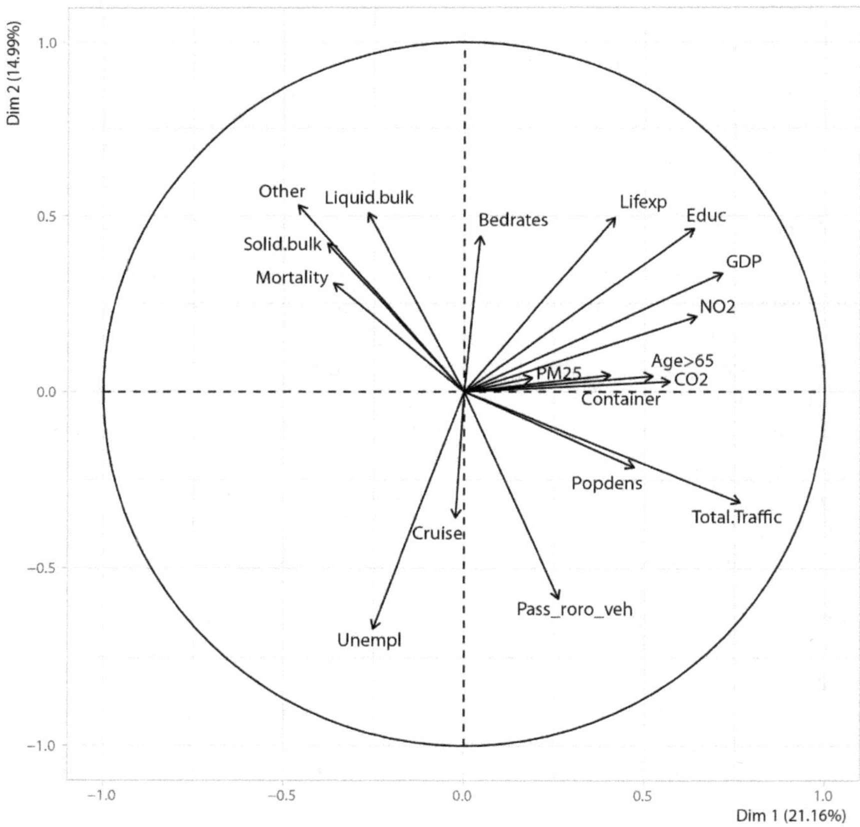

Figure 11.3 Results of the Principal Components Analysis (PCA)

on the Louisiana Mississippi Chemical Corridor (also known as "Cancer Alley"), Mah (2015) argues that the production, consumption, and routes of dangerous cargo, including bulk petrochemicals, reproduce a highly uneven geography of toxic risks, burdening the most marginalized and disadvantaged populations. It was also found that in Busan Gamcheon port, industrial activities stemming from bulk traffic are responsible for air pollution in adjacent areas because they produce relatively large volumes of PM and oxide dust due to their dusty nature and the processing of heavy cargo (Hwang and Kim, 2020). The authors established a causality between scrap metal and fine dust concentrations in the local unit. This can explain why "other traffic", which contains general cargo, participates in the observed trend. Although a PCA cannot account for causal relationships, mortality cannot cause traffic, so it is possible to confirm that traffic causes mortality, should it be directly (pollution from ships) or indirectly (pollution and hazards from related industries).

The third trend is a large group of variables projected on the right (positive) side of the first component (horizontal). This group is characterized by an intermingling of the three pollutions (CO_2, $PM_{2.5}$, NO_2) as well as large total traffic, container traffic, and population density. It is a profile of a large and modern port operating within a dense urban environment, so that port and city combine to create important emissions and congestion. At the same time, such port cities are positively characterized by a higher-than-average educational level, life expectancy, age over 65 years, and GDP. This is a typical profile of a metropolitan area, as in the case of regional and national capitals, which concentrate population and economic wealth, together with a healthy population despite congestion and pollution.

Those three trends actually correspond to three specific types of port cities based on average scores (Table 11.2) and the cartography of these types (Figure 11.4).

Among Metropolitan port cities, we find the main coastal capital cities where ports play a key role in global container shipping. They include Barcelona, Athens (Piraeus), Stockholm, London, Malta (Valletta), Amsterdam, Lisbon, Oslo, Helsinki, Tallinn, and Dublin. These capitals are the principal gateways of their home country. This category also includes regional capitals such as Antwerp, Rotterdam, Hamburg, and Bremen, which are hubs whose activity constitutes a major source of revenue for their belonged country.

Critical port cities possess industrial areas that play an important role in the national economy, specializing in liquid and solid bulk shipping. They include Rostock, Belfast, Middelburg, Huelva, La Coruña, Porto, Århus, Thessaloniki, Taranto, La Rochelle, Bordeaux, Lorient, Nantes, and Oostende. They are often small and medium-sized port cities located near important urban centers.

Between those two clusters, a third one is composed of a majority of the sample of port cities, coined tourism port cities due to their important cruise and passenger traffic. Among them, we find numerous insular port cities

Table 11.2 Three clusters of European port cities

	Critical port cities	*Metropolitan port cities*	*Tourism port cities*
CO_2	10.029	**11.309**	10.643
Container	12.049	**24.696**	17.493
Liquid bulk	**24.879**	7.729	11.016
Solid bulk	**18.558**	5.424	4.722
Cruise	6.914	10.843	**12.877**
Pass/roro/vehic	9.836	46.687	**48.190**
Other	**27.762**	4.621	5.703
Total traffic	15.695	**18.255**	17.130
PM2.5	0.969	**1.075**	0.926
NO_2	0.613	**1.300**	0.535
Life expectancy	0.995	**1.003**	0.995
GDP	0.821	**1.148**	0.852
Educational level	0.882	**1.072**	0.901
Unemployment	**1.097**	0.980	1.085
Bed rates	**1.045**	1.003	0.953
Mortality	**1.077**	0.934	1.075
Age > 65	0.041	**0.334**	0.036
Population density	0.603	**1.446**	0.898

Numbers in bold highlight the most important data.

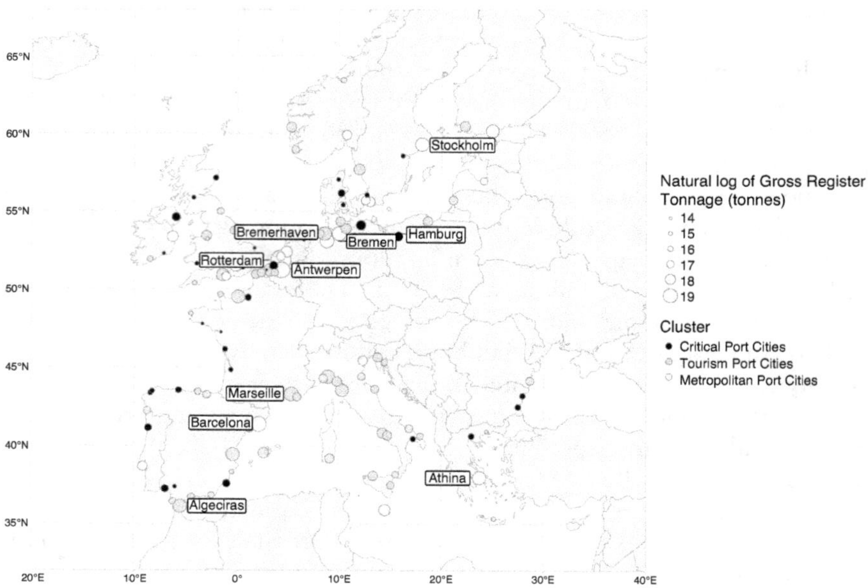

Figure 11.4 Typology of European port cities

such as in Sicily and Sardinia in Italy, Balearic Islands in Spain, and certain Greek islands (Chania). A large share of them is located in southern Europe, specializing in ro-ro and cruise, like Tarragona, Marseilles, Genoa, Naples, Brindisi, Split, etc. This cluster is also present in northern Europe, especially for cross-Channel traffic between Calais, mainland port cities, and the British Isles, as well as other port cities in Denmark, Norway (Trondheim), Sweden (Umea), Finland, and eastern Europe (Klaipeda, Rijeka).

Conclusion

Thanks to this analysis, three key points emerge in order to consider certain limits and to better understand the territorial dimension of these three types of port cities. First, it is possible to address an "environmental paradox". In the 1960s, port migration outside urban cores had been motivated by three elements: the lack of space to develop port-related industrial areas, the handling of bigger ships at deep-water sites, and the need for the city to "breath" again while removing negative externalities of shipping and ports. However, this separation has only displaced the problem of pollution, which has intensified through mass traffic to/from these new facilities (Lo Prete, 2023).

Second, there are methodological challenges to measure air pollution from ships. This pollution is mostly invisible and odorless (e.g., carbon monoxydes), so that human senses are often misleading (Lo Prete, 2023). Another difficulty is to identify the types of pollutants and to verify their link with shipping operations. Certain studies managed to distinguish several pollutants (i.e., SO_x, No_x, PM), and the fact that SO_x and NO_x emissions are particularly high during vessel berthing in the port (Lo Prete, 2023), while PM emissions are more related to cargo handling at berth (Ledoux et al., 2018), especially in the case of solid bulk. Lastly, there is also the difficulty to know which areas are the most affected by pollutions (Lo Prete, 2023). Wind is the principal vector to distribute emissions, and according to wind strength and directions, areas near the port are more or less vulnerable. The invisibility, amplitude, and borderless nature of ship emissions amplify the environmental vulnerability of not only port cities but also hinterland cities (INERIS, 2019).

Third, it seems important and necessary to link the port city typology with certain characteristics of maritime basins under study. In the Mediterranean, the three clusters are present, but there is a clear dominance of tourism port cities, for which cruise, passengers and ro-ro have an impact on environmental health. The first challenge is the territorial continuity among Med countries and notably islands (ferries and ro-ro), a condition for port cities to thrive, whatever their size. The second challenge is tourism, as the Med concentrates one-fifth of global cruise activity, and is the second most popular destination in the world, after the Caribbean (Lo Prete et al., 2024; Lo Prete and Kerbiriou, 2025). These traffics (ferry, ro-ro, cruise) thus target both territorial continuity and touristic benefits in the Med.

In the Black Sea, the majority of FUAs are critical port cities, mostly due to the fact that merchant vessels convey a huge share of global bulk traffic in this area, in relation to the industrialization of those port cities, notably with their strategic role for grain traffic. The Atlantic range possesses all three types of port cities, including a dominance of critical port cities. This relates to the presence of industrial activities in direct relation with maritime traffic, and to national strategies of port specialization to create functional complementarity. In the Channel and North Sea, port cities are very diverse, notwithstanding a strong role of ro-ro and ferry traffic in the Channel to link the mainland and British Isles (Lacoste and Lo Prete, 2024). In the North Sea, container traffic dominates, due to dominant hubs along the Northern Range.

To conclude, this diversity and complexity is not carved in stone, as the separation between port cities continues in various places. Port cities face more and more regulatory constraints, questioning their capacity to answer those multilevel rules and challenges. In fact, all new environmental regulations will have an impact on ship operations and, consequently, on operating costs. The cost implications will depend on the mitigation strategies implemented by shipowners and, to a large extent, on how the regulations are enforced in each port city (Lo Prete and Kerbiriou, 2025).

References

Abeal-Vázquez J.P., Moss S. L., Teira-Fachado A. (2024) The impact of cruise product consumption phases on cruise passenger spending in a non-overnight stay port: Implications for destination managers. *Tourism and Hospitality*, 5(4): 1182.

Agarwala P., Chhabra S., Agarwala N. (2021) Using digitalisation to achieve decarbonisation in the shipping industry. *Journal of International Maritime Safety, Environmental Affairs, and Shipping*, 5: 161–174.

Arlı E., Saygılı M.S., Ülker D. (2023) Analysis of the co-integration between the number of cruise Tourists and the World Unemployment Rate. *Journal of ETA Maritime Science*, 11(4): 242–250.

Athul S., Kuttippurath J., Patel V.K. (2025) Changes in global NO_2 pollution by shipping during the COVID-19 lockdown: Implication for sustainable marine operations. *Journal of Hazardous Materials*, 481: 136482.

Bauleo L., Bucci S., Antonucci C., Sozzi R., Davoli M., Forastiere F., Ancona C. (2019) Long-term exposure to air pollutants from multiple sources and mortality in an industrial area: A cohort study. *Occupational and Environmental Medicine*, 76(1): 48–57.

Bottasso A., Conti M., Ferrari C., Merk O., Tei A. (2013) The impact of port throughput on local employment: Evidence from a panel of European regions. *Transport Policy*, 27: 32–38.

Calgaro L., Giubilato E., Aghito M., Jalkanen J.P., Majamaki E., Ferrarin C., Hänninen R., Palamarchuk Y., Sofiev M., Semenzin E., Marcomini A. (2025) Influence of shipping activities on air and water quality in the Northern Adriatic Sea: A high-resolution modelling study. *Marine Pollution Bulletin*, 217: 118102.

Cao J., Chow J.C., Lee F.S.C., Watson J.G. (2013) Evolution of PM2.5 measurements and standards in the U.S. and future perspectives for China. *Aerosol and Air Quality Research*, 13: 1197–1211.

Chang Y.T., Park H., Liu S.M., Roh Y. (2016) Economic impact of cruise industry using regional input–output analysis: A case study of Incheon. *Maritime Policy and Management*, 43(1): 1–18.

Corbett J.J., Wang H., James J., Winebrake J.J. (2009) The effectiveness and costs of speed reductions on emissions from international shipping. *Transportation Research Part D: Transport and the Environment*, 14: 593–598.

D'Amico F., Ammoscato I., Gullì D., Avolio E., Lo Feudo T., De Pino M., Cristofanelli P., Malacaria L., Parise D., Sinopoli S., De Benedetto G., Calidonna C.R. (2024) Anthropic-induced variability of greenhouse gases and aerosols at the WMO/GAW coastal site of Lamezia Terme (Calabria, Southern Italy): Towards a new method to assess the weekly distribution of gathered data. *Sustainability*, 16(18): 8175.

Darbra R.M., Casal J. (2004) Historical analysis of accidents in seaports. *Safety Science*, 42(2): 85–98.

Englert B., Lam S., Steinhoff P. (2011) *The Impact of Truck Repositioning on Congestion and Pollution in the LA Basin*. California State University, Long Beach, METRANS Transportation Center (Calif.), https://rosap.ntl.bts.gov/view/dot/23264

Espinet-Rius J.M., García-Sánchez A., Gassiot-Melian A. (2024) Seasonality in the cruise industry: Activity, prices and regionality. *European Journal of Tourism Research*, 38: 3810.

Georgeault L. (2015) L'écologie industrielle et son pilotage dans la construction d'une politique publique d'aménagement du territoire en France. In: Alix Y., Mat N., Cerceau J. (Eds.), *Economie Circulaire et Ecosystèmes Portuaires*. Caen: EMS Editions, pp. 55–71.

Gianicolo E.A., Bruni A., Mangia C., Cervino M., Vigotti M.A. (2013) Acute effects of urban and industrial pollution in a government-designated "Environmental risk area": The case of Brindisi, Italy. *International Journal of Environmental Health Research*, 23(5): 446–460.

Gibbs D., Rigot-Muller P., Mangan J., Lalwani C. (2014) The role of sea ports in end-to-end maritime transport chain emissions. *Energy Policy*, 64: 337–348.

Hernández D., González-Olivardía F., Pinzón-Acosta C., Cruz E. (2024) Systematic review of the impacts of ship emissions in ports and nearby coastal areas. *9th International Engineering, Sciences and Technology Conference (IESTEC)*, IEEE, pp. 1–6.

Hoffmann J., Asariotis R., Assaf M., Benamara H. (2018) *Review of Maritime Transport*. New York: United Nations Publications.

Howitt O.J.A., Revol V.G.N., Smith I.J., Rodger C.J. (2010) Carbon emissions from international cruise ship passengers' travel to and from New Zealand. *Energy Policy*, 38: 2552–2560.

Hwang J., Kim S. (2020) Fine dust and sustainable supply chain management in port operations: Focus on the major cargo handled at the dry bulk port. *Journal of Marine Science and Engineering*, 8: 530.

INERIS (2019) ECAMED: A technical feasibility study for the implementation of an emission control area (ECA) in the Mediterranean Sea. *French National Institute for Industrial Environment and Risks (INERIS)*, with contributions from Cerema, Citepa and Plan Bleu (DRC-19-168862-00408A).

Jugović A. (2021) The impact of maritime passenger traffic on the development of seaports and their surroundings. In: Karanovic G., Polychronidou P., Karasavvoglou A.,

Ribaric H. M. (Eds.), *Tourism Management and Sustainable Development*. New York: Springer, pp. 143–159.

Kotowska I., Kubowicz D. (2019) The role of ports in reduction of road transport pollution in port cities. *Transportation Research Procedia*, 39: 212–220.

Lacoste R., Lo Prete M. (2024) Les ports secondaires rouliers et ferries en France: le tournant ferroviaire des pré et post acheminements de remorques non accompagnées. *Les Cahiers Scientifiques du Transport*, 82: 21–42.

Lansø A.S., Winther M., Steen S.J., Løfstrøm P. (2023) Impact on air quality from increasing cruise ship activity in Copenhagen port. *Environmental Research Communications*, 5(2): 021003.

Lecue M., Darbra R.M. (2019) Accidents in European ports involving chemical substances: Characteristics and trends. *Safety Science*, 115: 278–284.

Ledoux F., Roche C., Cazier F., Beaugard C., Courcot D. (2018) Influence of ship emissions on NO_x, SO_2, O_3 and PM concentrations in a North-Sea harbor in France. *Journal of Environmental Sciences*, 71: 56–66.

Lloret J., Carreño A., Carić H., San J., Fleming L.E. (2021) Environmental and human health impacts of cruise tourism: A review. *Marine Pollution Bulletin*, 173(A): 112979.

Lo Prete M. (2015) La vulnérabilité des villes portuaires méditerranéennes françaises et italiennes au prisme des contentieux. *Les Annales de la Recherche Urbaine*, Ville et vulnérabilités, 110: 206–215.

Lo Prete M. (2023) La pollution atmosphérique des navires: une cause majeure de vulnérabilité environnementale. In: Mathlouthi R. B., Pomade A. (Eds.), *Vulnérabilité(s) Environnementale(s): Perspectives Pluridisciplinaires*. L'Harmattan Environnement, pp. 229–250.

Lo Prete M., Kerbiriou R. (2025) Regard croisé entre villes portuaires méditerranéennes. Quelle évolution et emprise spatiale de la croisière? In: Kerbiriou R., Bazille A., Alix Y. (Eds.), *Les Ports Territoriaux: Ambition-Action-Anticipation*. Éditions EMS, Caen: Collection les Océanides, pp. 323–346.

Lo Prete M., Roche C., Dubois A., Chagnon Ph., Lacoste R. (2024) La croisière en Méditerranée: un levier de développement pour les ports mineurs? Le cas des villes-ports espagnoles, françaises et monégasques. *Géotransports*, 21: 41–57.

Mah A. (2015) Dangerous cargo and uneven toxic risks: Petrochemicals in the port of New Orleans. In: Birtchnell T., Savitzky S., Urry J. (Eds.), *Cargomobilities. Moving Materials in a Global Age*. London: Routledge, pp. 149–162.

McCarthy J. (2003) The cruise industry and port city regeneration: The case of Valletta. *European Planning Studies*, 11(3): 341–350.

McWay R. (2022) Cruising through school: General equilibrium effects of cruise ship arrivals on employment and education. *The American Economist*, 67(1): 5–23.

Mendoza-Lara O.O., Ortega-Montoya C.Y., Prieto Hinojosa A.I., López-Pérez A.O., Baldasano J.M. (2023) An empirical and modelling approach to the evaluation of cruise ships' influence on air quality: The case of La Paz, Mexico. *Science of the Total Environment*, 886: 163855.

Merico E., Cesari D., Gregoris E., Gambaro A., Cordella M., Contini D. (2021) Shipping and air quality in Italian port cities: State-of-the-art analysis of available results of estimated impacts. *Atmosphere*, 12(5): 536.

Merico E., Dinoi A., Contini D. (2019) Development of an integrated modelling-measurement system for near-real-time estimates of harbour activity impact to atmospheric pollution in coastal cities. *Transportation Research Part D: Transport and the Environment*, 73: 108–119.

Mueller N., Westerby M., Nieuwenhuijsen M. (2023) Health impact assessments of shipping and port-sourced air pollution on a global scale: A scoping literature review. *Environmental Research*, 216: 114460.

Navarro-Ruiz S., Casado-Díaz A.B., Ivars-Baidal J. (2020) Cruise tourism: The role of shore excursions in the overcrowding of cities. *International Journal of Tourism Cities*, 6(1): 197–214.

Nogué-Alguerό B. (2020) Growth in the docks: Ports, metabolic flows and socio-environmental impacts. *Sustainability Science*, 15: 11–30.

Olaniyi E.O., Prause G., Gerasimova V., Inkinen T. (2022) Clean cruise shipping: Experience from the BSR. *Sustainability*, 14(9): 5002.

Paoli C., Vassallo P., Dapueto G., Fanciulli G., Massa F., Venturini S., Povero P. (2017) The economic revenues and the energy costs of cruise tourism. *Journal of Cleaner Production*, 166: 1462–1478.

Rowangould D., Rowangould G., Niemeier, D. (2018) Evaluation of the health impacts of rolling back a port clean trucks program. *Transportation Research Record*, 2672: 53–64.

Santos M., Radicchi E., Zagnoli P. (2019) Port's role as a determinant of cruise destination socio-economic sustainability. *Sustainability*, 11: 4542.

Sathish M.N., Patterson J. (2025) The ecotoxicological implications and contamination profile of organochlorine pesticides (OCPs), organophosphorus pesticides (OPPs), and heavy metals, in Tuticorin, Southeast Coast of India. *Regional Studies in Marine Science*, *87*, 104237.

Sun L., Zhang J., Ducruet C., Itoh H., Liu X. (2025) The impact of shipping activities on air quality and residents' health in China's port cities. *Journal of Transport Geography*, 123: 104099.

Trozzi C., Vaccaro R. (2000) Environmental impact of port activities. In: Brebbia C.A., Olivella J. (Eds.), *Maritime Engineering and Ports II*. Southampton: WIT Press: 151-161.

Van Vianen T., Ottjes J., Lodewijks G. (2014) Simulation-based determination of the required stockyard size for dry bulk terminals. *Simulation Modelling Practice and Theory*, 42: 119–128.

Vayá E., Garcia J.R., Murillo J., Romaní J., Suriñach J. (2018) Economic impact of cruise activity: The case of Barcelona. *Journal of Travel & Tourism Marketing*, 35(4): 479–492.

Yu C.M., Chin M., Tan Q., Bian H., Colarco P.R., Yu H.(2025) Assessing COVID-19 lockdowns' impacts on global urban $PM_{2.5}$ air quality with observations and modeling. *Atmospheric Chemistry and Physics*, https://doi.org/10.5194/egusphere-2025-1750

Yuan C.S., Cheng W.H., Huang H.Y. (2022) Spatiotemporal distribution characteristics and potential sources of VOCs at an industrial harbor city in southern Taiwan: Three-year VOCs monitoring data analysis. *Journal of Environmental Management*, 303: 114259.

12 The relationship between maritime transportation and urban health in China

Sheng Zhang, César Ducruet and Liehui Wang

Introduction

Since China's reform and opening and its accession to the World Trade Organization, many Chinese ports have ranked among the world's top 100, and the Port of Shanghai, the country's largest, has surpassed 50 million 20-foot-equivalent units (TEUs) in container throughput. Port cities exemplified by Shanghai have taken the lead in green-transition initiatives, including shore-power supply, green-fuel bunkering, and automated terminals, placing them ahead of top domestic hubs in advancing the green-port agenda. Nevertheless, within China's overall urban-development strategy, the health implications of green development in port cities have not received sufficient attention. At present, port-development strategies still prioritize scale expansion, and green-port policies are more often treated as instruments to boost throughput than as health-centered, sustainability-oriented strategies.

As seaborne trade has multiplied, reducing or avoiding the health impacts of port activities on residents of port cities and their surrounding areas has become a central concern in green development. Evidence indicates that port-related air pollution is closely linked to cardiovascular disease, lung cancer, asthma, impaired lung function, and stroke (Loxham, 2021). Declining air quality not only increases mortality risk but also substantially diminishes quality of life. With rising life expectancy and expanding urban footprints, the adverse health effects of long-term pollution exposure are likely to intensify.

However, China's Healthy City strategy is largely organized by urban scale, categorizing policies for large, medium, and small cities (Qinghua University, 2024), and it lacks a systematic design for health issues specific to port cities and maritime transport. This study examines differences in health outcomes between residents of port and non-port cities and analyzes the potential individual-level impacts of port-related transport activities. We provide a systematic academic assessment of the mechanisms through which port transport affects disease-specific mortality, morbidity, and healthcare expenditures, and we further elucidate these effects by

DOI: 10.4324/9781003639589-16

integrating environmental and economic variables. The findings offer a theoretical foundation and decision guidance for the formulation, optimization, and refinement of policies in health management and environmental protection.

Literature review

Transport and health are linked through multiple pathways, with research to date focusing most often on road and urban transport (see Figure 12.1). As early as 2000, the World Health Organization undertook a systematic assessment of transport, environment, and health, highlighting road-traffic injuries, transport-related air pollution, psychological effects of mobility, active transportation (cycling and walking), and impacts on priority or vulnerable populations (Dora and Phillips, 2000). Widener and Hatzopoulou (2016) synthesized five principal domains of impact: the natural environment (e.g., traffic-related air pollution and its health linkages, contributions to climate change, and noise); health-supporting spatial infrastructure (especially accessibility of hospitals and other care resources); morbidity and mortality (from crashes and from indirect losses due to inadequate infrastructure); health behaviors (travel-mode choices and the surrounding built environment); and the diffusion of infectious disease through transport networks (Widener and Hatzopoulou, 2016). Glazener et al. (2021) further enumerated 14 urban pathways, including blue-green spaces, physical activity, accessibility, independent mobility, pollution, social exclusion, noise, urban heat islands, traffic injuries, community severance, and greenhouse-gas emissions. This framework provides an operational basis for indicator selection (Glazener et al., 2021). Nieuwenhuijsen and Khreis (2020) catalogued an extensive

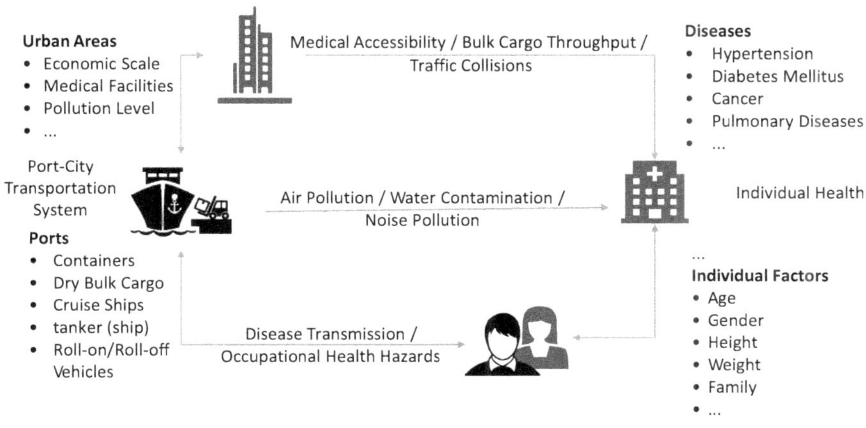

Figure 12.1 Research framework

set of mediators, such as pollution, noise, physical activity, and community segregation, and proposed policy instruments to guide future interventions (Nieuwenhuijsen and Khreis, 2020).

Current assessments of transport-related health impacts primarily evaluate urban transport systems, including road, rail, and even aviation. Consequently, studies of transport and health are often linked to urbanization, especially in rapidly developing China. Early debates in China focused on infrastructure expansion, such as the pollution and safety problems associated with rapid growth in highway mileage. As an authoritative venue in medicine, The Lancet has published work on transport and health in China, indicating that traffic injuries, physical inactivity, and pollution are the principal transport-attributable drivers of health loss (Jiang et al., 2017). Chinese scholars in the medical and environmental fields have synthesized evidence on Healthy Cities, concluding that urbanization over the past four decades has substantially shaped urban health and that noncommunicable diseases have become the dominant burden. They recommend integrating health into urban planning and advancing the "Healthy China 2030" goals (Yang et al., 2018). However, port cities, as a distinct urban typology, have not been explicitly incorporated into the Healthy China strategy. Although port cities account for a relatively small proportion of urban areas in China, with 53 out of 293 prefecture-level cities being coastal, they serve as national trade gateways, concentrate economic activities, and are densely populated. As a result, their impact on public health is profound.

Different transport modes exert heterogeneous health effects. Maritime transport underpins global connectivity, yet the proportion of cities directly engaged as seaports is relatively small. Accordingly, maritime transport constitutes an important component of both research on transport-related health impacts and policy design in China.

Research on the links between maritime transport and health generally follows two strands: evaluating the impacts of shipping on health, with air pollution treated as a key mediating channel; or examining how urban or individual health conditions influence the functioning of shipping and logistics, such as the effects of disease transmission on logistics and the effects of seafarers' physical and mental health on maritime operations. Yet research in port geography has largely neglected a systematic analysis within economic geography of the direct relationships between shipping and health.

Scholarship on maritime transport and health converges on three widely examined themes, namely adverse effects mediated by shipping-related pollutants, seafarers' health, and disease transmission associated with maritime transport. The first two themes primarily investigate the causal pathway from maritime activity to health outcomes. Determinants of health impacts include air, water, and noise pollution, traffic incidents and safety risks, and occupational hazards that arise directly from vessel operations and cargo handling. Additional, indirect effects stem from the socioeconomic consequences of maritime trade and from the spread of disease. Notably, health burdens that are maritime-related yet not confined to shipboard activity are often greater than those attributable to vessels alone and typically emerge at multiple points along the transport chain.

Existing research on the direct health impacts of port activity has focused primarily on air pollution, including the effects of port operations on local air quality (Sorte et al., 2020), the health burdens attributable to ship emissions (Corbett et al., 2007), the influence of port throughput on pollution and health (Sun et al., 2025), the health gains from environmental policy controls (Zhang et al., 2018), and the global health benefits of emission reductions in shipping (Jiang et al., 2017). Meta-analytical and empirical assessments quantify these effects. For example, Mueller et al. (2023) synthesized evidence on maritime transport, pollution, and health, estimating roughly 265,000 premature deaths associated with shipping emissions (Mueller et al., 2023). Kiihamäki et al. (2024) reviewed mortality linked to shipping-related ambient air pollution and reported excess all-cause mortality of one to five deaths per 100,000 person-years, with economic costs amounting to 0.06%–0.72% of gross domestic product (Kiihamäki et al., 2024).

A substantial body of study examined heterogeneity by region, pollutant, and exposed population. Regional case studies include the Port of Barcelona's contributions to air pollution and disease burden (Mueller et al., 2024) and the health impacts of shipping emissions in China (Luo et al., 2024). Pollutant-specific studies consider multipollutant co-exposure and its association with depression (Hao et al., 2025). Research on vulnerable or occupationally exposed groups highlights seafarers' health and occupational care needs (Zhang and Zhao, 2017) as well as mental health outcomes (Brooks and Greenberg, 2022; Jonglertmontree et al., 2022).

The most common "health to shipping" pathway concerns disease transmission and resulting logistics disruptions. The global configuration of maritime transport elevates transboundary infectious-disease risks, as seen in the spread of pathogens, interruptions to transport during COVID-19, and the persistence of post-COVID-19 effects on maritime logistics (Cullinane and Haralambides, 2021).

In economics, the focus typically lies on trade and health. Because maritime transport carries approximately 80%–90% of global merchandise trade, the literature is informative for understanding shipping–health linkages. Studies examine the direct health effects of imports (Adda and Fawaz, 2020), the relationship between trade liberalization and health in the United States (Pierce and Schott, 2020) and in China (Feng et al., 2021) and mortality effects associated with the trade war of the Trump era (Woolhandler et al., 2021). Related work on export shocks explores channels through employment, income, public services, taxation, and environmental pollution (Liu, 2018). Overall, rigorously identified evidence on the direct impacts of either trade or maritime shipping on health remains limited.

This study is organized into two parts that address spatial patterns and causal mechanisms. First, using chronic disease incidence as the focal indicator, we characterize the spatiotemporal variation of chronic disease across Chinese prefecture-level cities, examine the evolution of transport patterns, and assess the bivariate coupling between transport and disease. Second, we investigate causal mechanisms by estimating the direct effects of transport on health, including the impacts of 13 transport categories on 13 chronic disease outcomes.

Research data and methods

This study integrates a multiscale dataset encompassing individual, port, and urban levels. Individual-level data are drawn from the China Health and Retirement Longitudinal Study (CHARLS), a nationally representative survey capturing a broad spectrum of health and socioeconomic indicators. Port-level information is sourced from the Lloyd's List database, offering comprehensive insights into maritime activity. Urban-level data are supplemented with city statistical yearbooks and high-resolution satellite-derived gridded datasets, enabling fine-grained spatial and socioeconomic analysis. The primary variables employed in this study are as follows:

Individual-Level Survey Data: China Health and Retirement Longitudinal Study (CHARLS). CHARLS, available at https://charls.charlsdata.com, is a nationally representative, longitudinal social science survey jointly administered by the National School of Development and the Institute of Social Science Survey at Peking University. Designed to track the health, socioeconomic status, lifestyle, and aging-related issues of middle-aged and older Chinese adults (aged 45 and above), CHARLS provides rich micro-level data on households and individuals. Since its launch in 2011, the survey has been conducted every two to three years, with nationwide coverage spanning 28 provinces. For this study, we utilized data from the 2011, 2013, 2015, 2018, and 2020 survey waves.

The CHARLS dataset offers detailed information on dietary patterns and food consumption (e.g., daily food categories and intake quantities), household economic conditions, individual health indicators (e.g., body mass index, chronic disease prevalence, physical function), and lifestyle behaviors (e.g., smoking, alcohol use, physical activity). Its breadth and depth make it particularly suitable for analyzing health outcomes in relation to environmental and socioeconomic exposures at the individual level.

City Coverage in the Health and Nutrition Database: Port and Non-Port Urban Samples. The health and nutrition survey database includes data from 125 cities across China, among which 51 are identified as port cities. These port cities are further categorized into 28 inland river ports and 23 coastal ports.

Maritime traffic data is sourced from Lloyd's List Intelligence, a world leader in shipping information, which covers about 80% of the world fleet. Vessel traffic at ports is the product of call frequency and vessel capacity (in Gross Registered Tons). We aggregated port-level traffic at the city level, as a single city may contain several ports, such as Shenzhen (Chiwan, Shekou, Yantian). The 159 original vessel types were categorized as follows: containers, general cargo, solid bulks, liquid bulks, passengers and vehicles, port services, and other.

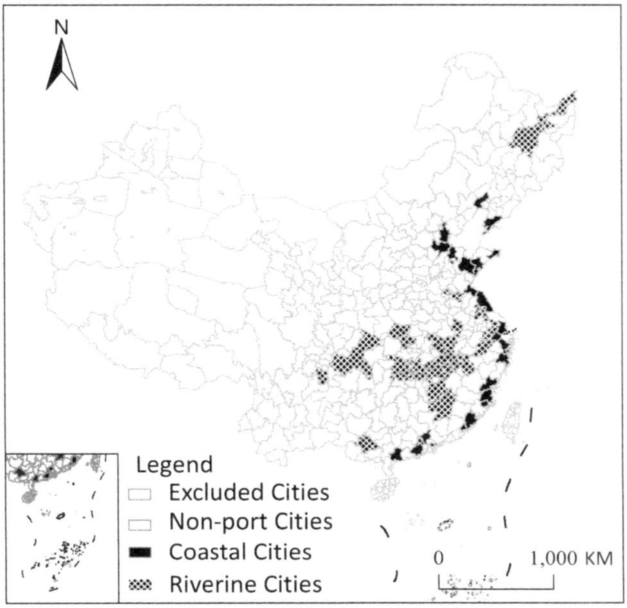

Figure 12.2 Study area

Note: The inland port cities represented in the dataset include: Anqing, Changde, Foshan, Ganzhou, Harbin, Hangzhou, Hefei-Chaohu, Huzhou, Huanggang, Ji'an, Jiamusi, Jingmen, Jingdezhen, Jiujiang, Nanchang, Nanning, Shangrao, Suzhou, Taizhou, Xiangyang (Xiangfan), Yangzhou, Yibin, Yichun, Yiyang, Yueyang, Changsha, Chongqing, and Xuzhou. The coastal port cities include: Binzhou, Cangzhou, Chaozhou, Dalian, Fuzhou, Guangzhou, Jiaxing, Jiangmen, Jinzhou, Lianyungang, Maoming, Ningbo, Ningde, Putian, Qingdao, Shanghai, Shenzhen, Taizhou, Tianjin, Weihai, Weifang, Yancheng, and Zhangzhou

This geographic distribution enables a comparative analysis between inland and coastal port cities, allowing the study to capture spatial heterogeneity in health outcomes and environmental exposures across distinct urban-port interfaces (Figure 12.2).

Result

Spatial patterns of chronic disease and maritime transport in Chinese port cities

Spatial patterns of chronic disease prevalence in Chinese cities

We use the CHARS database indicator "chronic (whether the respondent has a chronic disease)" to gauge individual health status. Figure 12.3 presents the spatial distribution of chronic disease prevalence for Wave 1 in 2011 and Wave 5 in 2020. To enable temporal comparisons, prevalence intervals are harmonized across the first and last survey years. Because the number of

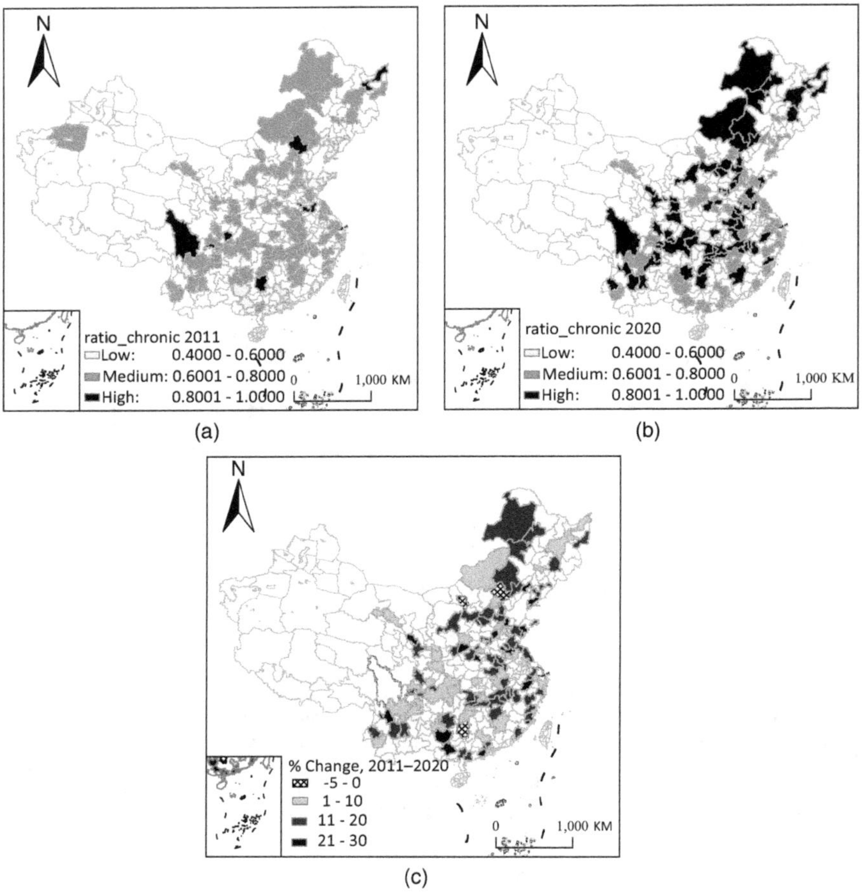

Figure 12.3 Comparison of changes in city-level chronic disease incidence in China between 2011 and 2020

Note: Because the survey population is not constant across cities, we define the incidence rate as the ratio of chronic disease cases to the total number of surveyed individuals in each city; accordingly, the reported incidence rates can be interpreted as the probability of disease under sampling. Although 2020 encompasses the pandemic period, chronic disease incidence is unlikely to have risen immediately in response to COVID-19

respondents varies by city and year, we measure city-level prevalence as the share of respondents with a chronic disease among all surveyed individuals in that city.

The results show a broad increase in prevalence from 2011 to 2020. In 2011, most surveyed Chinese cities fell in a medium band between 60% and 80%. By 2020, most cities had moved into a high-prevalence band above 80%. The increase is widespread across Northeast China, the North China Plain, the eastern seaboard, and several inland city clusters, while a small number of prefectures in the southwest and central regions show stable or declining patterns, indicated by hatched areas in the figure.

Although 2020 coincides with the COVID-19 pandemic, these findings align with national statistics. According to materials from China's National Health Commission, chronic disease prevalence is rising nationwide. Non-communicable diseases such as cardiovascular diseases and cancer account for more than 80% of deaths, with high prevalence, long duration, low effective control rates, and substantial economic burden that threatens population health and constrains socioeconomic development (CCTV News, 2024).

Over time, port cities exhibit lower chronic disease prevalence than non-port cities. A chi-squared test pooling all five survey waves from 2011 to 2020 indicates that the baseline prevalence in port cities is significantly lower than in non-port cities: 73.1% of residents in port cities have a chronic disease compared with 77.5% in non-port cities. Within the set of port cities, coastal port cities handle greater cargo throughput than riverine port cities, yet riverine port cities exhibit higher prevalence. In the top-ten prevalence rankings for 2011 and 2022, several inland river cities such as Cangzhou, Jiujiang, and Chongqing appear consistently, suggesting persistently high prevalence in parts of the inland river system with little improvement over time.

Maritime transport patterns of Chinese port cities

From the perspective of cargo movements, the hierarchy of Chinese port cities is broadly stable. Coastal ports such as Shanghai, Shenzhen, Ningbo, Qingdao, Dalian, Tianjin, and Guangzhou function as the principal comprehensive hubs, although their cargo portfolios differ. Shanghai, Ningbo, Qingdao, Tianjin, and Guangzhou are container-dominated, with containers accounting for more than 40% of total throughput. These ports are mixed in function, featuring a dominant cargo class, containers, alongside at least one additional class contributing no less than 20%. Shenzhen is a specialized container port where containers are overwhelmingly dominant. Suzhou and Taizhou are specialized dry-bulk ports. Ranked by the gross tonnage of vessel calls, Shanghai, Shenzhen, Weihai, Tianjin, and Guangzhou constitute the main passenger and cruise hubs. Although Weihai and Dalian are functionally mixed, passenger and cruise traffic is their leading activity, accounting for 54.72% in Weihai and 46.62% in Dalian. Among inland ports, Chongqing, while a local node, is a key energy port focused on oil, gas, and liquid bulk (Table 12.1).

Bivariate coupling of disease and transport

After analyzing disease patterns and transport patterns separately, we couple the two variables. Figure 12.4 presents a bivariate map contrasting the disease variable (Chronic) with the maritime transport variable (Throughput). The disease variable is derived from individual-level survey data in 2011 and 2020 and is defined as the share of respondents with a chronic condition in

Table 12.1 Transport profiles of coastal Chinese ports (regional hubs and above)

City	*Primary cargo type*	*Primary share*	*Secondary cargo type*	*Secondary share*	*HHI*	*Specialization*	*Hub level*
Shanghai	Containers	0.6010			0.4035	Mixed	Mega hub
Ningbo	Containers	0.5839	Dry bulk	0.2074	0.4133	Mixed	
Qingdao	Containers	0.4185	Dry bulk	0.2670	0.3073	Mixed	
Shenzhen	Containers	0.8528			0.7372	Specialized	
Tianjin	Dry bulk	0.3911	Containers	0.2479	0.2659	Diversified	Major hub
Guangzhou	Containers	0.5517	Dry bulk	0.2143	0.3686	Mixed	
Dalian	Passenger and cruise	0.4662	Energy (oil, gas, liquid bulk)	0.2251	0.2991	Diversified	
Suzhou	Dry bulk	0.7797	–	–	0.6258	Specialized	
Lianyungang	Dry bulk	0.6489	–	–	0.4556	Mixed	Regional hub
Fuzhou	Dry bulk	0.5991	–	–	0.4125	Mixed	
Taizhou	Dry bulk	0.8798	–	–	0.7817	Specialized	
Weihai	Passenger and cruise	0.5472	Dry bulk	0.273	0.3843	Mixed	
Jiaxing	Dry bulk	0.6228	Energy (oil, gas, liquid bulk)	0.2083	0.4456	Mixed	
Jinzhou	Dry bulk	0.4034	Energy (oil, gas, liquid bulk)	0.3513	0.3224	Mixed	
Cangzhou	Dry bulk	0.9418	–	–	0.889	Specialized	
Putian	Dry bulk	0.6826	Energy (oil, gas, liquid bulk)	0.2864	0.5488	Specialized	

Notes: Concentration is computed from the shares of six cargo classes, defined as each class share over the sum across the six classes. Ports are classified by Herfindahl–Hirschman Index thresholds as diversified (HHI < 0.30), mixed (0.30 ≤ HHI < 0.50), or specialized (HHI ≥ 0.50). Hub size is defined by 2019 total gross tonnage quantiles: P90 or greater indicates a mega hub, P75 or greater a major hub, P50 or greater a regional hub, and below P50 a local node. The table reports the dominant cargo type and its share, and any secondary types meeting the default threshold of at least 20%, up to two types. Empty cells indicate that no cargo type exceeds 20%.

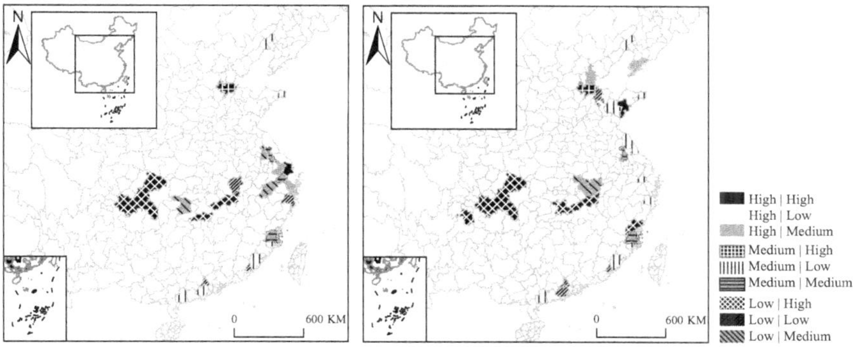

Figure 12.4 Bivariate map of disease incidence and maritime transport intensity

the surveyed population. The maritime transport variable is port throughput measured by vessel gross tonnage. The bivariate map cannot by itself establish causality or even correlation between maritime transport and health expenditure at the city or regional level. It does, however, reveal whether the two variables move upward or downward together, which enables an assessment of whether maritime transport scale and health expenditure exhibit dispersed or clustered development across cities, thereby informing classification-based urban governance.

The association between shipping and disease is concentrated in coastal port cities. Inland river ports such as Chongqing and Jiujiang also exhibit high chronic disease incidence, but their per capita cargo volumes are low. Consequently, in the data the strength of association between the two variables is weaker for inland than for coastal ports. After removing the confounding effect of city population size by using population as the denominator, Shanghai in 2011 falls into the joint high category for disease incidence and per capita cargo. By 2020 Shanghai's per capita cargo increases while its incidence declines to a low level. Shenzhen, Ningbo, Suzhou, and Guangzhou display a similar pattern of high transport volume and low chronic disease incidence.

Port cities around the Bohai Rim exhibit rising transport alongside worsening chronic disease. In 2011 the predominant categories are transport high with disease at medium or low and transport at medium with disease at medium. By 2020 many prefectures shift to transport high with disease high or transport at medium or low with disease high, with Tianjin and several Jiaodong Peninsula port cities being representative cases. This indicates that while port throughput remains high or at mid to high levels, chronic disease incidence in this area shifts upward relative to the national distribution.

Note: To enable matched comparison of the transport and disease indicators, we do not use the earlier scheme that applied common bins across both years. Instead, each indicator is partitioned by quantiles within each year. This permits within-year coupling analysis of the two variables but limits the comparability of growth across years

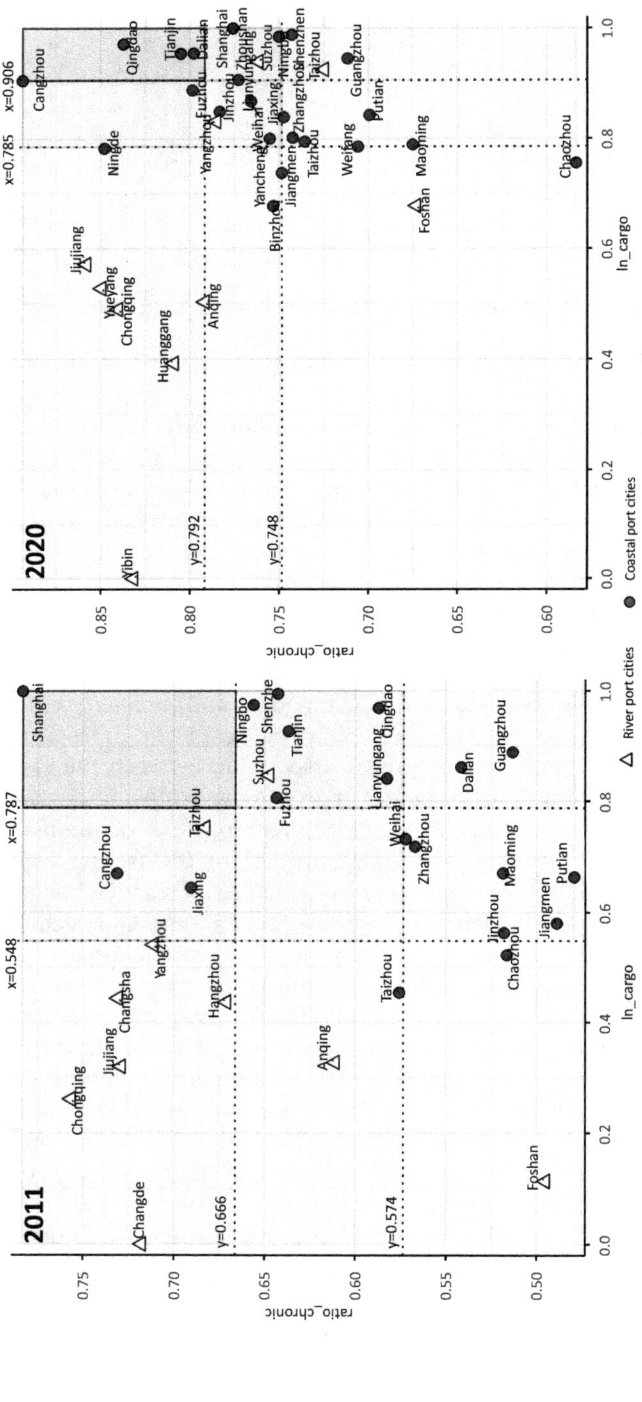

Figure 12.5 Bivariate scatter plot of disease incidence and maritime transport Throughput, 2011–2022

The scatter plot in Figure 12.5 further substantiates the spatial-coupling inference. Coastal hubs (e.g., Shanghai and Ningbo) sustain high maritime transport throughput while disease incidence is lower, whereas Bohai Bay port cities (Qingdao, Tianjin, Dalian, Cangzhou) show simultaneous increases in transport and disease. River ports exhibit weak transport-disease association and, despite relatively low throughput, often report high disease incidence (e.g., Chongqing, Yibin).

Effects of port transport scale and cargo type on individual health

Freight versus passenger transport: differential impacts on morbidity

Table 12.2 presents the results of principal component analysis applied to 13 categories of maritime transport variables. Dimensionality reduction was necessary because cargo volumes across different categories were highly correlated; for example, the correlation coefficient between Oil and General cargo was 0.782, between Other and Container 0.774, between RoRo and Vehicle 0.744, between Gas and Chemical 0.737, and between solid bulk and general cargo 0.732. Direct inclusion of these variables in regression models would therefore lead to severe multicollinearity. After dimensionality reduction, two principal components were retained. The first is a freight factor, dominated by industrial activities including oil and gas, chemicals, bulk commodities, and containers, representing a port function centered on material turnover. The second is a passenger factor, characterized by cruises, passenger transport, and roll-on-roll-off services, reflecting a port function oriented toward human mobility and tourism.

Table 12.2 Principal component scores extracted from different cargo types

Types of maritime transportation	*Freight factor*	*Passenger factor*
	(freight, energy-related transport, etc.)	*(passenger and roll-on–roll-off transport, etc.)*
ln_Oil	0.909	0.556
ln_General_cargo	0.881	0.564
ln_Other	0.768	0.788
ln_Chemical	0.883	0.551
ln_Port_services	0.836	0.686
ln_Other_tanker	0.786	0.516
ln_Cruise	0.399	0.841
ln_Roll_on_roll_off	0.668	0.884
ln_Solid_bulk	0.824	0.49
ln_Container	0.816	0.707
ln_Gas	0.844	0.548
ln_Vehicle	0.554	0.827
ln_Passenger	0.592	0.811

Note: The extraction method was principal component analysis, and the rotation method was Promax with Kaiser normalization.

The Poisson-GLMM results indicate that the health effects are primarily driven by freight transport. Calculation of the expected proportional change, exp(b) (incidence rate ratio, IRR), shows that the freight factor is strongly positive in Model 1 ($e^{0.3543} \approx 1.4251$, IRR = 1.4251, 95% CI: 1.3748–1.4773). After controlling for individual-level covariates, the effect diminishes but remains significant (Model 2: IRR = 1.0498, 95% CI: 1.0058–1.0957). When climate and macro-level variables are added, the effect becomes statistically non-significant while remaining positive (Model 3: IRR = 1.0205, 95% CI: 0.9766–1.0663). This suggests that the initial positive association between freight activity and chronic disease counts is largely explained by individual, medical, economic, climatic, and industrial structural factors. The independent effect of freight transport is therefore not robust, underscoring the difficulty of isolating the health impacts of maritime activity from broader natural and social determinants. A one-unit increase in freight-oriented port transport corresponds to an approximate 5% rise in chronic disease counts (multimorbidity).

By contrast, the passenger factor is consistently non-significant across all three models, indicating no robust association between passenger transport and chronic disease counts in China. Model fit improves markedly when covariates are included, with the Akaike information criterion (AIC) decreasing from 60,090 to 45,961.

At the individual level, age has a strong positive effect: each additional year increases expected disease counts by $e^{0.10} \approx 1.105$ (about +10.5%). The quadratic term of age (−0.0006) reveals an inverted U-shaped relationship, with disease counts rising initially and then leveling off. Self-rated health (SRH) is significantly negative ($b \approx -0.266$), indicating that better perceived health is associated with lower disease counts ($e^{-0.266} \approx 0.766$). Place of residence, pension insurance, and medical insurance coverage are also significant predictors (Table 12.3).

Heterogeneous effects of transport types on chronic disease prevalence

Table 12.4 indicates that growth in maritime scale materially affects individual health, increasing medical spending. Container shipping and general cargo are significantly associated with higher disease-related expenditures. For liquid bulk, coefficients for outpatient probability and chronic disease probability are not statistically significant, although the point estimates suggest a positive association with spending. Roll-on/roll-off, solid bulk, port services, and other port activities show no significant effects on these health outcomes. These patterns imply that the transport types with significant coefficients are linked to higher individual health burdens, reflected in greater chronic disease prevalence and outpatient demand. The results hold after controlling for regional economic development and healthcare accessibility, with community, city, and year fixed effects included to absorb region- and time-invariant factors.

Table 12.3 Impact of passenger and freight transport on the chronic count (Poisson generalized linear mixed model)

	Model (1)		*Model (2)*		*Model (3)*	
Predictors	b (log-link)	*CI*	b (log-link)	*CI*	b (log-link)	*CI*
(Intercept)	0.1542*	*0.0109–0.3192	*8.3532***	*9.4058 to *7.3006	*5.0036***	*6.4291 to *3.5780
factor1_freight	0.3543***	0.3183–0.3902	0.0486**	0.0058–0.0914	0.0203	*0.0237–0.0642
factor2_passenger	0.0078	*0.0319–0.0474	*0.0296	*0.0739–0.0148	*0.0134	*0.0572–0.0303
Age			0.1036***	0.0833–0.1239	0.1011***	0.0808–0.1213
Age^2			*0.0006***	*0.0008 to *0.0005	*0.0006***	*0.0008 to *0.0005
Education			*0.0022	*0.0252–0.0208	*0.0052	*0.0281–0.0178
Gender			*0.0446*	*0.0907–0.0015	*0.0409*	*0.0869–0.0051
Marry			*0.0297	*0.0887–0.0292	*0.0273	*0.0862–0.0316
self_rated_health			*0.2657***	*0.2844 to *0.2470	*0.2678***	*0.2865 to *0.2490
Rural			*0.0815***	*0.1404 to *0.0226	*0.0873***	*0.1454 to *0.0292
pension_insurance			0.0798***	0.0414–0.1183	0.0764***	0.0380–0.1149
health_insurance			0.0595	*0.0151–0.1342	0.0650*	*0.0098–0.1398
family_size			*0.0075	*0.0182–0.0032	*0.0056	*0.0163–0.0051
pc gdp 100 k			0.0046	*0.0037–0.0128	0.0051	*0.0037–0.0139
ln doctors			0.5685***	0.4766–0.6603	0.2882***	0.1794–0.3969
ln precip					0.0494	*0.0382–0.1370
Temp Max					0.0105***	0.0041–0.0170
ln wind					*0.1193	*0.3611–0.1226
secondary_va_pct					*0.0125***	*0.0177–*0.0073
budget exp pct					1.6271***	0.8217–2.4326

(*Continued*)

Table 12.3 (Continued)

	Model (1)	*Model (2)*	*Model (3)*
Random effects			
σ^2	0.4829	0.4652	0.4652
τ_{00}	0.2470 city_num 0.6806 ID_num	0.1466 city_num 0.3895 ID_num	0.0778 city_num 0.3873 ID_num
ICC	0.6576	0.5354	0.4999
N	36 city_num 6703 ID_num	36 city_num 6032 ID_num	36 city_num 6032 ID_num
Individual/City control	Y	Y	Y
Observations	20,273	15,895	15,895
Marginal R^2/ Conditional R^2	0.084/0.686	0.262/0.657	0.230/0.615
AIC	60,090.483	46,048.145	45,960.559

*$p < 0.1$, **$p < 0.05$, *** $p < 0.01$.

Note: In the regression results, a positive coefficient b indicates that a one-unit increase in the independent variable raises the log expected value of the dependent variable by ***b***. On the original count scale, the expected value is multiplied by exp(b); a negative coefficient implies the reverse. For an intuitive percentage interpretation, use 100 × [exp(b) − 1]; exp(b) is the incidence rate ratio (IRR) and is used throughout. Model (1) includes no control covariates. Model (2) adds individual-level covariates and baseline city covariates. Model (3) further incorporates city natural environment data and an expanded set of city socioeconomic indicators.

Table 12.4 Effects of different types of maritime transport on individual disease counts

	Model (1)		*Model (2)*		*Model (3)*	
Predictors	b (log-link)	*CI*	b (log-link)	*CI*	b (log-link)	*CI*
ln_Oil	*0.0094**	*0.0172 to *0.0017	*0.0074*	*0.0149–0.0002		
ln_Chemical	*0.0065**	*0.0127 to *0.0002	*0.0063**	*0.0124 to *0.0002		
ln_Gas	*0.0038	*0.0100–0.0024	*0.0031	*0.0090–0.0029		
ln_Other tanker	0.0076**	0.0003–0.0148	0.0072**	0.0001–0.0144		
ln_Solid bulk	0.0199***	0.0118–0.0280	0.0174***	0.0095–0.0254		
ln_Container	0.0083***	0.0036–0.0129	0.0070***	0.0024–0.0116		
ln_Vehicle	*0.0031	*0.0079–0.0017	*0.0018	*0.0064–0.0029		
ln_Roll on roll off	0.0003	*0.0052–0.0059	0.0018	*0.0035–0.0071		
ln_General cargo	0.0040	*0.0026–0.0107	0.0050	*0.0015–0.0114		

(*Continued*)

Table 12.4 (Continued)

	Model (1)		*Model (2)*		*Model (3)*	
ln_Cruise	*0.0004	*0.0057–0.0049			*0.0012	*0.0064–0.0039
ln_Passenger	*0.0069**	*0.0133 to *0.0005			*0.0032	*0.0089–0.0026
ln_Port services	0.0087**	0.0016–0.0157			0.0041	*0.0018–0.0100
ln_Other	*0.0012	*0.0077–0.0053			0.0002	*0.0060–0.0064
Random effects						
σ2	0.4652		0.4652		0.4652	
τ00	0.1895 city_num 0.3932 ID_num		0.1919 city_num 0.3933 ID_num		0.1553 city_num 0.3943 ID_num	
ICC	0.5560		0.5571		0.5416	
N	36 city_num 6032 ID_num		36 city_num 6032 ID_num		36 city_num 6032 ID_num	
Individual/city control	Y		Y		Y	
Observations	15,895		15,895		15,895	
Marginal R^2/conditional R^2	0.266/0.674		0.266/0.675		0.263/0.662	
AIC	46,095.605		46,097.951		46,118.966	

*p < 0.1, **p < 0.05, ***p < 0.01.

Transport-type effects across specific chronic conditions

This study utilizes the CHARLS database, which includes 14 categories of diseases recorded as binary indicators of disease incidence. These 0–1 variables were employed as dependent variables y to examine the effects of different types of cargo throughput. Consistent with the previous specification, both individual- and city-level covariates were controlled, and each outcome was analyzed using a Logit generalized linear mixed model (Logit-GLMM). To mitigate collinearity among predictors, the 13 cargo categories were transformed using isometric log-ratio (ILR) coordinates, allowing each cargo type to be evaluated relative to the geometric mean of all other categories. Results are reported as log odds ratios [log(OR)], with statistical significance determined after multiple-testing adjustment using the Benjamini–Hochberg procedure; non-significant estimates were set to zero for clarity.

Figure 12.6 illustrates the effects of different transport shares (the proportion of a specific cargo type relative to all others) on chronic diseases. Overall, the heatmap reveals pronounced heterogeneity between passenger and freight transport. Certain cargo categories are positively associated with specific chronic diseases, whereas others show negative or non-significant relationships. The results indicate that the relative shares of some cargo types

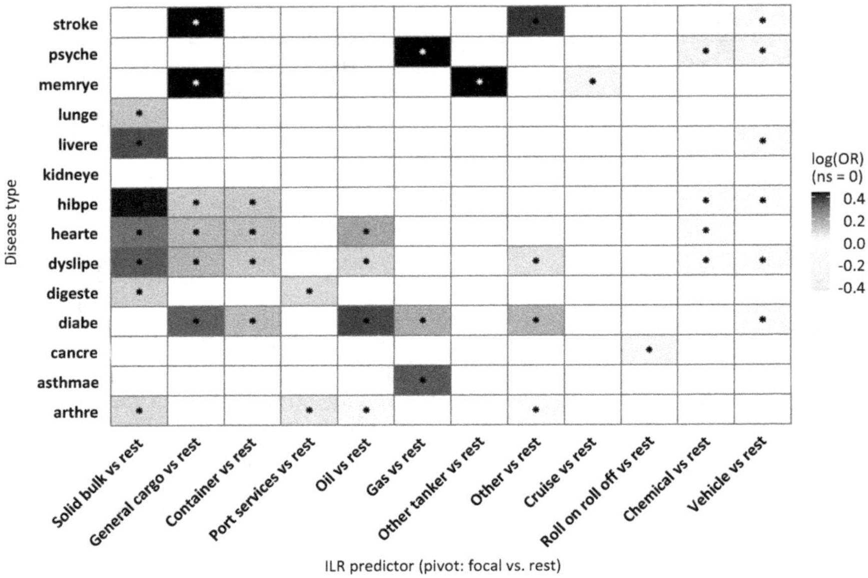

Figure 12.6 Effects of freight transport composition on different diseases

are strongly linked to respiratory conditions. For example, increases in the shares of gas and "other oil products" are significantly associated with higher risks of lung disease and asthma, consistent with the adverse impacts of their atmospheric emissions. In contrast, larger shares of containers and general cargo are positively related to cardiovascular and metabolic diseases such as hypertension, heart disease, and dyslipidemia, suggesting indirect health risks associated with high-intensity port logistics. Conversely, higher shares of cruise and vehicle transport exhibit negative associations with certain diseases (e.g., asthma and memory-related disorders), reflecting potential health benefits arising from transport restructuring, specifically, the transition of ports from freight-dominant to passenger-oriented functions, which may reduce emissions and generate structural substitution effects conducive to public health improvement.

The findings suggest that diversification is an inevitable trajectory for major hub ports, and adjustments in the relative structure of port transport are closely intertwined with the port city's path toward green development. The use of ILR transformation highlights this structural feature of trade-offs, whereby an increase in the share of one cargo type necessarily corresponds to a decrease in others. The health effects documented in this study should therefore be understood within this compositional context. From a policy perspective, identifying cargo categories that contribute disproportionately to the health burden can inform more targeted emission-reduction strategies and accelerate the transformation of ports toward healthier and more sustainable futures.

Discussion and conclusion

Future research into urban maritime transport and individual health can expand along several promising directions. First, given that cities differ substantially in maritime activity and associated health profiles, future studies should focus on complex combinations of influencing factors, including interactions among various disease types, transportation modes, and mediators such as specific air pollutants. Second, while our current study primarily emphasizes the relationship between transport volume growth, disease incidence, and healthcare expenditures, future research might further investigate China's role within the global maritime network. This could include distinguishing health impacts among global transshipment hubs, major export gateways, and multipurpose ports that maintain extensive international market connections. Third, since China's reform and opening up, numerous major ports and terminals have been developed. Investigating how policy interventions across this transition, from initial construction to full operational status, affect disease incidence and healthcare costs is an important research direction.

Based on these analyses, we propose **several policy recommendations.** First, we advocate incorporating "healthy port cities" as a distinct urban typology into China's national Healthy China strategy. Port cities, characterized by unique geographic and economic conditions, face particular health challenges. Recognizing them explicitly within urban health policy will better address their dual roles: domestically, as critical infrastructure hubs that intensify environmental challenges such as air and water pollution, and internationally, as gateways to global markets requiring specialized health strategies to enhance their openness and resilience. Second, maritime pollution management must shift from solely regulating dockside ship emissions toward comprehensive oversight of the entire transport and trade chain, actively promoting cleaner fuels and widespread adoption of shore-side power supply systems. Moreover, port city health should be explicitly integrated into urban planning goals, through strategic interventions such as improved maritime infrastructure, expanded green space, and enhanced healthcare facilities, all designed to mitigate adverse health impacts from maritime activities. Given the complex, nonlinear interactions identified in this study, health strategies should adopt a layered, segmented approach tailored specifically to varying city contexts.

After the preceding analyses, it is important to acknowledge that several port adjacent prefecture-level cities in China cover extensive administrative territories, and the spatial separation between ports and urban centers can be considerable. Even when port cargo is transported inland or port-related industrial activities occur, their direct influence on the city may be limited. Including such cities may therefore dilute the estimated relationships and weaken the measured effects. To alleviate attenuation bias caused by spatial mismatch, future work could apply port exposure weights that incorporate distance and prevailing wind direction, or aggregate health and disease outcomes at finer spatial units such as grid cells or counties and relate them to port throughput. These approaches require more granular morbidity data, which remains a substantial challenge.

References

Adda J., Fawaz Y. (2020) The health toll of import competition. *The Economic Journal*, 130(630): 1501–1540.

Brooks S.K., Greenberg, N. (2022) Mental health and psychological wellbeing of maritime personnel: A systematic review. *BMC Psychology*, 10 (1): 139.

CCTV News (2024) Chronic diseases on the rise in China, responsible for 80%+ of all deaths, https://news.cctv.cn/2024/09/12/ARTI1uiaQICinOmYL8uioAt5240912.shtml

Corbett J.J., Winebrake J.J., Green E.H., Kasibhatla P., Eyring V., Lauer A. (2007) Mortality from ship emissions: A global assessment. *Environmental Science and Technology*, 41(24): 8512–8518.

Cullinane K., Haralambides H. (2021) Global trends in maritime and port economics: The covid-19 pandemic and beyond. *Maritime Economics & Logistics*, 23 (3): 369–380.

Dora C., Phillips M. (2000) *Transport, Environment and Health*. WHO Regional Office Europe.

Feng J., Xie Q., Zhang X. (2021) Trade liberalization and the health of working-age adults: Evidence from China. *World Development*, 139: 105344.

Glazener A., Sanchez K., Ramani T., Zietsman J., Nieuwenhuijsen M.J., Mindell J.S., Fox M., Khreis H. (2021) Fourteen pathways between urban transportation and health: A conceptual model and literature review. *Journal of Transport and Health*, 21: 101070.

Hao Y., Xu L., Peng M., Yang Z., Wang W., Meng F. (2025) Synergistic air pollution exposure elevates depression risk: A cohort study. *Environmental Science and Ecotechnology*, 23: 100515.

Jiang B., Liang S., Peng Z., Cong H., Levy M., Cheng Q., Wang T., Remais J.V. (2017) Transport and public health in China: The road to a healthy future. *The Lancet*, 390(10104): 1781–1791.

Jonglertmontree W., Kaewboonchoo O., Morioka I., Boonyamalik P. (2022) Mental health problems and their related factors among seafarers: A scoping review. *BMC Public Health*, 22(1): 282.

Kiihamäki S., Korhonen M., Kukkonen J., Shiue I., Jaakkola J.J.K. (2024) Effects of ambient air pollution from shipping on mortality: A systematic review. *Science of the Total Environment*, 945: 173714.

Liu K.H. (2018) *Does Export Expansion Affect Health?* Nankai University (Tianjin).

Loxham M. (2021) Preventing disease in port cities, https://www.southampton.ac.uk/news/2017/07/preventing-disease-in-port-cities.page

Luo Z., Lv Z., Zhao J., Sun H., He T., Yi W., Zhang Z., He K., Liu H. (2024) Shipping-related pollution decreased but mortality increased in Chinese port cities. *Nature Cities*, 1(4), 295–304.

Mueller N., Cirach M., Ambros A., Daher C., Nieuwenhuijsen M., Basagaña X. (2024) Health impact assessment of port-sourced air pollution in Barcelona. *PLoS One*, 19(8): e305236.

Mueller N., Westerby M., Nieuwenhuijsen M. (2023) Health impact assessments of shipping and port-sourced air pollution on a global scale: A scoping literature review. *Environmental Research*, 216: 114460.

Nieuwenhuijsen M., Khreis H. (2020) *Advances in Transportation and Health: Tools, Technologies, Policies, and Developments*. Academic Press.

Pierce J.R., Schott P.K. (2020) Trade liberalization and mortality: Evidence from US counties. *American Economic Review: Insights*, 2(1), 47–63.

Qinghua University (2024) Tsinghua city health index 2024, https://iugsd.tsinghua.edu.cn/news/view?id=857

Sorte S., Rodrigues V., Borrego C., Monteiro A. (2020) Impact of harbour activities on local air quality: A review. *Environmental Pollution*, 257: 113542.

Sun L., Zhang J., Ducruet C., Itoh H., Liu X. (2025) The impact of shipping activities on air quality and residents' health in China's port cities. *Journal of Transport Geography*, 123: 104099.

Widener M.J., Hatzopoulou M. (2016) Contextualizing research on transportation and health: A systems perspective. *Journal of Transport and Health*, 3(3): 232–239.

Woolhandler S., Himmelstein D.U., Ahmed S., Bailey Z., Bassett M.T., Bird M., Bor J., Bor D., Carrasquillo O., Chowkwanyun M., Dickman S.L., Fisher S., Gaffney A., Galea S., Gottfried R.N., Grumbach K., Guyatt G., Hansen H., Landrigan P.J., Lighty M., Mckee M., Mccormick D., Mcgregor A., Mirza R., Morris J.E., Mukherjee J.S., Nestle M., Prine L., Saadi A., Schiff D., Shapiro M., Tesema L., Venkataramani A. (2021) Public policy and health in the trump era. *The Lancet*, 397(10275): 705–753.

Yang J., Siri J.G., Remais J.V., Cheng Q., Zhang H., Chan K.K.Y., Sun Z., Zhao Y., Cong N., Li X., Zhang W., Bai Y., Bi J., Cai W., Chan E.Y.Y., Chen W., Fan W., Fu H., He J., Huang H., Ji J.S., Jia P., Jiang X., Kwan M., Li T., Li X., Liang S., Liang X., Liang L., Liu Q., Lu Y., Luo Y., Ma X., Schwartländer B., Shen Z., Shi P., Su J., Wu T., Yang C., Yin Y., Zhang Q., Zhang Y., Zhang Y., Xu B., Gong P. (2018) The Tsinghua–Lancet commission on healthy cities in China: Unlocking the power of cities for a healthy China. *The Lancet*, 391(10135): 2140–2184.

Zhang Y., Loh C., Louie P.K.K., Liu H., Lau A.K.H. (2018) The roles of scientific research and stakeholder engagement for evidence-based policy formulation on shipping emissions control in Hong Kong. *Journal of Environmental Management*, 223: 49–56.

Zhang P., Zhao M. (2017) Maritime health of Chinese seafarers. *Marine Policy*, 83: 259–267.

13 Towards a multilevel port performance indicator considering economy, environment, and health

Charbel Alkhoury

Introduction

Shipping nowadays represents about 80% of global trade by volume (World Bank, 2023). The increase in trade activities has led to a significant rise in greenhouse gas emissions from the shipping industry, which accounted for 2.2% of global CO_2 emissions in 2012 (International Maritime Organization [IMO], 2014). If there are no measures in place to mitigate these emissions, this figure might soar by 250% by mid-century (IMO, 2014). In response to these concerns, the International Maritime Organization aims to reduce GHG emissions by 50% by mid-century (IMO, 2018).

However, it is important to note that the expansion of global trade and increased GHG emissions are linked to GDP growth in various countries (El Weriemmi and Bakari, 2024). For instance, due to the growth of the Chinese economy, China shipping industry's emissions have increased (Zheng, Kwon, and Wang, 2014). As a result of sulphur oxides emissions (SO_x), nitrogen oxides (NO_x), and particulate matter (PM) from ships, ports, and related industries as well as logistics, the impacts of maritime transportation on the environment and human health have received increased scrutiny (Corbett et al., 2007; Viana et al., 2020). Ships' emissions, such as nitrogen oxides (NO_x) and sulphur oxides (SO_x), can badly impact the air quality and create some health problems such as respiratory diseases (U.S. Environmental Protection Agency [USEPA], 2016). The detrimental effect of atmospheric pollution on public health can indirectly influence economic development by increasing the disease burden (Prüss-Üstün et al., 2016).

Moreover, pollutions disproportionately hurt socially and economically deprived populations, which often live near port areas. A study by Gillingham and Huang (2021) found that each new ship arrival at the port causes more unplanned hospital visits for Blacks residents than for Whites. Residents near ports like Los Angeles have higher rates of asthma, heart disease, and depression (Human Impact Partners, 2010). According to the World Health Organization, ambient (outdoor) air pollution caused approximately 4.2 million premature deaths worldwide in 2019. Despite these significant health risks,

DOI: 10.4324/9781003639589-17

academic research has primarily focused on measuring pollution itself rather than the direct effects on health and social disparities. The very few case studies explicitly addressing health impacts, mainly focusing on the Mediterranean region (Vigotti et al., 2014), remain insufficient to date. In addition to that, most literature still tackles traditional measures of economic performance and growth, and remains ignorant of wider societal and ecological effects.

As a result, a new perspective on development is suggested. Amartya Sen, the Nobel Prize winner in 1998 (Nobel Prize, 1998), changed economic theory by creating the Capability Approach. It was first established by him in "Commodities and Capabilities" (1985), serves as a comprehensive and general framework that extends beyond economic and development applications, which lies in redefining development and justice by focusing on expanding individuals' real freedoms to achieve "valuable beings and doings" or what is called functionings, rather than relying on income or resource measures. This approach looks at how socio-economic and environmental conditions affect people's ability to live meaningful lives (Sen, 1999). In 1990, the UNDP implemented these ideas by introducing the Human Development Index (HDI), a multidimensional instrument that moves beyond traditional economic metrics (Human Development Report, 1990; Sen, 1992).

Although significant progress has been made, there is no single, fixed method for measuring the capability approach, because its practical application requires context-specific value judgements, such as choosing relevant capabilities and assigning weights, and should be adapted to cultural, institutional, and historical contexts. This study is based on Sen's Capability Approach and involved estimating health impacts from ports. It develops the PPCI, which integrates the various ways in which ports affect human well-being and sustainable development into its definition of port performance, moving beyond traditional performance measures in ports. Port operations positively influence the economy and human development (HDI); however, they also increase air pollution, which could negatively impact both the economy and society. Social outcomes can also influence the growth of the economy, suggesting that these factors are closely linked and affect each other in a cycle (see Figure 13.1).

This chapter will explore the concepts and theoretical underpinnings of the approach. Container shipping is the focal modality of the conceptual approach, but other types of shipping and modalities, for instance, bulk and cruise shipping are included when relevant. We choose to construct the PPCI at the national level rather than at the individual port level. This choice is motivated by the high challenge to obtain consistent and reliable local-level indicators. Therefore, the PPCI will be aggregated and measured at the national scale, reflecting the overall capability of a country's port system to generate economic, environmental, health, and governance outcomes.

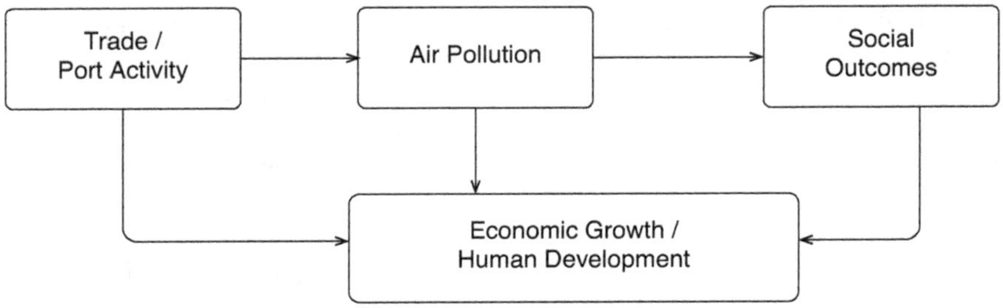

Figure 13.1 Socio-economic and Environmental Health Effects of Port Activity: understanding the cycle

Source: Own elaboration

Literature review

The existing and "classic" port performance indicators (PPIs)

PPIs are not a new topic for port managers or maritime scholars. In the late 1970s, the UNCTAD proposed that signatory countries should adopt and follow certain PPIs (UNCTAD, 1976). The initial schemes for PPIs were focused on quantitative aspects, measuring the operational and financial performance of ports by means of objective and measurable metrics, organized by an initial taxonomy proposed by UNCTAD (1976), which categorized these indicators into three sectors, namely, ship performance, cargo handling performance, and financial performance. The ship performance indicators included average ship turnaround time, berth occupancy ratio, and waiting time; the cargo handling indicators included cargo dwell time, labour productivity, and crane rates; and the financial indicators included cost per ton handled and revenue per employee. In building on this taxonomy, De Monie (1987) operationalized indicators such as tonnage per ship call, berth throughput, and handling time per unit cargo, with emphasis on ensuring that comparisons were made between ports with similar characteristics, for commensurability. Numerous studies on the subject of port performance and efficiency have compared some selected ports using certain performance and efficiency criteria, for example, studies by the Australian Bureau of Industry Economics (1993) and the Australian Transport Advisory Council (1992). The UNCTAD (2022) has created a series of key indicators to measure port performance, such as the number of port calls, turnaround time, port waiting time, cargo handling, throughput volume, crane productivity, and liner shipping connectivity. The liner shipping connectivity index is defined based on the number of port calls, their container-carrying capacity, the number of services and companies, the size of the largest ship, and the number of other countries connected through direct liner shipping services (UNCTAD, 2022).

The vessel turnaround time, which is the time vessels spend in port, is adopted by the World Bank to assess port performance and published in The Container Port Performance Index (World Bank, 2025). Slack et al. (2018)

also underscore the importance of vessel turnaround time in port operations. Their review suggests that port performance can influence the time ships spend in port; more efficient ports tend to turn ships around faster even under high volumes (see also Ducruet and Itoh, 2022). Karnoji et al. (2021) also highlighted the importance of vessel turnaround time as an indicator of performance in their examination of its predictors. Similarly, Adeyanju and Ojekunle (2014) discuss this concept. In another work, Chen et al. (2016) use a unique group of indicators: ship traffic, container throughput, berth utilization, and terminal productivity. They define ship traffic as the number of ships arriving at a terminal during a period of time, container throughput as the number of containers handled during a period, berth utilization as the percent of time berths occupied, and terminal productivity as the number of containers handled per hour.

Econometric studies, such as Tongzon (1995), examined crane productivity, terminal operating efficiency, and ship/terminal turnaround time to shed light on port competitiveness. Like Slack, Tongzon's study is academic and employs rigorous quantitative methods; while most of the literature came from consulting firms and was only interested in operational benchmarking rather than theory. Most studies produced in this timeframe involve measuring performance with numbers (e.g., cost, time, throughput, etc.). However, based on information provided from the results that they measure, the qualitative aspects (e.g., governance, environmental sustainability, social impact, etc.) are not evaluated or neglected. Many performance measures and PPIs are not systematically available, and when they do exist, they often vary widely across data sources or depend heavily on the specific context. The overall literature provides useful information, but they are often narrow and fragmented, presenting only partial view of port performance and not explaining the critical factors that truly drive efficiency and effectiveness (Table 13.1).

Environment, health, governance, and connectivity indicators for ports (developed and used more recently)

Beginning in the 2010s, port performance evaluation developed to include both quantitative and qualitative indicators that illustrate growing attention towards sustainability, governance, and public health. UNCTAD (2021) reorganized PPIs into seven categories: governance, human resources, financial, resilience, vessel operations, cargo operations, and environmental sustainability. Tezcan and Kan (2023) presented a "sustainable PPI framework" that combined various quantitative operational metrics (e.g., measurements of berth utilization and emissions reductions) with more qualitative metrics measuring stakeholder satisfaction and transparency of governance. Zis et al. (2023) focused on "green guidelines" when identifying performance indicators by measuring fuel efficiency, pollution, and carbon footprint. In addition, Notteboom et al. (2020) identified social and resilience dimensions i.e. employee training, innovation capacity, and involvement with the

Table 13.1 Port Performance Indexes (PPIs) and descriptions

Category	*Author/source (year)*	*PPI name*	*Definition/description*
General/ Composite	UNCTAD (1976/ Rev.1987)	General Port Performance Indicators	Recommended adoption of standardized PPIs grouped under ship performance, cargo handling, and financial efficiency.
Traffic/ Connectivity	UNCTAD (1976/ Rev.1; 2022)	Liner Shipping Connectivity Index (LSCI)	Calculated based on number of port calls, container-carrying capacity, number of services and companies, largest vessel size, and direct shipping connections to other countries.
Traffic/Vessel Movements	UNCTAD (1976/ Rev.1)	Port Calls/Number of Calls	Frequency of vessel arrivals at a port within a given period as a proxy for port activity.
Operational/ Time Efficiency	UNCTAD (1976 / Rev.1)	Turnaround Time	Total time a vessel spends in the port area from arrival to departure.
Operational/ Time Efficiency	UNCTAD (1976/ Rev.1)	Port Waiting Time	Time ships wait before being serviced at berth.
Operational/ Cargo Handling	UNCTAD (1976/ Rev.1)	Cargo Handling Indicator	Measures handling performance in terms of throughput and tonnage per time unit.
Operational/ Berth Utilization	UNCTAD (1976)	Berth Occupancy Rate	Share of time a berth is occupied relative to its availability.
Operational/ Cargo Handling	UNCTAD (1976)	Cargo Dwell Time	Time cargo remains in the terminal before clearance or further transport.
Labour/ Productivity	UNCTAD (1976)	Labour Productivity Indicator	Quantity of cargo handled per labour unit.
Operational/ Berth Utilization	Australian Business Council (1988)	Berth Occupancy Ratio	Ratio of time berths are actively used versus idle.

(*Continued*)

Table 13.1 (Continued)

Category	*Author/source (year)*	*PPI name*	*Definition/description*
Operational/ Cargo Handling	De Monie (1987, 1989)	Tonnage per Ship Call	Total tonnage handled per vessel visit.
Operational/ Cargo Handling	De Monie (1987, 1989)	Handling Time per Cargo Unit	Average time required to handle one unit/ ton of cargo.
Operational/ Time Efficiency	Marconsult (1991)	Ship Waiting Time	Time ships spend queued before berthing.
Labour/ Productivity	Australian Bureau of Industry Economics (1993, 1994)	Labour Utilization Indicator	Efficiency of labour deployment in port operations.
Operational/ Cost	Australian Transport Advisory Council (1992)	Port Charges/ Cost-Based Indicators	Measures related to port tariffs and cost per ton handled.
Operational/ Time Efficiency	Slack et al. (1992)	Vessel Turnaround Time	Time spent by a vessel inside port limits; more efficient ports turn ships around faster, even under congestion.
Operational/ Terminal Productivity	Tongzon (1995)	Crane Productivity	Number of container moves per crane per hour.
Operational/ Terminal Productivity	Tongzon (1995)	Terminal Efficiency Index	Composite index linking operational productivity (such as crane moves and turnaround time) to port competitiveness.
Operational/ Time Efficiency	Adeyanju and Ojekunle (2014)	Turnaround Time (Operational Efficiency)	Highlights turnaround time as a decisive metric to assess port productivity.
Operational/ Terminal Productivity	Chen et al. (2015)	Ship Traffic	Number of ships arriving at a terminal over a time period.
Operational/ Terminal Productivity	Chen et al. (2015)	Container Throughput	Total number of containers handled over a specified time.
Operational/ Berth Utilization	Chen et al. (2015)	Berth Utilization	Percentage of time berths are occupied by vessels.

(*Continued*)

Table 13.1 (Continued)

Category	*Author/source (year)*	*PPI name*	*Definition/description*
Operational/ Terminal Productivity	Chen et al. (2015)	Terminal Productivity	Containers handled per hour or per handling unit.
Operational/ Time Efficiency	World Bank (2018)	Container Port Performance Index (CPPI) – Turnaround Metric	Uses vessel time in port as a core metric to rank port efficiency globally.
Operational/ Time Efficiency	Karnoji et al. (2020)	Turnaround Time (as performance metric)	Evaluates operational efficiency through factors affecting time spent in port.

Source: Own elaboration.

Note: The table shows that in the most recent phase (2010s–2020s), the development of indicators focused on global benchmarking, connectivity, and trade facilitation (e.g. Liner Shipping Connectivity Index [LSCI] and Container Port Performance Index [CPPI]), further recognizes the increasing discussion and importance of integration in global trade and the use of digital, data-driven evaluation methods. Overall, there was a shift towards more context-specific indicators that better capture the complexity of globalization. However, aspects such as governance, sustainability, and social dimensions of port performance are still not well integrated into practice.

community when defining performance indicators. Similarly, UNCTAD (2004) introduced the Liner Shipping Connectivity (LSCI) under the leadership of Jan Hoffmann to quantitatively define the connections between the ports (Fugazza and Hoffmann, 2017). Liner shipping connectivity serves as a measure for assessing a port's integration into the global maritime transport system. Some recent contributions in the literature have developed this measure using analytical frameworks from graph theory, social network analysis, and complex network science that are treating ports as nodes and shipping routes as links in a network of global interconnectedness (Faure and Ducruet, 2025). In this sense, the notion of connectivity has introduced an array of new network-based metrics to capture the multidimensionality of port connectivity: degree centrality indicates the number of direct links a port has; betweenness centrality finds ports that are acting as intermediaries or transshipment points along a shipping route; closeness centrality indicates how easy it is for a port to be reached by other ports; eigenvector centrality examines how influential a port is within the network based on connectivity; and the clustering coefficient measures the degree of connectivity of neighbouring ports. Combined, these metrics provide a means of thinking about connectivity in structural and relational ways rather than simply counting services or capacities. As noted by Faure and Ducruet (2025), the transition from descriptive to structural strategies represents a significant methodological advancement for the study of maritime networks, providing new insights into how the port connectivity influences trade, economic integration, and systemic resilience.

Tezcan and Kan (2023) included air pollution management, clean energy use/deployment, green equipment, and community relations as qualitative indicators including quantitative measures of CO_2, NO_x, SO_2, and particulate matter (PM_{10} and $PM_{2.5}$) as indicators. The former emissions are associated with health effects related to cardiovascular and respiratory health, such as occupational safety incident rates, the incidence of port-centric illnesses, and health considerations at the community level (ShahrulAlfian et al., 2024). Modern Key Performance Indicator frameworks (KPI) presented by Zis et al. (2023) also included economic, social, environmental, and health KPIs, such as operational expenditures, emissions, accidents, and public health complaints. As stated by Parvasi et al. (2025), the multidimensionality and variations of this system provide evaluative measures of sustainability and competitiveness factors. In this way, it is a progress towards a holistic Environmental, Social, Governance (ESG), and health integrated model of port performance measurement. From the socio-economic point of view, ports can no longer be considered facilitators of trade alone but must be assessed with regard to contributions and implications of social and environmental health (Table 13.2).

Table 13.2 Modern Port Performance Indicators (PPIs) integrating sustainability, governance, environment and health

Category	*Author/source (year)*	*PPI name*	*Definition/description*
Operational/ Governance	UNCTAD (2021)	7 PPI Categories	Reorganizes PPIs into governance, human resources, financial, resilience, vessel operations, cargo operations, and environmental sustainability.
Operational	UNCTAD (2021)	Vessel Operations Indicators	Measures average time at berth and number of port calls to assess operational efficiency.
Operational	UNCTAD (2021)	Cargo Operations Indicators	Focuses on container dwell time and cargo handling rates as core performance indicators.
Environmental	UNCTAD (2021)	Environmental Sustainability Indicators	Measures CO_2 emissions per ton handled and terminal energy consumption.

(*Continued*)

Table 13.2 (Continued)

Category	*Author/source (year)*	*PPI name*	*Definition/description*
Operational/ Governance	UNCTAD (2021)	Liner Shipping Connectivity Index (LSCI) – Expanded	Measures global connectivity through ship calls, capacity, destinations, and competition, with extended scope towards sustainability governance.
Environmental	Zis (2021)	Green Performance Indicators	Includes fuel efficiency, pollution levels, and carbon footprint as environmental performance metrics.
Operational	World Bank (2022)	Container Port Performance Index (CPPI) – Turnaround and Waiting Time	Uses quantitative metrics such as vessel turnaround time and waiting time, complemented by qualitative assessments of infrastructure resilience and digital management.
Operational/ Environmental/ Social	Tezcan (2023)	Sustainable PPI Framework	Combines quantitative operational metrics (berth utilization, emission reduction) with qualitative dimensions (stakeholder satisfaction, governance transparency).
Social/Resilience	Wee and Notteboom (2023)	Social and Resilience Indicators	Highlights dimensions such as employee training, innovation capacity, and community engagement.
Social/Resilience	Parvasi (2023)	Resilience and Social Sustainability KPIs	Introduces resilience-related metrics and social engagement indicators to measure port-community integration.
Environmental/ ESG	Zis et al. (2023)	Integrated Sustainability KPIs	Proposes multidimensional KPIs addressing emissions, fuel management, safety, and environmental compliance.

(*Continued*)

Table 13.2 (Continued)

Category	*Author/source (year)*	*PPI name*	*Definition/description*
Environmental/ Health	Tezcan and Kan (2024)	Environmental and Community Health Indicators	Includes qualitative indicators like air pollution management, clean energy adoption, eco-friendly equipment, and community relations, alongside quantitative emissions (CO_2, NO_x, SO_2, PM_{10}, $PM_{2.5}$).
Health	Shahrul Alfian et al. (2024)	Health-Related Port Indicators	Connects emissions to respiratory and cardiovascular outcomes, proposing indicators such as occupational safety rates, incidence of port-related diseases, and community health impacts.
ESG/Integrated	Wee et al. (2024)	ESG-Oriented KPI Framework	Integrates economic, social, environmental, and health KPIs including operating expenses, emission levels, accident frequency, and public health complaints.
ESG/Integrated	Parvasi et al. (2025)	ESG & Health-Driven Competitiveness Indicators	Advocates for a holistic evaluation model combining economic performance with sustainability and health indicators to assess port competitiveness and socio-environmental responsibility.

Source: Own elaboration.

Note: The table demonstrates the continued progression of PPIs from performance measures that privilege efficiency, to frameworks linked with sustainability, governance and health aspects. Although the UNCTAD model of 2021 and World Bank model of 2023 included operational efficiency and connectivity, the latter frameworks began to incorporate environmental and social aspects, such as emissions reduction, stakeholder consultation, and resilience. From 2023 onwards, research has increasingly integrated ESG and health aspects in metrics that reference broader community and environmental outcomes from port operations. These shifts are reflective in the frameworks being proposed by Tezcan and Kan (2023) and Parvasi et al. (2025), which extends the portfolio of port PPIs and emphasizes holistic evaluation of competitiveness and socio-environmental outcomes. For the most part, there is evidence of transition from narrow performance measures based purely on operational criteria towards an increasingly multidimensional, capability-based approach to port performance directly linked to, and evidencing, the conceptual fields for the Port Performance Capability Index (PPCI) presented in this chapter.

From economic growth (GDP) and well-being (HDI) to economic development: adopting and adapting Sen's capability approach

GDP and HDI

Although GDP is the leading growth measure researchers for many decades believed that this metric does not fully reflect welfare, structural change, or durability (Baumol, 1967; Hartwig, 2012). Some evidence shows that structural change reduces productivity growth while the level of GDP grows (Foster-McGregor and Verspagen, 2016), while other studies suggest that innovation-based growth differs from imitator-based growth, as illustrated by China (Zhou et al., 2021). Additional studies persistently demonstrate that the growth of GDP correlates strongly with larger ecological footprints and carbon emissions, raising concerns for the environmental consequences (Cui et al., 2023; Neagu, 2020). To compensate for some of these deficiencies, the HDI has been advanced for the purposes of considering not only income but also the health and educational accomplishments.

Although broader than the GDP, HDI also suffers from deficiencies. Researchers note that qualification for the "very high" HDI category almost always relies upon income levels consistent with high emission and consumptive practice, generating ecological pressures (Hickel and Kallis, 2020). While governance, GDP, and HDI remain the predominant measures of economic performance, each has significant limitations. Governance remains important for the formation of institutions and long-lived developmental outcomes, although there still remains disagreement about the eventual causality and size of governance (even the authors disagree on the size of effects) (Acemoglu et al., 2001; Glaeser et al., 2004).

In an environment of increased complexity and heightened global interdependencies surrounding trade and maritime issues, it is increasingly important to develop a framework that allows us to examine the role of ports in the context of globalization, and how they interact with global markets to produce economic, social, or environmental outcomes as a contribution to economic performance. Early forms of PPIs had been characterized by operational and efficiency measures mostly like throughput, waiting time, and turnaround time, which kept their evaluation within a relatively narrow economic conception. The newer approaches, as clearly evidenced by the multidimensional PPCI method discussed in the next sections, enable assessment at a number of scales ranging from global (comparative competitiveness among maritime regions), to national (port systems and economic integration), to local (well-being of community and environmental quality), either simultaneously or longitudinally, helping to more holistically understand how ports influence development trajectories.

The capability approach

Developing the Capability Approach further, this research proposes a multidimensional PPCI combining micro-level factors such as emissions, operational productivity, connectivity, health, and the level of social achievements and contextual factors at the macro level including national environment and governmental authority. As a result, the PPCI not only merely measures how successful a particular port functions but also the broader consequences for the level of development for humans, pointing out both the positive contribution and potential negative effects. The concept of sustainable development became the prime concern for the level of policy for decision-makers, scientists as well as a broad community of stakeholders. The literature offers many definitions of sustainable development (e.g., Pearce et al., 1989; Pezzey, 1992). Frequently economists use a simple formulation in a working paper for the World Bank, which characterizes sustainable development trajectory as if the total level of well-being does not decrease over time (World Bank, 1997).

One notable turning point for the international discourse came when the report *Our Common Future* (World Commission on Environment and Development [WCED], 1987) by the World Commission on Environment and Development, chaired by Gro Harlem Brundtland, the former prime minister of Norway, came out in 1987. The report placed the principle of sustainable development on the international policy agenda when it framed it as the capability "to meet the needs of the present without compromising the ability of future generations to meet their own needs" (WCED, 1987, p. 16). Sen's Approach provides a deeper understanding of development. Instead of simply focusing on income or economic output, Sen (1999, 2000) argues that development is the expansion of people's capabilities, such as the real freedoms they are able to enjoy to lead lives that they value.

This approach also draws attention to the fact that individuals with the same income can experience vastly different levels of well-being depending on their health, social context, and environment (Sen and Muellbauer, 1988). For example, Sen makes the comparison of lives in Britain during World War II. While GDP suffered from the war, mortality rates were decreasing as resources were distributed more equally and public services were improved (Sen, 2000, pp. 50–51). This shows that GDP is a poor representation of progress when it is not coupled with more expansive measures of human flourishing. Similarly, other works of Sen and colleagues (Drèze and Sen, 1989) have advocated for government policies that strengthen the capability for access to public goods (health, education, environmental quality). In conclusion, GDP is a useful indicator of economic activity, but it is an insufficient measure of development.

A multilevel and multidimensional PPCI: an application to maritime ports

Port-level and country-level variables

Ports were considered natural monopolies in the early years of containerization as a result of their positional advantages and proximity to various containerized ship activities. However, containerization created a very competitive environment among neighbouring ports (Tongzon, 1995). While many ports around the world improved their performance in two major areas, cargo handling and berth operations, some ports have not fully tapped into the potential of maritime trade, regardless of their location (Notteboom and Rodrigue, 2008). As a response to this phenomenon, UNCTAD (2021) developed a Port Performance Scorecard as an initiative of their Port Management Programme. This Scorecard provides PPIs for port management and best practices. Between the years of 2015 and 2019, berth operations and cargo handling had the greatest mean effect on overall port performance to substantiate their importance in performance (UNCTAD, 2021). In this sense, port performance should be viewed not just as efficiency and throughput, but in terms of its role to streamline global supply chains and added value.

At the national level, areas of assessment regarding the performance and strategic relevance of ports are increasingly assessed with the use of macro indicators that encompass more than just pure throughput. This broadens the assessment to capture the economic, governance, environmental and health dimensions. Economic dimension macro variables include the national GDP, trade volume, trade openness, and foreign direct investment that are related to maritime logistics. These variables show the systemic ports' contribution in the national development context (Tongzon, 1995; World Bank, 2022). Governance became influential during the early 1990s, when underdevelopment came to be explained as much by weak institutions and negative structures of governance as by other factors (Leftwich, 1994). Simultaneously, governance indicators like regulatory quality, transparent decisions by port authorities, coordination with stakeholders, and efficiency of national governance systems related to ports have become paramount to understanding institutional arrangements that improve or restrict the performance of ports at a country level (UNCTAD, 2021).

Environmental indicators such as CO_2, NO_x, SO_2, and PM emissions from maritime transport are now incorporated into national emission inventories, reflecting growing concerns around port-related ecological pressures (IMO, 2018). In addition, new research contains health burden indicators, specifically, premature mortality, respiratory hospital admissions, and disability adjusted life years integrated with port air pollution, highlighting that ports not only represent economic nodes but also generate quantifiable negative health externalities at the country scale (WHO, 2024; OECD, 2025). Most multivariate forecasts have focused on macroeconomic variables (e.g., GDP, trade volume, and interest rates) with little attention paid to operational determinants specifically related to port performance.

More recently, studies of cargo port choice determinants from a shipper and shipping lines' perspectives have indicated that operational factors (e.g., berth productivity, storage, capacity, gate waiting time, and ship turnaround time, etc.) as critical operational influences on port performance (Omoke and Onwuegbuchunam, 2018). The focus of port performance should not only be on how many containers it handles but should also take into consideration how ports impact health, the environment, governance quality, and social welfare. Development indexes became more multidimensional over time, so should PPIs, become a measure of not only the volume of a port's performance, but how responsible or sustainable their performance is.

The full equation and its application to compare ports

In recent decades, maritime trade has increased with globalization and a disaggregated manufacturing environment (OECD, 2010). In Europe for instance, ports situated on international shipping routes provide unique platforms for environmental and public health issues not only related to economic development. This makes them ideal candidates for applying the multidimensional PPCI discussed below. Andersson et al. (2009), for instance, estimate that every year in Europe shipping-related air pollution contributes to 22,000 premature deaths.

The RAINS model developed by Jonson et al. (2015) takes a step further and quantifies health burden from shipping trade air pollution on local communities by estimating that those who live near major shipping routes are losing up to 0.2 Years of Life Lost (YOLLs). Countries differ in how they are administratively tackling shipping emissions, with some areas employing stricter local regulations and others strictly following international guidance. Another example of geographic differentiation is the presence of an Emission Control Area (ECA) in North Europe and its absence in the Mediterranean before 2025. While previous papers have established environmental PPIs or green port indices, these analyses remain single-dimensional and therefore limited in capturing and analysing the full spectrum of port-related capabilities.

In contrast, this chapter introduces a PPCI built on four interdependent pillars: economic, environmental, health, and social governance. Each subdimension is measured in isolation to record its particular impacts on collective capability, but collectively, the four sub-dimensions form a singular system that captures the combined expansion or contraction of collective capabilities created by port functions. Following Sen's logic, the relevance of performance indicators can differ depending on stakeholders' perspectives. Building on this idea and logic, the PPCI will be constructed starting with questionnaires and interviews with port experts, researchers, managers, and other stakeholders to identify the main indicators for each dimension. Every PPCI dimension will consider a number of potential variables that explain the indicator, and then the most applicable will be selected, justified by cultivation of expert opinion and/or the characteristics of reliable and available data.

Composite PPCI equation

Here, all dimensions are aggregated into one final Port Performance capability Index:

$$\mathbf{PPCI_j = f(Economic_j, Environmental_j, Health_j, SocialGovernance_j)}$$

Where each dimension is calculated from its **sub-dimensions** and variables:

Economic dimension ($PPCI_{econ}$)

$$\text{Economic}_j = f(\text{Throughput}_j, \text{TradeContribution}_j, \ldots)$$

Environmental dimension ($PPCI_{env}$)

$$\text{Environmental}_j = f(CO_{2j}, NOx_j, \text{EnergyUse}_j, \ldots)$$

Health dimension ($PPCI_{hlth}$)

$$\text{Health}_j = f(\text{RespiratoryAdmissions}_j, \text{OccupationalSafety}_j, \ldots)$$

Governemental dimension ($PPCI_{sogo}$)

$$\text{SocialGovernance}_j = f(\text{Transparency}_j, \text{CommunityEngagement}_j, \ldots)$$

This PPCI is designed with analytical flexibility:

1 when aggregated into a composite PPCI, it can be used as a dependent variable to evaluate the overall capability performance of ports;
2 when decomposed into sub-dimensions, it can serve as a set of independent variables to explain port activity growth, emissions, health, or governance quality.

This framework systematically parallels Sen's approach, which promotes the perspective that development should not be reduced to a single indicator but rather be construed as the expansion of multidimensional capabilities shaped by institutional, environmental, and social contexts.

Discussion and conclusion

Discussion

The PPCI illustrates that the value of a port goes beyond throughput and connectivity; it includes environmental, health, and governance aspects. In doing so, the PPCI exposes hidden trade-offs: a port may have high performance by traditional metrics but much poorer performance when pollution, health consequences, and governance quality are taken into account. For example, large hub ports in Northern Europe often have strong economic and connectivity pedigree but a high level of air pollution resulting from the amount of shipping traffic. Smaller ports in Scandinavia, while having low economic performance, provide a much more balanced performance because of strong regulation and community engagement. Therefore, the PPCI introduces a new element into the traditional question of "how well a port performs" to "for whom, and at what cost."

The varying economies of North versus South are clear, with northern ports generally having higher levels of financial capacity to invest in green technologies versus southern ports with smaller budgets. The geographical aspect affects the context as well: ports that have large hinterlands like Rotterdam and Antwerp have inherent economic benefits; island or peninsular ports like Greece or Finland are normally cruise/shore side traffic and that comes with significant environmental issues. Additionally, the PPCI suggests that bigger is not always better. Large gateway ports may contribute to national economies, but they also provide a concentrated pollution and congestion centre, while intermediate ports will have responses to policy that must be sensitive to context. Therefore, understanding performance requires a multidimensional understanding about how operational performance interacts with quality of governance, environmental responsibility and social well-being.

Conclusion: limitations of the study, further research envisaged

This chapter has presented the PPCI as a multidimensional framework for evaluating the performance of ports, such as in Europe, from economic, environmental, health, and governance perspectives. However, it involves several comparable shortcomings. The first is in relation to data availability and consistency. Although many economic data sources (especially trade data) exist, information on health impacts, environmental externalities, and governance practices remains paltry and inconsistent across ports. Second, even though the PPCI includes a multidimensional structure, it still utilizes a subjective weighting and aggregation of a number of diverse indicators, which very likely present overly simplified sets of causal relationships between port activities, environmental pressures, and community outcomes.

Lastly, this chapter is itself mostly theoretical at this point; to operationalize the framework properly we need to most importantly validate the framework empirically from real-world data and discuss values and opinions with local stakeholders. Future research will focus on translating the PPCI from theory to practice through a participatory process involving surveys and interviews with port authorities, experts, researchers, and managers to identify the most relevant and context-specific indicators for each dimension. One ultimate goal of this research is to provide policymakers with an integrated, evidence-based tool to advance equitable and sustainable port development, ensuring that ports not only serve as engines for economic growth but are also integral actors in environmental protection and public health.

References

Acemoglu D., Johnson S., Robinson J.A. (2001) The colonial origins of comparative development: An empirical investigation. *American Economic Review*, 91(5): 1369–1401.

Adeyanju J., Ojekunle J. (2014) *Perspectives in Seaport and Shipping Developments in Nigeria*. Lambert Academic Publishing.

Andersson C., Bergström R., Johansson C. (2009) Population exposure and mortality due to regional background PM in Europe: Long-term simulations of source region and shipping contributions. *Atmospheric Environment*, 43: 3614–3620.

Australian Bureau of Industry Economics (1993) *International Performance Indicators — Waterfront.* Australian Government Publishing Service, https://www.sfu.ca/~poitras/PORTS2.pdf

Australian Transport Advisory Council (1992) *Port Performance Indicators.* Australian Government Publishing Service, https://www.bitre.gov.au/sites/default/files/report_084.pdf

Baumol W.J. (1967) Macroeconomics of unbalanced growth: The anatomy of urban crisis. *The American Economic Review*, 57(3): 415–426.

Chen L., Zhang D., Ma X., Wang L., Li S., Wu Z., Pan G. (2016) Container port performance measurement and comparison leveraging ship GPS traces and maritime open data. *IEEE Transactions on Intelligent Transportation Systems*, 17(5): 1227–1242.

Corbett J.J., Winebrake J.J., Green E.H., Kasibhatla P., Eyring V., Lauer A. (2007) Mortality from ship emissions: A global assessment. *Environmental Science & Technology*, 41(24): 8512–8518.

Cui C., Li S., Zhao W., Liu B., Shan Y., Guan D. (2023) Energy-related CO_2 emissions in 40 emerging economies: Trends, drivers, and inventories. *Earth System Science Data*, 15: 1317–1328.

De Monie G. (1987) *Measuring and Evaluating Port Performance and Productivity.* UNCTAD, https://digitallibrary.un.org/record/147442?ln=en

Drèze J., Sen A. (1989) *Hunger and Public Action.* Oxford University Press.

Ducruet C., Itoh H. (2022) Spatial network analysis of container port operations: The case of ship turnaround times. *Networks and Spatial Economics*, 22(4): 883–902.

El Weriemmi M., Bakari S. (2024) The impact of CO_2 emissions, domestic investment and trade openness on economic growth: New evidence from North African countries. *MPRA Paper No. 122152,* University Library of Munich.

Faure M.A., Ducruet C. (2025) The blue connection: A systematic and critical review of shipping network research. *Networks and Spatial Economics*, https://doi.org/10.1007/s11067-025-09705-y

Foster-McGregor N., Verspagen B. (2016) The role of structural change in the economic development of Asian economies. *Asian Development Review*, 33(2): 74–93.

Fugazza M., Hoffmann J. (2017) Liner shipping connectivity as determinant of trade. *Journal of Shipping and Trade*, 2(1): 1–17.

Gillingham K., Huang P. (2021) Racial Disparities in the Health Effects From Air Pollution: Evidence From Ports, ZEW Discussion Paper Nr. 21-058, Mannheim.

Glaeser E.L., La Porta R., LopezdeSilanes F., Shleifer A. (2004) Do institutions cause growth? *Journal of Economic Growth*, 9(3): 271–303.

Hartwig J. (2012) Testing the growth effects of structural change. *Structural Change and Economic Dynamics*, 23(1): 11–24.

Hickel J., Kallis G. (2020) Is green growth possible? *New Political Economy*, 25(4): 469–486.

Human Impact Partners (2010) *Los Angeles and Long Beach Maritime Port Health Impact Assessment (HIA) Scope (Working Draft).* U.S. Environmental Protection Agency, Region 9.

International Maritime Organization (IMO) (2014) *Third IMO GHG Study 2014*. IMO, https://www.imo.org/en/OurWork/Environment/Pages/Greenhouse-Gas-Studies-2014.aspx

International Maritime Organization (IMO) (2018) *Initial IMO Strategy on Reduction of GHG Emissions from Ships*. IMO, https://www.imo.org/en/MediaCentre/HotTopics/Pages/Reducing-greenhouse-gas-emissions-from-ships.aspx

Jonson J.E., Jalkanen J.P., Johansson L., Gauss M., Denier van der Gon H.A.C. (2015) Model calculations of the effects of present and future emissions of air pollutants from shipping in the Baltic Sea and the North Sea. *Atmospheric Chemistry and Physics*, 15(2): 783–798.

Karnoji D.S., Gurudev V., Dwarakish G.S. (2021) Factors affecting the vessel turnaround time in a seaport. *Paper Presented at the HYDRO2020 International Conference*, https://www.researchgate.net/publication/350654572_Factors_affecting_the_Vessel_Turnaround_time_in_a_Seaport

Leftwich A. (1994) Governance, the state and the politics of development. *Development and Change*, 25(2): 363–386.

Neagu O. (2020) Economic complexity and ecological footprint: Evidence from the most complex economies in the world. *Sustainability*, 12(21): 9031.

Nobel Prize (1998) The SverigesRiksbank Prize in Economic Sciences in Memory of Alfred Nobel 1998 – Amartya Sen, https://www.nobelprize.org/prizes/economic-sciences/1998/sen/facts/

Notteboom T., Rodrigue J.P. (2008) Containerisation, box logistics and global supply chains: The integration of ports and liner shipping networks. *Maritime Economics & Logistics*, 10(1–2): 152–174.

Notteboom T., van der Lugt L., van Saase N., Sel S., Neyens K. (2020) The role of seaports in green supply chain management. *Sustainability*, 12(4): 1688.

OECD (2010) *Globalisation, Transport and the Environment*. OECD Publishing, https://doi.org/10.1787/9789264072916-en

OECD (2025) *Health at a Glance 2025: OECD Indicators*. OECD Publishing, https://doi.org/10.1787/8f9e3f98-en

Omoke V., Onwuegbuchunam D.E. (2018) Determinants of interport competition: A case of coastal ports in West Africa. *Journal of Shipping and Ocean Engineering*, 8(2): 43–53.

Parvasi S.P., Lam J.S.L., Psaraftis H.N. (2025) Redesigning logistics systems towards sustainability: The impact of autonomous green-fueled ships. *International Journal of Physical Distribution & Logistics Management*, https://doi.org/10.1080/03088839.2025.2574673

Pearce D., Markandya A., Barbier E.B. (1989) *Blueprint for a Green Economy*. Earthscan Publications.

Pezzey J. (1992) Sustainable development concepts: An economic analysis. *World Bank Environment Paper No. 2*, World Bank.

Prüss-Üstün A., Wolf J., Corvalán C., Bos R., Neira M. (2016) *Preventing Disease through Healthy Environments: A Global Assessment of the Burden of Disease from Environmental Risks*. World Health Organization.

Sen A. (1992) *Inequality Reexamined*. Harvard University Press.

Sen A. (1999) *Development as Freedom*. Oxford University Press.

Sen A. (2000) *Development as Freedom*. Anchor Books.

Sen A., Muellbauer J. (1988) Economic factors and social welfare. In: Sen A. (Ed.), *The Standard of Living*. Cambridge University Press, pp. 1–38.

ShahrulAlfian H.A., Zakaria A., Md. Arof A. (2024) Green port performance indicators for dry bulk terminal: A case study of Port Klang. *Journal of Sustainable Marine Structures*, 8(1) 19–28.

Slack B., Comtois C., Wiegmans B., Witte, P. (2018) Ships time in port. *International Journal of Shipping and Transport Logistics*, 10(1): 45–62.

Tezcan Ö., Kan E. (2023) Meta-synthesis of research on green port performance evaluation criteria. *Pomorstvo*, 37(2): 227–239.

Tongzon J. (1995) Determinants of port performance and efficiency: Economic and operational perspectives. *Transportation Research Part A*, 29(3): 245–255.

UNDP (1990) *Human Development Report 1990*. Human Development Report 1990, https://hdr.undp.org/content/human-development-report-1990

United Nations Conference on Trade and Development (UNCTAD) (1976) *Port Performance Indicators: Report by the UNCTAD Secretariat*. United Nations Conference on Trade and Development, https://unctad.org/system/files/official-document/tdbc4d131sup1rev1_en.pdf

United Nations Conference on Trade and Development (UNCTAD) (1987) *Manual on a Uniform System of Port Statistics and Performance Indicators*. United Nations Conference on Trade and Development, https://unctad.org/system/files/official-document/shipd185rev2_en.pdf

United Nations Conference on Trade and Development (UNCTAD) (2004) *Review of Maritime Transport 2004*. United Nations Conference on Trade and Development, https://unctad.org/publication/review-maritime-transport-2004

United Nations Conference on Trade and Development (UNCTAD) (2021) *Review of Maritime Transport 2021: Chapter 4 – Key Performance Indicators for Ports and the Shipping Fleet*. United Nations Conference on Trade and Development, https://unctad.org/webflyer/review-maritime-transport-2021

United Nations Conference on Trade and Development (UNCTAD) (2022) *Review of Maritime Transport 2022: Key Performance Indicators for Ports and the Shipping Fleet* (Chapter 4). UNCTAD, https://unctad.org/system/files/official-document/rmt2022ch4_en.pdf

U.S. Environmental Protection Agency (USEPA) (2016) *The Health Effects of Air Pollution from Ships*. USEPA, https://www.epa.gov/ports-initiative/health-effects-air-pollution-ships

Viana M., Rizza V., Tobías A., Carr E., Corbett J., Sofiev M., Karanasiou A., Buonanno G., Fann N. (2020) Estimated health impacts from maritime transport in the Mediterranean region and benefits from the use of cleaner fuels. *Environment International*, 138: 105670.

Vigotti M.A., Mataloni F., Bruni A., Minniti C., Gianicolo E.A. (2014) Mortality analysis by neighbourhood in a city with high levels of industrial air pollution. *International Journal of Public Health*, 59(4): 645–653.

World Bank (1997) *Advancing Sustainable Development: The World Bank and Agenda 21*. World Bank.

World Bank (2018) *The Changing Wealth of Nations 2018: Building a Sustainable Future*. World Bank Group, https://www.worldbank.org/en/news/feature/2018/01/30/the-changing-wealth-of-nations-2018

World Bank (2023) *The Container Port Performance Index 2022: A Comparable Assessment of Performance Based on Vessel Time in Port* (Technical Paper No. 182). World Bank, https://documents1.worldbank.org/curated/en/099051723134019182/pdf/P1758330d05f3607f09690076fedcf4e71a.pdf

World Bank (2025) *The Container Port Performance Index 2020–2024: A Comparable Assessment of Performance based on Vessel Time in Port.* World Bank, https://openknowledge.worldbank.org/server/api/core/bitstreams/695e8bdc-eb9a-439a-a8d5-228593831ce8/content

World Commission on Environment and Development (WCED) (1987) *Our Common Future.* Oxford University Press, https://sustainabledevelopment.un.org/content/documents/5987our-common-future.pdf

World Health Organization (WHO) (2024) *Ambient (Outdoor) Air Pollution and Health.* October 24, World Health Organization, https://www.who.int/news-room/fact-sheets/detail/ambient-(outdoor)-air-quality-and-health

Zheng S., Kwon H., Wang S. (2014) Air pollutant emissions from ships in China's ports and coastal areas: Inventory and policy implications. *Atmospheric Environment*, 89: 74–84.

Zhou X., Cai Z., Tan K.H., Zhang L., Du J., Song M. (2021) Technological innovation and structural change for economic development in China as an emerging market. *Technological Forecasting and Social Change*, 167: 120671.

Zis T.P.V., Psaraftis H.N., Reche-Vilanova M. (2023) Design and application of a key performance indicator (KPI) framework for autonomous shipping in Europe. *Maritime Transport Research*, 5: 100095.

14 The impact of Chinese ports on cities' air pollution and public health

Ling Sun

Introduction

Maritime shipping is the backbone of global trade, accounting for about 80% of international freight volume (Zhang et al., 2025). It has inadvertently become a major contributor to global pollution. As international maritime trade flourishes and ports worldwide expand, many environmental concerns have emerged, including declining air quality and noise pollution. These issues further threaten public health and the well-being of local residents (Lim et al., 2019). Bailey and Solomon (2004) point out that sulfur oxides, volatile organic compounds, nitrogen oxides, and PM all seriously affect the health of local residents, with the smallest PM causing the greatest harm. Extensive research has found that daily variations in PM pollution can have fatal effects (Bailey and Solomon, 2004). On the other hand, the expansion and prosperity of many cities globally are closely linked to the development and operational efficiency of their ports (Xu et al., 2025). In 2024, Chinese ports handled 17.6 billion tons of cargo and 330 million TEUs (Twenty-Foot Equivalent Units). According to the Chinese Ministry of Transport, both indicators rank first in the world. In terms of cargo and container throughput, China now holds eight positions in the global top ten ports, solidifying its status as a world-recognized port powerhouse (Ma et al., 2025). In China, coastal areas account for 14% of the country's land area but are home to about 40% of the national population and generate nearly 60% of the Gross Domestic Product (GDP) (Wang et al., 2020). This exposes China to more severe challenges regarding air pollution and health risks associated with maritime activities compared to other maritime nations.

Studies have found that the impact of urban form indicators on air pollution is heterogeneous among cities of different sizes (Li et al., 2020). Furthermore, socioeconomic characteristics such as income level, industrialization, and population density can exacerbate pollution and affect the implementation of environmental policies (Hou et al., 2025). However, although air pollution in different port cities has been widely discussed, much current academic research focuses on the overall environmental effects of port activities or conducts case studies on single cargo types. There is a lack of horizontal comparison regarding

DOI: 10.4324/9781003639589-18

the structural impacts of different cargo types. For example, what are the differences in air pollution generated and its impact on resident health between port cities dominated by different cargo types? Do coastal port cities or inland river port cities have a greater impact on environmental pollution and resident health? Do port cities with high or low population density have a greater impact on the environment and health? These are all questions worth exploring. For the sustainable development of ports, which cargo type should be recommended for development? Does the development of shipping in port cities ultimately have a positive or negative impact on residents' health?

Therefore, this chapter examines the impact of different cargo structures on urban air pollution and public health using panel data from 35 Chinese port cities from 2013 to 2023. The sample includes major ports across coastal and inland regions, ensuring representativeness. A two-way fixed effects panel model is applied, with core explanatory variables being container, liquid bulk, and dry bulk throughput. The empirical analysis consists of three parts. The chapter is structured as follows: Section "Literature review" reviews the literature, Section "Data and methodology" describes data and methodology, Section "Results and discussion" presents and discusses empirical results, and Section "Multiple linear regression model" concludes with policy implications.

Literature review

Air pollution in port cities with different cargo types

In recent decades, container ports have become much more important in global shipping. Over 90% of non-bulk cargo is moved by containers. Container shipping makes up about 60% of all maritime trade. Container terminals need to cut CO_2 emissions, their main source of pollution (Olgay, 2023). Some studies link container ports to air pollution. For example, Rødseth et al. (2020) show how Norwegian ports reduced CO_2 emissions relative to container growth, studying why environmental efficiency changed. Park et al. (2023) predicted PM_{10} and $PM_{2.5}$ concentrations at container ports. These studies generally indicate a positive correlation between container ports and air pollution. Based on total cargo volume transported, dry bulk accounts for over 50% of all loaded cargo, compared to containers (about 16%) and liquid bulk (about 30%). In 2013, approximately 4.3 billion tons of dry bulk goods were shipped. Five major commodities (iron ore, coal, grain, bauxite/alumina, and phosphate rock) make up about 57% of all dry bulk shipments (Rahman et al., 2019). Bulk cargo ports hold a unique and critical role in global logistics and complex supply chains. They specialize in handling large volumes of unpackaged goods like coal, grain, minerals, and crude oil seamlessly (Lv et al., 2025). However, dust pollution from these operations, particularly particles smaller than 2.5 μm ($PM_{2.5}$), seriously affects air quality and public health in coastal cities (Shen et al., 2024).

Consequently, global demand for switching from coal to Liquefied Natural Gas (LNG) to reduce carbon monoxide (CO) has been increasing. LNG exports from the United States have grown rapidly in recent years. Imports of LNG by Asian countries like China, Japan, and South Korea are being consumed as a supplement to renewable energy and a clean energy source for key industries. Notably, in 2022, Europe's LNG imports replacing Russian gas increased by 60% (Chen et al., 2024). However, the full lifecycle climate impact of LNG as a marine fuel must be carefully evaluated. Balcombe et al. point out that while LNG can achieve 20%–30% CO_2 reduction and nearly eliminate sulfur oxide emissions, its greenhouse gas reduction benefits can be affected by methane slip. The extent of this impact varies by engine type (Balcombe et al., 2019). This reveals a direct climate risk during LNG's application phase. Therefore, analyzing liquid bulk cargo is also very important (Seo et al., 2024).

Public health issues in port cities

Research on public health in port cities focuses on two main areas: environmental pollution and residents' health. Regarding pollution, studies show port activities significantly affect air quality. For example, Tokaya et al. (2024) simulated European ports and found that shipping emissions greatly impact urban air. Yang et al. (2022) used satellite data to show that China's emission policies influence NO_2 and SO_2 levels in ports. Zhang et al. (2022) found multiple factors affect $PM_{2.5}$ in Yangtze River Delta port cities, while Barregard et al. (2019) showed public exposure to ship pollution depends on pollution levels and population density.

For health impacts, studies indicate clear risks and costs. Rahim et al. (2024) found air pollution near ports raises heart disease hospital visits, especially for the elderly and men. Cases show ship emissions cause about 70 early deaths yearly in Durban, with $71 million losses (Manqele et al., 2024). In London, short-term exposure to ship-related particles increases death rates (Piper et al., 2024). In Brindisi, PM10 and NO_2 pollution raise hospital visits (Gianicolo et al., 2013). These highlight the need to control port emissions. WHO estimates air pollution caused 4.2 million early deaths in 2019, with shipping playing a key role.

Summary

Existing research shows shipping emissions are a key source of port city air pollution, with $PM_{2.5}$, NO_2, and SO_2 as major pollutants. Health impact methods now quantify impacts precisely, not just correlate broadly. Studies link port-area pollution to higher hospitalizations, premature deaths, and costs. Short-term exposure to carbon particles also raises mortality.

However, most studies ignore cargo type differences. Ports are often treated as the same, or only container emissions are studied. Bulk port dust and liquid bulk fuel risks are rarely compared. This study focuses on how different cargo types—dry bulk, liquid bulk, and containers—affect environment and health. Using a two-way fixed effects model, it compares their impacts and examines drivers like economic level and pollutant mix. The goal is to provide evidence for targeted policies and green port development.

Data and methodology

Study area

China has over 50 coastal port cities. Based on data availability and sample representativeness, this study selects 35 port cities from different clusters, as illustrated in Figure 14.1. These include major seaports along the Bohai Rim (e.g., Dandong and Dalian), the Yangtze River Delta (e.g., Shanghai and Ningbo), and the Pearl River Estuary (e.g., Guangzhou and Shenzhen), as well as key inland river ports along the Yangtze River (e.g., Nanjing and Yichang). In 2023, their total throughput accounted for over 80% of China's total port throughput.

Variable selection

Selecting appropriate variables is essential for the research. This study is based on the stepwise regression model and identifies relevant variables by reviewing the literature. Factors such as industrial SO_2 emissions, industrial smoke and dust emissions, and doctor density all affect urban air pollution and public health. Following the principles of scientific validity, data availability, practicality, relevance, and completeness, 11 variables are chosen. These include three core independent variables: container throughput, dry bulk throughput, and liquid bulk throughput, which reflect port operational structure and intensity. Two dependent variables—AQI and mortality—are used to measure air pollution and health levels in port cities. Six control variables are also included: per capita GDP, population density, doctor density, industrial SO_2 emissions, industrial smoke and dust emissions, and wind speed. Doctor density reflects regional medical resources and capacity.

1. Container Throughput
   Containerization promotes trade by consolidating goods into standard units, revolutionizing maritime transport. Container throughput (in TEU) measures port activity and economic vitality, and its growth directly drives economic development (Akinsolu and Krmac, 2025). Container trucks connect ports and hinterlands. In 2021, heavy-duty diesel trucks accounted for 76.1% of motor vehicle NOx emissions in China (Zhao et al., 2024).
2. Dry Bulk Throughput
   Dry bulk throughput refers to the volume of unpackaged solid bulk cargo (e.g., coal, ore, grain) handled at a port, usually measured in 10,000 tons. Dry bulk ports are key nodes connecting land and sea

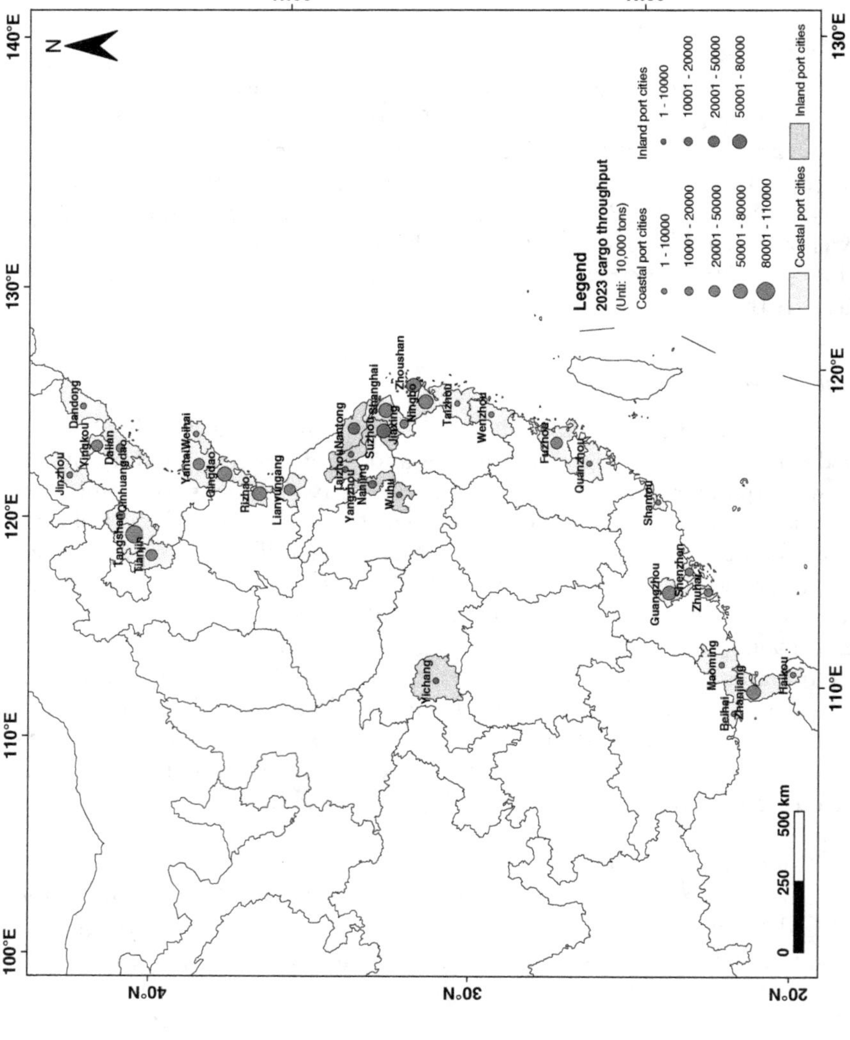

Figure 14.1 Geographical location of selected port cities and their throughput

transport (Wang et al., 2024). However, dust from these operations harms air quality and public health (Liu et al., 2023; Zhang et al., 2023).

3 Liquid Bulk Throughput
Liquid bulk throughput refers to the volume of unpackaged liquid cargo (e.g., crude oil, chemicals, LNG) handled at a port, measured in tons or m^3. Most liquid bulk is shipped via specialized vessels due to its physical properties (Zhang, 2015). The use of traditional fuels (diesel, gasoline) in transport emits harmful pollutants (Khan et al., 2015).

4 Air Quality Index (AQI)
AQI is a composite index based on six pollutants: $PM_{2.5}$, PM_{10}, SO_2, NO_2, CO, and O_3. A higher AQI indicates worse air quality (Dong et al., 2025). In China, AQI is calculated according to the "Technical Regulation on Ambient Air Quality Index".

5 Mortality Rate
Mortality rate is a key health indicator (Sun et al., 2024). Long-term exposure to shipping emissions raises risks of respiratory and cardiovascular diseases and increases mortality (Shi et al., 2024; Kiihamki et al., 2024).

6 Per Capita GDP
Per capita GDP reflects regional economic output and living standards. Studies show it is negatively correlated with air pollution levels (Wang et al., 2021).

7 Population Density
Population density measures the number of residents per unit area (persons/km^2). It is closely related to urban health and environmental quality (Yun et al., 2019).

8 Doctor Density
Doctor density refers to the number of licensed (assistant) physicians per 1,000 people. It reflects the availability of medical resources in a region.

9 Wind Speed
Wind speed measures how fast air moves horizontally (m/s). It affects pollutant dispersion; low wind speeds can lead to pollution accumulation.

10 Industrial SO_2 Emissions
Industrial SO_2 emissions refer to the total SO_2 released from industrial processes (tons). They are a major source of air pollution and acid rain (Table 14.1).

Methodology: two-way fixed effects panel model

As a cross-sectional and time-series study (2013–2023), panel data regression analysis is the best method to test our hypotheses. This model was chosen primarily because it helps reduce omitted variable bias when information on

Table 14.1 Description of research variables

Variable name	*Variable*	*Description*	*Unit*
Share of Container Throughput	TEU	Proportion of container throughput in total throughput	10,000 teu
Share of Dry Bulk Throughput	BULK	Proportion of dry bulk throughput in total throughput	10,000 tons
Share of Liquid Cargo Throughput	LIQ	Proportion of liquid bulk throughput in total throughput	10,000 tons
Air Quality Index	AQI	Dimensionless index quantitatively describing air quality status	Dimensionless
Mortality Rate	DEATH	Number of deaths in a period (usually a year) divided by the average population	%
Per Capita GDP	PGDP	Gross domestic product per capita	Yuan
Population Density	PD	Number of inhabitants per unit land area	persons/km^2
Physician Density	DOCTOR	Number of licensed (assistant) physicians per 1,000 population	persons/1,000
Wind Speed	WIND	Horizontal distance air moves per unit time	m/s
Industrial Sulfur Dioxide Emissions	SO_2	Total sulfur dioxide gas emitted to the atmosphere from industrial processes	tons

variables correlated with both the explanatory and dependent variables is missing, and these variables do not change over time or across individuals. We ran two models:

a A fixed effects regression model including time and individual fixed effects.
b A random effects regression model.

Based on the Hausman test, we ultimately selected the fixed effects model. Since the model includes a time-invariant variable (the Emission Control Area dummy variable), we used the equivalent Least Squares Dummy Variable model variant, which is as effective as the demeaning method. For the most recent year's data (2023), we applied factor analysis and hierarchical cluster analysis to describe the overall (static) trends and identify different types of port areas. Based on the preceding theoretical analysis, and to quantify the impact of different cargo types on air quality and public health, the basic two-way fixed effects panel model is given as:

$$AQI_{it} = \beta_0 + \beta_1 TEU_{it} + \beta_2 BULK_{it} + \beta_3 LIQ_{it} + \gamma Controls_{it} + \mu_i + \lambda_t + \varepsilon_{it}$$

$$DEATH_{it} = \beta_0 + \beta_1 TEU_{it} + \beta_2 BULK_{it} + \beta_3 LIQ_{it} + \gamma Controls_{it} + \mu_i + \lambda_t + \varepsilon_{it}$$

where i denotes the city, and t denotes the year.

Core independent variables: TEU (share of container throughput), BULK (share of dry bulk throughput), LIQ (share of liquid bulk throughput);

Control variables: $Controls_{it}$ include: per capita GDP (PGDP), population density (PD), doctor density (DOCTOR), wind speed (WIND), and industrial sulfur dioxide emissions (SO_2);

μ_i represents city fixed effects, controlling for time-invariant city characteristics;

λ_t represents year fixed effects, controlling for time trends and macroeconomic shocks;

ε_{it} is the random error term.

Results and discussion

Background statistics

Figure 14.2 and Table 14.2 provide basic statistics about the distribution of key variables across Chinese port cities, before presenting the results of the models in the following sections.

Research based on time series data from 2013 to 2023

From Figure 14.3, we can see that AQI dropped sharply from 2013 to 2014. All three port city types saw declines. Among them, dry bulk ports had the highest AQI, followed by container ports; liquid cargo ports had the lowest.

Figure 14.4 shows the mortality trends for the three types of port cities. The main conclusions are: Dry bulk (DBC) ports have the heaviest health burden. Their mortality rate is consistently the highest, showing the worst health outcomes for residents. Container (TEU) ports have the best health status. Their mortality rate is the lowest in most years. Liquid bulk (LIQ) ports show a puzzling trend. Although their air quality greatly improved after 2015, their mortality rate did not drop at the same rate. Instead, it sometimes came close to or even exceeded the rate in dry bulk ports. This is a key and noteworthy signal.

Dry Bulk Ports: High Pollution → High Mortality. Data shows they have the worst air quality and the highest death rates. Long-term exposure to dust pollution harms heart and lung health, creating a "pollution-health vicious cycle." Container Ports: Low Pollution → Low Mortality. Data shows they have the best air quality and the lowest death rates. Low pollution, combined with the economic benefits of these ports, improves healthcare, income, and

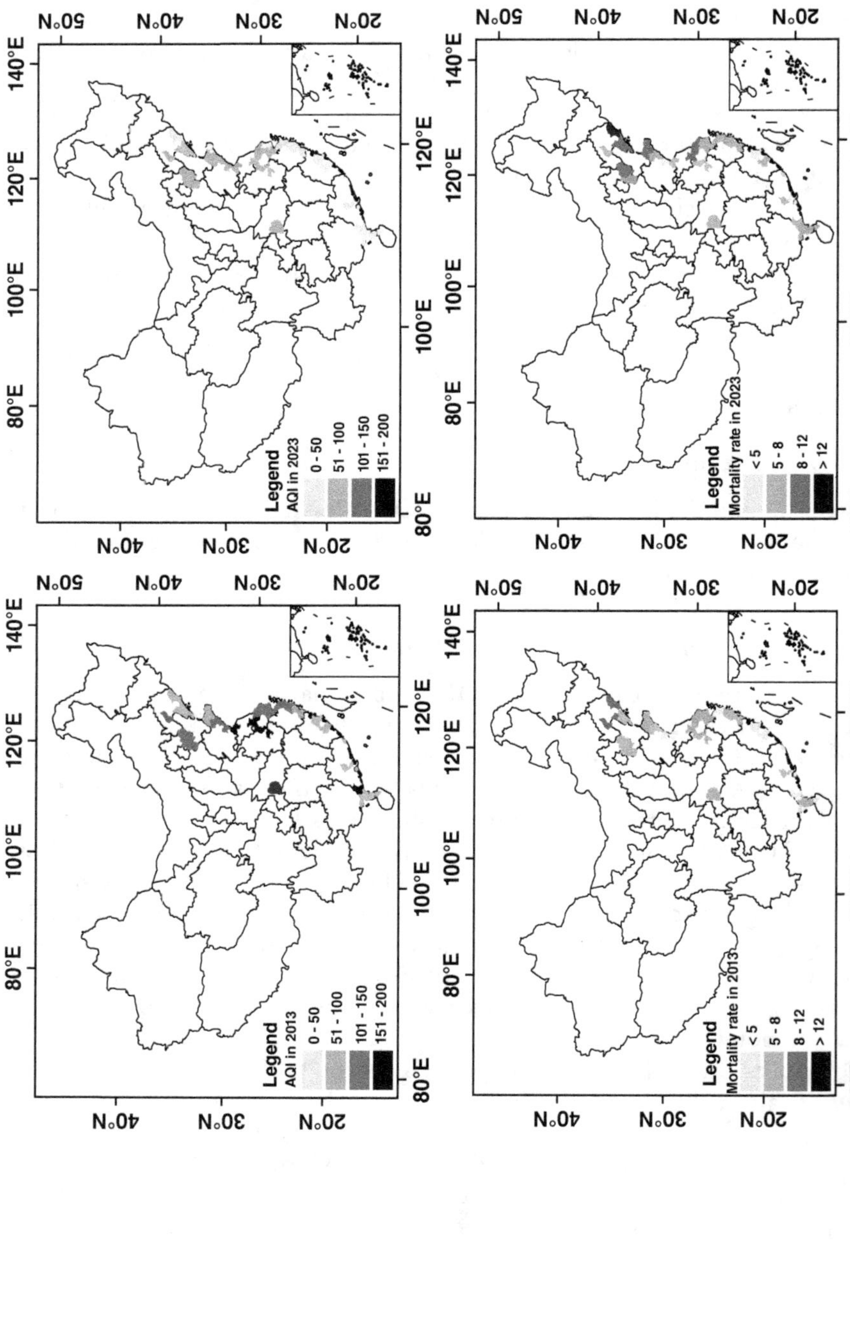

Figure 14.2 AQI and mortality rate index of port cities in 2023

Table 14.2 The descriptive statistics of variables

Variable	*Number*	*Mean*	*Median*	*Srd.Dev*	*Min*	*Max*
LnTEU	385	4.0454	5.1216	4.155	*6.9078	8.4962
LnLIQ	385	*1.1619	*6.9078	6.9507	*6.9078	9.1801
LnBULK	385	1.8612	6.319	7.3533	*6.9078	11.3754
LnCARGO	385	9.4546	9.6173	1.2821	4.6405	11.3371
LnAQI	385	4.117	4.1001	0.3529	3.3262	5.2095
LnDEATH	385	1.8086	1.8405	0.4095	*0.9416	3.1398
LnDOCTOR	385	3.2906	3.3084	0.2446	2.4611	4.0007
LnPGDP	385	11.381	11.4565	0.4674	10.1512	12.2234
LnPD	385	6.3286	6.2299	0.7219	4.7034	8.3957
LnWIND	385	2.3356	2.355	0.1819	1.7966	2.7496
$LnSO_2$	385	9.4154	9.4116	1.3769	3.091	12.5525

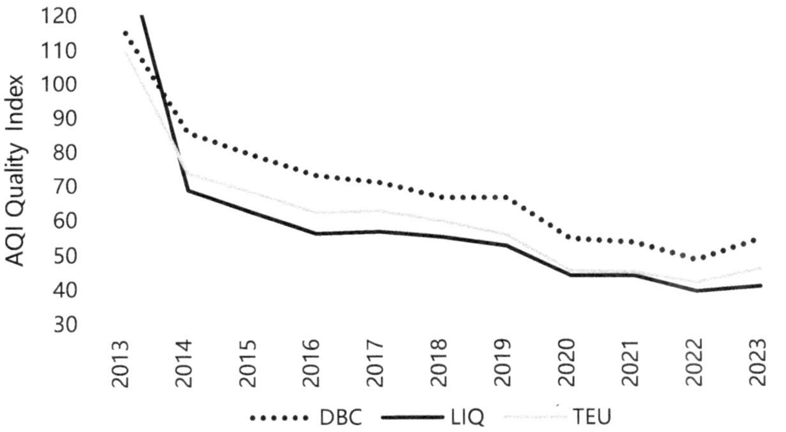

Figure 14.3 AQI of port cities by dominant cargo type (2013–2023)

health awareness, forming a positive cycle. Liquid Bulk Ports: While air quality greatly improved after 2015, the death rate did not drop significantly. This reveals the complex link between pollution and health: the lag effect of past pollution, specific toxic pollutants, and other industrial or socioeconomic factors can still impact health.

Multiple linear regression model

To reduce heteroskedasticity and nonlinearity, all continuous variables in this study were transformed using natural logarithms. For variables containing zero values (such as LIQ, Bulk, and TEU), zeros were replaced with 0.001 before log transformation (i.e., ln(x + 0.001)) to avoid missing values, following common practice in the literature. Descriptive statistics of the variables

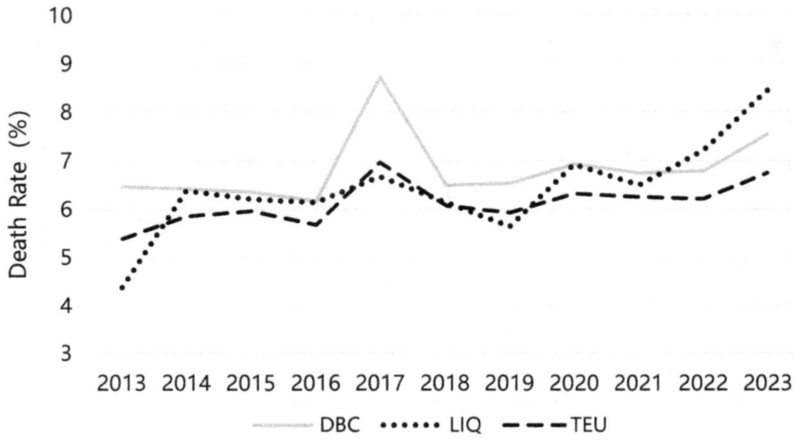

Figure 14.4 Death rate of port cities by dominant cargo type (2013–2023)

are shown in Table 14.2. Total cargo throughput (Ln_Cargo) exhibits the most concentrated and stable distribution, while other core port variables show high dispersion.

To assess the reliability of correlations between variables, a correlation coefficient test was conducted (results in Table 14.3). Additionally, Variance Inflation Factor (VIF) testing ruled out multicollinearity concerns (mean VIF 2.27, maximum 3.74, all below 10), with detailed results in Table 14.4. Finally, a unit root test was performed on the time series data to identify and address potential non-stationarity, ensuring the accuracy and reliability of the model estimates (Table 14.5).

The Hausman test in this study yielded a chi-square statistic of 44.12, with $p < 0.01$, indicating that the null hypothesis is rejected at the 1% significance level. This suggests that the fixed effects model is preferred over the random effects model. Therefore, it can be concluded that the panel data are suitable for the two-way fixed effects model, which controls for both individual and time effects simultaneously. Table 14.6 reports the stepwise regression results. Model 1 includes only the control variables, with a within R^2 of 0.9065, indicating that the model explains 90.65% of the variation in air quality within cities. Economic development level (LnPGDP) shows a significant negative correlation with air quality ($\beta = *0.2324$, $p < 0.01$), while population density (LnPD) has a significant positive effect on air quality ($\beta = 0.7684$, $p < 0.01$). Industrial emissions ($LnSO_2$) are marginally significant at the 10% level ($\beta = 0.0293$, $p = 0.058$). Model 2 adds port-related variables to Model 1. The within R^2 increases by only 0.0006–0.9071, and none of the three port variables (container, liquid cargo, and dry bulk) show significant coefficients (all p-values > 0.35). These results suggest that the expansion of port cargo volume is not a direct driver of urban air pollution. Meanwhile, the

Table 14.3 Correlation coefficient test

	LnTEU	*LnLIQ*	*LnBULK*	*LnCARGO*	*LnAQI*	*LnDEATH*	*LnDOC*	*LnPGDP*	*LnPD*	*LnWIND*	*LnSO$_2$*
LnTEU	1										
LnLIQ	0.1779*	1									
LnBULK	0.2111*	0.3262*	1								
LnCARGO	0.6459*	0.4498*	0.5757*	1							
LnAQI	−0.1114*	−0.1575*	0.2798*	−0.0023	1						
LnDEATH	−0.1111*	−0.0344	0.2052*	0.0097	0.199*	1					
LnDOCTOR	0.193*	0.1334*	0.0961	0.2786*	−0.3311*	0.1123*	1				
LnPGDP	0.2085*	0.0919	−0.04	0.3173*	−0.1854*	−0.1391*	0.5307*	1			
LnPD	0.4044*	0.0018	−0.2659*	0.2454*	−0.2330*	−0.5213*	0.0051	0.4601*	1		
LnWIND	0.3314*	0.1953*	−0.0532	0.3441*	−0.1916*	−0.1833*	0.09	0.3936*	0.3276*	1	
LnSO$_2$	0.0189	−0.1167*	0.3348*	0.1264*	0.7443*	0.1846*	−0.4633*	−0.1324*	−0.1538*	0.0073	1

* Significant correlation (greater than 0.1)

Table 14.4 Results of the VIF test

Variable	*VIF*	*1/VIF*
LnCARGO	#	0.267609
LnDOCTOR	2.66	0.375245
LnPGDP	2.52	0.397443
LnBULK	2.38	0.419493
LnPD	2.22	0.450531
LnTEU	2.14	0.467866
$LnSO_2$	1.92	0.520998
LnWIND	1.44	0.692519
LnLIQ	1.44	0.696602
Mean VIF	2.27	–

Table 14.5 Panel unit root test results

Variable	*IPS*			
	Level	*First-order differences*	*Second-order differences*	*Conclusions*
LnTEU	−1.352	0.989	0.009***	Stationary
LnLIQ	−1.544	0.000***	–	Stationary
LnBULK	−4.517***	–	–	Stationary
LnCARGO	−3.407***	–	–	Stationary
LnAQI	−2.415***	–	–	Stationary
LnDEATH	−1.725*	–	–	Stationary
LnDOCTOR	−1.868**	–	–	Stationary
LnPGDP	−1.46	0.002***	–	Stationary
LnPD	−0.553	0.003***	–	Stationary
LnWIND	−2.258***	–	–	Stationary
$LnSO_2$	−1.852**	–	–	Stationary

*, **, *** level of statistical significance

Table 14.6 Regression results

Variable	*(1) Control variable model*	*(2) Full variable model*
LnTEU	–	0.002 (0.0021)
LnLIQ	–	−0.0008 (0.0018)
LnBULK	–	−0.0026 (0.0038)
LnDOCTOR	−0.0696 (0.0772)	0.0681 (0.0781)
LnPGDP	−0.2324*** (0.0677)	−0.2416*** (0.067)
LnPD	0.7684*** (0.2121)	0.6998*** (0.202)
LnWIND	−0.0589 (0.1446)	−0.0545 (0.1473)
LnSO2	0.0293* (0.015)	0.0299* (0.015)
Year Fixed Effects	Yes	Yes
City Fixed Effects	Yes	Yes
Within R^2	0.9065	0.9071
Observations	385	385
Number of Cities	35	35

*, **, *** level of statistical significance

Table 14.7 Robustness tests

Variable	*(1) Control variable model*	*(2) Full variable model*
LnTEU	–	−0.0026 (0.0024)
LnLIQ	–	−0.0006 (0.0018)
LnBULK	–	−0.0002 (0.0014)
LnDOCTOR	−0.069 (0.0773)	0.0697 (0.0777)
LnPGDP	−0.1737 (0.1029)	−0.1722 (0.1031)
LnPD	0.3982 (0.3003)	0.4040 (0.0777)
LnWIND	0.0396 (0.1381)	0.0466 (0.1388)
LnSO2	−0.0035 (0.0065)	−0.0034 (0.0065)
Year Fixed Effects	Yes	Yes
City Fixed Effects	Yes	Yes
Within R^2	0.6657	0.6663
Observations	385	385
Number of Cities	35	35

coefficients of the control variables remain highly stable in Model 2, indicating good robustness of the model specification. Robustness tests were conducted in Table 14.7.

The empirical results of this study indicate that the growth of port throughput has no statistically significant direct impact on a city's overall average air quality (AQI). A plausible mechanism is that port pollution is highly localized, and its effect is diluted by the city-wide measurement of AQI. Therefore, our findings do not deny that port activities generate local pollution, but rather suggest that their intensity is not yet sufficient to significantly alter the average air quality at the city level. Next, a subgroup analysis will be conducted. The sample will be divided based on the following dimensions. By geographical feature: into coastal port cities and inland port cities. By port size: into port cities with larger throughput and port cities with smaller throughput. By PD: into port cities with higher PD and port cities with lower PD.

Impact of coastal and inland cities on environment and health

Table 14.8 shows that coastal city development is closely tied to the economy and medical resources, while inland river cities show a more complex and unstable pattern. In coastal cities, economic growth (GDP per capita) does not come at the cost of short-term health (mortality rate). Coastal port cities have poorer air quality, but their health outcomes are better than those of inland river port cities. Coastal cities produce most of the country's industrial output, but their water pollution levels are clearly higher than in inland cities.

Impact of port cities with large or small throughput on environment and health

Table 14.9 uses K-means cluster analysis to divide the 37 port cities into two categories. The categories are cities with relatively large cargo throughput and

Table 14.8 Regression results of hierarchical clustering analysis in 2023

		CONT	*LIQ*	*BULK*
Coastal port cities	Death	−0.166 (−0.860)	−0.102 (−0.494)	0.145 (0.731)
	AQI	0.124 (0.785)	0.002 (0.012)	0.596 (3.665)***
	Doctor	0.918 (9.401)***	−0.263 (−2.516)***	0.152 (1.514)
	SO2	0.154 (0.953)	−0.09 (−0.519)	0.604 (3.647)***
	pcGDP	0.6 (3.897)***	0.098 (0.597)	0.015 (0.098)
	pd	0.660 (4.370)***	−0.235 (−1.454)	−0.091 (−0.587)
		CONT	LIQ	BULK
Inland River Port Cities	Death	0.704 (1.390)	−1.962 (−1.331)	1.789 (1.193)
	AQI	−0.693 (−2.007)	−1.496 (−1.488)	0.988 (0.967)
	Doctor	−0.078 (−0.563)	2.275 (5.624)	−1.512 (−3.673)
	SO2	−0.586 (−4.414)	−2.112 (−5.463)	1.747 (4.441)
	pcGDP	−0.43 (−2.456)	1.934 (3.794)	−1.23 (−2.372)
	pd	−0.295 (−1.091)	2.173 (2.761)	−1.480 (−1.849)

Table 14.9 Regression results of hierarchical clustering analysis in 2023

		CONT	*LIQ*	*BULK*
Port cities with relatively large throughput	Death	−0.033 (−0.074)	−0.180 (−0.460)	0.305 (0.699)
	AQI	0.144 (0.41)	0.005 (0.016)	0.720 (2.069)
	Doctor	0.727 (3.71)**	−0.466 (−2.681)*	0.074 (0.380)
	SO2	0.204 (0.592)	−0.169 (−0.552)	0.747 (2.192)
	pcGDP	0.124 (0.592)	−0.246 (−0.797)	−0.52 (−1.514)
	Pd	0.633 (2.589)*	−0.39 (−1.801)	−0.098 (−0.407)
		CONT	LIQ	BULK
Port cities with relatively small throughput	Death	−0.341 (−1.708)	−0.4 (−0.198)	0.239 (1.254)
	AQI	−0.072 (−0.349)	−0.212 (−1.022)	0.296 (1.505)
	Doctor	0.468 (2.572)*	0.179 (0.975)	−0.151 (−0.868)
	SO2	−0.141 (−0.667)	−0.131 (−0.614)	0.202 (1.0)
	pcGDP	0.473 (2.496)*	−0.249 (−1.306)	−0.201 (−1.116)
	Pd	0.855 (7.45)***	−0.121 (−1.046)	−0.191 (−1.747)

cities with relatively small cargo throughput. There are 27 cities with small cargo throughput, with an average of 128.1653 million tons. There are ten cities with large cargo throughput, with an average of 613.9052 million tons.

Changes in national port cargo throughput is one of the most important indicators for describing national port activity (Li et al., 2020). It includes the transport of goods and commodities through ports within a specific country. This includes inbound and outbound movements across seaports, which are important nodes for trade and transport. This field involves many categories of cargo. These include containers, bulk commodities like coal and grain, liquid bulk items like oil and chemicals, and general cargo like machinery and vehicles.

Table 14.10 Regression results of hierarchical clustering analysis in 2023

		CONT	*LIQ*	*BULK*
Small population density per capita	Death	0.499	−0.995	0.139
	AQI	1.037	−0.87	−0.371
	Doctor	1.075	−0.388	0.049
	SO2	1.013	−0.908	−0.292
	pcGDP	0.693	0.545	0.394
Large population density per capita		CONT	LIQ	BULK
	Death	−0.013 (−0.058)	−0.161 (−0.673)	0.122 (0.614)
	AQI	0.297 (1.578)	−0.210 (−1.045)	0.549 (3.310)**
	Doctor	0.642 (3.420)**	−0.243 (−1.213)	0.179 (1.084)
	SO2	0.296 (1.535)	−0.297 (−1.443)	0.534 (3.138)**
	pcGDP	0.317 (1.473)	0.032 (0.14)	−0.065 (−0.343)

Comparison of port cities with large and small population densities

Table 14.10 uses K-means cluster analysis to divide the 37 port cities into two categories. The categories are cities with relatively large PD and cities with relatively small PD. In Auckland, communities with higher PD often have poorer air quality and more diseases related to air pollution. Communities with higher PD usually have higher population-weighted NO_2 and ambient $PM_{2.5}$ concentrations (Wrightson et al., 2025). There is a debate about the effect of PD on sustainability, between a belief that compact cities tend to emit less carbon, and the opposite view where.

Conclusion and policy implications

This study used regression analysis on panel data from 35 Chinese port cities (2013–2023). It examined the linear and nonlinear relationships between port function and city-level AQI and mortality rates.

Our results show that dry bulk cargo has the greatest negative impact on the environment. Container throughput is positively correlated with economic development. Developing dry bulk in coastal port cities can easily cause environmental problems. These cities should focus on developing container operations. Inland river ports could consider developing liquid bulk cargo. For ports with large throughput, dry bulk is strongly linked to environmental pollution. They need to strengthen environmental technology to develop this business potential. For ports with small throughput, container and liquid bulk operations can be moderately developed if there is industrial demand. They must also build proper safety and environmental protection facilities.

This study has some limitations. First, due to data collection limits, we mainly used AQI to describe air pollution. We did not study the main pollutants released from port activities in detail. Second, due to a lack of data directly related to public health, we used the mortality rate as a proxy for health status. A more accurate assessment would require more detailed indicators, such as the incidence rates of specific diseases.

References

Akinsolu O., Krmac E. (2025) Analyses of the container throughput: Case study on the selected ports of Europe and China. *Transportation Research Procedia*, 83: 244–250.

Bailey D., Solomon G. (2004) Pollution prevention at ports: Clearing the air. *Environmental Impact Assessment Review*, 24(7/8): 749–774.

Balcombe P., Brierley J., Lewis C., Skatvedt L., Speirs J., Hawkes A., Staffell I. (2019) How to decarbonise international shipping: Options for fuels, technologies and policies. *Energy Conversion and Management*, 182: 72-88.

Barregard L., Moln`ar P., Jonson J.E., Stockfelt L. (2019) Impact on population health of Baltic shipping emissions. *International Journal of Environmental Research and Public Health*, 16(11): 1954.

Chen X., Zhou J., Wang Y. (2024) Marine fuel restrictions and air pollution: A study on Chinese ports considering transboundary spillovers. *Marine Policy*, 163: 106136.

Dong X., Li D., Wang W., Shen Y. (2025) BWO-CAformer: An improved Informer model for AQI prediction in Beijing and Wuhan. *Process Safety and Environmental Protection*, 195: 106800.

Gianicolo E.A.L., Bruni A., Mangia C., Cervino M., Vigotti M.A. (2013) Acute effects of urban and industrial pollution in a government-designated "environmental risk area": The case of Brindisi, Italy. *International Journal of Environmental Health Research*, 23(5): 446–460.

Hou Y., Wang Q., Tan T. (2025) Evaluating drivers of PM2.5 air pollution at urban scales using interpretable machine learning. *Waste Management*, 192: 114–124.

Khan M.I., Yasmin T., Shakoor A. (2015) Technical overview of compressed natural gas (CNG) as a transportation fuel. *Renewable and Sustainable Energy Reviews*, 51: 785–797.

Kiihamki S.P., Korhonen M., Kukkonen J., Shiue I., Jaakkola J.J.K. (2024) Effects of ambient air pollution from shipping on mortality: A systematic review. *Science of the Total Environment*, 945: 173714.

Li Y., Zhu K., Wang S. (2020) Polycentric and dispersed population distribution increases PM2.5 concentrations: Evidence from 286 Chinese cities, 2001–2016. *Journal of Cleaner Production*, 248: 119202.

Lim S., Pettit S., Abouarghoub W., Beresford A. (2019) Port sustainability and performance: A systematic literature review. *Transportation Research Part D: Transport and the Environment*, 72: 47–64.

Liu B., Peng Y., Wang W., Mao N. (2023) Robust optimization for designing air quality monitoring network in coal ports under uncertainty. *Atmospheric Environment*, 304: 119792.

Lv Y., Gao Y., Liu J. (2025) Dual strategies-based resilience enhancement in a bulk cargo port under dynamic machinery failure scenarios with reinforcement learning. *Ocean and Coastal Management*, 260: 107484.

Ma Q., Li S., Jia P., Kuang H. (2025) Is port integration a panacea for regions green development: An empirical study of China port city. *Transport Policy*, 160: 15–28.

Manqele M.N., Moolla R., Ramsay F.L. (2024) The health and economic impacts of exposure to marine mobile emissions from ships in Durban port, South Africa. *Atmospheric Environment: X*, 24: 100277.

Olgay O. (2023) Carbon emission strategies for container handling equipment using the activity-based method: A case study of Ambarlı container port in Turkiye. *Marine Policy*, 149: 105480.

Park S., Woo S., Lim C.W. (2023) Predicting PM_{10} and $PM_{2.5}$ concentration in container ports: A deep learning approach. *Transportation Research Part D: Transport and Environment*, 115: 103601.

Piper R., Tremper A., Katsouyanni K., Fuller G.W., Green D., Font A., Walton H., Rivas I., Evangelopoulos D. (2024) Associations between short-term exposure to airborne carbonaceous particles and mortality: A time-series study in London during 2010–2019. *Environmental Pollution*, 360: 124720.

Rahim N.N.A., Zaki R.A., Yahya A., Wan Mahiyuddin W.R. (2024) Acute effects of air pollution on cardiovascular hospital admissions in the port district of Klang, Malaysia: A time-series analysis. *Atmospheric Environment*, 333: 120629.

Rahman N.S.F.A., Othman M.K., Sanusi I.A., Arof A.M., Ismail A. (2019) Evaluation of delay factors on dry bulk cargo operation in Malaysia: A case study of Kemaman port. *Asian Journal of Shipping and Logistics*, 35(3): 127–137.

Rødseth L.K., Schøyen H., Wangsness B.P. (2020) Decomposing growth in Norwegian seaport container throughput and associated air pollution. *Transportation Research Part D: Transport and the Environment*, 85: 102391.

Seo D.W., Jung D.H., Kwon J.T. (2024) Numerical investigation of subcooled two-phase flow and heat transfer characteristics in a liquefied natural gas cargo containment system. *Gas Science and Engineering*, 121: 205179.

Shen J., Liu Q., Feng X. (2024) Hourly PM2.5 concentration prediction for dry bulk port clusters considering spatiotemporal correlation: A novel deep learning blending ensemble model. *Journal of Environmental Management*, 370: 122703.

Shi J., Chen J., Chen H., Han W., Chen X., Xu J., Huang X., Yan T. (2024) Impact of China's ECA policies on air pollution in coastal cities: Empirical analysis based on synthetic-DID model. *Cities*, 148: 104871.

Sun L., Liu X., Hu Z., Zhang J., Ducruet C., Zhang W. (2024) Does just transition increase social and environmental risks? Evidence from global port cities development. *Environmental Impact Assessment Review*, 105: 107370.

Tokaya J.P., Kranenburg R., Timmermans R.M.A., Coenen P.W.H.G., Kelly B., Hullegie J.S., Megaritis T., Valastro G. (2024) The impact of shipping on the air quality in European port cities with a detailed analysis for Rotterdam. *Atmospheric Environment: X*, 23: 100278.

Wang J., Li R., Xue K. (2021) Analysis of spatio-temporal heterogeneity and socioeconomic driving factors of PM2.5 in Beijing–Tianjin–Hebei and its surrounding areas. *Atmosphere*, 12(10): 1324.

Wang W., Liu B., Tian Q. (2024) Predicting dust pollution from dry bulk ports in coastal cities: A hybrid approach based on data decomposition and deep learning. *Environmental Pollution*, 350: 124053.

Wang Z., Zhao L., Wang Y. (2020) An empirical correlation mechanism of economic growth and marine pollution: A case study of 11 coastal provinces and cities in China. *Ocean & Coastal Management*, 198: 105380.

Wrightson S., Hosking J., Woodward A. (2025) Higher population density is associated with worse air quality and related health outcomes in Tāmaki Makaurau. *Australian and New Zealand Journal of Public Health*, 49(1): 100213.

Xu J.H., Chen J.H., Zhao Q.F., Shi J., She S., Chen H. (2025) The impact of port-city interaction on urban economic development: An empirical study based on coastal port cities in China. *Cities*, 159: 105770.

Yang Z., Rui Z., Jihong C., Rangel-Buitrago N. (2022) The effectiveness of emission control policies in regulating air pollution over coastal ports of China: Spatiotemporal variations of NO_2 and SO_2. *Ocean & Coastal Management*, 219: 106064.

Yun G., He Y., Jiang Y., Dou P., Dai S. (2019) PM2.5 spatiotemporal evolution and drivers in the Yangtze River Delta between 2005 and 2015. *Atmosphere*, 10(2): 55.

Zhang G. (2015) An analysis of several legal issues in the carriage of seaborne liquid bulk cargoes. *World Shipping*, 38(04): 55–58.

Zhang Y., Li C., Dai T. (2025) Port sustainability: Synergistic pathways and perspectives for air pollution control and carbon mitigation. *Journal of Environmental Sciences*, https://doi.org/10.1016/j.jes.2025.09.053

Zhang Y., Yang Y., Chen J., Shi M. (2023) Spatiotemporal heterogeneity of the relationships between $PM_{2.5}$ concentrations and their drivers in China's coastal ports. *Journal of Environmental Management*, 345: 118698.

Zhang Y., Zhou R., Xu D., Chen J., Xu L. (2022) Modelling driving factors of $PM_{2.5}$ concentrations in port cities of the Yangtze River Delta. *Marine Pollution Bulletin*, 184: 114131.

Zhao H.M., He H.D., Lu D.N., Zhou D., Lu C.X., Fang X.R., Peng Z.R. (2024) Evaluation of CO_2 and NO_x emissions from container diesel trucks using a portable emissions measurement system. *Building and Environment*, 252: 111266.

Part 4

Governance and policies

15 Seafarer health safety and security challenges in global shipping

Claude Comtois, Serge Novikov and Sarah Lutfy

Introduction

The capacity of port and marine transport to adapt to changes is a key issue in sustaining their competitiveness. The opportunities for the constituents of maritime shipping to respond to new global challenges in epidemiological hazards are likely to be manifold in the next decade. A major constituent of the shipping industry pertains to vessel crew security, safety, health and welfare. This raises a series of key questions. How are factors of epidemic threats attributable to poor working and living conditions of seafarers? How is the industry responding to pressures imposed by the building blocks governing health regulations for global shipping? How can seafarer safety and security concerns associated with innovations be developed?

In this chapter these issues are first addressed by identifying how viral pathogen transmission may affect vessel crew. This is followed by an examination of the applicable international regulations for the prevention of epidemic risk in maritime transport. In interpreting these regulations, a detailed analysis is made of the impact of the Maritime Labour Convention 2006 on crew health conditions. Finally, the chapter reviews the contribution of information technologies in enhancing the maritime industry safety and security working environment.

Health risks of seafarers

In 2024 the total world fleet stood at 109,000 vessels of greater than 100 gross tonnes (United Nations Conference on Trade and Development [UNCTAD], 2024). The capacity of global shipping is increasing as the demand for global flow of goods, and the burgeoning cruise industry is leading to longer shipping routes and higher demands for international seafarers.

Seafarers are key actors underpinning world shipping. The worldwide number of sea workers is estimated at 1,892,720 seafarers comprising 857,540 qualified officers and 1,035,180 skilled crew members (Baltic and International Maritime Council [BIMCO] & International Chamber of Shipping [ICS], 2021). The risk of an outbreak of infectious diseases emanating from crew members can be high. First, the global maritime workforce

DOI: 10.4324/9781003639589-20

is drawn from a wide range of countries with variable vaccination history schedules and coverage, different levels of immunization rates and where hygiene traditions and sanitary measures differ. Second, each month approximately 300,000 seafarers are involved in crew changeovers. About half of this number are repatriated home while the other half are waiting to embark on a ship. This turnover is considered essential to comply with international maritime regulations for safety, crew health and welfare and employment amid uncertainties on the potential spread of infectious diseases (Safety-4Sea, 2024). Third, the stopover in ports of call in various parts of the world increases the vulnerability of seafarers to epidemics with the transmission of pathogens introduced on board from land-based populations. Fourth, ships are semi-closed and densely populated environments with shared facilities and frequent social and operational interactions. Contaminated food and potable water, ineffective ventilation systems, invasive pest populations in ship's hold and cargo and contaminated environmental surface can be conducive for the spread of communicable diseases.

Applicable regulations

Maritime international conventions are sets of international regulations and practices that govern seafaring activities. There are various international legal frameworks defining rights and obligations of States to regulate the containment of cross-border transmission of virulent infectious diseases. Specific guidelines to ship sanitation are regulated by the International Health Regulations (IHR) of the World Health Organization (WTO) and by the BIMCO Infectious or Contagious Diseases (IOCD) Clauses for Time Charter Parties. Four pillars have been defined by the International Maritime Organization (IMO) to enhance the safety, the security, the environmental protection and the welfare of sea workers in the global shipping industry. These include the International Convention for the Prevention of Pollution from Ships (MARPOL), the International Convention for the Safety at Sea (SOLAS), the International Convention on Standards of Training, Certification and Watchkeeping for Seafarers (STCW) and the Maritime Labour Convention 2006 of the International Labour Organization (International Labour Organization [ILO], 2006).

The MLC 2006 sets out fundamental rights and principles of seafarers for almost all aspects of working and living conditions applicable to ships of over 500 gross tonnage engaged in international voyages or transiting in foreign ports. It includes a section entitled Regulations and Code referred to as Titles of which there are five. Critical measures of infectious disease control strategies rest with Title 4 covering health conditions of seafarers both onboard and onshore matters. It specifically addresses access to and financial responsibility for medical care, health and safety protection and accident prevention, welfare onshore and social security protection. The extent covered by the MLC 2006 is not to control the infectious diseases related to maritime shipping but to identify deficiencies and associated health issues in the conditions of ships and provide measures to ensure seafarers' health and general well-being. As of June 2024, one hundred and ten States accounting for 96.6% of the world gross shipping tonnage have ratified the Maritime Labour Convention 2006.

Compliance of vessels with the requirements of an international maritime convention is subject to flag State and port State control mechanisms. Flag State and port State control are integral parts of existing maritime laws (Comtois & Slack, 2005).

States that have signed MLC 2006 are required to implement and enforce the controls provided for in the convention, by national laws, regulations and measures on ships which bear their flag. A flag State is expected to conduct regular inspections of each vessel flying the flag of that State to ensure the safety and the security of the ship, its cargo and the crew members.

Port State control is a form of control given within States that are signatories to MLC 2006. Conformity to the convention is not dictated by the shipowners or charterers' agreement but by the port authorities. Under this inspection regime each port authority has the right to inspect the compliance of any ship to the convention, regardless of their flag, so long as they voluntarily enter that port. Official shipboard inspection, monitoring, reporting and legal proceedings are conducted in ports by port State control officer and regulated by a set of guidelines defined by the IMO and the International Labour Organization (ILO). The objective is to identify substandard ships sailing around the world and enforce measures upon vessels which are in non-conformity to the requisites of MLC 2006. Violations of the requirements of the convention can lead to sanctions imposed by the port State control officer, the necessity to adopt corrective measures or detention of the ship until shortcomings are remedied before the vessel is allowed to sail. Nine regional port state controls, each incorporated in a Memorandum of Understanding (MOU), have been established since the 1980s aimed at standardizing inspections and sharing information (Table 15.1). It is important to underline that even vessels from non-ratified States calling at ports of ratified States must give access for inspections.

Table 15.1 Regional port State control memorandums of understanding, 2025

Memorandum	*Entry into force*	*Region*	*Contracting states*
Paris	1982	Europe and North America	27
Vina Del Mar	1992	Latin America	16
Tokyo	1993	Asia and the Pacific	22
Caribbean	1996	Caribbean	20
Mediterranean	1997	Mediterranean	10
Indian Ocean	1998	Indian ocean	20
Abuja	1999	West and Central Africa	22
Black Sea	2000	Black Sea	6
Riyadh	2004	Persian Gulf	6

Source: International Maritime Organization (IMO) (2025).

Impacts of MLC 2006 on seafarers' health safety and security

In analysing the MLC 2006 several studies have focused on the limits of selected MOU (Grbić et al., 2015; Kara, 2016); the effectiveness of port State control inspections (Cariou et al., 2008, Cariou and Wolff, 2015); and on regional assessment of MOU (Graziano et al., 2018). A limited number of studies have examined the impact of the MLC 2006 on the working and living conditions of seafarers. Fotteler et al. (2020) have studied the implementation of the MLC 2006 through port State control statistics. The authors analysed the evolution in the number of inspections, deficiencies and detentions in relation to working and living conditions on board vessels for seven MOU for the period 2010–2017. Specific attention was given to deficiencies related to the MLC certificates and documents on the declaration of maritime labour compliance of vessels flying the flag of ratifying countries. The results of the study suggested general improvement in the working and living conditions in the shipping industry. The research indicates however the persistence of large variation among MOU demanding more harmonization of port State control procedures. Pan (2021) has analysed the protection of Chinese seafarers' rights and interests under MLC 2006. She points out the inadequacies of China's legal system, the deficit in the implementation of public policies and the lack of effective coordination mechanisms between government agencies. In examining the impact of the MLC 2006 in Iran, Yousefi (2025) ranked 14 challenges in the implementation of the MLC 2006. He observed that only the minimum age and the medical care are properly implemented in the country. Among the most important challenges are the low-income level of shipowners and crew and the inspection and verification system for seafarers' certificates of competency. His research suggested that major efforts must be undertaken to increase the support of port and shipping organizations by the control and inspection officers in the effective implementation of the MLC 2006.
Improvements in seafarers working and living conditions provide a good insight into the adjustments following the entry into force of the MLC 2006. No reference in the scientific literature however alludes specifically to the security and safety deficiencies pertaining to health conditions on board vessels. A major problem is that MOU statistics are tardy in their publications, characterized by an absence of some time series data and some restrictions in their information on precise deficiency nature. In gauging the impact of the MLC 2006 on seafarers' health safety and security this study adopts a two-pronged approach. Initially the key features of vessel inspections and detentions as recorded in the annual reports of nine port State control are summarized. This is followed by a more detailed examination of the deficiencies in labour conditions of seafarers related to health protection, medical care and social security for the period January 2019 to July 2025.

In 2019 a total of 73,299 inspections were recorded from vessels arriving in international ports under nine regional agreements on port State control.

Table 15.2 Vessel inspections and detentions by MOU 2019–2024

MOU		*2019*	*2020*	*2021*	*2022*	*2023*	*2024*
Tokyo	Total inspections	31,372	19,416	22,732	24,894	30,887	32,054
	Total detentions	983	493	526	725	1,334	1,189
Paris	Total inspections	17,916	13,168	15,402	17,304	16,769	16,508
	Total detentions	534	385	538	736	639	665
Via del Mar	Total inspections	n.a.	n.a.	5,172	6,796	7,762	8,835
	Total detentions	n.a.	n.a.	40	72	64	70
Mediterranean	Total inspections	5,349	3,670	4,988	6,132	5,976	5,993
	Total detentions	94	51	103	132	157	196
Indian Ocean	Total inspections	5,943	4,762	4,993	5,062	5,785	5,334
	Total detentions	232	218	198	200	247	225
Black Sea	Total inspections	6,036	5,721	5,624	4,972	5,294	4,587
	Total detentions	212	241	178	174	208	216
Riyadh	Total inspections	3,206	1,842	2,506	3,649	3,926	n.a.
	Total detentions	46	30	37	36	34	n.a.
Abuja	Total inspections	2,695	2,337	2,605	2,421	3,117	n.a.
	Total detentions	21	9	23	19	23	n.a.
Caribbean	Total inspections	782	293	316	461	540	n.a.
	Total detentions	11	7	8	10	9	n.a.

Source: Authors, using data compiled by MOU.

Evidence shows that after a general downward trend because of the severe impact of the coronavirus disease in 2019 on the shipping industry, the number of inspections is reversing upwards with 80,056 inspections being realized in 2023. As a result of thorough inspections, vessels characterized by deficiencies in respect to minimal norms of safety, security and environmental compliance under MARPOL, MLC, SOLAS or STCW conventions can be grounded for detention. Table 15.2 shows that ship detentions have increased from 2,133 to 2,715 vessels between 2019 and 2023, an average annual growth rate of 6.2%. In 2024 port State controls in countries participating in the Tokyo and Paris MOU accounted for 62% of total vessel inspections and 70% of total ship detentions. The analysis exposes the significance of long-distance shipping traffic and vessel movements between maritime hubs in East and Southeast Asia and Western Europe. This also indicates the strong support of inspection officials from Asia Pacific and European maritime shipping and port organizations. In addition, it is apparent that coordination and information sharing between the various port State control regimes bring about significant change in the number of ships subject to risk-based methodologies.

A major problem in interpreting these diverse regional experiences is that the deficiencies and detentions related to MLC alongside SOLAS, MARPOL, STCW and the Seafarer Bill of Rights are not isolated events in themselves but related to the world-spanning activities of the global maritime economy. All maritime carriers have varying patterns of market segmentation and yields, and thus divergent level of response to international maritime regulations.

Table 15.3 Health-related vessel detentions under regional agreements of port State control, 2019–2025

Year	*2019*	*2020*	*2021*	*2022*	*2023*	*2024*	*2025*
	151	195	252	386	359	305	165

Source: Authors, using data compiled by MOU.

To overcome the previous limitations, insights into the health safety and security conditions of seafarers is derived from analysing detentions recorded by all MOU under Title 4 of MLC 2006 with close examination of the nature of deficiency, the ship type, the flag of registry and the geographical location for the period 2019–2025.

Table 15.3 indicates that the number of detentions has increased from 2019 to 2022 followed by a relative decline since 2023. This points to a tightening of the application of the MLC 2006 by port State control in a quest for more requirements and control in vessel inspections. This is also the result of emerging infectious diseases and public health emergencies associated with many influenza outbreaks including the severe acute respiratory syndrome coronavirus 2 (SARS-CoV-2) virus infection and the global propagation of the COVID-19 disease having led to an alarming fatality rate around the world. The spread of these pandemics has drastically changed the overall approach to maritime transport-associated safety. The shipping industry currently includes in its understanding of transport safety and security a transport devoid of any viral infection risk.

Cooperation, coordination and communication between port State controls have allowed the development of common guidelines to standardize protocols and unify criteria in the performance of ship inspection before the issuance of a compliance certificate with international regulations. Vessel inspection reports thus provide a list of deficiencies under a unified code. Vessel detention because of health concerns refers to detention of a ship by a port authority on account of detrimental conditions on board for seafarers as defined by Title 4 of MLC 2006 related to health protection, medical care, welfare and social security protection. Title 4 enumerates 33 deficiency codes that can be grouped under five headings: equipment (14 deficiencies); medical and hygienic (seven deficiencies); hazard warning (five deficiencies); shipboard conditions (four deficiencies); and emergency protocols (three deficiencies).

An examination of the MLC 2006 related deficiencies as justification for detention for vessels inspected under the jurisdiction of nine regional agreements on port State control between 2019 and 2025 has permitted to record 1,813 deficiencies related to 30 items considered as health hazards to the safety and security of seafarers during roughly 400,000 inspections recorded from vessels arriving in international ports for the period 2019–2025.

Table 15.4 indicates that in considering health protection, medical care and social security, attention focuses on various factors arising out or in connection

Table 15.4 MLC 2006 health-related vessel deficiencies and detentions, 2019–2025

Deficiency code	*Nature of detention*	*Number of detentions*
18420	Cleanliness of engine room	362
18408	Electrical	223
18418	Winches and capstans	133
18425	Access/structural features (ship)	133
18407	Lighting (working space)	87
18409	Dangerous areas	87
18499	Procedure of inspection, reporting and correcting unsafe conditions and for investigating and reporting onboard occupational accidents	87
18416	Mooring ropes/lines and wires	83
18417	Anchoring devices	75
18410	Gas instruments	71
18401	Medical equipment, medical chest, medical guide	68
18424	Steam pipes, pressure pipes, wires (insulation)	62
18414	Protection machines/parts	60
18412	Personal protective equipment (PPE)	55
18415	Entry dangerous spaces	36
18428	Onboard programme for the prevention of occupational injuries and diseases	36
18432	Risk evaluation, training and instruction to seafarers	24
18426	Exposure to harmful levels of ambient factors	23
18421	Guards – fencing around dangerous machinery parts	20
18419	Adequate lighting – mooring arrangements	17
18427	Ship's occupational safety and health policies and programmes	16
18402	Access to onshore medical doctor or dentist	14
18413	Warning notices	10
18429	Procedure of inspection, reporting and correcting unsafe conditions and for investigating and reporting onboard occupational accidents	10
18431	Investigation after accident	7
18406	Medical care onboard or ashore free of charge	5
18422	Asbestos fibres	4
18430	Ship's safety committee	3
18411	Emergency cleaning devices	1
18423	Preventive information	1
Total		1 813

Source: Authors, using data compiled by MOU.

with any defect in equipment or installation required for ship operations that may directly or indirectly affect the safety and security of seafarers. Operations related to navigation account for approximately 10% of allocated duties of crew on board a commercial vessel. Work organization aboard ocean-going vessels is complex. In addition to shipping-related operations, shipboard duties are linked to a multitasking operational environment including inspection of steel cables, wires and ropes, vessel maintenance, repair and refuelling, docking and anchoring, loading and unloading of cargo, dry bulk and liquid bulk, maintenance and exploitation of engine room. Potential consequences of equipment failure can result in a greater likelihood of accidents, personnel injury, various health problems along with increased legal liability.

The most frequently recorded deficiency is "cleanliness of engine room» followed by «electrical", "winches & capstans" and "ship access and structural features". These deficiencies involve equipment failure on board for navigation or cargo handling that can bring about serious physical injuries and fatalities. These deficiencies outnumber "Medical equipment, medical chest, medical guide", "Access to onshore medical doctor or dentist" and "Medical care onboard or ashore free of charge". This suggests that more emphasis is placed on precaution and prevention by prioritizing measures avoiding potential harm to vessel crew. It involves identifying ship deficiencies to promote uniform vessel construction standards, strict operational requirements and high-quality equipment to meet crew's right and interest, efficient cargo operation and enhanced navigation safety.

In considering ship type, health-related efficiency objectives suggest there is noticeable difference between types of ships (Table 15.5) and efforts should concentrate on bulk carriers and general cargo ships as they account for

Table 15.5 MLC 2006 health-related vessel detentions by type of ship, 2019–2025

Ship type	*Number of detentions*	*Percentage of total detentions*
Bulk carrier	663	36.57
General cargo/multipurpose	650	35.85
Container	198	10.92
Oil tanker	85	4.69
Ro-Ro cargo	32	1.77
Tug	33	1.82
Other special activities	24	1.32
Chemical tanker	19	1.05
Ro-Ro passenger ship	18	0.99
Offshore supply	15	0.83
Refrigerated cargo	13	0.72
Vehicle carrier	13	0.72
Livestock carrier	10	0.55
Gas carrier	8	0.44
Wood-chip carrier	8	0.44
Commercial yacht	7	0.39
Passenger ship	6	0.33
Heavy load	5	0.28
NLS tanker	3	0.17
LPG tanker	2	0.11
Dredger	1	0.06
Total	1,813	100

Source: Authors, using data compiled by MOU.

Table 15.6 MLC 2006 health-related vessel detentions by age of ship, 2019–2025

Years of build	*Age of ship* (years)	*Number of unique ship detained*	*Percentage of detentions*
2021–2025	01-May	8	0.74
2016–2020	06-Oct	30	2.76
2011–2015	15-Nov	192	17.7
2006–2010	16–20	288	26.54
2001–2005	21–25	180	16.59
1996–2000	26–30	132	12.17
1991–1995	31–35	85	7.83
1949–1990	>35	170	15.67
Total		1,085	100

Source: Authors, using data compiled by MOU.

36.57% and 35.85% respectively of the total number of detentions. These figures can be explained by two reasons. First, these vessels represent 46.3% of the world fleet capacity and play a critical role in the global economy as they facilitate the movement of massive quantities of resources and commodities (UNCTAD, 2024). Second, the bulk shipping segment in developing country flags is characterized by limited fleet renewal while the general cargo ships have the oldest age profile of the global merchant fleet.

A further aspect of differentiation is that of age of vessels. Table 15.6 indicates that 52.26% of vessels being detained are more than 20 years old. Taking note of ship names and IMO numbers, the analysis permits to identify 1,085 vessels liable to detention over 1,813 cases mostly bulk carriers and general cargo ships. Several ships have been subjected to detention on numerous occasions due to potential risks to the health safety and security of seafarers over the period 2019–2025. Global fleet renewal is emerging as a key feature to comply with regulatory measures of MLC 2006. The marine industry sector is hard-pressed to keep up with growing demands for safe and secure working environment. Evidence suggests that the order book of strong-branded carriers with extensive global networks continues to flow. But the erosion of the balance sheet of several shipowners can lead to the deferment or cancellation of the deliveries of new vessels and more emphasis on second-hand markets thus limiting fleet renewal. An additional factor in fleet modernization hinges on the global shipping yards' commands of the latest naval technology to meet high-quality safety and security standards for seafarers.

The study reveals important differences between vessel's flag States. Three out of the 78 flag States accounted for 47.28% of detained vessels. Between 2019 and 2025 high detention rates under MLC 2006 health protection, medical care and social security were recorded for ships registered in Panama (273 detentions), Liberia (142 detentions) and Marshalls Islands (98

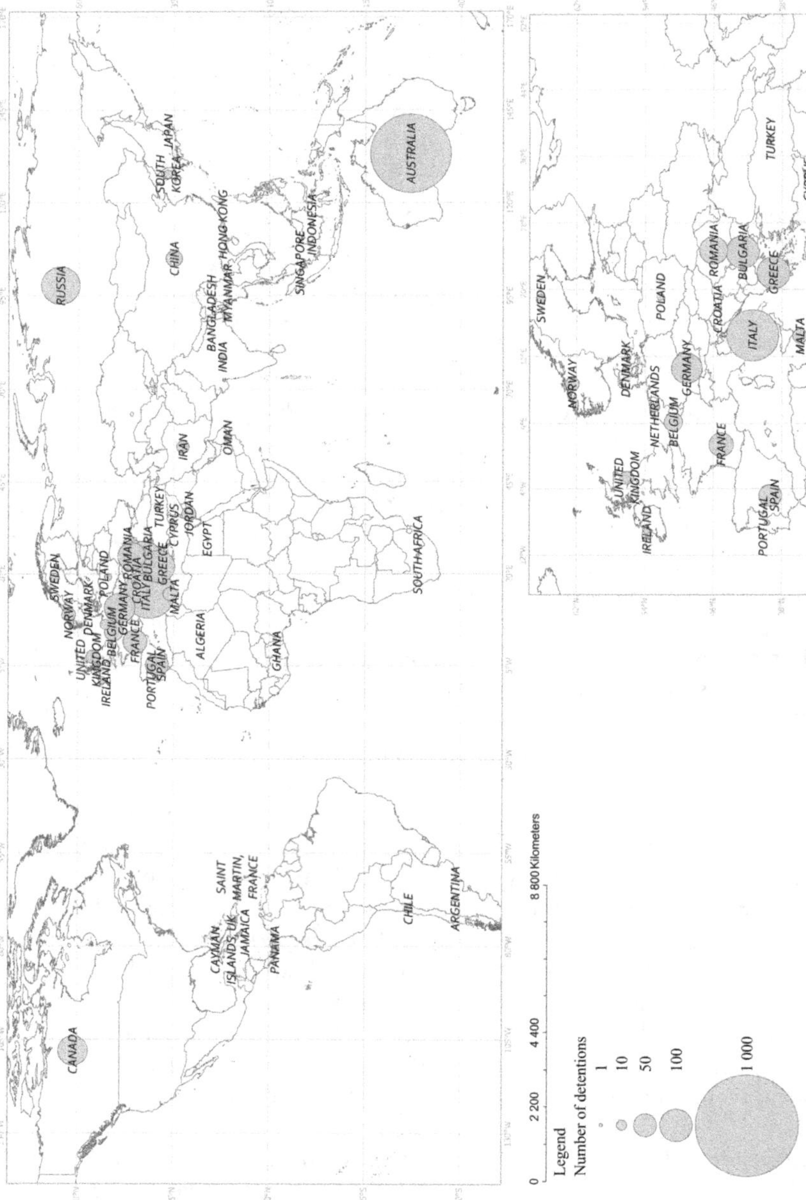

Production: Sarah Lutfy, 2025.
Source: Port State controls annual reports, 2019-2025

Figure 15.1 MLC 2006 health-related vessel detentions by port State controls, 2019–2025 detentions). The relationship between flags of convenience and MLC 2006 regarding health-related conditions on board ship is complex. Shipowners may choose a flag of convenience to avoid stricter regulations, potentially impacting the safety and security of seafarers. In sharp contrast the purpose of MLC 2006 is to establish standard requirements for medical safety, disease protection and healthcare safeguard of crew. The answer to this dilemma depends in technical terms on a common inspection procedures and uniform criteria under all regional MOU agreements and, in commercial terms, in the search for compromises between seafarer safety and security and cost-effectiveness of vessel equipment, operation and maintenance which often implies smaller financial return for shipowners and operators.

The total number of ships detained for deficiencies in health-related conditions under MLC 2006 exhibits important regional patterns among port State with a strong preponderance of port state controls in Australia, Europe and Canada (Figure 15.1). Australian and Italian ports account for the highest share of vessel detentions with 34% and 14% respectively for the period 2019–2025. The size of the share of bulk shipping in Australia's maritime industry is significant. In 2023–2024 crude materials which comprises mainly bulk freight, was 63% by weight and 25% by value of Australia's maritime trade estimated to be 1,669.8 million tonnes and $804 billion (Australian Government, 2025). Australia has a long tradition of marine safety and security surveillance encompassing the inspection of goods at border-crossing, confirmation of regulatory compliance and response plan which focuses on health-related assistance. Given the significance of the share of bulk shipping in Australia's maritime industry, the impact on seafarers' physical health and welfare has been given a high priority by the Australian port State control. Port State control performance in Italy surpasses all other countries adhering to the Paris MOU establishing records in the number of inspections and detentions of vessels calling at Italian ports. Several bulk and cargo vessels have been refused access to Italian ports and detained on numerous occasions over the past five years. Many of these ships are registered under flags of convenience showing excessive number of deficiencies, poor performance and very high-risk shipping practices. In addition, there are numerous detentions of vessels involved in humanitarian search and rescue operations in the Mediterranean.

Mitigating future health risks

Several measures are currently in place to respond to key epidemiological parameters associated with outbreaks of infectious disease or epidemics on board ships. Measures applied to seafarers include, but are not limited to education/training, vaccinations, pre-embarkation screening and treatment. The shipping industry is also taking actions applied to inanimate objects through inspection of cargo, cleaning and disinfecting ship surface and equipment and better ventilation systems. While certainly valid, the adoption of almost all these measures is coloured by the multifaceted impacts of the experience of recent pandemics. But the findings from the analysis of ship detentions in relation to health protection, medical care, welfare and social security protection points to defective equipment or improper vessel installations that may directly or indirectly affect the safety and security of seafarers. Rather than pursue suggestions that the protection of seafarers require new medical and hygienic practices, it is time to provide fresh insights by invoking the criticity of a ship's assets, information technology and automation.

The critical aspect of a ship relates to the relative importance of an asset due to its indispensable nature and the consequences of dysfunction on the continuous functioning of the vessel. The concept emphasizes the dependency of a ship on a specific component supporting its operations. The critical aspect thus varies in relation to the impact of a material support on the reliability of the vessel. The risks of failure of a ship's asset can be very varied. Equipment failure can be affected by different kinds of potential hazards: emergency, natural disaster, security breach, communication failure, technical breakdown, operational error, lack of maintenance, etc. There is a common understanding that the complexity and the existence of direct links between assets allow relatively small disruptions to degenerate into crisis.

It is generally admitted that considerations to determine the criticity of a ship's asset refer to the potential consequences of an incident that can compromise a ship asset and concomitantly the safety and security interests of seafarers. Four criteria are proposed: (1) functionality as an estimation of the level of performance of a ship asset in terms of efficiency and optimal capacities; (2) viability defined as the capacity of an asset to maintain its physical and operational characteristics during its service life; (3) interdependence interpreted as the degree to which the asset contributes to the safety of operations of other ship assets; (4) maintenance viewed as a measure of the work to be carried out on asset to reference standards. These indicators could be the benchmark used by the ship operator to measure the deficiencies in ship equipment and improve the safety and security aspects of seafarers.

As operational requirements, sensors and actuators can be fixed within equipment and linked to a digital network. Large amount of information on ship assets can be transferred to a computerized data processing system and be subject to data analysis. Ship asset conditions would be monitored and controlled in real-time during a vessel journey from the port of origin to the arrival at a foreign port. Critical situations arising from equipment failure can be anticipated and solutions proposed to many of the safety and security challenges facing seafarers. The vision of a digital ship can serve as a base for discussion between ship operators and port State controls. A long-term goal would be to enhance the role of port State control as data service provider. Shipowners willing to collaborate remain fully independent. Through digitization, the global network of port State controls would permit information flows to optimize the safety and security of seafarers by sharing good practices and innovative solutions within the network.

Seafarers' rights and interests under MLC 2006 can be further enhanced with ship automation. Over the years maritime carriers have increased in size, and the equipment required for cargo-handling systems has become more capital-intensive and automated. Automation of operations on board vessel, at sea and in ports of call can lead to important efficiency improvements and significant reduction of time and costs. An additional argument for the automation of ships pertains to human injury in the context of accidents. Automation allows a minimum crew number and contributes to the need to increase safety and security of seafarers. The minimum crew provision and their qualification are determined by the operational requirements of a vessel as defined by the International Maritime Organization. Seafarers aboard ship can be reduced as a result of progress in information and communication technologies and intensification of automation. Autonomous vessel manoeuvres can be monitored and controlled by land-based crew. This represents an alternative to the traditional work aboard to operate a vessel and contributes to improving living and working conditions of seafarers. By taking vessel automation to the largest possible degree, it will remove some issues in the regulations.

If these changes occur in the medium-to-long term, they will have triggered some positive developments to offset health-related issues affecting seafarers. Much will depend on the development of innovations benefiting the shipping industry. If an appropriate arrangement between shipowners and port State controls can be created, seafarers will be able to use their professional skills to the maximum advantage of the shipping industry.

Conclusion

A wide range of international regulations is in place to govern maritime activities. Inspections are a key element in assuring the health, safety and security not only of ships and seafarers but also on the oceans across which they ply as well as the ports they serve. This is the responsibility of port State control mechanisms. Over 80,000 inspections were carried out in 2023 of which 2,715 resulted in detentions. Differences are evident between the number of inspections and detentions by which port State control MOUs were applied. Health criteria considered in MLC 2006 also include safety and security measures in terms of equipment standards, hazard warning, shipboard conditions and contingency plans. These indicators have a greater impact on the well-being of seafarers than purely health criteria. The potential consequences of dysfunction can result in a greater likelihood of accidents and personnel injury, various health problems and loss of productivity of key personnel. In addition, data analysis has revealed important differences between vessel age and ship type in the numbers of detentions based on MLC 2006 health protection, medical care and social security.

The regime of international inspections must be maintained and improved. There is need for IMO to assure comparability between the MOUs and their application. The maritime industry is adapting to the inspections as older vessels are being retired. Improvement in shipping technologies and cargo handling are keys to improving health security and safety of seafarers. Information technologies and digitization can be applied to ship assets and operations. Scale economies are evident in all shipping. Increased vessel size in some bulk and container shipping is making use of technologies that require fewer seafarers. Full automation, resulting in the removal of the need for human control over navigation and engine management remains in its infancy, and there are still very significant legal challenges and labour issues. How far these disruptive technologies will go is still uncertain at present. The answer will come through a new management framework for the next generation vessel driven by the collaboration of the shipping and port State controls in developing a new business model of operational excellence and high-quality services.

References

Australian Government (2025) *Maritime. Australian Sea Freight 2023–24*. Canberra: Bureau of Infrastructure and Transport Research Economics Statistical Report, Department of Infrastructure, Transport, Regional Development, Communications, Sports and the Arts, 106 p.

Baltic and International Maritime Council (BIMCO) & International Chamber of Shipping (ICS) (2021) *Seafarer Workforce Report. The Global Supply and Demand for Seafarers in 2021*. London: Witherbys, 106 p.

Cariou P., Mejia Jr. M.Q., Wolff F.C. (2008) On the effectiveness of port state control. *Transportation Research Part E: Logistics and Transportation Review*, 44(3): 491–503.

Cariou P., Wolff F.C. (2015) Identifying substandards vessels through Port State control inspections: A new methodology for concentrated inspection campaigns. *Marine Policy*, 60: 27–39.

Comtois C., Slack B. (2005) *Restructuring the Maritime Transportation Industry: Global Overview of Sustainable Development Practices*. Québec: MTQ, 247 p.

Fotteler M.L., Bygvraa D.A., Jensen O.C. (2020) The impact of the Maritime Labor Convention on seafarers' working and living conditions: An analysis of port state control statistics. *BMC Public Health*, 20: 1586.

Graziano A., Cariou P., Wolff F.C., Mejia Jr. M.Q., Schröder-Hinrichs J.U. (2018) Port state control inspections in the European Union: Do inspector's number and background matter? *Marine Policy*, 88: 230–241.

Grbić L., Ivanešević D., Čulin J. (2015). Detainable maritime labour convention 2006-related deficiencis found by Paris MOU authorities. *Scientific Journal of Maritime Research*, 29: 52–57.

International Labour Organization (ILO) (2006) *Maritime Labour Convention 2006*. Geneva: ILO, 112 p.

International Maritime Organization (IMO) (2025) *Port State Control*, https://www.imo.org/en/ourwork/msas/pages/portstatecontrol.aspx

Kara E.G.E. (2016). Risk assessment in the Istanbul Strait using Black Sea MOU port state control inspections. *Sustainability*, 8(4): 390.

Pan H. (2021) *Protection on the Rights and Interests of Chinese Seafarers under MLC 2006*. M.Sc. dissertation, Maritime safety and environmental management, World Maritime University, 71 p.

Safety4Sea (2024) *IMO Publishes FAQ on Crew Changes and Seafarers Repatriation*, https://safety4sea.com/imo-publishes-faq-on-crew-changes-and-seafarers-repatriation/

United Nations Conference on Trade and Development (UNCTAD) (2024) *Review of Maritime Transport*. New York: United Nations, 166 p.

Yousefi H. (2025) Recognizing the challenges of the Maritime Labour Convention 2006 (MLC 2006) in Iran. *Transactions on Marine Science*, 1: 1–13.

16 Beyond port impacts

Quality of life as a framework for port–city governance

Sabah Zrari Djellid

Introduction

Chile's geography has made it a maritime nation whose development and international integration depend on port activity. Since the 1980s, Chile's export-oriented model has relied on maritime trade, which manages over 90% of foreign commerce. San Antonio and Valparaíso together handle more than one-fifth of national cargo and nearly one-third of maritime exports (DIRECTEMAR 2023).

This strong performance has consolidated Chile's position as one of Latin America's most competitive port systems, ranking among the region's top three in the World Bank's 2023 Logistics Performance Index. Despite major infrastructure investments and gains in port efficiency, living standards in Valparaíso and San Antonio have not kept pace. Indicators of housing, services, green areas, and mobility remain below regional and national averages, exposing a clear gap between port modernization and urban well-being. As argued elsewhere (Zrari 2021a, 2021b), port competitiveness must be reinterpreted through a territorial lens that balances global logistics imperatives with local well-being and governance equity.

Studies on port impacts have long focused on pollution, noise, congestion, and waterfront access, yet these explain only part of ports' influence on urban well-being. A broader framework is needed, one that integrates material, environmental, and perceptual dimensions.

This chapter argues that quality of life (QoL) should become a core principle of port–city governance, linking port performance to tangible improvements in everyday life. It pursues two objectives: (i) to reveal territorial disparities through Chile's QoL indicators; and (ii) to propose a governance model using these metrics to foster healthier, more equitable port–city relations.

The analysis draws on Chile's ecosystem of QoL observatories—ICVU, SIEDU, MBHT, and Fundación Piensa—to compare Valparaíso and San Antonio between 2011 and 2024. These reflections also stem from training programs at IIPC–AIVP (IIPC: International Institute of Ports and Cities, AIVP/IACP: International Association Cities and Ports), where port,

DOI: 10.4324/9781003639589-21

municipal, and civil-society professionals examine indicators to identify where ports and cities can act separately or jointly. Such experience revealed the lack of systematic QoL data in port territories and the need to shift from an impact-based view to a systemic approach that considers ports and cities as interdependent socio-territorial systems.

This chapter proceeds as follows: Section "Quality of life" discusses the conceptual link between QoL, health, and governance; Section "Measuring quality of life: Chile's observatory ecosystem" presents Chile's observatory system; Section "Port–city case studies: Valparaíso and San Antonio" compares Valparaíso and San Antonio; Section "From measurement to governance: port–city councils as policy laboratories" proposes a governance framework; and Section "Conclusions and recommendations" concludes with recommendations. The annexes complement this chapter by providing data tables from the Chilean observatories.

Quality of life

Since the 1960s, the notion of QoL has become consolidated as an interdisciplinary field, integrating material, subjective, and environmental dimensions. Although there is no consensus regarding its definition, Eduardo Lora, coordinator of the Inter-American Development Bank's 2008 report on QoL in Latin America, notes broad agreement on its multidimensional and contextual nature. A widely accepted definition combines equitable access to essential goods, security, civic participation, and perceived well-being.

Yet there is no consensus on which dimensions should be included, nor on how they should be selected or weighted to construct a synthetic measure of QoL. Lora (2008: 9) warns that such attempts risk homogenizing realities that are context-specific and culturally embedded. Building on this debate, the Quality of Life Program of the Kingdom of Saudi Arabia's Vision 2030 introduces new and forward-looking elements in its formulation:

> Quality of life is a compound experience of satisfaction with lifestyle, course and conditions, and with the necessary environment to develop and support new opportunities, overcoming constraints, for expanded liveable options.

This definition reframes QoL as a dynamic and adaptive experience, linking present living conditions with the capacity of individuals and territories to generate and expand opportunities for well-being.

Perceptions of QoL, however, vary across contexts and social strata, following distinct psychological and cultural patterns (Lora 2008: 4). As Lora highlights even though Chile ranks among the countries with the region's highest GDP per capita, its inhabitants appear among the least optimistic regarding various aspects of their lives.

Thus, while the concept of QoL is inherently multidimensional, its analysis requires operationalization through indicators capable of reflecting specific local contexts. An innovative feature of the UN Habitat QoLI lies in the construction of an index with a "global layer" encompassing universal domains—health, housing, education, governance, social cohesion, and environment—complemented by a "local layer" adaptable to the priorities and particularities of each city.

In port cities, QoL provides a bridge between environmental management, social equity, and public health. While port governance has long prioritized competitiveness and efficiency, residents' lived experience—their satisfaction, health, and sense of belonging—has often remained secondary. Yet in recent years, there has been a gradual evolution in the practices and communication of Chilean port authorities. In Valparaíso, a cooperation agreement was signed between the regional government, the municipality, and the port authority to promote joint action in areas such as urban integration and QoL.[1] A similar agreement is currently being prepared in San Antonio, explicitly incorporating QoL as one of its strategic axes. Reframing port–city relations through that lens thus builds on this emerging trend, placing human dimensions at the core of policy evaluation and territorial governance.

Measuring quality of life: Chile's observatory ecosystem

Chile has developed a robust ecosystem of QoL observatories that combine objective indicators and perception-based data to assess urban QoL. Each offers distinct yet complementary insights.

The Urban Quality of Life Index (ICVU), created in 2011 by the Pontificia Universidad Católica and the Cámara Chilena de la Construcción (2022, 2024), compiles over 40 indicators in six dimensions: labor, business, sociocultural conditions, connectivity, health, and housing. Over time, its methodology has evolved through adjustments in weighting and indicator selection, requiring caution when comparing results across years.

The Urban Development Indicators System (SIEDU), established in 2014 as part of Chile's National Urban Development Policy, the SIEDU is jointly developed by the National Statistics Institute (INE) and the National Council for Urban Development. It monitors eight national urban policy commitments.[2] Rather than a single index, it reports indicators on mobility, municipal capacity, public investment, and access to services. Its scope has evolved significantly over time: the first measurement included 81 indicators, the second 58, the third 12, the fourth 13, and the fifth and last one: 12 indicators.

The Territorial Human Well-Being Matrix (MBHT), developed by the Universidad Adolfo Ibáñez, the MBHT began in 2017 for 22 cities over 100,000 inhabitants and expanded nationwide in 2021 with the Undersecretary for Regional Development support. It integrates 18 territorial indicators grouped into four domains—material, socio-environmental, relational,

Table 16.1 Quality of life Chilean observatories

Observatory	*Institution*	*Website*	*Key dimensions*	*Geographical scale*	*Periodicity*
ICVU	Pontificia Universidad Católica de Chile/CChC	https://estudiosurbanos.uc.cl/documento/indice-de-calidad-de-vida-urbana-icvu-2024/	Labor, Business, Mobility, Health and Environment, Housing, Sociocultural conditions, Safety.	99 communes nationwide ≥ 50,000 inhabitants	Annual
SIEDU	INE/CNDU	https://www.ine.gob.cl/herramientas/portal-de-mapas/siedu	Public services and facilities; Planning; Cultural Heritage; Sustainable urban economy Housing, Environment, Mobility, Governance, Safety.	117 communes ≥ 50,000 inhabitants.	Source-dependent
MBHT	Universidad Adolfo Ibáñez	https://matrizbht.cl	Labor, Education, Accessibility to public equipments Health, Housing, Environment Safety	Nationwide coverage, urban blocks and rural entities.	Biennial
Fundación Piensa	Fundación Piensa	https://fundacionpiensa.cl/	Accessibility and Satisfaction to public equipments and facilities, Environment, Satisfaction with Life and Happiness.	Regional	Annual

Source: Own elaboration.

and accessibility to public facilities—and maps inequalities down to the level of urban blocks using satellite-based data from 2017 to 2020. The MBHT thus provides one of the most spatially detailed instruments for assessing local well-being. The Universidad Adolfo Ibáñez also collaborates with UN-Habitat's Quality of Life Initiative (QoLI), offering technical support to three Chilean cities, including Iquique, a port-city, in implementing the local layer of the index.

The Fundación Piensa, a think tank based in Valparaíso, conducts an annual Life Quality Survey covering the main municipalities of the Valparaíso Region. Implemented annually since 2014, this survey is based on face-to-face interviews with approximately 1,650 households, representative of the regional population. Between 2014 and 2024, the survey evolved from a broader model—covering dimensions such as Culture and Regional Development—to a more focused structure that emphasizes critical aspects as perceived by citizens, such as transport and safety. It captures satisfaction with public services, safety, municipal management, and happiness. For port–city governance, it helps prioritize interventions with the greatest perceived impact (public space, cleanliness, safety, participation).

Despite their differences, these observatories form a coherent system linking quantitative comparability with qualitative insight. Together, they enable correlations between environmental performance, institutional capacity, and citizen satisfaction—an approach consistent with the QoLI, which also combines global indicators with locally relevant variables. For port cities, this convergence provides a solid empirical foundation to link port activity with urban health and governance outcomes.

Table 16.1 summarizes the main observatories and their key characteristics.

Port–city case studies: Valparaíso and San Antonio

The next section focuses on Chile's two main port cities, Valparaíso and San Antonio. Drawing on the three observatories that provide indicator-level data—and using the ICVU as a national benchmark—it analyzes results from 2018 to 2020, complemented by the 2024 Fundación Piensa survey. Comparisons with neighboring communes, Viña del Mar and Santo Domingo,[3] help contextualize differences in QoL and territorial equity.

Port competitiveness and limited urban well-being: Valparaíso and San Antonio

Since the 1997 port reform, the ports of Valparaíso and San Antonio have shown sustained gains in productivity, reflected in shorter vessel turnaround times, higher cargo volumes handled per hectare, and improved coordination between logistics actors. According to the Observatorio Logístico of the Chilean Ministry of Transport and Telecommunications, San Antonio is the country's main port in terms of cargo throughput and trade value, handling around 23 million tons in 2024—more than one-fifth of Chile's total maritime cargo—followed by Valparaíso with approximately 8.4 million tons in the same year. These figures confirm the strategic primacy of San Antonio in national logistics chains, while Valparaíso remains a key hub for containerized and regional exports.

In contrast, the cities of Valparaíso and San Antonio have exhibited only limited progress according to urban QoL indicators. According to the ICVU 2011–2020, Valparaíso's composite score declined from medium-high in 2011 to medium-low in 2020, while San Antonio remained low. A selection of key indicators is presented below, which illustrate that statement.

Access to public facilities and services

According to SIEDU and MBHT data, access to public facilities and services continues to reflect structural disparities between the port cities and the regional average. Between 2018 and 2020, the MBHT confirms a persistent lag: Valparaíso remains below the regional average (11.49 years of schooling) in most indicators, with 11.19 years of schooling on average compared to 12.16 in Viña del Mar. The largest gaps for Valparaíso are found in the availability of sports facilities (0.58 m^2 per inhabitant versus a regional average of 1.32 m^2), health infrastructure (1.25 m^2 per inhabitant compared to 2.17 m^2), and housing quality and sufficiency (ISV = 0.95). In San Antonio, the main deficits concern the surface of public green areas per inhabitant (2 m^2, versus 3.27 m^2 regional average), the availability of sports facilities (0.83 m^2 compared to 1.32 m^2), and the average educational attainment of household heads (10.77 years versus 11.49 regional average).

Mobility

According to SIEDU data, the indicator "Ratio between travel time during peak and off-peak hours" reveals significant differences between the two main port cities, but not between them and their neighboring communes. Values close to 1 indicate stability between both periods, while higher values reflect greater congestion during peak hours. Valparaíso records a ratio of 0.83, suggesting even shorter travel times during peak hours, likely due to local traffic characteristics or methodological factors. Viña del Mar reaches 0.92, indicating relative stability and only slight variations between periods. In contrast, San Antonio registers 1.33, revealing clear congestion during peak hours. Transport surveys help explain this contrast: trucks bound for the Port of Valparaíso represent less than 15% of vehicles using the city's main access routes, while private cars exceed 70%, generating congestion mainly during morning and evening peaks. The construction of Camino La Pólvora in 2004 provided a direct freight corridor to the port, preventing trucks from circulating through the city center. San Antonio, by contrast, lacks a dedicated freight access, which causes heavy congestion on bridges and inter-municipal roads during rush hours.

In Valparaíso, the narrow sidewalk, the cliffs on one side, and the port perimeter on the other leave little buffer between pedestrians, cyclists, and port equipment, with visible emissions contributing to adverse local air-quality conditions. However, the Port of Valparaíso is including in the new concession contract a shift from diesel-based to electric equipment, to be implemented over a ten-year period starting in 2030, the expected beginning of the new concession. This clause would require the concessionaire to ensure that all yard operations are powered by electricity (Enrique Piraino, Development Manager at EPV, telephone interview, 2 December 2025).

In San Antonio, the juxtaposition between residential areas and large-scale port operations is even more pronounced. There is a direct visual and spatial overlap between low-income housing and container-handling infrastructure, reflecting the city's long-standing challenges of territorial inequality.

Socio-economic and institutional factors: persistent inequality under different dynamics

Residents of Valparaíso and San Antonio are poorer than the regional average and than those of their neighboring residential communes. The share of the population living in income poverty (2018–2019) reached 15.42% in Valparaíso and 7.71% in San Antonio, compared with 9.81% in Viña del Mar and 5.41% in Santo Domingo. This situation is also reflected in their greater dependence on the Municipal Common Fund (FCM), which exceeds the 30% threshold recommended by the National Council for Territorial Development. In 2018, the FCM accounted for 35.61% of total municipal revenues in Valparaíso and 46.32% in San Antonio, compared with only 7.63% in Viña del Mar and 9.31% in Santo Domingo. It is worth noting that the SIEDU considers 30% the upper limit for this indicator.

In the field of heritage building restoration, Valparaíso allocated almost half as much as Viña del Mar, despite its status as a World Heritage City (2018: Valparaíso 9.41%, Viña del Mar 17.9%). The SIEDU does not provide data for San Antonio or Santo Domingo. These gaps may be linked to the institutional and technical weaknesses of port-city municipalities in formulating projects, competing for national funds, and aligning local needs with national resource allocation mechanisms.

Subjective well-being and urban perceptions: from shared optimism to divergent paths

Historically, both cities reported high levels of self-perceived happiness, rooted in social cohesion and maritime identity. The Fundación Piensa Regional Life Quality Survey (2024) shows, however, a regional decline in perceived happiness: the average fell from 77% (2022) to 64% (2024). Valparaíso dropped from 85% to 65%, now slightly below both the regional mean (64%) and Viña del Mar (60%), whereas San Antonio remained stable (76 → 75%), exceeding Santo Domingo (68%).

This divergence suggests that subjective well-being is not linearly correlated with material conditions. Valparaíso's decline likely reflects frustration with urban management, safety, and cleanliness, while San Antonio's relative stability may stem from civic cohesion. Indeed, San Antonio shows a dense civic-organization network (≈ 6 per 1,000 inhabitants), which strengthens community participation. These results confirm that trust, identity, and belonging play as decisive a role in well-being as income or infrastructure—an argument for integrating perceptual data into port-city governance.

Recent port-development trends and future prospects

Both cities are entering a new cycle of port-infrastructure development that could reshape their urban and environmental interface. In San Antonio, the Puerto Exterior project plans the construction of two new terminals with a projected capacity of up to 6 million TEUs per year—around three times the port's current throughput. Environmental review is expected to conclude in 2026, paving the way for construction in 2028 and the first terminal's operation in 2036 (www.puertosanantonio.com, consulted on 30 September 2025). The project is under environmental review; a complementary addendum was submitted in June 2025 by the port authority that incorporates 20 mitigation measures and 48 voluntary commitments in response to over 2,000 citizen observations. Once operational, the port could handle 25%–35% of Chile's total seaborne foreign trade.

In Valparaíso, the Terminal 2 project involves a new berth and an esplanade redesigned to include urban-integration spaces such as a coastal promenade and viewing platforms. The environmental evaluation process began in 2024 and is projected to conclude by 2027 and, if approved, is expected to start operations in 2030, handling 12%–15% of Chile's national seaborne trade (www.puertovalparaiso.cl, consulted on 30th September 2025).

These expansion plans illustrate how both ports are entering a strategic phase where future competitiveness must align with environmental mitigation and social legitimacy. Their implementation will test the capacity of the City–Port Councils and local governance frameworks to ensure that economic growth translates into tangible QoL improvements for surrounding communities.

From measurement to governance: port–city councils as policy laboratories

QoL metrics introduce a governance perspective grounded in coordination among diverse actors. In Chile, this approach is embodied in the City–Port Coordination Councils (CCCP), created by Law 19,542 (1997) to promote "harmonious development between ports and cities." As noted in earlier studies (Zrari 2021a, 2021b), these councils emerged as compromise mechanisms within the 1997 port-modernization law—focused on competitiveness rather than territorial governance. Their limited mandate and absence of binding mechanisms explain their uneven and often discontinuous implementation across Chilean port cities.

Chaired by regional governments and including municipal and port authorities, the CCCP have recently begun to open sessions to civil-society representatives and to meet more regularly. Yet discussions remain mostly informative; integrating QoL indicators would strengthen their analytical role and transform them into genuine platforms of collaborative governance.

The debate over a royalty portuario—or territorial port levy—illustrates the need for such evidence-based coordination. Supported by associations representing Chile's port municipalities, the proposal seeks to compensate local externalities and reinforce municipal finances, arguing that while ports contribute substantially to national trade, benefits remain centralized as port cities bear environmental and social costs. Despite several legislative attempts—the latest in 2025—no bill has been approved, revealing persistent tensions over fiscal equity between port and inland territories.

Linking any future fiscal mechanism to QoL indicators would make redistribution strategic, rewarding measurable improvements in environmental quality, health, and governance. Within this framework, City–Port Councils could act as policy laboratories, aligning national development goals with local well-being. Empowered with reliable data and participatory methods, they could coordinate investments and mediate between competitiveness and community interests.

Although implementation remains uneven, Valparaíso and San Antonio illustrate encouraging trends. Both councils now include civil-society representatives and interact regularly with regional planning bodies. Embedding QoL metrics in their agenda would help turn these dialogues into measurable progress, ensuring that economic growth contributes to healthier, more equitable port-city environments. To operationalize the multidimensional concept of urban well-being in port contexts, Table 16.2 presents a proposed list of QoL indicators specifically adapted to port cities.

Conclusions and recommendations

Monitoring QoL offers Chile a path from diagnosis to strategy, balancing port competitiveness with urban health, equity, and cohesion. Despite modernization, Valparaíso and San Antonio still show deficits in environmental quality, safety, and services, revealing a disjunction between economic and social progress. The need to link port performance with social outcomes echoes earlier reflections on territorial equity in port governance (Zrari 2021a, 2021b).

Table 16.2 Proposed set of quality of life key indicators for port cities

Domain	*Indicator*	*Source (Chile)*	*Responsible actor(s)*	*Associated health or social outcome*
Air Quality	Annual average $PM_{2.5}$ concentration ($\mu g/m^3$)	SINCA/Ministry of Environment	Ministry of Environment, Municipality	Respiratory and cardiovascular diseases
Noise Exposure	Share of population exposed to high traffic or industrial noise	SECTRA/ Environmental Baseline Studies	Municipality, Port Authority	Sleep disorders, hypertension, stress
Mobility and Accessibility	Average commuting time (peak vs. off-peak)	SIEDU/SECTRA	Ministry of Transport, Municipality	Physical inactivity, pollutant exposure
Sustainable Transport	Share of trips by walking, cycling, or public transport	SECTRA/Mobility Surveys	Municipality, Regional Government	Physical activity, reduced obesity
Housing Sufficiency	Overcrowding index (0–1 normalized)	MBHT/INE	MINVU, Municipality	Infectious disease exposure, mental health
Public Space and Green Areas	m^2 of green areas per inhabitant	SIEDU/SINIM	Municipality, MINVU	Stress reduction, cardiovascular health
Urban Safety	Serious crimes against persons (per 10,000 inhabitants)	Carabineros/SIEDU	Ministry of Interior, Municipality	Injuries, mental well-being
Health Services Access	Primary care centers per 10,000 inhabitants	SIEDU/MINSAL	Ministry of Health, Municipality	Preventive and curative care
Employment and Income Security	Unemployment rate (%)	INE/CASEN	Ministry of Labor	Mental health, life satisfaction
Quality of Employment in Port Industries	Gender parity, contract stability, and occupational safety in port-related jobs	Port Authorities/ Ministry of Labor	Port Companies, Ministry of Labor	Economic security, inclusion, mental health
Social Cohesion	Civil-society organizations per 1,000 inhabitants	SIEDU/SINIM	Municipality, Community Organizations	Collective efficacy, social resilience

(*Continued*)

Table 16.2 (Continued)

Domain	*Indicator*	*Source (Chile)*	*Responsible actor(s)*	*Associated health or social outcome*
Governance and Institutional Coordination	Effectiveness of coordination among municipal, regional, and port institutions	CCCP/Municipal Records	Municipality, Port Authority, Regional Government	Policy coherence, implementation capacity
Citizens' Perception of Governance	Perceived fairness, participation, and trust in port decision-making	Fundación Piensa/ Local Surveys	Municipality, Port Authority	Legitimacy, civic trust, social capital
Cultural Heritage and Port Identity	Proportion of port-related heritage sites under restoration or reuse; participation in cultural programs that strengthen maritime identity; perception of pride and belonging linked to port heritage	MINVU/CMN/ Municipalities/ Fundación Piensa	Ministry of Culture, Municipality, Port Authority	Social cohesion, cultural identity, community pride
Environmental/ Operational Interface	Port emissions, noise, logistics intensity, and waterfront access	Port Authorities/SEA/ SINCA	Port Authority, Ministry of Environment	Exposure reduction, environmental justice
Social/Perceptual Interface	Frequency of cultural and community events linked to maritime identity; waterfront accessibility and visual connection to the sea; perceptions of fairness and transparency in port decision-making; participation in planning processes	Fundación Piensa/ Municipal Surveys	Municipality, Port Authority, Community Organizations	Well-being, belonging, trust in institutions
Environmental Risk	Population in tsunami or flood zones (%)	ONEMI/SINAPRED	Municipality, Port Authority	Mortality, displacement, trauma
Perceived Quality of Life	Overall satisfaction with city life (0–1,000)	Fundación Piensa	Fundación Piensa, Municipality	Subjective well-being

Source: Own elaboration.

Aligning Chile's observatories with the UN-Habitat QoLI transforms them into tools for prioritizing actions that most effectively improve life conditions and perceptions. Empowering City–Port Councils with these metrics can turn them into policy laboratories capable of coordinating investments, guiding fiscal innovation, and reinforcing transparency.

My personal experience as the academic director of AIVP–IIPC training programs reveals that, despite growing interest in sustainability metrics, few port-city systems have yet connected their governance frameworks to national or regional QoL observatories-a gap this chapter seeks to address.

It was in this pedagogical context that I first observed the absence of systematic information on urban QoL observatories, particularly in port territories, and the need to shift from an impact-based to a QoL perspective, consistent with a systemic view of port–city relations. As Carola Hein (2011) notes, the port city should be seen as a co-evolutionary system where spatial, economic, and cultural dynamics intersect. This approach provides a conceptual bridge between port competitiveness and the everyday well-being of urban inhabitants.

The following policy box illustrates how the QoL framework can be translated into actionable guidance for port-city governance, connecting conceptual advances to concrete policy instruments.

Policy box 1—key recommendations for healthy port–city governance

1 **Institutionalize QoL Monitoring**
Embed QoL indicators within City–Port Councils and municipal planning to ensure continuity and accountability.
2 **Adopt Port-Specific Indicators**
Include metrics that capture port-city dynamics and influence both objective and subjective well-being including indicators that reveal the psychosocial drivers of happiness and belonging.
3 **Use Data for Prioritization**
Employ observatory results to rank policy actions by their potential to improve health, safety, and sense of belonging.
4 **Link Fiscal Mechanisms to QoL Outcomes**
Design the *royalty portuario* or equivalent transfers so that funds reward measurable QoL improvements.
5 **Foster Participation and Transparency**
Broaden civil-society involvement in CCCP meetings and publish QoL data in accessible formats to build trust.
6 **Join the UN-Habitat Quality of Life Initiative (QoLI)**
Encourage Chilean port cities to become active QoLI participants, contributing port-city-specific expertise while gaining global methodological support.

Acknowledgments

The author wishes to express sincere gratitude to César Ducruet and Mariantonia Lo Prete for their invitation to contribute to this collective volume and for his valuable editorial guidance and constant encouragement throughout the process. Special thanks are also extended to Eduardo Goldstein, whose insightful comments and stimulating discussions greatly enriched the analytical depth of this chapter.

Notes

1 Available at: https://www.puertovalparaiso.cl/acuerdo-por-valparaiso.
2 Improved access to basic public services and facilities; improved access to sustainable mobility; improved quality of the urban environment; greater social integration and quality of neighborhoods and housing; more and better planning of cities and regions; more inclusive and sustainable economic growth for urban development; greater protection of cultural heritage; and stronger and more effective participation of civil society in urban development decisions.
3 According to the National Institute of Statistics of Chile (INE) estimates, the province of Valparaíso concentrates over 700,000 inhabitants, distributed mainly between Valparaíso (299,000) and Viña del Mar (324,000), while the province of San Antonio accounts for approximately 130,000 residents, the majority in San Antonio (101,000) and Santo Domingo (around 17,000).

References

Hein C. (2011) *Port Cities: Urban Planning, Heritage, and Development*. London: Routledge.
Lora E. (2008) Calidad de vida desde otro ángulo. In: Lora E. (Ed.), *Calidad de Vida, Más Allá de los Hechos*. Washington, DC: Banco Interamericano de Desarrollo, pp. 3–13.
Pontificia Universidad Católica de Chile & Cámara Chilena de la Construcción (2022) 10 años de calidad de vida.
Pontificia Universidad Católica de Chile & Cámara Chilena de la Construcción (2024) Índice de Calidad de Vida Urbana (ICVU): Una nueva generación de variables.
Zrari S. (2021a) Construir una gobernanza en las ciudades puerto de Chile para una mejor gobernabilidad. In: Alix Y., Castelein C., Morel S. (Eds.), *Océanides, Tome 7 – Ports, villes et territoires: vers de nouvelles alliances*. Le Havre: Fondation Sefacil, pp. 167–186.
Zrari S. (2021b) Los Consejos de Coordinación Ciudad Puerto: ¿Un instrumento de gobernanza territorial? *Revista Geográfica de Valparaíso*, 53: 92–105.

Interviews

Arturo Orellana (2025) Director of Instituto de Estudios Urbanos y Territoriales de Pontificia Universidad Católica de Chile. April 29th 2025.
Marcela Letelier, Luis Valenzuela, John Treimun (2025) Team in charge of MBTH Observatory, Universidad Adolfo Ibañez. October, 7th 2025.

17 'Collective place consciousness', coastal grabbing, and the 'toxic heritage' in the Venetian Lagoon

Matteo Nicolini and Giuseppe Rigobello

'Collective place-consciousness' and environmental-health concerns

The law has always been in a special relationship with space. Human geographers will consider this predicament a truism: not only has this relationship always been part of geographical research (see e.g. Lefebvre, 1991; Blomley, 1994; Braverman et al., 2014), but it continues to be investigated by human geographers (see e.g. Chiodelli & Moroni, 2025; Kymäläinen, 2025). Legal scholars, by contrast, have shown less interest in the law-space entanglement. By traditionally 'bracketing' the law (Blomley, 2015, p. 169), space counts only as a 'legal space' demarcating the validity of the law (Burchardt, 2022).

The mood has changed, though. Lawyers have adopted cross-disciplinary stance, conceiving of space as a (social) product (Lefebvre, 1991, p. 26) fabricated *also* through legal practices. Expressions such as 'lawscape' (Philippopoulos-Mihalopoulos, 2007; Graham 2011), 'nomoscape' (Delaney, 2005, p. 1), 'nomic setting' (Delaney, 2010, p. 59), and 'splice', all point to 'enacted encodings, which weave together spatial and legal meanings' (Bennett & Layard, 2015, pp. 410, 411). Implicated in the 'production' and 'construction' of the world (Nicolini 2022, 2024), the law thus contributes to producing 'a concrete geography' made up of 'wordless words deposited on the surface of the Earth, in cities and fields', coasts, and seas (Besse, 2020, p. 17; our translation).

This marine reference is fitting for this chapter, which examines how coastal communities legally produce their landscape through a complex intertwining of the physical-human interface. The law allowed them to impress their own place-specific socio-cultural meaning onto terrestrial and marine landscapes. In so doing, they shaped their own 'collective place-consciousness', i.e. the way they 'live collectively' *in that particular place*, because *there* they find the 'character of life' they have co-produced (Sennett, 2019, pp. 1–2). This character of life also encompasses the socially and environmentally healthy balance with the place that has become their own; theirs is indeed an ecosystemic approach that 'offers a [sensible] response to interlinked environmental and health challenges' (Morand, 2022) that populated the place as the

DOI: 10.4324/9781003639589-22

'repository' (Johnston, 1991, pp. 50–55) and the 'archive' (Godden, 2020, p. 140) of their situated legal practices.

Legal frameworks usually take into account – and shape – these interconnections, whose transformative potential is essential in terms of collective place-consciousness. Although the law seems 'to recede – or withdraw – from view, leaving its situational "lawscape" often not readily noticeable' (Bennet, 2019, p. 3), the 'place-space-environment nexus' is also produced through legal practices (Matthews & Herbert, 2008, p. 17).

Our predicament points to a process of spatial-legal production, within which the law helps to link the 'physical qualities of [the] area that are significant to' the coastal communities with 'the forms of use of the area' (Sauer [1925] 1969, p. 325). The whole process also resonates with the idea of cultural environment, which, in legal geographical terms, counts as 'nomic landscapes' (Delaney, 2005, p. 1).

The socially and environmentally health-related balance with places is also part of the situational 'lawscape' mentioned above. This interdependence is at the heart of this chapter, which will focus on how collective-place consciousness permits us to regain an 'appreciation that legal laws are sedimented quietly throughout the built environment alongside lots of other non-legal elements' (Bennet, 2019, p. 10), such as ecosystems and health-related practices. For centuries, traditional and deep-seated local rules have governed the sustainable relationships between communities and their coastal territories, outlining the 'deep topography' of marine areas (Hubbard, 2022, p. 18). Lying within the municipality of Venice and her lagoon, the industrial pole of Porto Marghera will be our case study; close to Venice and easily accessible from the sea, it has become one of the major logistic, industrial, and marine poles in northern Italy.

Marghera allows us to assess how the ecology of this place has been affected by urban, industrial, and infrastructural transformations often conflicting with its traditional character of life. As collective-place consciousness is rooted in the landscape, it is of the utmost importance to preserve the situated (environmental, legal, cultural, and health-related) practices that make up coastal areas.

Yet, the materiality and ecology of coastal landscapes have been severely affected by the dynamics of port governance. Owing to such industrial development, Marghera has also turned out to be a place where 'the environmental consequences were even more devastating' (Zazzara, 2019, p. 151). Since the 1960s, industrial facilities have been releasing 'fumes, dust or vapours harmful to human life into the air … poisonous substances into the water … vibrations and noise' (Chinello, 1975, p. 42; our translation). Porto Marghera is experiencing the dire impacts of our transnational and interconnected economic system: port restructuring, maritime supply chains, overtourism, and cruise shipping networks now literally build and manage coastal landscapes and turn them (and their environmental-cultural heritage) into financial assets. This chapter will examine 'coastal grabbing', i.e. the appropriation of large parts of these coastal territories by supra-local economic actors to meet their financial interests. By buying up docks and ports, international investors harvest profits on the basis of the (real or presumed) benefits that coastal communities will enjoy thanks to the investment of large amounts of capital. The outcome is the obliteration of the centuries-old socio-cultural ties underpinning collective place-consciousness at the expense of the healthiness of these places. We shall see how these processes have affected the ecology of the Venetian lagoon. Industrial, logistical, and marine-related activities have compromised the integrity of the cultural heritage of Porto Marghera, which now embeds the ongoing conflicts between global economic interests and local communities as regards the physical reconfiguration of Venice's port area.

The Venetian lagoon also bridges coastal grabbing and human health. The exploitation of the lagoon reappraises the relationship between the Venetian community and its socio-natural environment in terms of 'toxic heritage'. Today, the toxicity is both a detrimental element of the local ecosystem and part of a new 'collective place consciousness' of the community, which has always struggled for its health rights and for the preservation of its environment.

Changes in the coastal landscape and 'coastal grabbing'

The obliteration of the place-specific century-old relationships defining coastal places as repositories of deep-seated legal-cultural practices impacts both the production of 'collective place-consciousness' and the environmental dynamics making up the ecology of these areas. Through it, local communities produced the terrestrial-marine continuum as a unique landscape, whose essence lies 'in the largely unconscious intentionality that defines places as profound centres of human experience' (Relph, 1976, p. 43). Encompassing marine waters, shorelines, and lands, these areas have been made meaningful through spatial production. These communities have generated a true 'political landscape' evolving 'partly out of experience, partly from design, to meet some of the needs' of the communities 'in their political guise' (Jackson, 1986, p. 12). There are hints of territoriality here, inasmuch as the relation between these communities and *their* terrestrial-marine continuum leads to the construction of their concrete geographies. Territoriality is a cultural competence synthesising the result of the appropriation of morphological, anthropic, and economic data that make a given territory meaningful to its community. Its social and legal significance lies in the intrinsic political nature of the space lived by the communities that produce it. Building and dwelling in coastal areas certainly left human marks on shores, lagoons, and intertidal zones. At the same time, the community moulding the landscape avoided overexploiting the natural resources that could be extracted from them. As 'holistic' practices, these are also able to integrate health concerns in the relationships between the communities and their socio-natural environment, according to what is now called 'one health approach': 'the health of humans ... and the wider environment (including ecosystems) are' indeed 'closely linked and interdependent' (One Health High-Level Expert Panel [OOHLEP] 2022).

As 'a way in which space is both imagined and organized' (Storey, 2020, p. 6), this place-specific political landscape is not a self-contained process of spatial production. As a tract of land, it is usually under a given state authority; its social, economic, and environmental-geographical features fall under a broader territorial governance that allots power both *vertically* (i.e. among different orders of government) and *geographically* (i.e. among units whose boundaries are demarcated on a geographical basis). This is evident in Porto Marghera; located along the lagoon gutter on the mainland just north-west of Venice, this port area is part of the borough of Marghera, i.e. one of the six boroughs that make up the Municipality of Venice.[1]

Coastal areas are 'attractive places ... due to the richness of the biodiversity, the extraordinary natural resources, and logistical reasons' – not to mention the 'strategic advantages for trading generations' (Innocenti & Musco 2023, p. 1). From the mid-19th-century onwards, the advent of our capitalist, industrial, and trading economy brought about huge changes in the physical-legal landscape in many European states – and Italy was no exception (Sereni [1972] 2016, p. 429). Changes have affected the coastal landscape in various ways. Capitalist economy required industrial ports to be expanded; docks, ship loaders, and several other infrastructures were therefore built. To this end, land was massively reclaimed 'to expand and increase economic sectors such as tourism, oil and gas, aquaculture, and fishery' (Innocenti & Musco 2023, p. 1). This was evident when Porto Marghera was created (1917–1923: see Zazzara, 2017). In order to avoid Venice being negatively impacted by industrialisation, the north-western part of the lagoon (and its fishing valleys) located on the mainland and in front of the city, was reclaimed to set up a port area that would become one of the most significant industrial (mainly petrochemical) and commercial hub in southern Europe, as well as a major cruise terminal owing to its proximity to Venice (Soriani, 2024, p. 261).[2]

Porto Marghera completely reshuffled the way in which the lagoon, its valley, and traditional, deep-seated activities were both imagined and organised. In terms of decision-making, planning, and implementation, the whole project was a top-down process. Local communities and Venice municipality were marginalised (Zazzara, 2017, p. 210), so as to avoid any possible conflict between them and the 'superior' economic interests of the state-led capitalist enterprise in Marghera as regards the use of local resources (the land, the sea, and their ecosystem services). The impact of such national policies on the lagoon altered its collective place-consciousness. Take, for example, the workforce; the first workers were recruited from among the labourers employed in the reclamation and construction of the facilities; in the 1960s, the workforce for the petrochemical industries mainly consisted of young labourers living in the surrounding agricultural areas (Zazzara, 2017, pp. 214 and 222). New suburbia were built to accommodate the workforce, leading to a permanent conflict between the labour movement and the investors. This also resulted in social segregation; as Gilda Zazzara vividly writes, petrochemical waste was dumped into the lagoon: whose waters turned 'red'; 'the sky above Porto Marghera [was] constantly covered in smoke and the acrid smells associated with chemical production spread through the surrounding homes' (Zazzara 2019, p. 151; our translation). Consequently, the wider coastal community was destined to live in one of the most polluted and degraded areas of northern Italy.

Globalisation has made such conflicts more strained. Since the 1970s, Porto Marghera has been experiencing a decline in terms of its manufacturing industry and trading activities. The retreat from the waterfront left a 'vacuum, an abandoned doorstep, ... and a zone of pronounced dereliction and decay where once all had been bustle and interchange and activity' (Hoyle, 2000, p. 397). The vacuum has been filled by international investors, who acquire new lands for cruise terminals.

Not only do local communities now face a 'superior' interest, but they also have to cope with an 'external' one: an economic interest with no local roots at all. In the maritime areas, this process is called 'coastal grabbing': it consists precisely in 'the appropriation of coastal space – including sea and land – by interests external to the community' (Bavinck et al., 2017, p. 2). Far from being the measure of the relationships between a community and its (coastal) territory, through expropriation and planning the law has become a powerful instrument whereby local communities are dispossessed of their place-consciousness: the ownership, materiality, and ecology of their landscapes are now reshaped by external forces – mainly global investors and holders of capital.

Coastal grabbing can take two forms, the first of which refers to 'the effective exclusion of communities from the space and resources on which those communities depend' (Bavinck et al., 2017, p. 2). In this case, the power of law entails the physical separation between the community and part of its territory. In its second form, coastal grabbing affects the ecosystem balance of the territory as a whole with adverse consequences for the conservation of natural resources, environment, and health. This is evident as a consequence of toxic dumping, environmental incidents, and poisonings caused by the petrochemical industries: 'the situation was so alarming that the prefect ordered all workers to wear their gas masks at all times while at work' (Zazzara, 2019, p. 151; our translation). The sea and the coastlines are indeed some extremely fragile ecosystems. The lagoon is at the core of the ecological crisis: we are witnessing 'the slow strangulation of the sea from pollution, heat, acidification, and deoxygenation' (Braverman, 2023, p. 4). How can we as legal scholars approach coastal ecosystems? Irus Braverman (2023) calls for an 'amphibious legal geography', capable of overcoming the terrestrial-marine continuum making up coastal landscapes. And we will now consider the most 'amphibious' of all territories, namely the lagoon – the Venetian lagoon.

Coastal grabbing in the Venetian Lagoon

The features of the Venetian lagoon, as well as its ecology and landscape, are the results of complex historical interactions between physical geography and anthropogenic activities. The transformation of the natural landscape into a 'cultural' landscape (for more on these expressions, see Sauer, [1925] 1969, p. 333 et seq.) was made possible through 'the uninterrupted work undertaken by the *Serenissima Repubblica di Venezia*'. Without this work, the lagoon would be naturally transformed into a marine bay or would be buried, through eluviation, by 'the load of solid material discharged into the lagoon from its tributaries' (Ravera, 2000, p. 19). The Republic of Venice had a long history of environmental regulation and territorial planning, which helped to maintain the difficult ecological balance of the lagoon, its islands, and its 'terra firma' (i.e. the mainland: see Novello & McCann, 2017).

In the first two decades of the 20th century, the Venetian lagoon started experienced the huge processes of industrialisation, land reclamation, and transformation of the landscape described in the previous section. The consequences of such changes persist today. In the following subsections, we shall focus on two of the major environmental and social conflicts that – often adversely – have had (and still have) some bearing on the lagoon area: the establishment of petrochemical industries in Porto Marghera, and the cruise ships and large commercial vessels ('grandi navi' in Italian) sailing into the centre of Venice.

Atypical coastal grabbing? The creation of Porto Marghera

From a historical perspective, the industrial development of Porto Marghera is the most fitting example of how the Italian industrial-economic public policies were implemented at the expense of the ecological balance of the lagoon and the health of the workforce (Barca, 2012). It is a history of dispossession of large tracts of coastal land, as well as a tale of changes leading to a new 'collective place-consciousness'.

The creation of Porto Marghera as an industrial district does not fully match the definition of 'coastal grabbing' mentioned above. It is, in our opinion, an atypical coastal grabbing, since it reflected the needs of the Italian capitalist economy, also rooted in the Venetian context. The 1920s and the post-WWI economic context were completely different from the current phase of globalisation. As said, Marghera was a top-down state-led process, subsequently boosted by the advent of Fascist and its related economic model of self-sufficiency (so-called *autarchia*, autarchy: see Cerasi, 2007, p. 41). The establishment of an industrial port on the marine outskirts of the old city of Venice tallied the desired geographies of the Italian capitalist (and political) elite, in general, and of the Venetian-born Giuseppe Volpi (1877–1947), in particular. As a prominent politician and Minister of Finance during the Fascist regime, Volpi was the main 'sponsor' of the project (Zazzara, 2017, p. 211). As an economic enterprise, Porto Marghera elicited several deep-seated interests within the Venetian context, since it could provide the proletarian classes of the city with job opportunities and foster the urban development of both Venice and its lagoon.

The (urban, industrial, and port) development of Porto Marghera shares several features with the process of gentrification that still today affects global cities like Venice. In the view of the Venetian ruling class, the creation of the industrial port in the mainland would complement 'the consecration of the historic centre to cultural and tourist activities'; this dualism 'was supposed to integrate the development brought about by heavy industry with the heritage of the artistic tradition' (Cerasi, 2007, p. 38, our translation).

Built in the 1920s, the industrial area was enlarged in the aftermath of WWII, between 1953 and 1956. In the 1960s Porto Marghera also became the major district in the petrochemical and oil industries with thousands of workers employed in its refineries (De Ghantuz Cubbe, 2014).[3] Here lies a further anomaly of Porto Marghera's coastal grabbing. From the perspective of the local authorities, the expansion of the industrial area was an opportunity *also* for the local communities: it would favour the local economy without exposing it to health and safety risks. This objective, it goes without saying, 'clashed with the interests of large industrial groups', which aimed to replicate 'the highly advantageous experience achieved' in the 1920s: 'equipment, infrastructures, and services' had to be offered to them 'at the expense of public bodies ... in exchange for their establishment in the territory'. As Cerasi puts it (2007, p. 51), 'The result was the nullification of the planning proposals, because private companies, especially Edison and Montecatini, had in the meantime already set up on the land intended to be regulated by the plan'. Indeed, the regulatory plan (approved in 1963) explicitly allowed the unbridled realisation of polluting systems that could spread substances dangerous to the human life (Cerasi, 2007, p. 51).

The history of Marghera's industrial development became the history of what has been termed the 'Petrolkiller' (Bettin & Dianese, 2002). One hundred and fifty-seven workers died as a result of diseases related with the chemical manufacturing and the contamination of a large part of the lagoon and its coast (De Ghantuz Cubbe, 2014, p. 5; see also Gessoni et al., 2020). This dramatic situation developed in the Marghera community a sort of 'workers environmentalism', whereby

> the focus on workers' health extends to that of the entire population and the environment as a whole. In 1973, several strikes broke out over environmental issues. The role of workers' organisations, supported by young activist doctors, proved decisive in launching the first occupational health service within local public health structures.
>
> (Zazzara, 2019, p. 152, our translation)

Alongside a long struggle against the health and environmental disaster in the 1970s, the workers and the community of Marghera engaged in a legal battle in 1998; five executives of Montedison were prosecuted, tried, and finally found guilty of murder and environmental disaster in 2006 (De Ghantuz Cubbe, 2014, p. 8). This legal narrative is now fundamental to the collective identity of a community that carries on living in a complex situation, caught, as it is, between deindustrialisation and contamination residues.

'Grandi Navi' sailing into the lagoon

Unlike the industrial development of Porto Marghera, the highly contested sailing of extra-large cruises ships into the city of Venice, perfectly fit into the definition of coastal grabbing. As is well known, Venice is one of the most famous tourist sites in the world. Millions of people visit it every year, and this pressure has led to many tensions. Cruise tourism, in particular, is the most controversial form of tourism in Venice. It is a form of business with a significant impact, driven by external interests that are neither concerned with local development nor with the quality of life of the city's residents. In 2012 a large civic protest group was set up: the 'No Big Ships Committee' (*Comitato No Grandi Navi*, in Italian) frequently referred to the dominance of external interests and the heteronomy this creates. The interests of the powerful shipping sector sharply contrast with those of the city whose residents are shrinking, and who feel that their opportunities are decreasing. Venice is experiencing a paradox; the same trade that once brought wealth to Venice is now adversely affecting it. This is due to an increasingly outsourced supply chain; likewise, cruise tourism 'brings scant benefit to the port territory' (Schemmer, 2022, p. 387).

The passage of gigantic cruise ships raises several issues because it impacts on the landscape (the huge imbalance between ships' tonnage and the buildings of Venice) with harmful effects for the whole lagoon environment, leading to the erosion of its seabed and the contamination of both water and air, which is caused by harmful emission (Fabbri & Tattara, 2014, p. 18, 35–39). The Venetian communities also oppose cruise ships because of their being 'the symbol of the drastic impact that mass tourism can have' (Schemmer, 2022, p. 379).

The struggle against the ships sailing into Venice culminated with the Law Decree No. 103 of 2021, whereby the national executive turned the urban waterways of the St. Mark's Basin, St. Mark's Canal, and the Giudecca Canal into a 'national monument'. Large ships are therefore banned from these watery areas. This has made Porto Marghera even more palatable in terms of financial investments, because it is the 'natural' candidate for berthing large vessels, thus eliciting the appetites of shipping companies and terminal operators.

This kind of coastal grabbing represents the flip side of the coin compared to the coastal grabbing in Porto Marghera. As said, in the 20th century the economic development of the lagoon reflected the dualism between the mainland and its industrialised coastal areas, on the one hand, and the tourist-oriented economy on the islands, on the other. In both cases, the spaces (the city, the coast, and the lagoon) are not seen as places lived by their communities; rather, they are 'places of profit' for external investors. There, global capital is invested, and financial returns are harvested. The Metropolitan City of Venice eagerly endorses the interests of transnational actors as far as the lagoon is concerned, as Schemmer vividly states (2022, p. 380), 'the local field of tension is situated between the limits of popular discourses about the city, the spatialization of the industry, and the governance of these processes'.

The 'toxic heritage' in the Venetian lagoon

If we want to fully grasp how both Porto Marghera and the cruise ships problem changed the place-consciousness of the Venetian lagoon, we can refer to the concept of 'toxic heritage', i.e. the 'intersection of heritage as a field of discourse and practice, and the toxicity as a material and social reality' (Kryder-Reid & May, 2024, p. 1). If Venice is the 'heritage city' *par excellence*, the lagoon is its 'environmental heritage' that has been shaping the socio-cultural relationships of the communities living there. The history of both the city and the lagoon is tragically tied to toxic environmental and health threats due to economic development.

'Toxic heritage' is a twofold expression. It denotes 'the history of the processes and substances (toxins and toxicants) that create or threaten physical harm to environments and the life supported within them' (Kryder-Reid & May, 2024, p. 1). Take, for example, nuclear waste, whose harmful effects on human health last for centuries. The places where waste is stored hold memory of toxicity; alongside its effects, this memory is passed down through the generations, not unlike the transmission of a cultural meaning through the conservation of cultural heritage (Wollentz et al., 2020, p. 296). Toxic heritage is again related to health-related concerns: Porto Marghera is indeed a case in point, owing to the anthropogenic changes to its ecosystem. At the same time, the Venetian lagoon discloses a further denotation of 'toxic waste', that is, 'the intersections of that history of harm with both formal heritage institutions and informal memory practices'. In producing collective place-consciousness, 'the attention to memory practices, processes of heritagisation, lived experiences, and the ways in which interpretations of past environmental harm are entangled with fields of power centre this work within critical heritage studies' (Kryder-Reid & May, 2024, p. 1). Here, we consider toxicity for its relationship with cultural-environmental heritage and its role in the construction of a new 'collective place-consciousness' for the lagoon. Evidently, it does not coincide with the postcard-city we find in touristic guides.

The 'toxicity' of the lagoon has lot to do with its cultural heritage. The pollution produced by cruise ships is due to the attractiveness of Venice and the exploitation of its cultural heritage. Defining Marghera as an industrial area (and, to an extent, a 'sacrificial' area) was necessary to increase the 'touristification' of Venice. But, the 'toxification' of the lagoon has triggered several other forms of 'heritage making', such as the historical struggle against pollution in Porto Marghera and the contemporary social movement against the '*grandi navi*'. Both are now part of the identity of the broader community that co-produces the lagoon. They are in fact new (and conflicting) ways whereby the coastal community still assigns a meaning to its territory in response to the external interests.

A legal space for the Venetian lagoon. Concluding remarks

The physical features of the Venetian lagoon have undoubtedly nurtured a well-defined collective place-consciousness. Such a sense of belonging and commonness perfectly reflects the uniqueness of the place-specific 'character of life' the communities dwelling there have contributed to co-producing. This place-consciousness is the result of a distinctive process of landscape production: the terrestrial-marine continuum of the lagoon has indeed favoured the transformation of the natural landscape into a 'cultural' landscape with a fragile ecological balance. The place-specific century-old relationships that define the lagoon as the archive and repository of deep-seated legal-cultural practices have thus overcome the dichotomy between sea and land, and, in more recent times, it has also surpassed the divide that should distinct industrialisation, pollution and the protection of its cultural heritage.

We have seen how the development of Porto Marghera had (and still has) a strong impact on the 'collective place-consciousness' of the communities living there. Perceived as a terrestrial-marine continuum, the construction of the lagoon is not given once and for all; it is a dynamic process of spatial production. This is evident, as said, owing to the consequences of toxic dumping, environmental incidents, and poisonings caused by the petrochemical industries. The concept of 'toxic heritage' is decidedly apt to style the process whereby waste, pollutants, and their effects have infiltrated the ecology of the place to such an extent that we are now co-constitutive of the 'character of life' of the lagoon.

The lagoon landscape is also produced through legal practices. In the 1970s, the idea of the Venetian lagoon as a 'legal space' emerged at the administrative and legislative level to address the growing challenges it faced. Several 'special laws for Venice' (*leggi speciali per Venezia*) were thus enacted, the first of which dates back to 1973.[4] Enacted for the first time in 1904 as exceptional measures for the development of Southern Italy (Borgato, 2012, p. 7; Verrastro, 2021), the 'special law' is a piece of legislation lacking the 'general and abstract content' that usually characterises parliamentary legislation (Borgato, 2012, p. 12). It regulates a concrete and specific situation such as, for what matters here, the protection of the Venetian lagoon.

To address the problem of the unique natural and social environment of the lagoon, Parliament dismissed the traditional formalistic legal approach we mentioned in the introductory section (and that is typical of the liberal State), thus returning to a decision-making process engaging with the specificity of a given territory. It thus takes part in the process of legal-spatial production of the lagoon landscape, assigning a (legal) meaning to its concrete geography. In making the preservation of the lagoon a prominent national interest, Art. 1.2 of Law No. 171/1973 was a real act of geography and landscape production, providing for

> the protection of the landscape, historical, archaeological and artistic heritage of the city of Venice and its lagoon, safeguarding its hydraulic equilibrium, preserving the environment from atmospheric and water pollution and ensuring its socio-economic vitality within the framework of the general development.
>
> (our translation)

The territorial planning instruments provided by the law (such as the '*piano comprensoriale*' and the '*piano territoriale*': Arts 3 and 4 Law No. 171 of 1973) considered the lagoonal environment only a part of the wider area that constitutes its catchment. In declaring the St Mark's basin a national monument, the Law Decree No. 103 of 2021 added a new layer to the process of legal-spatial production by favouring a legal geographical correlation between administrative and the physical spaces of the lagoon.

Despite remaining incomplete in certain respects, the legal framework adopted for the preservation of Venice takes into account the complex ecosystem of the lagoon in environmental, cultural, health-related, and socio-economic terms. The 'toxic heritage' and the cruise-related coastal grabbing paradigm also percolate through the special legislation, which fights against pollution and, at the same time, preserves the cultural heritage of the lagoon. Again, the special legislation implements the idea of an 'amphibious' territory, of a marine-terrestrial continuum that stretches across shorelines, islands, and the brackish water. And, perhaps, this amphibious legal geography lies at the heart of the place consciousness of the Venetian communities, contributing to the unique, albeit fragile and intoxicated, character of life of both Venice and its lagoon.

Notes

1 See Art. 1.1. of the basic law of the Municipality of Venice. See also the municipal bylaw No. 64 of 2007 on the creation and demarcation of the six Venetian boroughs of Venzia-Murano-Burano, Lido-Pellestrina, Favaro Veneto, Mestre Carpenedo, Chirignago Zelarino, and Marghera.

2 Porto Marghera covers over 2,000 hectares, of which: 1,400 are used for industrial, commercial, and tertiary activities; 350 for navigable canals and basins covers; 130 for the commercial port. There are also 40 km of internal roads, 135 km of railway tracks, 18 km of port canals and approximately 40 hectares occupied by state-owned areas). The quays extend for 12 km, where fibre-optic cables are 7 km long. (Municipality of Venice, 'Porto Marghera' available at https://www.comune.venezia.it/it/content/larea-di-porto-marghera (accessed on 15 September 2025).

3 Those decades marked the apogee of Porto Marghera. The industrial activities and port facilities employed more 20,000 in the 1950s; the number of workers

peaked at 40,000 in the 1970s and then began to decline, settling at c. 10,000 in the 2010s.

4 Law No 171 of 1973 ('Measures to safeguard Venice'). See also Law No. 798 of 1984, No. 798 ('New measures for the safeguarding of venice'); and Law No 139 of 1992 ('Measures for the safeguarding of Venice and its lagoon').

References

Barca S. (2012) On working-class environmentalism: A historical and transnational overview. *Interface, a Journal for and about Social Movements*, 4(2): 61–80.

Bavinck M., Berkes F., Charles A., Esteves Dias A.C., Doubleday N., Nayak P., Sowman M. (2017) The impact of coastal grabbing on community conservation – A global reconnaissance. *Maritime Studies*, 16(8): 1–17.

Bennet L. (2019) Towards a legal psychogeography: Pragmatism, affective-materialism and the spatiolegal. *Revue Géographique de l'Est*, 58(1–2), https://journals.openedition.org/rge/7534

Bennett L., Layard A. (2015) Legal geography: Becoming spatial detectives. *Geography Compass*, 9(7): 406–422.

Besse J.M. (2020) *La Nécessité du Paysage*. Marseille: Éditions Parenthèses.

Bettin M., Dianese M. (2002) *Petrolkiller*. Milan: Feltrinelli.

Blomley N. (1994) *Law, Space and the Geographies of Power*. New York: The Guilford Press.

Blomley N. (2015) The ties that blind: Making fee simple in the British Columbia treaty process. *Transactions of the Institute of British Geographers*, 40(2): 168–179.

Borgato M. (2012) Una nuova legge speciale per Venezia. *Federalismi.it*, 14: 1–18.

Braverman I. (2023) Introduction. Amphibious legal geographies: Toward land–sea regimes. In: Braverman I. (Ed.), *Laws of the Sea. Interdisciplinary Currents*. Abingdon and New York: Routledge, pp. 1–24.

Braverman I., Blomley N., Delaney D., Kedar A. (2014) Expanding the spaces of law. In: Braverman I., Blomley N., Delaney D., Kedar A. (Eds.), *The Expanding Spaces of Law: A Timely Legal Geography*. Stanford: Stanford UP, pp. 1–29.

Burchardt D. (2022) The concept of legal space: A topological approach to addressing multiple legalities. *Global Constitutionalism*, 11(3): 518–547.

Cerasi L. (2007) *Perdonare Marghera. La Città del Lavoro nella Memoria Post-Industriale*. Milan: Franco Angeli.

Chinello C. (1975) *Forze politiche e sviluppo capitalistico. Porto Marghera e Venezia 1951–1973*. Rome: Editori Riuniti.

Chiodelli F., Moroni S. (2025) *The Legal and Political Geography of Pluralism. Supporting Diverse Public and Private Spaces in Contemporary Cities*. Bristol University Press.

De Ghantuz Cubbe M. (2014) La scienza nel processo penale: Porto Marghera. *Diacronie*, 20(4), https://doi.org/10.4000/diacronie.1707

Delaney D. (2005) *Territory. A Short Introduction*. Oxford: Blackwell.

Delaney D. (2010) *The Spatial, the Legal and the Pragmatics of World-Making: Nomospheric Investigations*. Oxford: Blackwell.

Fabbri G., Tattara G. (2014) *Venezia, la laguna, il porto e il gigantismo navale. Libro Bianco sul perché le grandi navi debbono stare fuori dalla laguna*. Bergamo: Moretti & Vitali.

Gessoni F., Maccio S., Amidei C.B., Simonato L. (2020) Study on the health status of the population living in Marghera (Venice, Italy) through the use of a Longitudinal Surveillance System. *Annali dell'Istituto Superiore Di Sanità*, 56(2): 157–167.

Godden L. (2020) Legal geography – place, time, law and method: The spatial and the archival in 'Connection to Country'. In: O'Donnell T., Robinson D.F., Gillespie J. (Eds.), *Legal Geography. Perspectives and Methods*. Abingdon and New York: Routledge, pp. 130–148.

Graham N. (2011) *Lawscape: Property, Environment, Law*. London: Routledge.

Hoyle B. (2000) Global and local change on the port-city waterfront. *Geographical Review*, 90(3): 395–417.

Hubbard P. (2022) *Borderland. Identity and Belonging at the Edge of England*. Manchester: Manchester UP.

Innocenti A., Musco F. (2023) Land–sea interactions: A spatial planning perspective. *Sustainability*, 15(12): 9446, https://doi.org/10.3390/su15129446

Jackson J.B. (1986) *Discovering the Vernacular Landscape*. New Haven: Yale UP.

Johnston R.J. (1991) *A Question of Place. Exploring the Practice of Human Geography*. Oxford: Blackwell.

Kryder-Reid E., May S. (2024) Toxic heritage: An introduction. In: Kryder-Reid E., May S. (Eds.), *Toxic Heritage. Legacies, Futures, and Environmental Injustice*. London and New York: Routledge, pp. 1–6.

Kymäläinen P. (2025) Legal geography II: The possibilities and disruptions of place. *Progress in Human Geography*, 49(3): 323–331.

Lefebvre H. (1991) *The Production of Space* (trans. Nicholson-Smith D). Oxford: Blackwell.

Matthews J.A., Herbert D.T (2008) *Geography. A Very Short Introduction*. Oxford: Oxford UP.

Morand S. (2022) One Health: An ecosystem-based ecology of health. *Field Actions Science Reports*, 24. Online since 07 October 2022, connection on 09 November 2022, https://journals.openedition.org/factsreports/6940

Nicolini M. (2022) *Legal Geography. Comparative Law and the Production of Space*. Cham: Springer.

Nicolini M. (2024) Geographies of law. In: Warf B. (Ed.), *The Encyclopedia of Human Geography*. Cham: Springer, https://doi.org/10.1007/978-3-031-25900-5_25-1

Novello E., McCann J.C. (2017) The building of the 'Terra Firma': The political ecology of land reclamation in the Veneto from the sixteenth through the twenty-first century. *Environmental History*, 22(3): 460–485.

One Health High-Level Expert Panel (OHHLEP) (2002) One health: A new definition for a sustainable and healthy future. *PLoS Pathogens*, 18(6): e1010537, https://doi.org/10.1371/journal.ppat.1010537

Philippopoulos-Mihalopoulos A. (2007) Introduction: In the lawscape. In: Philippopoulos-Mihalopoulos A. (Ed.), *Law and the City*. London: Routledge-Cavendish, pp. 1–20.

Ravera O. (2000) The lagoon of Venice: The result of both natural factors and human influence. *Journal of Limnology*, 59(1): 19–30.

Relph E. (1976) *Place and Placeness*. London: Pion.

Sauer C.O. ([1925] 1969) The morphology of landscape. In Leighly J. (Ed.), *Land and Life. A Selection from the Writings of Carl Ortwin Sauer*. Berkeley and Los Angeles: University of California Press, pp. 315–350.

Schemmer J. (2022) Social resistance and spatial knowledge: Protest against cruise ships in Venice. *NTM Zeitschrift für Geschichte der Wissenschaften, Technik und Medizin*, 30: 387–406.

Sennett R. (2019) *Building and Dwelling. Ethics for the City*. London: Penguin.

Sereni E. ([1972] 2016) *History of the Italian Agricultural Landscape* (trans: R. Burr Litchfield). Princeton: Princeton UP.

Soriani S. (2024) Porto Marghera: eppur si muove.... verso dove? In Soriani S. (Ed.), *Venezia tra Storia Sviluppo e Sostenibilità*. Bolonia: il Mulino, pp. 261–267.

Storey D. (2020) Territory and territoriality: Retrospect and prospect. In: Storey D. (Ed.), *A Research Agenda for Territory and Territoriality*. Cheltenham and Northampton: Edward Elgar, pp. 1–24.

Verrastro D. (2021) Nitti e gli interventi speciali per il Mezzogiorno del 1904. Per una comparazione tra il caso napoletano e quello lucano. *Democrazia e Diritti Sociali*, 2: 43–59.

Wollentz G., May S., Holtorf C., Högberg A. (2020) Toxic heritage: Uncertain and unsafe. In: Harrison R., DeSilvey C., Holtorf C., Macdonald S., Bartolini N., Breithoff E., Fredheim H., Lyons A., May S., Morgan J., Penrose S., Högberg A., Wollentz G. (Eds.), *Heritage Futures. Comparative Approaches to Natural and Cultural Heritage Practices*. London: UCL Press, pp. 294–312.

Zazzara G. (2017) I cento anni di Porto Marghera (1917–2017). *Italia Contemporanea*, 284: 209–236.

Zazzara G. (2019) La disparition de l'Italie industrielle: Porto Marghera en Vénétie (trans: X. Vigna). *Revue d'Histoire*, 4: 147–170.

18 Legal approach to taking public health issues into account in port governance

Marine Chouquet, Mariantonia Lo Prete and Catherine Roche

Introduction

The concept of environmental health, which assesses a population's physical and mental well-being through the health determinants of its living environment, is now at the heart of public health policies, notably through the UN's 'One Health' approach. Public authorities are now aware that changes to the ecosystems in which human beings live have consequences for their health. They are therefore required to integrate these considerations into their decision-making process. In areas where seaports are located, these health issues are particularly acute.

However, due to the great diversity of the French port landscape, these challenges will not arise in the same way throughout the country. First of all, health issues will vary depending on the types of activity carried out in ports. Fishing ports and marinas are therefore less affected by these issues than commercial harbours, which are first in line, due to the volume of maritime traffic and the proximity of industrialized port areas. Furthermore, decision-making authorities will differ depending on whether the port is a territorial (i.e. a generally small or medium-sized port managed by a local authority) or a state port (i.e. one of the 11 major maritime ports in mainland France and its overseas territories, which are administered by public state institutions). However, the difference in legal configuration does not prove to be a particularly convincing criterion for distinguishing between ports in terms of health issues. Indeed, the traditional tendency to centralize public health powers in the hands of state authorities plays a unifying role in this area: port authorities rarely have control in this field, whether they operate in a state-owned port or a decentralized one. The state's omnipotence on health issues will also be a recurring source of friction with local authorities, who feel the discomfort of their 'public helplessness' to deal with phenomena specifically affecting their constituency (e.g. cruise tourism in the Mediterranean Sea) or when their population is threatened by particularly virulent health crises (such as COVID-19).

The unique nature of public health issues in seaports has in recent years led national and international authorities to issue specific regulations in an

DOI: 10.4324/9781003639589-23

attempt to limit the effects of port activities pollution on the health of populations in their territories and to contain the various health risks associated with maritime transport. However, these regulations have not been drafted with a comprehensive approach structured around public health issues. Rather, they are based on a sectoral, fragmented and undeniably piecemeal approach. However, from an environmental health protection perspective, all threats posed by port activities to local populations' health should be taken into account in decision-making processes relating to maritime port activities development (Bley et al., 2022).

This can explain the lack of comprehensive consideration of health risk assessment issues in port areas: much of the relevant legislation stems from laws that are not specific to seaports. This is particularly true of health risks attributable to the presence of industrial port areas. Large seaports have significant land reserves, which have enabled them to host numerous industrial activities (Gougeon & Sandrin, 2015). In Europe, many ports are home to industries (such as Dunkirk in France, where 460 industries are already established),[1] whose effects on the health of the neighbouring population can impact mortality (Bauleo et al., 2019). Some of these industrial establishments are subject to ICPE (*Installations Classées pour la Protection de l'Environnement*) regulations and are sometimes classified as 'Seveso' (particularly dangerous for people and the environment). In general, industrial ports are no longer just places of transit, but have also become production sites. These ports now also accommodate industrial shippers (Magnan, 2016), for example in the steel and petrochemical industries. Some of these activities are not related to maritime flows (Magnan, 2016). However, not all industrial facilities are subject to ICPE regulations (warehouses, for example); but they are subject to other rules. While the issue of accidents is better known in relation to ICPEs, Article L.511-1 of the French Environment Code cites human health among the interests protected by this regulation and therefore raises the issue of environmental nuisances and pollution that impact health. Classified facilities located in port areas are not themselves subject to specific provisions. At most, the facility location will be taken into account in order to impose specific requirements, such as the establishment of special protection perimeters or other control procedures. It should be noted that when an ICPE is subject to an impact assessment, the latter must also include a health risk assessment. The Technological Risk Prevention Plan (PPRT) is drawn up at port level, which in this case represents a single industrial site (Art. R.515-39 of the Environment Code). The PPRT is mandatory for high-threshold Seveso-type establishments. Its purpose is to limit accidents that could jeopardise public health, either directly or through environmental pollution (Art. L.515-15 of the Environmental Code). It defines areas of urbanization control or regulations.

Although port authorities do not have specific jurisdiction over ICPEs, they do have jurisdiction over the choice of industries that set up in the port hinterland. Their role as land managers leads them to define a genuine industrial strategy in the port area, thereby enjoying a very direct lever for preventing health risks when they favour the establishment of non-polluting industries to replace former high-emission activities (see, for example, the project to demolish the former thermal power plant located in the port of Le Havre). In line with France's 2021 National Port Strategy, ports are now focusing on attracting carbon-free or decarbonizing industries (Cornot, 2023) and renewable energies (ISEMAR, 2022). The port of Dunkirk, for example, presents itself as a 'pioneer in the decarbonized industry'[2] and in 2023 became one of the first industrial port areas to be selected for the ZIBAC (Low-Carbon Industrial Zones) call for projects. Although the word 'health' is rarely used, this move towards decarbonization, which will result in lower pollutant emissions, can only have a positive impact on the surrounding populations. The decarbonization of port industries goes hand in hand with the ongoing decarbonization of maritime transport (Bordereaux & Roche, 2024), which will also have beneficial consequences for local residents' health.

Indeed, beyond the industrial risks generated by industrial port activity (Marquès et al., 2020), the main source of health risks for the population of port areas comes from maritime transport. Both the ship itself and its cargo therefore pose potential threats to the health of people living in port cities and areas. It is around this issue that the problem of understanding health risks in ports is now crystallizing, through regulations that aim to limit the threats attributable to ships, and those emanating from the human beings they carry, who can be vectors for the spread of disease.

Health risks from ships

Maritime transport can pose a threat to the health of populations in port cities. Ports are seen as gateways for health risks and, as such, need to be made safe. Here we will analyse some of the 'vectors' for the spread of health risks that have a direct impact on populations' health. These pollution sources have gradually been taken into account by international and European law, which form the basis of the applicable law.

Ships in operation – air pollution: a key legal concern

While oil pollution has long been a concern following various disasters, air pollution (whether or not linked to climate change) has been subject to later regulations because it is less spectacular (Lo Prete, 2021). In the port context, industrial emissions, which are subject to specific regulations, must also be considered, as well as emissions from non-maritime transport. However, the maritime sector contributes significantly to air pollution from particulate matter (PM) and gaseous pollutants through shipping transport and port-related activities, particularly near ports and surrounding coastal areas. In Europe, shipping contributes less to PM_{10} levels than $PM_{2.5}$, as the particles created through combustion processes are generally of fine or ultrafine sizes (diameters <0.3 and 0.1 microns) (Gregoris et al., 2021). The literature linking both maritime emissions and health impacts in European coastal towns is limited, with only a few studies available. More literature has been published assessing the relative contribution of shipping to PM concentrations in the European region. However, methodologies in collecting pollution data are variable. A particular challenge is the disaggregation of shipping and port-related emission sources with other sources such as urban road traffic. A recent example of a study linking shipping emissions to health outcomes by Viana et al. (2020), used observational data from 2003 to 2015 to create a model correlating long-term shipping-related $PM_{2.5}$ exposure with adverse health outcomes (premature mortality, cardiovascular and respiratory hospital admissions). Data was collected in eight Mediterranean seaport cities: Barcelona (Spain), Melilla (Spain), Athens (Greece), Brindisi (Italy), Genoa (Italy), Venice (Italy), Msida (Italy) and Nicosia (Cyprus). Exposure to $PM_{2.5}$ from shipping and oil-combustion sources accounted for 0.3%–1.8% of total mortality in these cities, with the highest incidence rate (3.9%) in Athens. Shipping-related emissions contributed 1%–10% of PM_{10} concentrations and 2%–17% of $PM_{2.5}$ concentrations in these coastal cities. However, there are several limitations to this study, including challenges in distinguishing between shipping and general oil-combustion sources and comparing pollution data collected at heterogeneous locations between the study cities.

Within the port, a number of studies managed to disentangle emission sources. A comparative analysis (Merico et al., 2017) concluded that road transport surpassed maritime transport for non-methane volatile organic compound (NMVOC) emissions in Brindisi, Patras, Venice and Rijeka, while SO_2, NO_x and $PM_{2.5}$ predominantly originated from shipping, while PM_{10} emanated from road transport.

Emissions of sulphur-containing compounds occur from the combustion of petroleum-derived fuels such as petrol and diesel fuel and contribute to the composition of ambient PM that can pose risks to human health and contribute to ocean acidification, hence harming aquatic ecosystems (WHO, 2021). According to the International Maritime Organisation (IMO), 'the share of shipping emissions in global anthropogenic emissions (including carbon oxide (COx), sulphur oxide (SOx) and nitrogen oxide (NOx) emissions) has increased from 2.76% in 2012 to 2.89% in 2018' (IMO, 2020). The European Union and then the IMO took this issue into account. It was within the framework of the Green Deal that the European Union set its climate neutrality target and that directives and regulations were adopted, replaced or amended. The IMO has adopted several international treaties to protect the marine environment, while reducing air and water pollution in coastal communities and seaports. Under the IMO, the Marine Environmental Protection Committee (MEPC) is responsible for environmental protection and enforces the Convention for the Prevention of Pollution from Ships (MARPOL and its annexes).[3] The MEPC also adopted new standards for marine fuels and a global mechanism for pricing atmospheric emissions in

2025. Some regional conventions also address the issue (Barcelona Convention, Helsinki Convention). Listing all applicable EU directives aimed at preventing marine and atmospheric pollution would be too long here.

Annex VI of the MARPOL Convention contains specific limits for gaseous and PM pollutants for the maritime industry, and has designated emission control areas (ECAs), which have stricter limits to reduce sulphur oxides and/or nitrogen oxides. Three of these regions are in the WHO European Region: the SECAs (sulphur emission control area) in the Baltic, North Sea and Mediterranean Sea. The Norwegian Sea will become one in 2026, and the North-East Atlantic is expected to be the next, following a proposal for 2025. The latest IMO regulation reduced the global sulphur content in shipping fuels from 3.5% to 0.5% outside ECAs, whilst 0.1% remains the standard value for ships operating within ECAs, including ports. In the European Union, pursuant to Directive 2016/802 of 11 May 2016 on the reduction of the sulphur content of certain liquid fuels, ships that remain at berth for more than two hours must use the same fuel or turn to an electrical connection. Several of these ECA areas are nitrogen emission control areas where nitrogen emissions are limited.

Ships in operation – noise pollution: the forgotten issue

Noise pollution can significantly impact health, well-being and the maritime ecosystem. Exposure to transport noise can disturb sleep quality, increase annoyance levels, contribute to cognitive and hearing impairments and increase the risk of developing cardiovascular diseases (WHO, 2018). In the European Economic Area, exposure to environmental noise from road traffic, railways, aircraft and industry is estimated to contribute to 48,000 cases of ischaemic heart disease and 12,000 premature deaths annually (EEA, 2020). The evidence-base for cause-effect relationships between transport noise exposures and health outcomes has been systematically reviewed in the WHO Environmental Noise Guidelines for Europe (2018) (WHO, 2018). However, these guidelines do not include industrial noise exposures, including those in communities living close to ports with linked industrial sites. In the WHO European Region, the burden of disease from environmental noise is the second highest after air pollution. However, lack of noise exposure data in the central and eastern parts of the WHO European Region mean that disease burdens cannot be quantified for the whole region. Low-level continuous noise generated by maritime traffic, oil and gas prospecting and dredging devices, which fall below thresholds for human health, can nevertheless disturb marine wildlife and associated ecosystems (Shannon et al., 2016).

The European Commission Environmental Noise Directive (END) 2002/49/EC requires EU member states to establish action plans to control and reduce the harmful effects of noise exposure for major urban areas (>100,000 inhabitants), major roads, railways, airports and industries. The port is not taken into account as such, but rather in terms of the industries that are located in the hinterland. The International Labour Organisation Code of Practice for the 'Safety and health of ports' recommends noise monitoring measures at source. Several EU initiatives have integrated noise mapping at seaports, such as the NoMEPorts project (2005–2008), which successfully created noise plans for six major seaports across Europe.

Only a few studies specifically attribute shipping and port-related noise to health and well-being outcomes in European seaports. However, it is suggested that low-frequency noise pollution from shipping ports affects sleep quality and overall well-being (Alves et al., 2015). Mandatory reporting of noise levels begins at 55 dB Lden (day-evening-night noise indicator) and 50 dB Lnight (night-time noise indicator), yet harmful effects to health have been reported at lower levels (EEA, 2020), suggesting that the health impacts of noise are likely greater than reported through this Directive.

Ships in distress

The health of populations in port cities can also be affected by accidents related to maritime navigation. Oil spills can pose a risk to public health,[4] especially for volunteers helping with clean-up or bird rescue operations without the appropriate equipment (INERIS, 2000). This risk is taken into account by the competent authorities, particularly in France, in the implementation of the ORSEC (*Organisation des Secours*) emergency response plan. However, the issue also arises for other pollutants and has been highlighted in particular in cases where a ship in distress is looking for a place of refuge or port of refuge. In fact, the United Nations Convention on the Law of the Sea does not provide for any access right to ports for ships, even in the event of damage. It was following the sinking of the oil tanker Prestige in 2002 (https://wwz.cedre.fr/Ressources/Accidentologie), which was unable to enter a port despite being damaged, that the European Union addressed this issue in the 27 June 2002 amended Directive 2002/59/EC, which implemented a Community vessel traffic monitoring and information system. The IMO also adopted two successive (non-binding) resolutions in 2003 and 2023 (Resolution A 33/Res.1184). In France, the Transport Code (Articles L. 5331-3 and R. 5331-27) empowers the maritime prefect or the Government delegate for State action at sea (overseas) to order 'if necessary, the port authority to accommodate a ship in need of assistance', after 'consulting the prefect or senior defence and security official'. While for the European Union the Community vessel traffic monitoring system is intended to minimize accidents and their consequences for human health, accommodating ships in distress in a place of refuge is considered in terms of its consequences for 'public safety' (We do not mention environmental issues here). The word 'health' is not mentioned, but is undoubtedly included in this concept of safety. The IMO states that in designating a place of refuge or port of refuge, particular consideration must be given to 'the risk to safety and/or human health' (point 2.5.5.2.2). The French Transport Code does not mention any criteria to be taken into account, which prompted much criticism (Rézenthel, 2012). However, pursuant to the 24 April 2012 Instruction (NOR: DEVT1222485J), inter-prefectural decrees relating to the interface between maritime, zonal and departmental ORSEC plans (maritime prefecture websites) provide for the application of the risk analysis grid proposed by the IMO, which includes public health, in the event of a request from a ship.

Health risks associated with transport activities

Depending on their nature, the commodities handled are themselves a source of pollution in the form of dust, such as cereals and coal, during ship loading/unloading. The case of grain is specific, as it may be mixed with contaminated earth (e.g. fertilizers, pesticides used in agriculture, mycotoxins and micro-organism flora), which disperse through the air in the absence of filters between silos and ships. Conveyor belts carrying coal (i.e. between ports and power plants) or iron ore, if not closed, cause spillage and fugitive dust emissions at feeding, transfer and discharge points. Especially during the loading/unloading of tanker ships, Volatile Organic Compounds (methane and non-methane) contribute to the greenhouse effect. Among them, the heavier components (NMVOC) contribute to low-level petrochemical oxidants, such as ozone, impacting human health, food production and the environment.

Individuals on ships, whether passengers or crew members, are also vectors for the spread of disease. As such, their passage through a port area, which marks their entry into a territory, is subject to public authority control. Health checks on people arriving by sea are not simply an option for the port State, but are considered a genuine obligation under international regulations. The International Health Regulations adopted by the WHO in 2005 lay down binding standards for combating the international spread of disease, with particular attention paid to ports and airports as points of entry for travellers into the territory. These obligations are transposed into French law in Articles L. 3115-1 et seq. and R. 3115-1 et seq. of the Public Health Code. States undertake, in particular, to establish a system for issuing health certificates to ships engaged in international voyages when they call at their ports. These take the form of health inspection exemption certificates if the inspection carried out on board the ship has not found any threat to public health, and health inspection certificates when such threats have been identified and satisfactory corrective measures have been taken.

The diversity of health protection measures

Health inspections of ships are a regular and traditional means of containing the risk of infectious diseases spreading from one port of call to another while ensuring the continuity of maritime navigation. However, in the event of a serious and identified threat to public health, public authorities can enforce a range of more targeted and restrictive measures. They may thus choose to systematize health inspections of all ships in the event of a public health emergency (Article R. 3115-27 of the Public Health Code – CSP), to prohibit free practice (i.e. to refuse the ship concerned entry into port and to carry out disembarkation operations), to immobilize ships for the duration of investigations or the implementation of health measures deemed necessary (Article L. 3115-4 CSP), or even to decide to divert ships that pose a threat to public health (L. 3115-6 CSP). Finally, specific health checks on travellers from an infected area may be implemented by authorities, who may go so far as to order the confinement in a specialized medical facility of persons carrying infectious diseases (L. 3115-8 CSP). Travellers' isolation or quarantine, which historically were the first measures adopted by authorities to try and protect populations from health scourges carried by maritime transport (Belanger, 1981), is still being applied today (L. 3115-10 CSP). Various recent events show that states see this as an effective means of containing the health threat when faced with a large-scale epidemic risk or a particularly serious disease. The most emblematic illustration of this is undoubtedly the decisions taken by various governments around the world during the COVID-19 crisis, notably the highly publicized quarantine of cruise passengers and crew members on *the Diamond Princess* off the coast of Japan in February 2020. Even more drastically, some states went so far as to ban ships carrying a significant number of passengers from their coasts to protect themselves from the risk of COVID-19 spreading. This was one of the first measures adopted in France by the Prime Minister under the powers granted to him by the new state of health emergency regime established to deal with the COVID-19 crisis (Law No. 2020-290 of 23 March 2020).

Thus, the 23 March 2020 Decree No. 2020-293, famous for imposing lockdown on the French population in its Article 3, also included in its Article 4 restrictions on access to French seaports for ships most likely to contribute to the spread of the epidemic, namely cruise ships and ships carrying more than 100 passengers, which were banned from calling at French ports for nearly two months (Rézenthel, 2020a). Fears of the Ebola epidemic have also led West African states to adopt similar measures in recent years, ranging from banning access to their ports to organizing coordinated health checks on ships arriving from risk areas (Rebora, 2014). And even if health consequences are not as serious, simple outbreaks of gastroenteritis, now referred to as 'cruise ship viruses' (Lloret et al., 2021) given the recurrence of cases (see the record rates reached in 2024 by gastroenteritis epidemics on cruise ships according to records from the US public health agency Centres for Disease Control and Prevention: https://www.cdc.gov/vessel-sanitation/cruise-ship-outbreaks/index.html), can make authorities very reluctant to allow cruise passengers to disembark at their ports. This was the case, for example, with the British ship *Aurora* in autumn 2003, which was turned away from port after port during its Mediterranean cruise in autumn 2003, while carrying hundreds of passengers struck down by norovirus. Its journey even ended in a minor diplomatic incident, when Spain decided to close its land border with its British neighbour, Gibraltar, which had granted it the right to dock on its shores.

An arrangement of powers in favour of state authorities

Clearly, health checks on passengers arriving by sea at ports are prime issue for the state. Such health powers centralization in state authorities' hands is hardly surprising; public health matters are a classic exception to the decentralization movements that have swept through France since the 1980s. Actually, public health today remains a 'matter for the state' (Apollis & Truchet, 2022), with local authorities granted only 'marginal' powers (Renaudie, 2020). Attempts by local authorities to intervene in the health threat posed by the COVID-19 epidemic have ended in failure. For example, the municipal decrees adopted in March 2020 by the mayors of the four ports on the Marie-Galante island in Guadeloupe, which prohibited passengers docking and disembarking from any ship for fear of the spread of COVID-19, were suspended by the administrative judge on grounds they excessively infringed on freedoms (TA de Basse-Terre, order of 27 March 2020, no. 2000294; Bottini, 2020). In general, the administrative judge left little room for mayors to intervene during the health crisis. *The Commune de Sceaux* order specifically stipulated this: the exercise of general administrative police powers at local level must not compromise 'the consistency and effectiveness' of the measures adopted by 'the competent State authorities', thereby drastically reducing the scope of powers that could be exercised by local authorities during that period (CE, 17 April 2020, *Commune de Sceaux,* No. 440057, Lebon). This refocusing of powers in favour of state authorities was also to the detriment of port authorities, since the texts adopted during the health emergency period resulted in 'depriving the authority vested with port police powers of its competence to authorise cruise ships movements in the port' by transferring to the department prefect the power to grant exemptions from port access bans (Article 4 of the aforementioned decree; Rézenthel, 2020b). The effects are particularly significant in decentralized ports that have retained port police powers (Article L. 5331-6 CT), since for state-owned ports and other decentralized ports not vested with port police powers, such measures were already a crucial matter for the state.

Outside the specific framework of the state of health emergency, reorganizing powers is not unusual when dealing with a particularly acute health threat. The common law regime thus concentrates powers in the prefect's hands to adopt any measures necessary to prevent the spread of diseases originating from a ship (refusal of access to the port, diversion or immobilization of the ship, quarantine or isolation of its passengers: Articles L. 3115-4 and L. 3115-6 of the CSP and R. 3115-3-1 of the CSP; extension of health checks to all ships in the event of a public health emergency: Article R. 3115-37

CSP). It is the prefect who is responsible for drawing up the response plan for public health emergencies in ports (Article R. 3115-12 CSP).

Ultimately, port authorities prove to play a merely auxiliary role to the state's public health powers. They provide the necessary infrastructure to deal with health risks, i.e. secure areas for passengers medical care (Article D3115-19 CSP), in their capacity as 'managers of points of entry' into the territory (R. 3115-7 CSP) – a term that refers to the executive of local authorities in decentralized ports or the chair of the board of directors for state-owned ports (Article L. 5331-5 CT). However, even outside health crisis periods, it is agents authorized by the department prefects who are responsible for carrying out health checks at borders (Article L 3115-1 CSP). Local authorities, whether acting as port police authorities in the most decentralized ports (Article L. 5331-8 CT) or as the police authority responsible for public order in a territory (Article L. 2212-2 CGCT), will only have residual and subsidiary decision-making powers to deal with situations in which state authorities have not yet responded.

Conclusion

The health of populations seems to have been largely overlooked in the texts on the safety of ships docking in ports. Beyond the provisions relating to epidemic prevention, the health issue proves to be a fragmented legal corpus. Taking health into account in port cities would require further consideration if we are to comprehensively address the impact of port activities on the health of people living or working in their vicinity. This calls for the identification of an 'exposome' (Vineis et al., 2020) specific to port cities, encompassing all environmental determinants likely to influence their populations' health, and for an analysis of the most appropriate form of governance to implement this health policy effectively.

Last but not least, there is a lack of an integrated assessment approach that includes shipping, port/terminal, city/industry, and hinterland. Strategic urbanism documents increasingly consider environmental and health issues, including industrial hazards. City health workshops and open days reinforce the dialogue between port and city and between actors and populations, to try and solve discontent arising from exposure to pollutions. Such documents can result from joint studies between port cities and regional public health agencies, whose common goal is to lower socio-spatial inequalities, poverty and over-mortality.

Notes

1 https://dunkerquelenergiecreative.fr/choisir-dunkerque/entreprendre-et-innover-a-dunkerque/territoire-dindustrie/.
2 https://www.dunkerque-port.fr/port-du-futur/port-decarbone/industries-decarbonees/.

3 https://www.imo.org/en/about/conventions/pages/international-convention-for-the-prevention-of-pollution-from-ships-(marpol).aspx.
4 https://ncceh.ca/resources/subject-guides/oil-spills-and-health.

References

Alves J., Silva L., Remoaldo P. (2015) The influence of low-frequency noise pollution on the quality of life and place in sustainable cities: A case study from Northern Portugal. *Sustainability*, 7(10): 13920–13946.

Apollis B., Truchet D. (2022) *Droit de la santé publique*. Dalloz.

Bauleo L., Bucci S., Antonucci C., Sozzi R., Davoli M., Forastiere F., Ancona C. (2019) Long-term exposure to air pollutants from multiple sources and mortality in an industrial area: A cohort study. *Occupational and Environmental Medicine*, 76(1): 48–57.

Belanger M. (1981) Les actions de protection sanitaire en mer ou au port. *DMF*, 394: 579–589.

Bley D., Marano F., Squinazi, F. (Eds.) (2022) Santé-environnement. Quinze ans de politiques publiques. *ADSP*, 120: 70 p., https://stm.cairn.info/revue-actualite-et-dossier-en-sante-publique-2022-4?lang=fr

Bordereaux L., Roche C. (2024) Chronique littoral & milieu marin. *Revue Juridique de l'Environnement*, 3(49): 689–704.

Bottini F. (2020) Covid-19: Des mesures de police manifestement disproportionnées en matière de transport maritime de passagers outre-mer. *DMF*, 824: 429–437.

Cornot S. (2023) *La sidérurgie européenne se prépare pour être à la pointe de la décarbonation*. Notes de l'Ifri, Ifri, janvier 2023.

EEA (2020) *Environmental noise in Europe*. Publications Office, https://data.europa.eu/doi/10.2800/686249

Gougeon M., Sandrin M. (2015) L'industrie portuaire. *Annales des Mines – Réalités Industrielles,* Novembre, 2015(4): 30–34.

Gregoris E., Morabito E., Barbaro E., Feltracco M., Toscano G., Merico E., Grasso F.M., Cesari D., Conte M., Contini D., Gambaro A. (2021) Chemical characterization and source apportionment of size-segregated aerosol in the port-city of Venice (Italy). *Atmospheric Pollution Research*, 12(2): 261–271.

IMO (2020) Fourth IMO Greenhouse Gas Study 2020, Full Report, International Maritime Organisation, London, 495 p.

INERIS (2000) Evaluation du risque sanitaire de la marée noire consécutive au naufrage de l'Erika. Dossier Erika, Rapport 6 version modifiée, https://www.ineris.fr/sites/default/files/contribution/Documents/rapport6bis.pdf

ISEMAR (2022) Les ports maritimes et le défi énergétique. Note de Synthèse n°244 – Octobre.

Lloret J., Carreño A., Carić H., San J., Fleming L.E. (2021) Environmental and human health impacts of cruise tourism: A review. *Marine Pollution Bulletin*, 173: 112979.

Lo Prete M. (2021) *Onshore and Offshore Solutions from an Environmental and Health Perspective. Webinar on 'Environment and Health in Seaport Cities'*. World Health Organization (WHO) and Union for the Mediterranean (UfM), June 2021.

Magnan M. (2016) *La production et la gestion de l'espace portuaire à vocation industrielle et logistique. Les grands ports maritimes français: gestionnaires d'espaces infrastructurels*. Architecture, aménagement de l'espace. Université Paris 1 Panthéon Sorbonne.

Marquès M., Domingo J.L., Nadal M., Schuhmacher M. (2020) Health risks for the population living near petrochemical industrial complexes. 2. Adverse health outcomes other than cancer. *Science of the Total Environment*, 730: 139122.

Merico E., Gambaro A., Argiriou A., Alebic-Juretic A., Barbaro E., Cesari D., Chasapidis L., Dimopoulos S., Dinoi A., Donateo A., Giannaros C., Gregoris E., Karagiannidis A., Konstandopoulos A.G., Ivošević T., Liora N., Melas D., Mifka B., Orlić I., Poupkou A., Sarovic K., Tsakis A., Giua R., Pastore T., Nocioni A., Contini D. (2017) Atmospheric impact of ship traffic in four Adriatic-Ionian portcities: Comparison and harmonization of different approaches. *Transportation Research Part D: Transport and Environment*, 50: 431–445.

Rebora J.F. (2014) Ebola, nouveau danger maritime? *DMF*, 764: 965.

Renaudie O. (2020) Collectivités territoriales et compétences en santé publique: sortir de l'ambiguïté? *RFDA*, 4: 901–912.

Rézenthel R. (2012) Le décret du 2 février 2012 et l'accueil des navires en difficulté: Une décision lourde de conséquences pour les gestionnaires de ports. *DMF*, 735: 378–385.

Rézenthel R. (2020a) Les conséquences de la pandémie de Covid-19: Interdiction pour certains navires de mouiller dans les eaux intérieures et d'entrer dans les ports d'outre-mer. *DMF*, 823: 378–382.

Rézenthel R. (2020b) Les ports à l'aube d'un « autre monde » (l'état d'urgence sanitaire et après?). *DMF*, 827: 764–771.

Shannon G., McKenna M.F., Angeloni L.M., Crooks K.R., Fristrup K.M., Brown E., Warner K.A., Nelson M.D., White C., Briggs J., McFarland S., Wittemyer G. (2016) A synthesis of two decades of research documenting the effects of noise on wildlife. *Biological Reviews*, 91(4): 982–1005.

Viana M., Rizza V., Tobías A., Carr E., Corbett J., Sofiev M., Karanasiou A., Buonanno G., Fann N. (2020) Estimated health impacts from maritime transport in the Mediterranean region and benefits from the use of cleaner fuels. *Environment International*, 138: 105670.

Vineis P., Robinson O., Chadeau-Hyam M., Dehghan A., Mudway I., Dagnino S. (2020) What is new in the exposome? *Environment International*, 143: 105887.

WHO (2018) *Environmental Noise Guidelines for the European Region*. World Health Organization & WHO Regional Office for Europe,

WHO (2021) *WHO Global Air Quality Guidelines: Particulate Matter ($PM_{2.5}$ and PM_{10}) , Ozone, Nitrogen Dioxide, Sulfur Dioxide and Carbon Monoxide*. World Health Organization, https://apps.who.int/iris/handle/10665/345329

19 The COVID-19 pandemic and port resilience

The IAPH-WPSP Port Economic Impact Barometer as an early survey-based response

Theo Notteboom, Athanasios Pallis and Patrick Verhoeven

Introduction

COVID-19 as a major disruption to ports

The COVID-19 pandemic led to the second global disruption since the 2009 financial crisis with a significant impact on global supply chains at every level, including the port industry.

While the world economy entered a post-COVID-19 phase by early 2022, a series of other major disruptions started to impact seaport operations, such as the Russian invasion of Ukraine (Erol, 2024), the Red Sea Crisis (Notteboom et al., 2024; Wang et al., 2024; Yap and Yang, 2024) and rising geopolitical tensions (Notteboom and Haralambides, 2025; Yap et al., 2025). This new array of disruptions meant that the seaport industry returned neither to the previous setting nor to clear and consistent normal demand patterns.

Academic literature on the impact of COVID-19 on seaports reveals a multifaceted disruption to maritime logistics, port operations, and financial resilience, with studies focusing on both short-term shocks and long-term strategic adaptations.

Notteboom et al. (2021) provide a comprehensive analysis of how the pandemic reshaped port operations, cargo volumes, and vessel calls. They also examine the role of port authorities in leading adaptation efforts, including risk mitigation and policy responses to maintain operational continuity. Mańkowska et al. (2021) delve into the tactical responses of terminal operators during the pandemic, emphasising how operational flexibility, labour practices and digitalisation became essential tools for coping with disruptions. Guerrero et al. (2022) examine shifts in the global maritime network due to COVID-19, noting reduced connectivity and uneven impacts across ports. Cariou and Notteboom (2023) examine the impact of the COVID-19 pandemic on containerised import flows within the U.S. port distribution system.

DOI: 10.4324/9781003639589-24

Cullinane et al. (2023) offer a broader perspective by analysing both the short-term effects and longer-term implications of COVID-19 on international shipping and port industries. In a more localised context, Leviäkangas et al. (2023) assess the financial resilience of Finland's seaports during the pandemic.

Together, these studies illustrate that COVID-19 not only disrupted seaport operations but also catalysed innovation and strategic rethinking in maritime logistics. The literature reflects a growing recognition of the need for resilience, flexibility, and digital transformation in port management to prepare for future global disruptions.

Objective and scope of the chapter

The existing body of literature discussed in the previous section predominantly adopts an ex-post analytical approach to examining the impact of the COVID-19 pandemic on seaports. These studies generally assess the consequences of the crisis after its onset, focusing on retrospective evaluations of operational, logistical, and economic disruptions. However, in practice, the abrupt emergence of the pandemic took seaport communities by surprise, leaving them unprepared for the scale and immediacy of the challenges they faced.

As the situation rapidly evolved, port authorities and stakeholders worldwide were compelled to navigate considerable uncertainty, often without precedent or established protocols. This urgency generated a pressing need for real-time data and insights into the evolving conditions and response strategies being implemented at other ports. Consequently, there was a heightened demand for timely information sharing and comparative analysis to inform decision-making during the unfolding crisis.

This chapter examines the response of the International Association of Ports and Harbors (IAPH) and its member organisations to the challenges posed by the COVID-19 pandemic. Established in 1955, IAPH is a non-profit global alliance currently comprising 201 ports and 175 port-related entities across 94 countries. Collectively, its member ports handle over one-third of the world's sea-borne trade and well over 60% of the world container traffic. As a consultative non-governmental organisation, IAPH maintains formal engagement with several United Nations agencies, including the International Maritime Organization (IMO). In 2018, it launched the World Ports Sustainability Program (WPSP), an initiative aligned with the 17 UN Sustainable Development Goals, aimed at fostering sustainability and international collaboration across the maritime supply chain.

In response to the pandemic, IAPH and WPSP established a COVID-19 Task Force in March 2020 to monitor the evolving impacts on port operations and to facilitate the exchange of best practices among ports worldwide. The Task Force members included ports from different continents, i.e., Central and South America, North America, Europe, Northeast Asia and Southeast Asia. One of the first task force's key initiatives was the creation of the "IAPH-WPSP Port Economic Impact Barometer", designed to collect real-time data on short-term impacts of COVID-19 on ports in the areas of vessel calls, hinterland transport, distribution activities, procedural adaptations, and workforce availability. A dedicated portal to help ports worldwide handle the challenges they were all facing by disseminating information, best practices, and the industry's collective recommendations to governments was a second initiative. In early 2021, the newly formed Risk and Resilience Committee of IAPH integrated the work of the COVID-19 Task Force into its broader mandate.

Between April 2020 and April 2021, 17 Barometer reports were produced, based on surveys conducted among global ports. This chapter provides a synthesis of the principal trends and insights derived from these reports, offering a comprehensive overview of how ports navigated the operational and economic challenges in the first year of the pandemic.

The survey set-up

The IAPH-WPSP survey on the impact of COVID-19 was launched in early April 2020 to monitor the current situation in world ports and trends compared to previous weeks. The survey was sent to port authorities and port operators, with responses sent anonymously on a weekly basis. The first survey results were collected in week 15 of 2020 (April 6). The survey initially consisted of six identical questions, each associated with a scale of potential answers:

1. How would you best describe the number of vessel calls in your port in the past week, compared to what would be expected in the same week under normal conditions for this period?
2. Were there any extra restrictions on vessels introduced in the past week, for either cargoes or ship crews?
3. Were there any extra delays during the past week due to changes in port call procedures (hygiene inspections, distancing of workforce, disruption of port or related services, etc.)?
4. How has hinterland transport been affected by the COVID-19 situation compared to normal activity during the past week?
5. What is this week's situation in terms of capacity utilisation, including warehousing and distribution activities in your port?
6. What was the availability of port workers last week?

Beginning in week 23 of 2020, the survey was distributed on a bi-weekly basis, with its scope narrowed to four core questions. Grounding on the changing conditions, in particular the easing of economic interactions in several economies worldwide, this revision excluded questions 2 and 3, which had previously addressed restrictions on vessels and port call procedures.

On top of these four themes, several questions appeared one or a few times in the Barometer reports, such as questions on the status of crew changes in ports, the status of planned port infrastructure projects, and the trends observed in planned investments in environmental sustainability.

The eleventh Barometer report, released in mid-July 2020, was initially intended to conclude the series. However, the renewed surge of COVID-19 cases globally, alongside the emergence of initial outbreaks in several regions, prompted the IAPH COVID-19 Task Force to resume the Barometer initiative on a monthly basis. From 2021 onward, the reporting frequency was further adjusted to a bi-monthly schedule until the last Barometer report published in April 2021.

Participation level of world ports

The total number of valid answers varied throughout the survey period between 48 and 104. From week 15 to 21 of 2020, the number of responses fluctuated between 67 and 79, with an outlier of 90 in week 16. In week 23, a peak of 104 answers was recorded. Only 58 valid answers were received in week 29, which could be explained by the holiday season and some signs of survey fatigue. The lowest number of responses was recorded in April 2021, with 48 valid answers.

Throughout the survey period, Europe remained the leading region, with a total share ranging from 30% (week 6 of 2021) to 54% (week 15 of 2020). The number of responses received from Central and South American ports increased significantly from week 18 onwards. However,

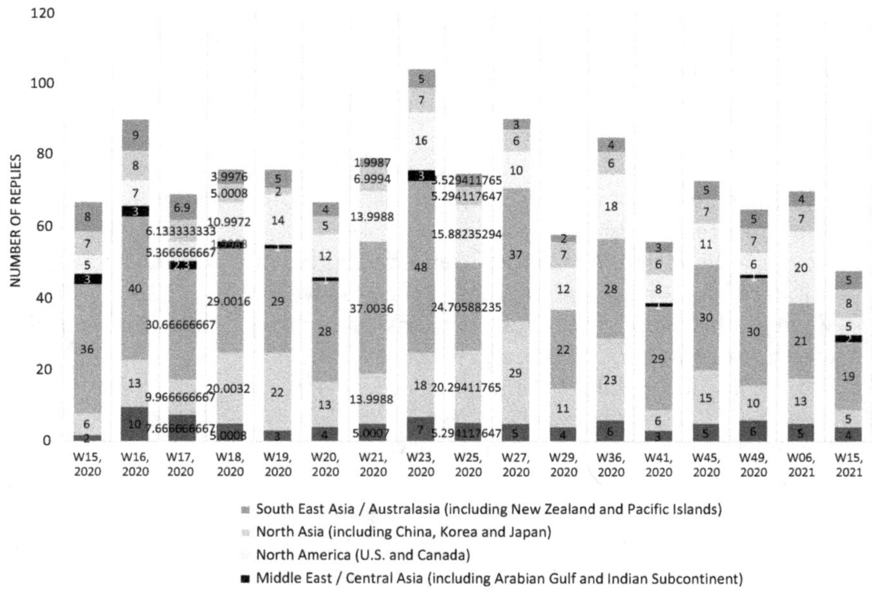

Figure 19.1 Geographical distribution of responses to the survey

the participation of this region dropped suddenly in a few survey weeks (such as in October 2020 and April 2021). North America was represented well in mid-2020 (21% share) and in February 2021 (29%), with its share fluctuating between 10% and 15% in most other weeks. A limited number of ports from North Asia, South East Asia, and Australasia took part in the surveys, but the ones who participated did so consistently. Except for April 2020 and April 2021, the share of these regions in the total never exceeded 20%. African ports remained under-represented throughout the entire Barometer exercise, while answers were received from ports of the Middle East or Central Asia on an occasional basis only (Figure 19.1).

Some of the main results of the Barometer are discussed in the following sections. The analysis also includes a regional comparison between the regions with the highest number of responses, i.e., Europe, Central and South America, and North America.

Impact of the crisis on vessel calls

The first survey topic deals with the vessel activity in ports. The bar charts in Figure 19.2 provide the distribution of answers per vessel category since the publication of the half-year Barometer report in September 2020. The line graph in Figure 19.3 provides an overall picture of the percentage of ports that

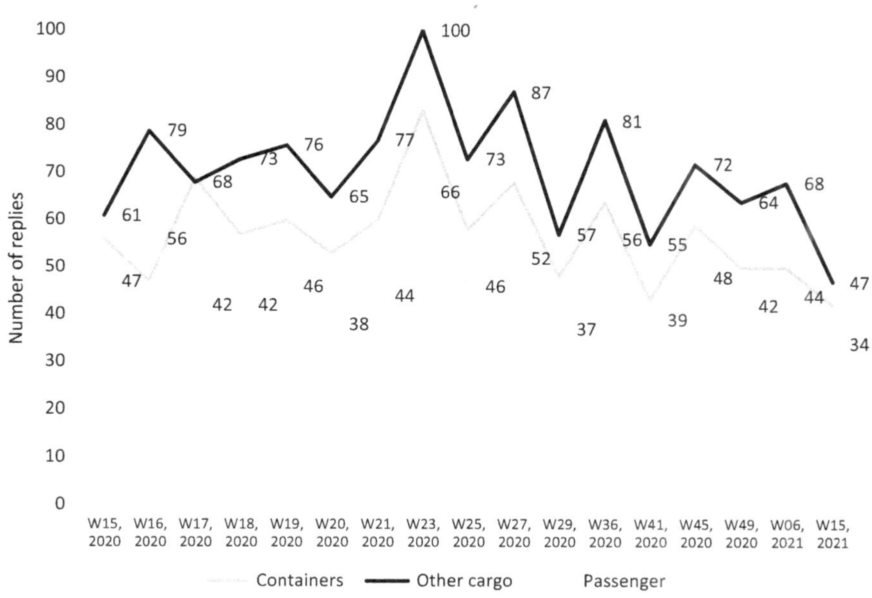

Figure 19.2 "How would you describe the number of vessel calls in your port in the past week, compared to activity during normal conditions?"—Answers per vessel category

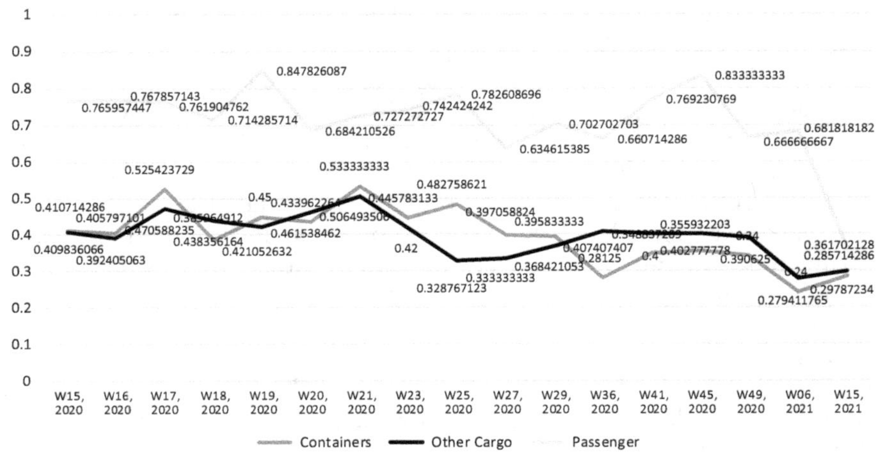

Figure 19.3 Ports where the number of ship calls is lower than in normal conditions (%)

reported more than a 5% decrease in vessel calls per market each week since the first survey of the COVID-19 pandemic implications in early April 2020.

Container vessels

Blank sailings, mainly on trade routes with the Far East, heavily affected the weekly results for container vessels throughout the first half of the survey period. In the period between early April and mid-July 2020, between 40% and just over 50% of all respondents indicated that container vessel calls were down by more than 5% (Figure 19.4). However, the situation improved considerably by September 2020 (week 36) to reach a much lower 28%. In April 2021, some 29% of the ports reported that the number of container vessel calls fell by more than 5% compared to a normal situation. This figure is much lower than the peak of 53% in week 21 and below the 40%–41% in the first weeks of the survey. In the last three months of 2020, this figure still stood at around 35%.

The share of ports facing a significant drop (over 25%) in container vessel calls reached 4.8% in April 2021, a figure that is about half of the results of weeks 17, 18, and 20 (Figure 19.5). About two-thirds of ports reported that vessel calls are similar or even higher compared to the same period the year before. The evolution continued to evolve positively, given the surge of container volumes on some trade routes (e.g., transpacific), combined with a sharp decrease in idle container vessel capacity observed in July/August 2020. Given the sharp decline in the number of blank sailings, an increasing number of ports were heading to almost similar numbers of calls compared to the same period the year before. At the same time, maritime trade volumes also started to increase, as several economies, or major parts of them, had returned to operations with an increase in the number of transactions.

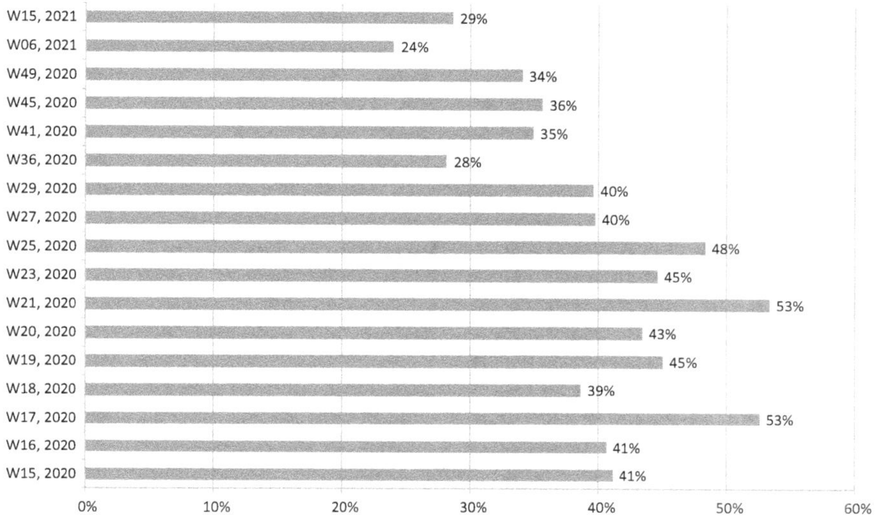

Figure 19.4 Percentage of ports with more than 5% decrease in container vessel calls

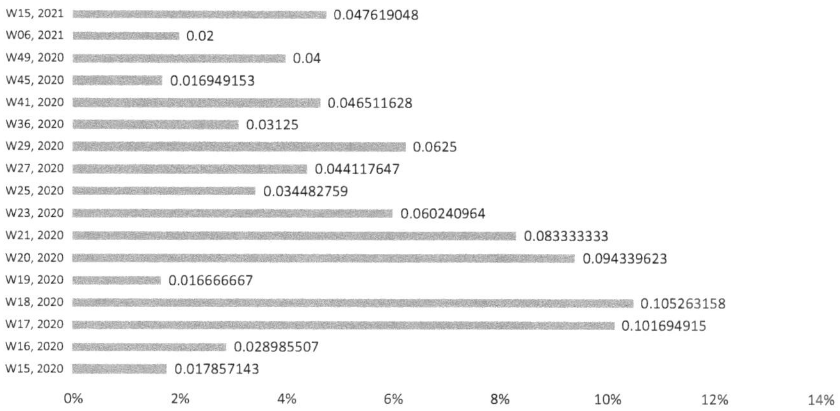

Figure 19.5 Percentage of ports with more than 25% decrease in container vessel calls

Other cargo vessels

The share of ports reporting reductions in other cargo vessel calls of more than 25% gradually decreased from 16% in week 21 to 4% in week 25, which is also far below the 12%–15% observed throughout weeks 16–20 (Figure 19.6). Since September 2020, the figure was consistently around 4%–6%. Thus, the overall evolution since September 2020 was a positive

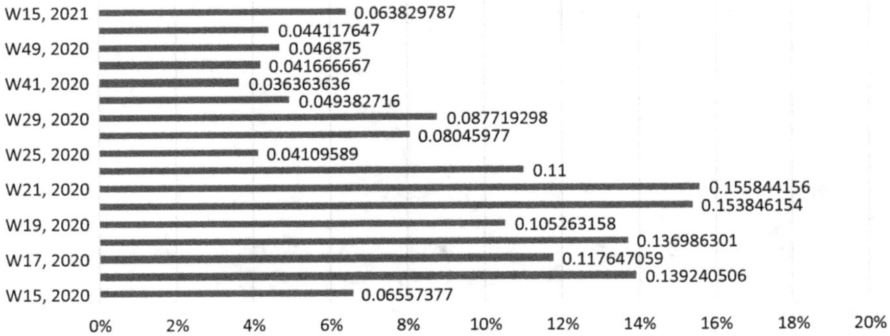

Figure 19.6 Percentage of ports with more than 25% decrease in other cargo vessel calls

one, with only a small minority of all ports reporting reductions in other cargo vessel calls of more than 25%.

In the first half of the survey period, cargo vessel calls were not only impacted by the economic downturn but also by a series of measures. For example, at the start of the survey exercise, some countries in regions such as South East Asia imposed trade restrictions. This meant that even though ports were operating normally, only essential cargoes were permitted for delivery. Only certain window periods were allowed for the delivery of non-essentials to and from the port. Container vessels calling at these ports carrying import cargo for local consumption faced delays, and most cargoes were still stored in port storage areas. In the same cases, tanker and ro-ro calls fell significantly due to restrictions on direct deliveries.

At the beginning of 2021, other cargoes were on a par with, if not above, the expected levels for that period of the year. Cargo vessel traffic was getting back to normal. There was a recovery in goods related to several industries, such as exporting/importing for the steel industry or the movement of automotive units. Compared to 2020, the percentage of ports reporting a minor decrease in traffic was low. The cases of ports continuing to face the significant downward trend of their traffic (i.e., at more than 25% compared to pre-COVID-19) were few. Yet, the normalisation of the number of calls was not universal, as a total of 30% of the reporting ports continued to face a lower number of calls than a year before. For some of them, this was a surprise. Having expected an increase in cargo movement with the roll-out of the vaccinations, ports serving other cargoes than containers saw a decline in cargo vessels (import/export) during the early months of 2021.

Cruise/passenger vessels

The cruise/passenger market was the most affected by the COVID-19 contagion. In week 15 of 2021, 32% of respondents indicated that passenger vessel calls were down more than 50%, in many cases even down more than 90%. This was a sharp decline compared to the 69% in November 2020. From week 20 to week 25, this figure was 61%–62%, while in weeks 15–18, this figure amounted to two-thirds of respondents, with a peak of 76% in week 19. In late August 2020, only a few cruise operators had resumed some cruise activity, albeit on a very small scale compared to normal activity levels. For some ports, this implied that cruise ship calls no longer remain at near-zero levels.

In the early weeks of the Barometer reporting, these figures were caused by a virtual full cessation of cruise activities. Cruise lines decided to cease operations, and cruise vessels ended up at berth for lay-up (no passengers, only crew), with some ports limiting the number of crew remaining on board. In the early days of the pandemic, measures applied to all cargo and passenger ships included vessels with suspected cases onboard remaining in quarantine for 14 days with testing afterwards. Other measures included foreign crew not being permitted ashore unless due to a medical emergency, and requests for crew medical certificates with elementary health checks by VTS operators before permitting entry. Aside from the overall ban by authorities on foreigners in many ports, neither passengers nor crew of cruise vessels were or are still allowed to go on land.

On the one hand, in several countries, ports were still under an order from the government not to allow international cruise ships to berth at their terminals. On the other hand, as vaccination progressed and cruise lines returned, one after another, to operations in some other countries, ports developed efforts and protocols to host again cruise calls.

Cruise shipping did not seem to resume evenly in different countries and continents, even in those cases where it was expected to start. For a group of ports located in countries that advance the return of cruising, cruise vessels were berthing only for lay-up or shipyard. Another significant development was the decision of cruise lines to use only turnaround ports for departures and arrivals of the so-called “cruises to nowhere” or “blue cruises”. These are cruises in which guests embark on a vessel and remain onboard and at sea for the entire cruise without the vessel visiting intermediate ports of call.

A year after the pandemic outbreak, passenger vessels had yet to return to normal in some parts of the world. RoPax vessels were still in layby due to COVID-19-related border restrictions. Others had no passenger activities beyond essential services as citizens remain restricted within municipality borders, and there was still no maritime traffic between regions of the country and/or to and from the islands. Passenger ships in operations continued with half the number of passengers on board, as the restrictions preventing these vessels from carrying more than 50% to 60% of their capacity continued to apply. There were still cases where, due to the applied restrictions on people’s movements, the passenger vessels were used mainly for carrying cargo (Figure 19.7).

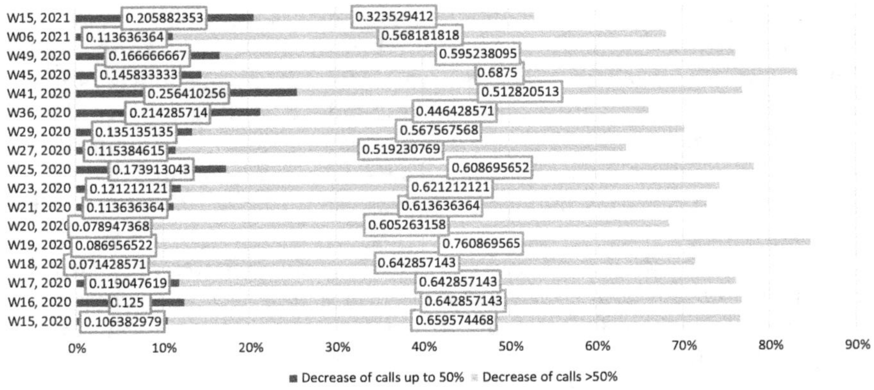

Figure 19.7 Percentage of ports with a decrease in passenger vessel calls

Extra restrictions on vessels

COVID-19 resulted in some extra restrictions on vessels. The survey focused on this issue from week 15, 2020, to week 21, 2020. The overall results show that the share of ports imposing restrictions on container and other cargo vessels started to decrease in week 19 of 2020. In week 21, about nine out of ten ports did not impose any restrictions on container vessels and other cargo vessels. The situation for passenger vessels also improved strongly by week 21: 80% of the responding ports did not impose additional restrictions (same as in week 20; 69% in week 19, and 44% in week 15). The share of ports imposing extra measures on all incoming passenger vessels reduced from 35% in week 15 to 9% in week 21, the lowest figure in the time series (Figure 19.8).

All vessel operations were performed in accordance with local biosecurity procedures to avoid any impact on terminal performance. In some cases, vessels were inspected alongside. In other cases, vessels were all inspected before berthing when the medical team boarded the vessel. The green light for the vessel to berth was given only after checking that there were no suspected cases. There were no extra restrictions on vessels as long as health declarations remained clear. In many cases, only the truck drivers were allowed to board ferries. Health protocols were, in most cases, designated by the national health authorities.

Permissions for crew to disembark remained limited. In some countries, due to the preventive measures adopted by governments for port facilities, it is recommended that no member of the crew should leave their ship, unless it is deemed necessary for operational reasons and in accordance with security measures to prevent the spread of COVID-19. In other cases, the crew is restricted to four-hour shore leave for essential purposes only.

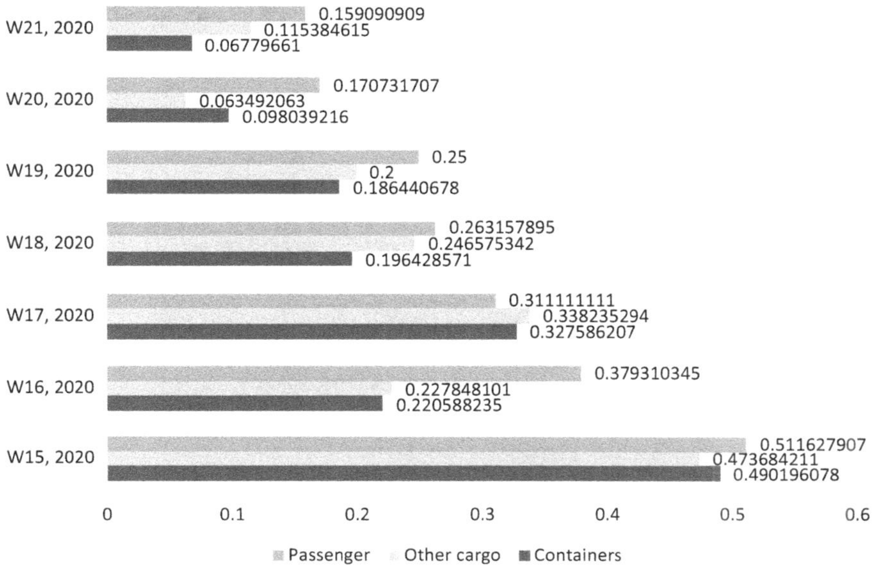

Figure 19.8 "Were there any extra restrictions on vessels introduced in the past week, for either cargoes or ship crews?"

Extra delays due to changes in port call procedures

In the first Barometer report of early April 2020, nearly seven out of ten ports with inland barge operations reported no extra delays during the past week due to changes in call procedures (e.g. hygiene inspections, distancing of workforce, disruption of port or related services), while some two out of ten ports reported minor delays (longer than six hours). For container vessels and other cargo vessels, more than 90% of the ports indicated zero or only minor delays. Also here, the worst situation was found in the passenger sector: 40% of the ports discontinued this type of operation, while nearly half of the ports reported no additional delays (Figure 19.9).

By week 21, the situation had changed. For inland barge operations, approximately 80% of ports reported normal or back-to-normal activities, with no additional delays due to changes in call procedures over the past week, down from a record 92% in week 20, 2020.

For container vessels and other cargo vessels, slightly fewer ports reported delays or major disruptions, which were mainly caused by a decline in the share of respondents facing minor delays. The passenger segment remained the most affected vessel category, and the improvement observed in week 20 continued throughout week 21 of the year.

The reported delays were only those minor ones that take place due to the sanitary controls that were being carried out on ships, land transport, and

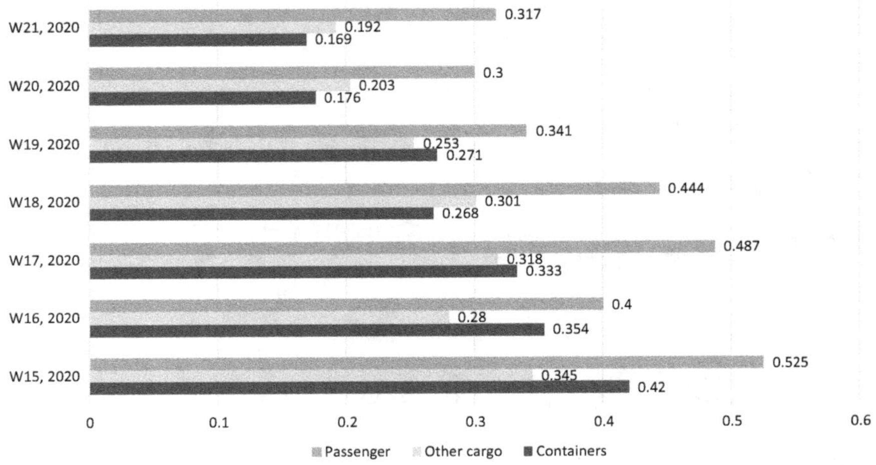

Figure 19.9 "Were there any extra delays during the past week due to changes in port call procedures?" (hygiene inspections, distancing of workforce, disruption of port or related services, etc.)

port workers to prevent the spread of COVID-19. Beyond these, there were no reasons for delays and regular conditions applied. Workers in many ports are at normal numbers, and operations have therefore not suffered disruptions. The presence of fewer ships and fewer vessels than expected also naturally helps the case of avoiding delays.

However, in specific countries, delays were caused by landside operations. For instance, the mandatory testing of truck drivers in the short run resulted in a slowing of turnaround times. In some ports, all truck drivers were required to have a COVID-19-free certificate, with testing taking relatively longer than expected. This was affecting truck turnaround time. Further reopening of the economies saw these problems ease off. Nonetheless, there were also concerns that it might result in the implementation of new procedures in the respective countries.

Impact on the availability of port-related workers

The measures to fight the COVID-19 outbreak did affect the availability of port-related workers. However, the level of impact limiting ports' capacity to operate was relatively small. The shock of the first weeks resulted in some severe difficulties, with shortages at all levels of personnel and workers reaching their peak in week 18 of 2020. These initial shortages were due to dockers and administrative personnel remaining at home for the first weeks following the COVID-19 pandemic. At the same time, the impact of any workforce shortages was alleviated by several industries linked with ports remaining inoperative, with less goods transported to and/or from ports. Since then,

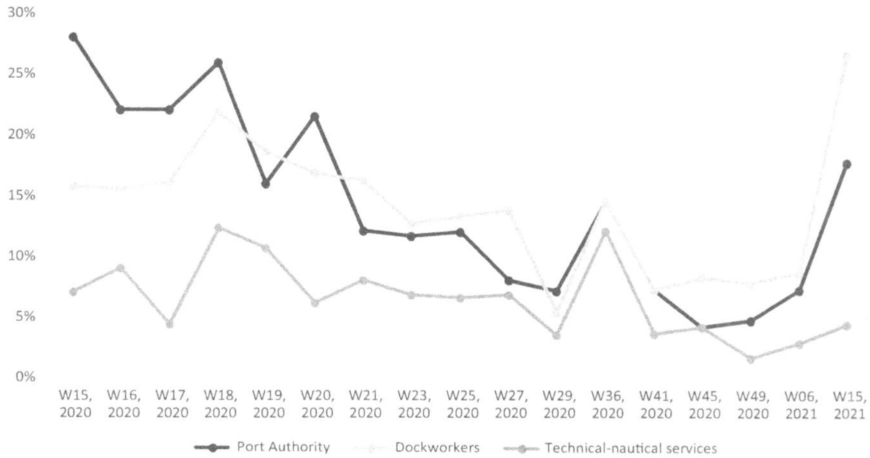

Figure 19.10 Ports reporting shortage of port-related workers (%)

shortages decreased, with the most improved situation occurring in early July 2020 and at the end of 2020. However, staff availability issues resurfaced in early 2021, although the share of ports reporting shortages remains below the peak figures of April 2020 (Figure 19.10).

Dockworkers

Between May 2020 and mid-July 2020, the ports facing shortages of dockworkers declined from 22% to 5%. From October 2020 to February 2021, this figure remained very low at only 7%–9%. However, April 2021 brought a sudden sharp rise, with more than a quarter of ports now facing dock worker availability problems.

Dockworkers were soon to return to work, although a few of the ports reported that a number of the dockworkers stayed home longer due to lack of work, with the State paying part of their salary. Working on site normally took place with some extra safety arrangements in place, and in some ports only dockworkers under 60 years of age were allowed to return to work. Given the lack of cruise calls, some dockworkers serving these operations were among those who stayed at home receiving social security support. The surge in dock worker availability problems in early 2021 had several causes, which differ greatly among ports: COVID-19 outbreaks among dock workers, port strikes and/or shortage of dock workers to handle the demand surge in containerised cargo.

Technical-nautical staff and harbour master services

The COVID-19 crisis had a moderate impact on the availability of port-related workers for the delivery of technical-nautical services (pilots, towage, mooring). In April 2021, only 4% of the sample faced shortages in the delivery of technical-nautical services. This figure peaked at 11%–12% in late April/early May 2020 (weeks 18 and 19).

Problems with harbour master services (including VTS operators) were also low throughout the pandemic, never exceeding 10%. In April 2021, only 2% of the sample ports faced a minor shortage of personnel for harbour master services.

Port authority personnel

In April/May 2020, major difficulties were observed in the case of port authority personnel. Between 20% and 30% of ports experienced such difficulties following the COVID-19 outbreak, when government-enforced rules and lockdowns forced staff to work from home, with only essential staff working from the port. Adjusting to teleworking and social distancing took some weeks. The peak of the problem was week 15 of 2020, when nearly 30% of ports were experiencing difficulties.

Teleworking expanded, transforming working from home into a regular practice, especially for employees in administrative services. Working in shifts became another adopted practice, in order to avoid a whole section/department being quarantined should one of the staff suffer infection. Operational workers attended work as usual despite port workers having to respect safety measures (i.e. longer checks, personal protection equipment, etc.) to prevent direct contact (e.g. social distancing). As adaptation to the "new normal" continued, shortages since then were limited to approximately 15% of the ports or less. Since early June 2020, port authorities have been confronted with personnel shortages ranging between 4% and 15%.

However, April 2021 was an outlier with almost one out of five ports reporting availability issues, a sharp increase compared to previous months. In three continents, ports reported that COVID-19 cases were present and increasing. Hinterland municipalities returned with more severe restriction measures (such as lockdowns) due to rising case numbers, deaths, and hospital occupancies. Emergency plans to delay the spread of the virus were reactivated in those countries where the number of cases was rising. In some ports, this led to dockworker and port authority employee shortages without actually resulting in disrupted operations. As reported, ports were even planning to help municipalities to accelerate vaccination and analyse the solutions together with private sector initiatives aiming to increase their resilience to any further "wave" of COVID-19 cases.

Truck drivers

Following an initial period of considerable shortages, i.e. at 21% in lockdown conditions in many economies (week 17 of 2020), the situation improved. By mid-June 2020, only 3% of ports faced shortages of truck drivers. Since then, the availability of truck drivers remained high, with less than 10% of the surveyed ports facing some moderate shortages. However, also here, April 2021 was an outlier with almost one out of five ports reporting availability issues.

Impact on planned port infrastructure projects

A major crisis, economic or otherwise, might have long-term effects on both the development and operations of world seaports. Plans and investments in upgrading existing infrastructures, or constructing new ones, might be revisited, advanced earlier or later than had been initially scheduled, even cancelled and/or replaced by new ones that emerge as essential with the new situation. These effects are not present during the outbreak of the crisis, when the necessity for ports to remain operational and serve essential trade prevails. However, they might emerge later in time, when the magnitude of the crisis is further realised.

Six months after the day that the World Health Organisation declared COVID-19 a pandemic, in early September 2020 (week 36), 69% of the surveyed ports reported that the majority of their investment plans had been delayed in some way or even amended. Forty-one percent of the reporting ports informed that the delays in investment had been, at least for the moment, minor. Due to the changing conditions, major investment delays were occurring in 19% of the ports. A few ports (4%) decided to shelve or cancel existing investment plans, while 3% of respondents had already decided to replace specific investments with other ones. Notably, three of the surveyed ports reported that, given the emerging conditions, they decided to accelerate their existing investment plans and execute them faster than initially scheduled (Figure 19.11).

Despite a diminished appetite for completing investment projects during the COVID-19 pandemic, the delays observed did not significantly hinder cargo or vessel traffic flows. In many instances, postponements were attributed

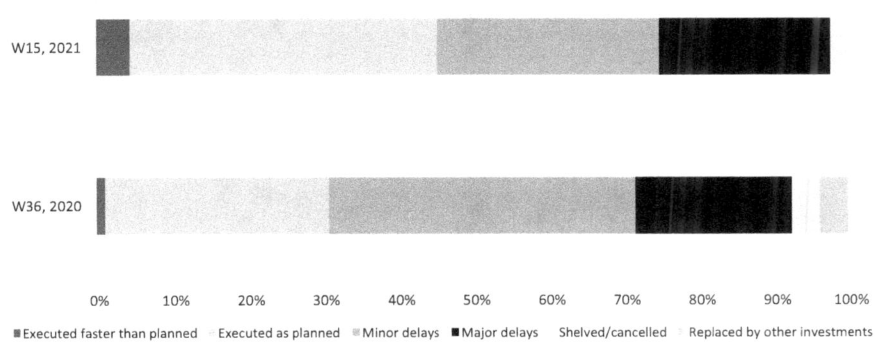

Figure 19.11 Status of the majority of planned port investments

to administrative challenges in securing authorisation from regional, federal, or national authorities. Other delays stemmed from third-party contractors, likely due to workforce shortages linked to pandemic-related disruptions. These setbacks predominantly affected smaller-scale initiatives—such as terminal crib repairs or pipeline maintenance—while larger infrastructure projects, including new container terminals, experienced only minor delays and generally proceeded as scheduled.

In specific ports, however, delays appeared to reflect broader strategic recalibrations. Some authorities opted to defer planned investments pending a clearer understanding of the pandemic's long-term implications for market demand and social dynamics. While projects initiated prior to the pandemic largely continued, new investments were frequently placed on hold, with some ports explicitly postponing them by a year. Investment plans related to cruise infrastructure faced particular scrutiny, as uncertainty surrounding the sector's recovery led several ports to suspend or reconsider terminal developments. In some cases, deliberations remained ongoing; in others, projects were formally shelved until clearer prospects emerged. These developments underscore the need for continued monitoring of port investment trajectories in the post-pandemic context.

Impact on crew changes

For three weeks, i.e. weeks 27 and 29 of 2020 and week 6 of 2021, the Barometer included a question on crew changes. Figure 19.12 shows the results. On a global scale, 44% of ports that provided information on crew changes reported no crew changes had taken place in week 6 of 2021, down from 55% in week 27. In a quarter of ports, a very limited number of crew changes occurred (less than 5) compared to one-third in week 27.

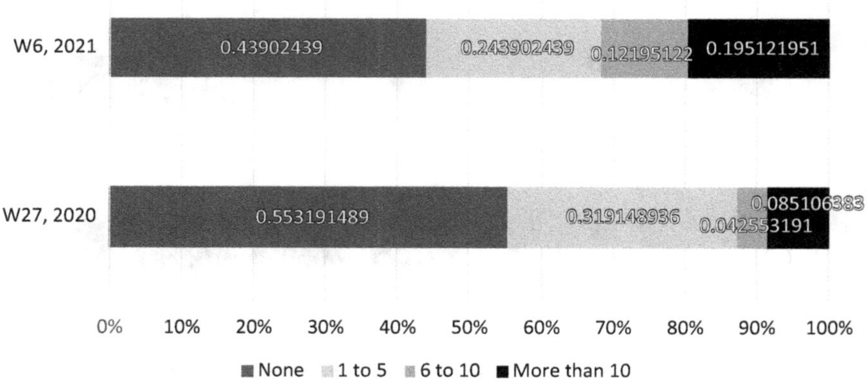

Figure 19.12 Crew changes in world ports

When comparing regions, European ports showed the best picture in terms of the crew change situation. In North America, crew changes remained at a low level, with 50% of ports indicating there were no crew changes in week 6 of 2021. This figure is comparable to the 57% in week 27 of 2020. Overall, the crew change situation remained more precarious in the Americas compared to Europe.

Crew changes were reported in several participating ports, with the vessel's flag state playing a significant role in determining applicable procedures in certain jurisdictions. Despite these regulatory variations, all crew changes that occurred were executed successfully. Domestically flagged vessels continued to conduct crew rotations routinely, while foreign-flagged vessels experienced no notable delays or complications.

Some ports indicated that crew changes were feasible, although no vessel calls specifically for crew changes had taken place during the reporting period. Survey responses also underscored that ports themselves had limited authority over crew change decisions and implementation, which remained under the jurisdiction of external regulatory bodies and administrative procedures.

Conclusions

The COVID-19 pandemic produced complex temporal and spatial disruptions across global ports, triggering a severe economic crisis with profound consequences for supply chains, maritime transport, and port operations. An initial supply shock in Asia in early 2020 was followed by a demand shock driven by lockdowns in Western economies. Yet, from mid-2020 onward, trade volumes rebounded sharply, particularly in sectors typically vulnerable during economic downturns. As consumer behaviour shifted towards home-centred activities, demand surged for durable goods such as electronics, furniture, and office equipment, despite reduced discretionary spending. This shift, coupled with an e-commerce boom, placed significant strain on supply chain management.

The first half of 2020 was marked by blank sailings and declining port throughput, while the latter half saw mounting challenges related to container shortages, constrained vessel capacity, and terminal congestion. These disruptions were compounded by external events, notably the Suez Canal blockage in March 2021. From a supply chain perspective, the pandemic represented an unprecedented disruption, leaving port managers with limited foresight and requiring rapid adaptation across terminals, storage facilities, and inland transport networks. Despite these challenges, ports demonstrated remarkable resilience, maintaining operations under evolving commercial and regulatory conditions.

The crisis underscored the critical importance of information exchange, best practice sharing, and coordinated action among stakeholders. Enhancing risk management and resilience within the global port community has emerged as a continuous and essential endeavour. In this context, the

IAPH-WPSP COVID-19 Economic Impact Barometer played a pivotal role. Through regular input from IAPH member ports, the Barometer documented the pandemic's effects on vessel calls, hinterland transport, warehousing, labour availability, procedural restrictions, and investment planning. Covering the first year of the pandemic, the Barometer provided valuable insights to support preparedness and strategic planning for future disruptions, including those related to climate change and security.

The Barometer provided the established IAPH Task Force with the latest factual information, as well as the background to subsequently develop relevant risk and resilience guidelines (IAPH, 2023). It also facilitated international organisations, which, given the scale of the pandemic, started investigating the actual implications of the events and the best ways to address similar challenges in the future. The UN broader programme "Transport and trade connectivity in the age of pandemics", its publications, and website to promote resilient maritime logistics in the face of disruptions, is one of these cases.

The findings emphasise the need for a holistic supply chain perspective in port strategy development, extending beyond the ship-port interface to encompass landside logistics and nautical services. Bottlenecks at any point in the chain can undermine maritime transport efficiency, highlighting the necessity for integrated monitoring systems that address maritime, in-port, and landside operations.

Looking ahead, the IAPH Risk and Resilience Technical Committee is advancing efforts to establish early warning systems and real-time intelligence frameworks. In the aftermath of the pandemic, the Committee produced a generic set of risk and resilience guidelines for ports (IAPH, 2023) and is now working on specific guidance tools related to other major disruptions occurring in the post-pandemic era.

Although this chapter discussed the case of the Barometer, the initiative continued in an expanded though different format after 2021, as the World Ports Tracker reports. Six issues were published between May 2022 and March 2024. The latest iteration of the World Ports Tracker of IAPH occurred in 2025. The report "IAPH World Ports Tracker 2025: Sustainability and Market Trends" was published in May 2025 as an IAPH initiative to monitor and evaluate critical developments shaping the global port industry, as they evolve. The report is designed to provide ports with timely insights into strategic opportunities and challenges that emerge regionally and globally. As such, digitalisation, sustainability and market indicators are combined to support the evolving needs of the global port sector.

References

Cariou P., Notteboom T. (2023) Implications of COVID-19 on the U.S. container port distribution system: Import cargo routing by Walmart and Nike. *International Journal of Logistics Research and Applications*, 26(11): 1536–1555.

Cullinane K., Haralambides H., Notteboom T. (2023) Short-term effects and longer-term impacts of the COVID-19 pandemic on the international shipping and port industries. *International Journal of Transport Economics*, 50(1–2): 45–88.

Erol S. (2024) The early impact of the Russia-Ukraine war on seaborne trade and transportation in the Black Sea. *International Journal of Shipping and Transport Logistics*, 18(3): 305–323.

Guerrero D., Letrouit L., Pais-Montes C. (2022) The container transport system during Covid-19: An analysis through the prism of complex networks. *Transport Policy*, 115: 113–125.

International Association of Ports and Harbors (IAPH) (2023). *Risk and Resilience Guidelines for Ports*. Antwerp: IAPH.

Leviäkangas P., Ojala L., Paik S.M., Pekkala V. (2023) COVID-19 and the financial resilience of Finland's seaports. *Journal of Shipping and Trade*, 8: 29.

Mańkowska M., Pluciński M., Kotowska I., Filina-Dawidowicz L. (2021) Seaports during the COVID-19 Pandemic: The terminal operators' tactical responses to disruptions in maritime supply chains. *Energies*, 14(14): 4339.

Notteboom T., Haralambides H. (2025) Seaports in a tense geopolitical environment: Key agents or sitting ducks? *Maritime Economics & Logistics*, 27: 1–24.

Notteboom T., Haralambides H., Cullinane K. (2024) The Red Sea Crisis: Ramifications for vessel operations, shipping networks, and maritime supply chains. *Maritime Economics & Logistics*, 26(1): 1–20.

Notteboom T., Pallis T. (2021) *IAPH-WPSP Port Economic Impact Barometer One Year Report: A Survey-Based Analysis of the Impact of COVID-19 on World Ports in the Period April 2020 to April 2021*. Antwerp: IAPH.

Notteboom T., Pallis T., Rodrigue J.P. (2021) Disruptions and resilience in global container shipping and ports: The COVID-19 pandemic versus the 2008–2009 financial crisis. *Maritime Economics & Logistics*, 23(2): 179–210.

Wang Z., Fang Z., Yu J., Hu X., Gong J. (2024) Red Sea crisis impacts on maritime shipping networks. *Heliyon*, 10(22): e40384.

Yap W.Y., Xiao Z., Fan Z., Feng H. (2025) Shipping network disruption, vulnerability and resilience amidst geopolitical tensions. *Maritime Business Review*, 10(3): 260–281.

Yap W.Y., Yang D. (2024) Geopolitical tension and shipping network disruption: Analysis of the Red Sea crisis on container port calls. *Journal of Transport Geography*, 121: 104004.

Afterword

A value case approach for the importance of well-being in port city territories

Carola Hein

Port city symbiosis is understood as the visible and invisible interplay of forms of capital—natural capital, industrial capital, human capital, cultural capital, social capital and creative capital—connecting port and urban functions on water and land (Jansen and Hein, 2023). Port cities thrive through shipping, but maritime transport has long been closely associated with public health concerns. As traced by chapters in this book, diseases spread along maritime corridors and through port cities. As hubs for the import and export of food, tools, and energy, port cities have experienced a broad range of evolving health challenges, exacerbated by polluting industries clustered in ports—especially the petroleum industry. Ports and shipping are not goals in themselves: they serve the people who benefit from the commodities and energy that pass through them. Despite the public health risks posed by shipping and ports, port cities have long attracted people to gather, work, and innovate.

Port city symbiosis goes beyond technology, economics, and quantitative measurements. Economic, social, and cultural factors are equally important to health in port cities, understood here in line with the WHO's 1948 definition of health as "a state of complete physical, mental and social well-being and not merely the absence of disease or infirmity." As discussed in many chapters in this volume, advancing the quality of life in port cities requires technical solutions and the reduction of air, water, and noise pollution. Academic research and pilot projects in ports, cities, and regions, often funded with grants, have been addressing these challenges. From new sensors to legal intervention, attempts to improve port–city relations have often focused on technical and policy-related solutions. Improving public health in port cities, however, also requires new spatial and sociocultural approaches to port cities and their territories (Hein et al., 2020).

What about broader strategies to balance urban life with the demands of global trade? A value case approach includes tools and methods that can be used to connect spatial, social, and cultural conditions and their change over time. Such a comprehensive understanding can help facilitate societal change and guide political decision-making. (Re)imagining port cities and their adjacent territories requires strategies that acknowledge multi-scalar, multi-stakeholder approaches and adopt a long-term perspective—which is essential when addressing transitions, including those of energy, sustainability, and digitalization. In addition to the approaches showcased in the book's chapters, several dimensions merit further attention.

Space matters: While all port city territories host similar ships and facilitate comparable forms of transshipment, their spatial form and regional embeddedness vary greatly (Hein et al., 2023). Local morphologies, infrastructures, historic development, and heritage create distinct conditions that offer both opportunities and challenges. Spatial analysis requires an advanced understanding of port city territories as unique intersections of urban development, communities, and waterfront environments. To facilitate the local integration of global functions, it is important to understand the spatial implications of port and city practices on water and land, including in relation to flows of water that are in constant flux. Sustainable and resilient development depends on engagement with local conditions, including nature-based solutions. For example, the Dutch Ministry of Environment and Infrastructure initiated Room for the River, which provides more space to rivers to improve flood resilience. The sand motor, also developed in the Netherlands, uses natural forces of wind, waves, and tides to redistribute sediments along the coast in a cost-effective way that limits ecological disturbance, creating improved living environments for humans and non-humans.

Personae matter: Stakeholder analysis often focuses on recognized actors, such as municipalities and port authorities, in the transformation of port–city relationships. However, there are many more actors—public and private institutions, individuals, and other human-and non-human actors—that are linked to, or can be linked to, port city spaces and territories, each with their own interests. Network analysis is a commonly used tool to represent these relationships, yet it is often framed as part of a "business case" focused on economic outcomes rather than a more-encompassing "value case." Exploring a wider array of interests can help identify new interests and potential coalitions. Placing a person or object – personae – at the center of such a network and exploring specific interests and needs associated with values and their potential conflicts can lead to a better understanding of local practices and stakeholder dynamics. Developed over six years, the Blue Limassol Forum approach provides a model for a new form of territorial engagement, understood as an ongoing, place-based dialogue connecting research, policy, and local stakeholders.

Values matter: Engaging more diverse personae can help expand cultural integration and buy-in for port city development. There may not be unanimity regarding values, but understanding distinct qualities and shared values is key to resilient port city territories. Paris provides a compelling example of changing values in the redesign of port city territories and public health. The 2024 Olympics brought renewed attention to the Seine—where ambitions for swimming in the river now intersect with tourist cruises and the logistical operations and activities managed by the port authority. As part of the broader Seine Axis, ports connect Paris to maritime hubs like Le Havre and

Rouen, sustaining flows of goods, materials, waste, and energy that remain central to the city's economic metabolism. Javel Bas Port, recently awarded special mention by the AIVP Antoine Rufenacht Prize for its exemplary port-city interface design, demonstrates how multifunctional waterfronts can harmonize operational, civic, and ecological values.

Time matters: Spatial, social, and cultural practices change over time. The past—history and heritage—remains relevant for the design of the future as it provides a reference framework embedded in spatial form, institutional practices, and culture (Hein et al., 2023). The historical development of space, society, and culture can lead to value conflicts and opportunities; future transformations require knowledge of these conditions to support the smooth implementation of new plans and projects. Understanding historical conditions as "big data" of the past, recognizing path dependencies and potential lock-ins, and understanding the value of heritage as leverage for the future are key elements in facilitating transitions. Historic examples such as floating markets or nocturnal shipping can inspire contemporary circular practices, including nocturnal river-based deliveries from supermarkets and big box retailers in major cities, including Paris. Achieving sustainable futures in port city territories requires a clear, robust, and shared value-based vision.

Design matters: A comprehensive analysis—including spatially annotated maps, persona mapping, and long-term cultural analysis of local practices and stakeholder configurations—can make visible diverse and overlapping processes of value accumulation, displacement, and transformation. It can facilitate the identification of symbiotic and parasitic relationships and new shared values and novel approaches to (re)imagining the relationship between ports, cities, territories, and public health. Such an approach can provide the foundation for new vision and mission statements and interventions that promote well-being in port city territories from a holistic, sociocultural, long-term ecosystem perspective, in line with the UN Sustainable Development Goals.

References

Hein C., Luning S., van de Laar P. (2020) Port city cultures, values, and maritime mindsets: Defining what makes port cities special. *CPCL*, 4(1): 7–20.

Hein C., van Mil Y., Azman-Momirski L. (2023) *Port City Atlas: Mapping European Port City Territories: From Understanding to Design*. nai010/TU Delft Open Books.

Jansen M., Hein C. (2023) Port city symbiosis: Introduction to the special issue. *Maritime Economics & Logistics*, 25(2): 211–229.

Index

www.ingramcontent.com/pod-product-compliance
Lightning Source LLC
LaVergne TN
LVHW010652300926
849161LV00005B/1106
* 9 7 8 1 0 4 1 0 7 2 5 5 3 *